The HEART *of the* GREAT WESTERN

The HEART of the GREAT WESTERN

Adrian Vaughan

Silver Link Publishing Ltd

In memory of Dr Jack Hollick MD, who loved people and railways

First published in December 1994
Reprinted May 1995
First published in paperback March 1999

British Library Cataloguing in Publication Data

A catalogue record for this book is available from the
British Library.

ISBN 1 85794 117 9

Silver Link Publishing Ltd
The Trundle
Ringstead Road
Great Addington
Kettering
Northants NN14 4BW

Tel/Fax: 01536 330588
email: sales@slinkp-p.demon.co.uk

Printed and bound in Great Britain

Photographs credited 'AVC' are from the Adrian Vaughan
Collection, and signal box diagrams credited 'SRS' appear
by courtesy of the Signalling Record Society

The line drawings at the heads of the chapters are taken
from *The 10.30 Limited*, published by the GWR in 1923.

Frontispiece The Brunellian ancestry of the Great Western
Railway's Oxford station can be appreciated in this view of a
section of the down platform. What shows here is the standard,
wooden overall roof style of a 'Brunel' station, a design repeated at Banbury, Frome and Exeter St Thomas, to name but a
few. The station's nameboard is comprehensively informative
and, in a way, gives a potted history of the whole place. Noon
on 5 May 1935. *GWR*

Title page Oxford station looking north along the down platform. The symmetrically balanced arms pendant from the
canopy are Oxford Goods Shed's (later Oxford Station South)
No 50 (left hand) and 51, the latter routing out to the Down
Main via the 'scissors'. 5 May 1935. *GWR*

Below No 3304 *Oxford* with a train of 'salmon and chocolate'
L&SWR coaches in the up platform at Oxford, *circa* 1903; the
view is from the down platform, looking north. The engine is
one of the 'Badminton' Class, built in September 1898 with 6 ft
8 in driving wheels, and it is sen here in its original condition.
Passengers took the GWR's high standards of production very
seriously, and over the years many were misled by the beautiful
nameplates bearing the names of towns. The engine would run
past them on the platform, bearing the name *Wolverhampton*, or
wherever, and, thinking that these were very high-quality destination boards, they would either get into the train thinking it
was going to that town or would not get on to the correct train
thinking that it was going to a destination they did not wish to
visit. Consequently all these 'town' names were removed in May
1927. Note that the up 'scissors' crossings have their signals at
the north end of the platform, not at the centre. *AVC*

CONTENTS

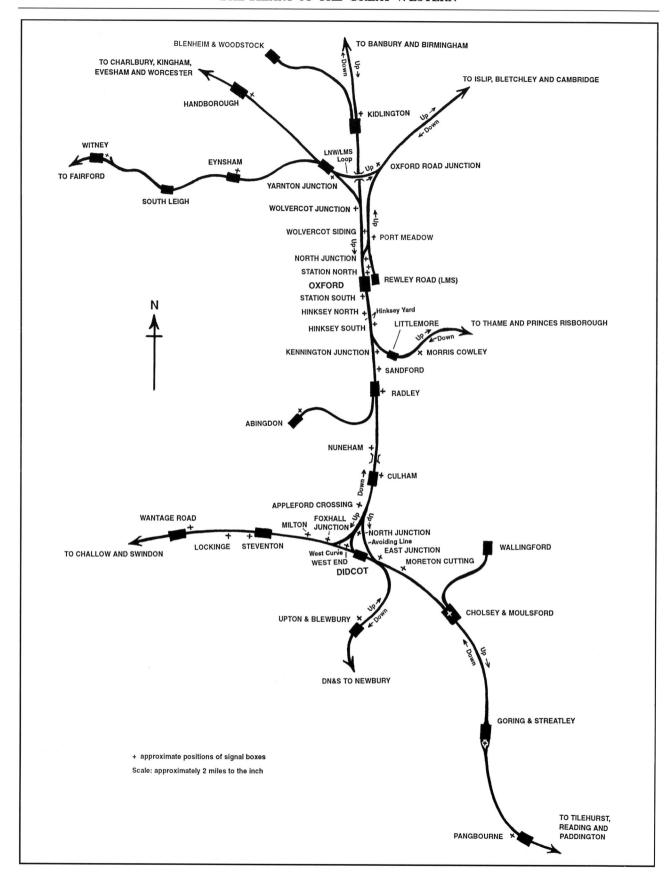

Map of the railways in the Oxford area showing the stations and signal boxes covered by this book.

INTRODUCTION

A railway is only as good as the men and women who work it, and their high morale is what makes it work well. This is why the steam-hauled railway, suffering from every conceivable disadvantage of 'inefficiency' and lacking even the most basic computer services, carried vast amounts of traffic and kept the country running even under wartime conditions. Indeed, according to the people who did the job during wartime, morale rose in proportion to the difficulties. Nowadays some companies send their staff on 'outward bound' courses to improve their desk-wise performance - the steam-hauled, hand-operated railway was one vast 'outward bound' course from the moment a person joined the service; that is why the job worked as well as it did, and why morale rose in proportion to difficulty.

The Heart of the Great Western was the men and women who did the job. I claim no special virtue for the railway at Oxford. A book in this vein could be written about Chester or Plymouth or Swindon. My home station, Challow, was closer to Swindon than Oxford, and I did some interviewing work with old-hand GWR Swindon men, but by chance I was drawn more towards Oxford.

The biographies of Oxford railwaymen herein are accurately rendered from the notes I took, or the tapes I made, when I went to visit them in their homes. One has to trust the accuracy of their recollections. Their individual memories cannot be checked, but when they recollected life on the engine shed, or certain locomotives, or other details in the common knowledge of all the Oxford men of their generation, their individual recollections tallied with those of one another. I am sure that each man I interviewed was anxious to leave an honest impression of his time working on the Great Western Railway.

The railwaymen worked for a common purpose and believed in the public service they were providing - even in 'Company' days they (and Management too)

thought of themselves in this way. They were like the General Post Office or the Police - a great public institution. There was a feeling of 'togetherness', especially on the engine shed where the men congregated and formed a social life beyond that of simply coming in to work trains.

Railway work was classed as 'unskilled' by outsiders who could not see beyond the dirt and the heavy work, but goods guards, shunters, signalmen, platelayers and, of course, locomotivemen were very skilled - otherwise the railway would have come to a stand. Their skill was not something learned at university or 'City Tech' - so there was no skill! 'One year's learning and 44 years' repetition,' I was told by a newly arrived (from University) Manager.

The work of the various departments of the steam-hauled or hand-operated railway was mentally and physically demanding, but, because the job was secure for life, people could, and did, give it their lives - only breaking off to volunteer for such interruptions as the Great War or Hitler's War. For me, a large part of the attraction of working on the railway was the people I worked with.

The staff of the railway were diverse and interesting people. Mr Roberts, who worked as a coal heaver on the coaling stage at Oxford, was an Alderman of the City. Reg Warrel was a Hinksey goods guard, working local trips to leave him time for his duties as Labour Councillor on the City Council, Chairman of the City Health Committee, Member of the Oxford Hospital Board, Sheriff of Oxford for 1953-54 and publican of the New Inn in Nelson Street! Signalman Edgar Smewin, who became a Traffic Regulator in Oxford Station North during 1939-46, then Platform Inspector, did his year as Mayor of Oxford and was a Justice of the Peace.

There were the worthy, the eccentric, the boozy or sober, the studious, the 'worriers' and, indeed, the decidedly carefree. They were not all paragons of virtue and good cheer - but while rolling stones gather no moss, stationary stones gather much moss, and there were a lot of very mossy characters on the railway.

Railway work used to be 'for life', 45 or 50 years' service, often within one job. Nowadays a person is considered odd by his superiors if he or she stays in one job all their life ('Have you no ambition?'), but once one would have been respected for loyal, long service, and the experience that had been gained would have been considered valuable. Technology makes experience redundant, since systems and procedures change so quickly, and skills once developed by an individual are now built into an electronic machine. Loyalty is no defence in so rapacious and inhuman world as this, where everyone is racing on the unstoppable treadmill of 'cost effectiveness', and rather than 45 years' service a person is likely to be discharged when he or she reaches the age of 45!

Besides leaving a record of the sort of people who formed the Heart of the Great Western, still at work long after Nationalisation, I also want to leave an account of the way they worked heavy traffic, and Oxford is as good a place as any to take as an example.

I first went to Oxford station in 1960. The station and its district was an astonishing and, to an enthusiastic railwayman, a beautiful sight. A very heavy traffic called at or passed through the station; 178 passenger and parcel trains and 150 goods trains in a normal weekday 24 hours, not counting any 'specials' that might have run. Of these, 54 started from Oxford, 52 terminated and 50 made a call. All regular booked trains stopped, only 'specials' and some Saturdays-only passenger trains went through without stopping for passengers, and of these many would stop to change engines. Of the 150 freight trains, 120 called at South End or Hinksey Yard and, on average, 2,200 wagons a day were put off, re-marshalled and sent on.

The track layout was insufficient to cope properly, so operating the station was, for the signalmen, hectic, and, for the passengers, frequently accompanied by delay. Some people called the place 'Cemetery Junction' for reasons that will become apparent later.

The predominant locomotive types in 1960 were of course ex-Great Western, just about any class, including the streamlined diesel railcars, but not the 'Kings'. This misfortune was mitigated to some extent by the large minority of types from the former Southern, LMS and LNE railways. It was normal at Oxford in 1960 to enjoy Bulleid 'Pacifics', 'King Arthurs', 'Lord Nelsons', 'Crabs', 'Black Fives', 'Jubilees', 'B1s', 'V2s', 'K3s', ex-GER 'B12' 4-6-0s and 'D16' ('Claud Hamilton') 4-4-0s. At times there were no GWR engines in sight, but there might be an ex-LNWR 'Super D' 0-8-0 on the Up Middle Road with a freight for Hinksey Yard and a 'Lord Nelson' alongside in the Up Platform with a Birkenhead-Dover passenger, while an LMS '8-freight' pulled noisily out of the goods loop from the South End Yard, across all roads, across the bows of the up trains, taking a freight for 'downhill'. The permutations of locomotive types were seemingly endless and variety was the keynote of the place.

Platform staff carried suitcases, wheeled barrows of parcels (sometimes two days after they had been handed in, it must be said), directed passengers to the correct coach of the train or to the correct platform. Brake vans were loaded and guards made lists of their loads. Engines or footplate crews were changed, carriages or vans were attached and detached, incoming branch trains were shunted to sidings or into the opposite bay. The signals changed and trains took their correct routes - the only visible sign of the complicated work carried on over the bells and telephones by the signalmen.

This, then, was the steam-hauled, 'by-the-seat-of-your-pants' railway.

Sources and Acknowledgements

The information in this book is drawn from GWR 'working books' and GWR internal correspondence, in private collections, and eye-witness accounts collected from the railwaymen concerned, during their working lives and after they retired. Your author was a signalman (and amateur footplateman), and almost all the people who helped me with information and advice for this book were GWR - or at least Steam Age - railwaymen and women.

The 'working book' sources were:

(a) GWR No 1, No 3 and No 15 Section Working Timetables, and BR(WR) No 1 Section Working Time Table 1953
(b) GWR Sectional Appendices (Local Instructions) 1922 and 1932
(c) GWR 'Regulations for Train Signalling' 1936
(d) GWR Book of Acts of Parliament, leases, amalga-

mations, dates of opening of lines, 1926 (for which work the author, P. R. Gale, of the Chief Goods Manager's Office, Paddington, received a gratuity of £50 from the Company)

GWR internal papers consulted were:

(a) Traffic Census papers and correspondence
(b) 'Additional Instructions' for the signal boxes concerned (also early BR(WR) Instructions)
(c) Train Register, Oxford Station North signal box, 1946
(d) Oxford Station Passenger shunting schedule, 1946

GWR Working Timetables can be seen at the Public Record Office, Kew, London, under RAIL 937. Sectional Appendices can also be seen at Kew under RAIL 1136, pieces 25-38.

Mr R. A. Cooke's *Track Plans: Oxford*, Vol 27, was indispensable, as were the Signal Box Register and signal box diagrams of the Signalling Record Society (SRS), which copied them from GWR Signal & Telegraph Department records. Thanks are due to my friends Ray Caston, archivist of the SRS signal box diagrams, and John Morris, also of the SRS, who drew almost all of the diagrams I have used. Anyone wishing to join the SRS should write to the Membership Secretary, Gordon Grubb, Gribdae Cottage, Kirkcudbright DG6 4QD.

I am particularly indebted to Mr Larry Crosier (ex-GWR) for his very kind and patient assistance over the years. Larry shared with me his archive of GWR papers on signalmen's pay and signal box work census, and called my attention to various matters. I would also like to thank Mary Crosier for her hospitality.

Published books consulted were:

MacDermot's *History of the GWR*, Vols 1 & 2; Paul Karau's *GWR Branch Line Termini*, combined volume; Richard Lingard's *Princes Risborough-Thame-Oxford-Railway*; Karau, Parsons & Robertson's *The Didcot,* *Newbury & Southampton Railway*; Laurence Waters's *Rail Centres: Oxford*'; and Harold Gasson's *Footplate Days*.

My thanks are due to Mike Christensen for kindly drawing my attention to and allowing me to use his research for the 'World War 2 Study Group'; and also to photographers David Anderson, Peter Barton, H. C. and R. M. Casserley, Ray Simpson, David Chipchase and John Smith (Lens of Sutton). I must also thank Mr Peter Webber for his assistance from his private collection of GWR working books, and also Mrs Webber for her hospitality.

In the field of oral archives I am deeply indebted to the many signalmen and engine drivers I have known over the years who brought me up in their traditions of railway life. Many of them, sadly, have died, but two in particular, Special Class Relief Signalman Stan Worsfold and Driver Charlie Turner, are still very much alive, complete with photographic memories. Their assistance has been of *vital* importance; thanks, too, to Kathy Turner for her hospitality.

I also have to thank Signalman Albert Walker, for his assistance on Wolvercot, Kennington and Cowley, and his wife, Margaret; Signalman Basil Marchant, for his help with 'Cheddar' Wilson, Sandford and Station North boxes; Driver Charlie Arkell, for his assistance on the Fairford line ATC, and Drivers Don Kingdom, Harry Mears, Bill Whiter and Fireman Harold Gasson; and Brian Horton, an ex-GWR Oxford fireman who also helped me with recollections of 'Cheddar' Wilson.

Thanks largely to the ebullient Molly Eagle I have been able to give an impression of railway communications before Oxford caught up with the 20th century. Molly's pride in 18 years' service with the GWR, 1930-48, is as strong now as it ever was, and her memories of those days are as bright as the copper cap on an Oxford 'Castle's' chimney. I am also grateful for the help I received in the telegraph section from ex-GWR communications technician Peter Harris, from David Collins, Chief S&T Engineer GW ISU, and from ex-Porter David Castle, who also kindly supplied a photograph.

A Short Glossary of Signalling Terms

'In advance of' This must be taken according to the forward direction of travel. If a train is travelling from east to west it would be 'in advance' of a signal or signal box - or anything else for that matter - when it was on the western side of it. 'Ahead of' has the same meaning - to have run forwards in the nor-mal direction of travel and to have passed *beyond* the object.

'In rear of' When the train is still *approaching* a signal (or whatever) it is 'to the rear' of it. These are extremely important terms to understand, and it is surprising how many people, interested in railways, are confused by them! Forgive me, then, if I appear to labour the point.

'Clearing point' This is a spot 440 yards in advance of the Home signal. Under standard, double-line signalling regulations, the signalman must not give 'Line Clear' to the box in rear when the clearing point is fouled either by a vehicle(s) or when point within the clearing point are not safely set.

'Line Clear' (Regulation 4) When the signalman at the box in rear asks the signalman in advance 'Is Line Clear?' on the block bell, the signalman receiving that signal will only return 'Line Clear' - and thus permit the train to approach from the rear - if he has an unfouled clearing point.

'Line Clear to Clearing Point Only' (Regulation 4A) When signal boxes are so close together that the Distant signal for Box B is placed below the Home or other stop signal of Box A to the rear, and the distance from Box A's Distant signal to his Home signal does not give sufficient braking distance, then the signalman as B must not give 'Line Clear' to A - even if his clearing point is clear - until he has obtained 'Line Clear' from Box C, in advance of his own. If he is unable to obtain 'Line Clear' from the box in advance, signalman B will reply to 'Is Line Clear?' from signalman A with the 'Line Clear to Clearing Point Only' bell code, 2-2-2. Signalman A will then hold his stop signals at 'Danger' until the approaching train has passed his Distant signal at 'Caution'. Thus A's Distant signal is acting also as a Distant signal for B, and the requisite stopping distance is provided.

The Warning Acceptance (Regulation 5) If the use of this Regulation was authorised by the Divisional Superintendent, as shown in the 'Additional Instructions' to the signal box, a signalman could accept a train when the clearing point was fouled. The signalman at B replied to the 'Is Line Clear?' with the bell code 3-5-5. Signalman A, receiving this, could refuse it or accept it. If he accepted it he returned 3-5-5 to B, who then pegged his instrument to 'Line Clear'. Signalman A then warned the driver by bringing him nearly to a stand and exhibiting a green hand-signal, which meant 'Section clear, station or junction ahead blocked'. This was acknowledged by a 'toot' on the whistle. If the hand-signal was not acknowledged, the train was brought to a

stand at the Starting signal, which was then lowered. If there was no signal in advance of the box, the driver was stopped dead and told. This working was *not* permitted during fog or falling snow.

Fog working In some cases the 'footnotes' laid down the 'fog marking point' - if they did not do so, the signalmen chose a signal post about 200 yards from the signal box, or failing that some other convenient object sited at that range. When the 'fog marker' became obscured by fog or falling snow, the signalman was bound to call for his fog signalmen, and until they were on duty at his Distant signals - 'shooting' the trains with their detonators - he was obliged to operate his block signalling routine in accordance with the fog working instructions.

These laid down that a signalman could not give 'Line Clear' to the box in rear until he had an unobstructed clearing point, that he had received 'Train out of Section' from the box in advance for the previous train, and he had placed two detonators on the rail outside the signal box; he could do this last by reversing his detonator placer lever. When he was able to lower his signals, having obtained 'Line Clear' from the box in advance, he removed the detonators. If the box in advance was close, half a mile or less, then the signalman had to have his clearing point unobstructed and also to obtain 'Line Clear' from that box before he could return 'Line Clear' to the box in rear.

Notes on the use of BR(WR) 'Additional Instructions' in this book

The standard routine of train signalling was laid down in the 'Regulations for Train Signalling'. This formed the 'ground rules', and every signal box in GWR days displayed, boldly printed on a very thick card, the 'Additional Instructions' (or 'footnotes' as they were usually called) for that place. These 'Additional Instructions' modified the standard rules, made exceptions, placed special prohibitions on a place - whatever was needed under the local circumstances.

Few of the purely GWR additional instructions have survived because when BR(WR) had to make alterations, the old cards were removed and replaced by sheets of paper. However, these sheets contained all the old GWR instructions except where they had been modified or abolished. In this book I have made use of the oldest surviving 'Additional Instructions', some of them dating from 1944.

A HISTORY OF THE RAILWAYS OF OXFORD

The Broad Gauge arrives

Brunel's route for the Great Western Railway from Bristol to London was not the most direct, but it was the fastest and the only possible route for a strategic railway. Brunel intended it to be a main trunk from which important main lines would branch off or extend to serve South West England, South and West Wales (for Ireland), the English Midlands and the North West. The line to Oxford was mentioned in the Great Western Railway's prospectus of 1834 as 'a probable branch', but it was not included in the Act of Parliament obtained on 31 August 1835 incorporating the GWR and authorising its route.

The GWR was opened by stages and reached Steventon (for Oxford) on 1 June 1840*. In the year 1842, 12,620 tons of freight were handled at the station and 77,567 passengers used the station. Most of these would have been travelling to or from Oxford and would have used the horse-drawn coaches taking 1½ hours for the 10-mile journey and charging each person 3 shillings for a single trip.

The landowners between the GWR main line and Oxford and the University authorities had successfully opposed the various attempts at getting an Act for a branch to Oxford, but after three years of horse coaches or 'Shanks's pony' to and from Oxford, the

objectors realised the advantage of trains and ceased to object. With some clauses to 'protect the morals' of undergraduates and those holding the 'Bachelor' degree, the Act to build the railway was passed on 11 April 1843.

The work of building the 9¾-mile branch proceeded swiftly, in spite of two crossings of the Thames, the need for a 45-foot bridge over a backwater near the Oxford terminus and the construction of several stations, including the junction station at Didcot.

The landowners co-operated with the Company and no unnecessary hindrances were met with - except for the cheeky chancer with a legalistic turn of mind. This character managed to delay the construction of the bridge carrying the Abingdon turnpike over the line and very nearly delayed the opening of the line. He erected a timber framework on or close to the intended line of the railway, had covered the sticks with brown paper and placed a fireplace within. He then claimed that this was his home and demanded compensation from the Company for the depreciation in the value of his property.

On 8 May 1844 notice of opening for 12 June was given in Jackson's *Oxford Journal*; in the same issue there was a letter attacking the Broad Gauge as unnecessarily expensive, and another saying that when the line finally got through to Rugby, could the GWR make the break of gauge at Oxford since this would increase the trade of the town?

* John Henry Newman mentions Steventon as the station for Oxford in his semi-autobiographic novel *Loss and Gain*.

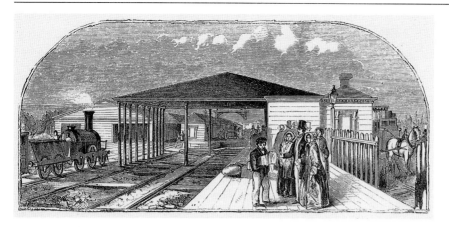

Oxford station, 1844-52, situated on the line of the existing Marlborough Road, on the south bank of the Thames west of Folly Bridge on the Abingdon Road. AVC

things on a wet or freezing day, and it was a very poor or very thoughtless person who did not wear heavy clothing for the journey. But even in July sunshine can turn to torrential rain, and passengers not sufficiently well dressed in a 2nd or 3rd Class carriage risked a soaking and subsequent illness, or even death from exposure - as is well recorded in contemporary newspapers.

The branch duly opened on 12 June 1844. It swung north from the main line at a new station at the 53rd milepost, near a little village called Didcot, and terminated in a swampy field belonging to Brasenose College, on the south bank of the Isis (or Thames) about 300 yards west of Folly Bridge, which carried the Abingdon turnpike across the river. There were some wharves and a steam mill on the north bank, but the station site was in virgin meadows. The only known illustration of it shows a very simple wooden station - obviously a temporary arrangement because the ultimate destinations of the line had always been known to be Worcester and Rugby. In July Brunel was holding meetings with farmers in the Cherwell valley to make out his route to Banbury for Rugby.

On the opening day 'the greatest bustle and excitement prevailed' as thousands gathered to witness the first and subsequent trains. The fields around the railway were turned into a fairground carnival with games taking place and tents housing eating and drinking places. The official party of 50 - sundry Directors, Brunel the Engineer, Saunders the Company Secretary and their wives - came down from London, and on arrival - to hearty cheers from the crowds lining the track - they betook themselves to the Angel hotel in the city where they partook of a sumptuous dinner.

The line was described as 'a remarkably easy one through beautiful and interesting countryside'. The same commentator (The Editor of Jackson's *Oxford Journal*) remarked that the railway fares were very high and asked, 'Who would care to pay ten shillings to travel by train to Town when for six one can go to London behind Charles Holmes and his splendid greys?'. While the railway 1st Class fare was indeed 15 shillings single, the passenger was conveyed in a well-upholstered vehicle over a road infinitely more comfortable than that traversed by the stage coach. The 2nd Class fare was 10 shillings, for travelling in a roofed but otherwise open carriage; these were deadly

The time for the 63 miles to and from London varied - the fastest down train took 135 minutes, with a change at Didcot, and the slowest 155 minutes - and there were ten trains each way every day except Sunday. However, London was at least 6³/4 hours away by road coach.

Careful examination of old surveys in Oxford City Library suggests that the present day Whitehouse Road (not the alluringly named 'Western Road') lies on the line of the original station approach from the Abingdon main road, and the junction of Whitehouse and Marlborough Roads approximates closely to the station forecourt. The railway ran over land now taken up with the back gardens of the houses on the west side of Marlborough Road. No 264 in this road had, in the 1930s, a set of ancient 'stop blocks' in its back garden, and another had a locomotive water supply tank in its back yard. The track bed still exists along the eastern edge of the reservoir known as Hinksey Lake* and merges with the modern trackbed at the 62 milepost**, about 400 yards north of the old Abingdon Road bridge.

The first station north of Didcot was at Appleford, at approximately 54 miles 70 chains, near the existing Appleford Crossing. There is a rectangular grassy area between the east side of the line and a lane, with a row of 'railway-looking' cottages at the north end. Perhaps this grassy area may once have been the site of the old station and its sidings and maybe the cot-

* The lake was formed when the GWR removed gravel for making embankments. The property of the Earl of Abingdon , it contained good drinking water that was piped away to the City. The Earl offered to sell the water acreage to the City Council, but in 1852 he exchanged the reservoir for an equal acreage of 'good producing land' in Botley Meadows.

** Mileage from Paddington via Didcot station. Trains to Oxford via the Didcot Avoiding Line travelled 10 chains (¹/8 mile) less.

tages were built because the station was there. This station was closed and demolished in 1849.

About 800 yards north of Appleford Crossing the aforementioned lane crosses the line by a brick arch, and Appleford Halt, 55 miles 17 chains, flanks the rails, butting up against the south face of the bridge; the Brunellian Broad Gauge shape of this arch is immediately apparent to the discerning eye.

A little way north of this bridge the Thames was crossed on a timber viaduct similar to those used by Brunel on the Swindon-Gloucester line, built simultaneously with the Oxford branch. This timber bridge was replaced in 1860 by a pair of wrought iron plate girder bridges, closely side by side, the girders resting on large-diameter cast-iron cylinders driven into the river bed. These cylinders slowly sank, and by the mid-1920s the ballast on the bridge was piled up high in order to keep the bridge tracks at something approximating to the level of the tracks on each side. In 1929 this bridge was replaced with the existing 'bow and string'-style steel riveted bridge.

Exactly 1 mile north of Appleford Halt is Culham station, 56 miles 17 chains, called 'Dorchester Road' on the original plans and in practise called 'Abingdon Road' until re-named because of the opening of Abingdon station in 1856. Culham is now the sole remaining example of that particular Brunellian style drawn up around 1838, and which is featured by J. C. Bourne in his *History of the Great Western Railway* of 1842, using Pangbourne as an example. Just north of this survivor of early Victorian technology is the Government's space exploration laboratory, the 'Astrophysics Research Centre'.

The meandering Thames had to be crossed again north of Culham at Nuneham. This bridge has the same history as the one near Appleford, except that it was replaced in 1907, supposedly because it was sinking more rapidly than the other. Approximately 500 yards north of the Nuneham bridge the Abingdon branch made a junction with the main line, the single track swinging in on a sharp curve from the west. The branch was opened on 2 June 1856 and was then 1 mile 70 chains long. There was no station at the junction, merely passenger interchange platforms between the down main line and the branch and alongside the up main (the same system was used at Kemble, where the old main line to Cirencester branched away from the new main line to Gloucester). The Abingdon branch was always a profitable one*, and as traffic built up the lack of facilities at the junction was a serious hindrance to trade and passengers.

During 1873 a proper station was built, at 58 miles 36 chains, about three-quarters of a mile north of the old interchange, to serve the village of Radley and to be the junction station for Abingdon; the branch was extended, parallel to the down main line, to the new station. On 8 September 1873 the new system was brought into use and the old junction and interchange were abolished.

A little more than 2½ miles north of Radley the branch from Thame, opened on 24 October 1864*, crossed the Isis (as the Thames is called in the Oxford area) on a three-span 'bow and string' steel bridge and joined the main line, at 61 miles 12 chains, in the water meadows below the village of Kennington.

In the early 1840s the railway companies saw the need for a connection from the Midlands and North to the South Coast. Rugby was the gateway to the North at that time, over the Midland Counties, North Midland and York & North Midland railways. Deputations from heavy industry interviewed the GWR Directors on the subject and also talked of forming independent companies to make the line - 'The Grand Connection Railway', for instance.

Thus the GWR was forced to undertake an Oxford to Rugby railway simply to prevent some hostile company from doing so. Simultaneously the Company was approached by the industries and mines of South Staffordshire for a line from Wolverhampton through Worcester to Banbury on the Oxford & Rugby; the southern destination was soon altered to join the O&R 3 miles north of Oxford. These two proposed railways from Oxford to Rugby and Wolverhampton provoked many years of expensive litigation outside, and more expense inside, Parliament, as other competing lines were proposed on the GWR's southern flank. This was the 'Battle of the Gauges', which set the railway companies against each other and cost their shareholders their dividends.

The London & Birmingham was the Great Western's chief opponent in the Midlands. The L&BR connected at Birmingham with the Grand Junction Railway, which ran north to Warrington for Liverpool and Manchester and Preston under the management of Captain Mark Huish (late of the East India Company's army). Huish forced the amalgamation of the L&BR and the GJR (and several minor companies) into the London & North Western Railway by issuing a notice to his shareholders suggesting that the GJR was thinking of co-operating with the GWR by laying the broad gauge from the intended GWR/Oxford, Worcester & Wolverhampton Railway

---

* The Abingdon Railway Co (ARC) was purchased by the GWR on 1 July 1904. ARC shareholders got £20 of GWR stock for every £10 of ARC stock!

* The 'Wycombe Railway' opened from Maidenhead to High Wycombe on 1 August 1854, and to Thame 1 August 1862.

Looking north from the 'Red Bridge', Abingdon Road, in November 1875. From 1942 until 1973 Hinksey South signal box and marshalling yard stood here, the signal box about where the engine is standing and the yard on the land to the left. Tuckwell's Crossing footbridge can be seen amongst the trees. The signals are operated by Kennington Junction; the semaphore on the left is the Up Main Distant and the 'disc and crossbar' signal acts as the Up Branch Distant signal. Framed between the signals, the main line curves left, while the original route to Oxford can be seen above the engine, going away towards housing on the right.

station at Wolverhampton to Warrington and beyond. This would almost certainly have been impossible without the vast expense of widening the works of the GJR, but of course Huish never had any intention of laying the broad gauge - he simply wished to frighten his prey, in his own words (to Parliament in 1853) 'to bring about an immediate arrangement between the LBR and GJR and to obtain for the GJR a large sum of money as the price of it'.

Having blackmailed the L&BR into amalgamation - and removing a 'large sum of money' from its coffers

The original passenger train service between Oxford and Dudley via Worcester. 1 August 1853. AVC

Facsimile of working time-table of Oxford, Worcester and Wolverhampton listed the member of the staff, to whom it was issued.

DOWN. — WEEK DAYS / SUNDAYS

† This train shunts at Droitwich for the 8 0 a.m. Passenger Train from Worcester.

Railway. This time-table was printed on glazed linen, so that a copy could be subjected to rough usage, although subjected to a considerable time.

UP. — WEEK DAYS / SUNDAYS

(The detailed timetables of train departure and arrival times for the DOWN and UP services between Oxford, Worcester, and Dudley are reproduced as facsimiles and are not transcribed in full.)

in the process, Huish became General Manager of the LNWR and for over 20 years waged a financially ruinous 'war' of competitive railway proposals into Oxfordshire and Worcestershire in opposition to the broad gauge GWR.

The Oxford & Rugby Railway Bill became law on 4 August 1845; it was a mixed gauge line, the standard gauge rail laid within the broad gauge. On 3 August 1846 another act was gained for the purely broad gauge Birmingham & Oxford Junction Railway. This was to leave the Oxford & Rugby line at Knightcote, 2 miles north of Fenny Compton, and go through Leamington to the LNWR near Curzon Street, Birmingham, with a branch to a GWR station at Snow Hill, Birmingham. The Oxford & Rugby Company was amalgamated with the GWR on 14 May 1846, but the 15½ miles of route from Rugby to Knightcote was abandoned in August 1849, with only a quarter of a mile of embankment built, heading north-east from Knightcote, but the line south to Banbury and Oxford was completed. The first section to be opened was the 24½ miles of broad gauge, (temporarily) single track, from Millstream Junction to Banbury, on 2 September 1850. Trains to and from Banbury and London had to reverse in and out of the Oxford terminus. An observant person standing on the old Abingdon Road bridge and looking north, can (or could in 1973) see the 'kink' in the line, where, in 1850, the new line turned just a few points northwest, away from the original track, to pass around the west side of the city.

During the next two years a new 'through' station for Oxford was built at 63½ miles immediately north of the Botley Road. The line was extended from Banbury to Birmingham (Snow Hill) as a double track mixed gauge railway and the old single track south to Millstream Junction was doubled, using the mixed gauge; the original line from Millstream Junction into the old terminus remained purely broad gauge to the end. The new line from Millstream Junction to Birmingham Snow Hill was opened on 1 October 1852, together with the new Oxford station. At this point the old terminus was closed to regular passenger traffic, but remained in regular use as a goods station. It was also occasionally used to accommodate excursion trains to some local carnival; for instance, on 13 June 1863 special trains carrying spectators from Abingdon and Didcot to the annual riverside boat show used the old station because 'it was convenient for the river' (Jackson's Oxford Journal).

Expansion and rivalries

The new station at Oxford consisted of a long row of single-storey timber offices flanking both sides of four tracks which passed beneath a Brunellian wooden train shed with a glazed windscreen at each end; a similar building had been erected at Banbury.

Originally there were three stations between Oxford and Banbury; going north these were Woodstock, 71 miles 30 chains (renamed Woodstock Road in May 1851), Heyford, 75¼ milepost, and Aynho, 80¼ milepost. In 1855 two new stations were opened: Somerton (Somerton (Oxon) from 2 July 1906 and Fritwell & Somerton from October 1907), 78 milepost, and a new 'Woodstock Road' at the 69th milepost; at this point the original Woodstock Road was renamed 'Kirtlington'. King's Sutton station, 82 miles 55 chains, was opened in 1872. On 19 May 1890 the Woodstock Railway, 3 miles 56 chains, was opened from Woodstock Road station, which was then renamed 'Kidlington, Junction for Woodstock', while Kirtlington station was renamed 'Bletchington' in October 1890. The Woodstock Railway was absorbed into the GWR on 1 July 1897.

On 1 May 1851 the so-called Buckinghamshire Railway Company (the London & North Western in disguise) opened its line from Bletchley to Banbury. On 20 May the section from Verney Junction to Oxford (Rewley Road) was opened, the latter station alongside the GWR's new facility, then under construction.

The LNWR, running westwards, came to the 27¾ milepost from Bletchley and here it crossed the Oxford-Banbury Road. At the 28 milepost it swung to the south and came downhill at 1 in 204, through Wolvercot tunnel, 145 yards long starting from the 28¾ milepost, crossed the Oxford Canal and reached virtually level track at the 30 milepost. The LNWR tracks were closely parallel to the GWR for the last 1½ miles into Rewley Road terminus. The line entered the station on a swingbridge over 'Duke's Cut', a waterway connecting the Oxford Canal with the Isis.

This line was part of a policy of the LNWR's Captain Huish to cut across the northwards extension of the broad gauge GWR and to compete with that

Company. It seems incredible that he should even attempt such an impossible feat as to run Euston-Oxford trains - but that was the kind of competitive man he was. In 1851 the LNWR ran five services each way between Euston and Oxford, all with a reversal at Bletchley. The fastest was the 10 am Euston-Oxford, taking $2^1/2$ hours; this was only 15 minutes longer than the 10.15 am Paddington-Oxford, so if they were both on time they arrived together - one from the north and one from the south. The 3.30 pm Euston arrived at 5.45 and the 4.50 pm Paddington arrived at 6.15.

The Oxford, Worcester & Wolverhampton Railway opened from the GWR at Wolvercot Junction, 66 miles 32 chains, on 4 June 1853. This was a very unfortunate company that had taken ten years to build the 89 miles from Wolvercot to Wolverhampton. The line had been intended as a broad gauge extension into the industrial Midlands, and was engineered by I. K. Brunel; funded in large part by the GWR, that Company also guaranteed a $3^1/2$ per cent dividend on the £1.5 million capital. Six out of 16 Directors were nominated by the GWR, so GWR interests ought to have been secure, but the London & North Western and Midland companies exerted their enormous influence against any northward extension of Brunel's maverick gauge.

The OWWR, under its first Chairman, Rufford, got into deep financial trouble, in part because Brunel (as usual) grossly under-estimated the capital required to build the line. By 1850 the Company had run out of money with the line far from complete, and in October it fell into the hands of the sharpest contractor/financial 'fixer' of the period, Samuel Morton Peto. He became one of the two main contractors for the line, he found new capital and took a seat on the Board while placing his creature, a dishonest solicitor inaptly called Parson, as Chairman. Parson was subsequently to commit perjury in an effort, which was in itself illegal, to get rid of the GWR and the broad gauge.

Brunel was then employing Peto on his works at Fenny Compton, the first time Peto had worked for Brunel since the Wharncliffe and Pangbourne contracts of 1835/38. Under Peto and Parson the OWWR became an enemy of the GWR, and Brunel ceased to advise the Company's Directors on *new* works from the end of 1850. In June 1851 Brunel, acting under orders from the OWWR Directorate (which included Peto), used Peto's navvies from Fenny Compton to violently and illegally evict the contractor of the Mickleton tunnel, as a result of which Peto took over the tunnel contract. Brunel resigned completely from the OWWR in March 1852.

Parson, directed by his master Peto, did everything possible to get rid of legal ties between the OWWR and GWR so as to sell out to the LNWR; thus the GWR was forced to waste time and money in the fight to preserve its interests. An example of money-wasting forced upon the Company by this unscrupulous pair was the London & Mid-Western Railway, a very typically Peto-esque production designed to dazzle the greedy and the gullible with money to invest or with enough credit at their bankers to raise a loan. The line cut through the middle of empty territory between the GWR and LNWR so as to make a competitive threat to one or both companies. It was to use the OWWR to Oxford, then go by Thame and High Wycombe to Hounslow on the London & South Western, with a branch around North London to the Eastern Counties Railway, in which Peto was deeply involved, and into London's growing dockland, much of which was being built by Peto and his friends.

The promotion of such a line, which was only one amongst many similar frauds between 1851 and 1864, gave ample opportunity to gamblers in shares - such as Peto - but only weakened established companies trying to run an honest railway. The GWR beat the Parson/Peto axis in the end and the OWWR remained under GWR control - but only after great expense.

The OWWR was opened on 4 June 1853 as a mixed gauge railway, but except for the Board of Trade inspection train, no broad gauge train ever ran on it, while the standard gauge trains of the OWWR came over GWR metals as far as Oxford station where there were bay platforms for them and 'narrow gauge' sidings for their stock. The OWWR had powers to use the GWR goods station if it laid its own third rail, but instead it chose to run into Rewley Road over the link line described below.

On 1 April 1854 the LNWR opened a 1-mile 49-chain link line to connect its 'Buckinghamshire Railway' with the OWWR. The junction - 'Oxford Road Junction' - was 27 miles 69 chains from Bletchley, near the level crossing of the Oxford-Banbury road, after which the new line continued westwards, climbing at 1 in 600 to a level crossing of the Oxford-Woodstock road, almost three-quarters of a mile from the junction. The line then dropped at 1 in 225 for a quarter of a mile, crossing the Oxford Canal, then less steeply over the GWR's Birmingham line, finally rising to the OWWR at 'Buckingham Junction' - Yarnton. A few yards east of the Woodstock Road level crossing a west-to-south curve was built to connect the new line with the 'Buckinghamshire Railway' line, making a junction just north of Wolvercot tunnel. This enabled up OWWR goods trains to use the LNWR goods yard at Oxford rather than go through the crowded GWR

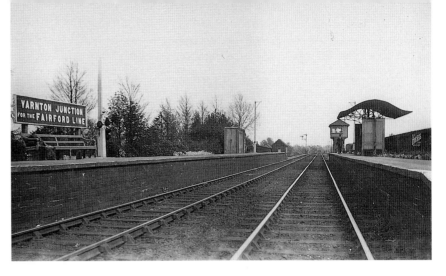

A station was opened at Yarnton Junction in 1861. This was the view looking towards Oxford some time between 1929 and 1935, with the 'North Western' loop junction signal on the horizon. *Locomotive & General 13789*

station to Millstream Junction and there reverse into the old passenger station. OWWR goods trains used the curve daily from 1854 until 1861, but that Company's passenger trains only used it (on a regular basis at any rate) from October to December 1857.

In October 1854 the LNWR opened a curve ('the Worcester curve') from just south of Bletchley station to its 'Buckingham Railway'. The junction faced Euston, and by this the distance from Euston to 'Buckingham Junction', or Yarnton, was 76 miles, while from Paddington to the same spot was 67 miles 12 chains, making the distance from Euston to Worcester 129 miles, against 120 by the GWR and OWWR. The curve was mainly for goods traffic, but one express train per day in each direction - Euston-Worcester-Wolverhampton - used it, covering the 129½ miles to Worcester in 4 hours.

There was originally no station at Yarnton Junction. Passengers to and from the LNWR and the OWWR, or those LNWR/OWWR passengers wishing to change trains for the GWR south of Oxford, did so at 'Handborough Junction', a wayside station 3¼ miles from Yarnton, towards Worcester; the OWWR ran a shuttle service to and from Oxford station and Handborough.

Relations between the OWWR and the GWR were very difficult owing to the perjured and perfidious nature of the OWWR's Directorate and their strong inclination to allow the LNWR to come into the GWR West Midlands over a route built - to a substantial degree - with GWR money. The OWWR passenger service out of Oxford (GW) to Worcester was very slow in order to prevent the GWR profiting from the line it had funded and to ensure that long-distance passengers used the LNWR route. Such is the result of competition!

On 1 June 1860 the OWWR absorbed the Newport, Abergavenny & Hereford and purchased the Worcester & Hereford companies to form the 'West Midland Railway' (WMR). This enlarged system maintained its hostility to the GWR and in 1861 launched its third or fourth attempt to build a railway from Yarnton to London. At each attempt the route varied a little, and this one announced its intention of going via Thame, Risborough, Amersham, Beaconsfield and Uxbridge to a terminus in Sloane

Square. At the same time the GWR was supporting a railway to occupy the ground between High Wycombe, Thame and Oxford.

The LNWR, which had been happy to use the OWWR/WMR, did not want a new, competing railway, and joined forces with the GWR in opposition, whereupon the WMR withdrew its Bill from Parliament and agreed to a lease by the GWR preparatory to a full take-over. The lease took effect on 1 July 1861 and the GWR purchased the WMR under the Great Western Railway (West Midland Railway) Act of 13 July 1863. On that day the junction of the Woodstock curve at the Wolvercot tunnel end was taken out of use, leaving the line as a long siding off the LNWR loop for wagon exchange between the GWR and LNWR.

However, Euston remained the London terminal for Worcester passengers for a while longer. In October 1852 the mixed gauge was laid between Oxford and Birmingham Snow Hill, and during 1856 it was extended from Oxford to Reading West Junction and Basingtoke; standard gauge trains from Birmingham to the South Coast began running on 22 December. On 1 October 1861 the mixed gauge was opened from Reading West Junction to Paddington. With the standard gauge now complete between Worcester and Paddington and under one management, Paddington superseded Euston as the London terminal for Worcester. The GWR Worcester expresses had 9½ miles less to travel than by Euston and Bletchley, but the GWR service was 'miserably slow. . . well over 4 hours for 120 miles'* (slow speeds actually were GWR policy at that time). The continuous standard gauge also enabled the South Eastern Railway to co-operate with the GWR in running a Dover-Birkenhead service via Redhill, Reading, Oxford and Birmingham, while the LSWR was able to run freight to and through Oxford without the expensive and time-consuming nuisance of transhipment.

The broad gauge was abolished between Wolver-

* E. T. MacDermot, *History of the Great Western Railway*, Vol 2.

hampton, Birmingham and Oxford via Banbury on 1 April 1869, and between Oxford and Didcot North Junction on 26 November 1872. The old Oxford terminus closed at the same time, and the site remained derelict until the late 1880s when the present housing was erected on the site.

The standard gauge branch line from Yarnton (OWWR) to Witney gained its Act as 'The Witney Railway Co' on 1 August 1859. The branch had its roots in a plan, going back to 1846, to drive a competing line from London to Cheltenham, and thus allow the Midland and LNWR into GWR territory in the same way as the OWWR tried to let the LNWR into Worcester. The 8-mile 13-chain single track was opened on 14 November 1862. The East Gloucestershire Railway Company, incorporated by Act of Parliament on 7 August 1862, opened the 14 miles 10 chains from Witney to Fairford on 15 January 1873.

With the opening to Kennington of the line from Thame, Princes Risborough, High Wycombe and Maidenhead on 24 October 1864, most of the routes directly affecting Oxford had thus been completed. All that remained to be added was the relatively insignificant Woodstock Railway in 1890.

In 1896 the Great Western began a progressive era with new managers that was to take it to the forefront of railway developments by 1914. This was most obviously shown by getting rid of the last remnants of the broad gauge, but more importantly with the introduction of steam-heated corridor coaches, restaurant cars, very much more powerful four-coupled express passenger engines and non-stop expresses between Paddington and Birkenhead, Bristol and Newport (Mon). The first 'corridor express' at Oxford was the Birkenhead service, commencing on 7 March 1892.

In 1891 the GWR and LSWR began running through passenger trains between Southampton and north-western destinations via Basingstoke and Oxford - Southampton via Newbury began in 1892 and Oxford-Folkestone in 1897.

Very few regularly scheduled trains passed Oxford non-stop, but there were some. The first was in 1896, a Paddington-Birmingham-Aberystwyth express, summer season only, which was scheduled to cover the 106 miles from Paddington to Leamington, start to stop, in 120 minutes. In the up direction (only) this train slipped a coach at Oxford. In 1897 the 2.10 pm Paddington-Birmingham began to run non-stop with a slip coach for Leamington, and was booked to cover the $129\frac{1}{2}$ miles to Birmingham in 147 minutes; in 1902 the schedule to Birmingham was reduced by 7 minutes. The first Worcester express booked non-stop through Oxford was the 1.40 pm Paddington, which began running in 1900 and was scheduled to cover the $120\frac{1}{2}$ miles, non-stop, in 135 minutes down and 140 minutes up; perhaps the extra 5 minutes were allowed for climbing Honeybourne bank. All these fast trains were formed with corridor stock, and up to 1910 they would usually have been hauled by the magnificent 7 ft 8 in Dean 'Singles'; No 3027 Worcester worked on these expresses from 1895. From 1910 the fastest Worcester expresses were hauled by the 'City' Class 4-4-0s with better adhesion and the much more powerful Churchward boiler.

As the very powerful four- and six-coupled Churchward express engines came into use, so journey times were reduced. The accompanying table gives an idea.

The GWR transferred its fastest Birmingham expresses from the Didcot-Oxford-Aynho route to the 'New Line' - Aynho Junction-Bicester-Old Oak Common - in 1910 (of which more later).

My friend, the late Dr Jack Hollick, studied medicine at Oxford in 1928-32. He spent a large part of his spare time on Oxford station or riding on trains from Oxford in company with the guard and Travelling Ticket Collector (TTI). He was fascinated with the com-

A Churchward-boilered Dean 'Single' comes through Oxford with a non-stop express, perhaps the 1.45 pm Paddington-Worcester, in about 1903. The view is from the down platform looking south. A horse box is standing on the wagon turntable with the Goods Shed (later Station South) box beyond. Engine Shed's (later Station North) Distant is 'off', which means that North box's Distant will also be 'off' - they have the road right through. On the up line the bracket signal applies only to trains on the up platform line; the signal for the up main is on a separate post, above the loco's cab roof. AVC

	Miles	1888	1900	1912
Paddington-Oxford	63½	78	77	70
Paddington-Worcester	120½	180	135	129
Paddington-Hereford	144¼	None	200	193
Paddington-Leamington	106	133	117	91*
Paddington-Birmingham	129¼	162	145	120*

* via Bicester

plications of the station's operation: the marshalling and re-marshalling of passenger trains, the way that the carriage sets were utilised for the different services, and also the complicated formation within certain trains - in particular the inter-company, cross-country services (for example, the 2.37 pm Newcastle-Bournemouth had five coaches from Newcastle, two from Leeds attached at Nottingham, and a Brake Composite from Bradford). These trains had several sections, each for different destinations, so it was of the utmost importance to the passengers that they sat in the right coaches; it was really a matter of marshalling the passengers, and this would be done between Oxford and Banbury. Jack travelled with the TTI and became very expert - he actually produced a guide book for the use of the ticket staff on and off the trains!

Handling the traffic

An event of great significance for Oxford was the opening on 13 August 1900 of the Great Central Railway link from that Company's main line at Woodford Halse to Banbury. This sounds a long way off, but it brought about a great deal of extra complication for the station by introducing more inter-company, cross-country workings, adding to the intricacy of carriage workings and engine changes at Oxford. Trains were now coming not only from Birkenhead and Chester, but also from Newcastle, York and Nottingham.

Quite a few of the passenger trains arriving at Oxford had to have an engine change, or coaches detached or attached from other trains from another route, or parcels, or milk or horse box traffic attached; this was done by the train engine or the Station Pilot. All these services, freight and passenger, had then to be found 'paths' through the double-track bottleneck south to Didcot, where a few passengers and more freight took the West Curve for Swindon, Weymouth, Plymouth and Penzance. From 1892 a through service began between Oxford and Southampton via Compton and Winchester, making a connection out of a northern train heading to the South Coast via Reading and Basingstoke.

In 1901 a couple of GC expresses, with restaurant cars to and from Leicester and Oxford, ran between Leicester and Southampton via Compton and Winchester. These or similar workings, slow and tedious south of Oxford, ran until September 1939. Most inter-company traffic went east to Reading where the flow split for London or for Kentish destinations via Guildford and Redhill, or for the South Coast resorts via Basingstoke. These passenger services were additional to the Worcester and Birmingham express trains, the Paddington/Reading-Oxford locals and semi-fasts, the Didcot-Banbury locals, the Oxford-Worcester locals, the 'stoppers' to Paddington via Thame, and the branch trains to Abingdon, Fairford and Woodstock. All these trains had to be accommodated at Oxford's too few platforms - while the goods trains crept through the Middle Roads as and when they could. From April 1910 the Birmingham expresses went via the 'New Line' (see the next section), so the situation would have been eased - for a while - but I have no doubt that other, slower, traffic developed to take the spare 'paths'. Thus Oxford (in steam days) handled enough traffic to justify four through platforms, but basically it was the 1852 layout that was made to suffice in spite of every pressure of traffic.

The 1852 station was reconditioned in 1890/1. This entailed removing the Brunel overall roof, improving passenger facilities - including the provision of flushing lavatories - and refurbishing the passenger subway. The up platform was extended by 110 feet at the north end, making the up bay 440 feet long, but the down platform was left untouched, with an ancient wagon turntable servicing some very short sidings at the south end. Between 1907 and 1908 this ancient device was demolished and the down platform extended at both the north and south ends. The northerly extension brought the down platform-end close to the 'Duke's Cut' bridge. The track to and from the down bay (known locally as 'Binsey') previously joined the down main without first crossing the river, but now that the platform was extended an extra span had to be added to carry the bay track over

The down platform from the up, looking south on 17 October 1935. 'Binsey Sidings' can just be seen through the gap on the right, and there is a clerestory coach in Binsey bay. The two sets of 'scissors' crossovers halfway along each main-line platform can be clearly seen. *GWR*

in one direction. From February 1932 there was a direct connection from Down Main to shed, but still many engines ran to North box to go on to the depot.

In about 1910 Oxford Running & Maintenance Depot and its staff had to service 36 of its own engines every day (rising to 65 in wartime), in addition to the others that came to the shed from terminating trains or off inter-company trains, from the LNER or Southern. Even in 1900 the depot was old-fashioned and difficult to operate due to the very badly sited coaling stage; this was replaced in November 1944, but the actual wooden engine shed, opened in 1862, was never replaced. It closed at the end of steam haulage after 102 years' service on 3 January 1966.

The vitally important coaling stage was situated very close to the single track by which engines arrived and departed, from and to the station. Engines coming to the shed took coal at once and this could lead to the points to the bypass* becoming obstructed by engines awaiting coal. Engines then went from the coal stage to the far side of the site for fire-cleaning or fire-dropping. The coal stage was built to a height suitable for low-sided 19th-century locomotive tenders and low-sided coal wagons. By 1923 locomotive-coal wagons were larger, and from 1926 this also applied to an ever-increasing number of locomotive tenders. The consequences of this were serious for some of my old friends who recalled matters ruefully and in detail.

The doors of larger 20th-century 12-ton coal wagons would not fully open when brought alongside the platform inside the coal stage, which meant that the coalers had to remove the coal by hand, from the top of the load, until such time as they reached the floor and had a smooth surface along which to shovel; by that time the wagon would be more than half-empty.

the water to its junction with the down main on the north side of the Cut. It is likely that two extra sidings for carriages were added at this time; they were called 'Binsey Sidings' and cut through space once occupied by the mysterious 'Bay' signal box.

The new up platform was 306 yards long and the down platform 305 yards 2 feet long. The platform face to Binsey bay was 440 feet and the up bay - to which local railwaymen never granted a nickname - was 450 feet long. Halfway along each main line platform a pair of 'scissors' crossovers were installed to connect the Up Platform and Up Main and the Down Platform and Down Main. The 'loops' thus formed by these intermediate crossovers held an engine and five coaches and were useful when passenger trains were parted, the front half for one destination, the rear half for another

There was always a great deal of engine-changing at Oxford, but until February 1932 direct access to and from the engine shed was not available from the Down Main, Up Platform or Up Bay. Engines off trains in the Up Bay reversed to Jericho, drove forwards to the Up Main clear of the crossover, then reversed to the shed. An engine off a train at the south end of the Up Platform ran back 'wrong road' along the Up Main and thence to the shed, or they crossed to the Down Main at the south end of the station, ran along the Down Main and into the Down Platform through the 'scissors'.

The 1922 Local Instructions for Oxford recommended that 'as far as possible' all engines going to shed should do so at North box. One good reason for this was that the exit from the shed was a single track, and therefore it was safest if all engines using it went

* At least until 1910 the track on which locomotives stood to receive their coal was a dead-end siding. Each engine had to reverse off the siding to make way for the next. See R. A. Cooke's *Track Plans: Oxford*.

Coal from the wagons was thrown or shovelled into iron trams that were wheeled across the floor and the fuel dropped on to the tender below by up-ending the tram. But the new 4,000-gallon tenders were too tall to allow the tram to be tipped, so coal had to be carried in shovelsful, or in wicker baskets, across the floor and thrown on to the tender.

If there was a co-incidence of 'un-openable' wagon door and high-sided tender, the reader can perhaps imagine the miserable labour involved in coaling up the handsome 'Hall' or 'Castle' Class engine. Engines of these classes that were allocated to Oxford were specially equipped with small tenders, but a visiting engine would have the normal, high-sided tender. The reader might like to imagine doing this job in darkness with a freezing wind, or maybe in the dust and sweat of a sweltering summer day. But yet - there was Mr Roberts, an Alderman of the City of Oxford, struggling away on nights, in the dust-laden, gas-lit gloom of the coal stage. Nor was Oxford, important depot though it was, unique in these shortcomings - the even more important depot of Worcester had the same problems. The GWR was fortunate that its staff made up the deficiency by being very well equipped with determination and courage.

During the Second World War, when locomotive work was doubled and trebled, a steam crane, placed elsewhere in the yard, was used as additional coaling capacity, the crane swinging hand-filled skips of coal on to the loco tenders. Under these great difficulties the coalers continued to service not only the shed's allocation of 65 locomotives, but all the 'foreign' engines that came on to the shed. This situation was only rectified between December 1944 and January 1945, when a proper coaling stage was erected, and 'Incoming' and 'Outgoing' roads were installed connecting at the station end to the Down Main and Platform lines (see the layout diagram on page 173).

The main road to Wantage, Faringdon and Swindon passed under the line at the south end of the station, but there was also a road/rail level crossing immediately south of the underpass. On the south side of this level crossing, on the down side of the line, there

were carriage sidings extending south to the cemetery and a footbridge over the line. These were always known as 'West Midland Sidings' in remembrance of the original owning company. Opposite, on the up side, there were some more sidings. The one next to the Up Goods Loop was an engine line called 'Mark's Hole', and those behind it were officially Beckett Street sidings, but actually 'Top Yard', across to the Beckett Street wall; these held coal traffic for local coal merchants. They were reached either from South End Yard or by backing across from the Down Main, and were serviced once or twice a day by the Transfer Pilot. The goods shed for Oxford's own traffic was situated on the up side 150 yards further south, and the South End Yard was south of and also at the back of this.

While on the subject of siding nicknames at Oxford, having already mentioned that the down bay and its associated sidings were always known as 'Binsey', on the up side there was the 'Up Bay', and alongside were 'Dock West', 'Dock East', 'No 2', 'No 1' and 'Back Road'. 'Dock West' was always the stabling point for the gas tanks on their flat-bed wagon, the gas being used to replenish the tanks on restaurant cars and the lighting in some carriages.

Just north of 'Duke's Cut', on the up side, there were two long 'Exchange' sidings lying between the Up Goods Loop and the LMS. Until 1940 the only connection between the GWR and the LMS was through these sidings. The line nearest to the LMS was always known as 'Jericho', presumably because it was the nearest one to the district of Oxford of that name surrounding St Barnabas's church, on the other side of the Oxford Canal. The next was 'Jericho Middle', then 'Jericho Loop'.

On the opposite side of the line, north of the engine shed yard, were some carriage sidings on the

The view looking south-east from the Osney Lane footbridge on 21 November 1929, with the GWR goods shed on the right, and coal and other wagons in South End Yard in the background. In the foreground are No 1688 and shunters, and the Oxford Ice Co's office. *Dr Jack Hollick/AVC*

No 3614, on Pilot duties in about 1930, has entered Station North section from the South End with a nod from the signalman. The shunter is George Viner, and he will take the gas tanks off the back of the down milk train, and assist in running the engine around the vehicle so as to be able to reverse it into the Up Sidings. The tanks have come from Swindon, changing trains at Didcot, and the gas will be used to re-charge the kitchen cars of passenger trains, especially those of the cross-country trains based at Oxford. *Dr Jack Hollick/AVC*

site of the old North End Yard, and these, from around 1948/50, were known as 'Miller's Sidings', to give honour to the man who was first the Assistant Station Master, then Station Master, and won everyone's affection and respect by leading from the front, getting his hands dirty when occasion demanded, and helping out with the passenger train shunting when the times were busy and the men hard-pressed.'He would turn his hand to anything,' said Ken Smewin, who spent a lifetime at Oxford station.

In 1895 and until 1942 there were two goods yards at Oxford - North End and South End Yards. As already mentioned, the former was on the down side of the line just beyond the engine shed, while the latter was on the up side south of the station. It might be supposed that all up freights having business at Oxford would call at the South End and all down freights would use the North End. This was, however, not the case. Goods trains with traffic for the City of Oxford or that required to change trains could stop at either of the yards to put off traffic. A down train with City of Oxford traffic might go through to the North End and drop the wagons, which would then be 'tripped' back to the South End later. Or perhaps this down train might stop on the Down Main at the South box, leave its tail behind and go on - leaving the South End Pilot to come out at once and collect the standing wagons and take them back into the yard. Or perhaps the train would stop at the Goods Shed box and shunt the front part of its train across all roads into the South End. There was no rule - it depended on the official marshalling instructions of trains, modified at times by the necessities of the moment. For example, South End might be too busy to accept traffic.

In 1904 Oxford had three Pilot engines: No 1, the South End Pilot, which came off shed at 5.30 am on

Monday and shunted continuously until 7 am the following day, returning to shed after being replaced by another engine; No 2, the Passenger Pilot, which 'tailed' passenger trains, removing or adding coaches and vans to passenger trains and being ready to take over a train in the case of an engine failure; and No 3, the North End Pilot, booked to work from 5 am to 2.30 pm each day.

To put this in perspective, at Reading in 1904 there were 10 Pilot engines. Six were goods shunting engines, at work 24 hours a day, designated West Junction Up Yard, West Junction Down Yard, West End, East End, Coal Yard and the Transfer Trip engine, booked on 8 am to 6 pm daily. There were four Passenger Pilot engines at Reading.

By 1922 traffic at Oxford had increased, and shunting requirements were greater:

Passenger Pilots
No 1   6.45 am to 4.30 am
No 2   7.30 am to 10.15 pm
On Sundays passenger train engines will act as Pilot.

Goods Pilots
No 1   6 am off shed for South End Yard*
No 2   6 am off shed for North End Yard*
No 3   3.30 am off shed for Transfer trips between North End and South End Yards and exchanges between GW and LNW. 4½ hours a day
No 4   Mileage Yard. 4 hours a day.'

* 24 hours each weekday and 14 hours on Sundays

In 1936 there were 17 scheduled transfer trips between the yards between 1 am and 11.45 pm. The following are two examples of the working from 1936. First is the 10.30 pm South End to North End trip, which took wagons forward that had been dropped from the following trains:

12.55 pm Banbury-Stoke Gifford
2.50 pm Moreton Marsh-Oxford*
9.05 am Bordesley-Oxford**
4.50 pm Banbury to Oxford

* Pick-up goods, all stations to Oxford South End Yard; arrive 8.05 pm
** Pick-up goods, all stations to Oxford South End Yard; arrive 7.30 pm

At North End these wagons were attached to:

2.10 am Basingstoke-Oxley
2.00 am Reading-Oxley
1.50 am Park Royal-Worcester
3.20 am Oxford-Pontypool*
5.50 am Oxford-Fairford
8.30 am Oxford-Moreton Marsh**
12.05 pm Oxford-Bordesley***

* Goods and coal empties via Yarnton, Honeybourne and Cheltenham
** Pick-up goods, all station to Moreton Marsh
*** Pick-up goods, all stations to Bordesley.

The second example is the 3.45 pm trip from North End to South End, which took wagons off the 3.55 am Slough to Oxford and from the LMS transfer siding. At South End these were attached to:

5.50 pm Yarnton-Didcot
3.30 pm Worcester-Paddington
12.01 am Oxford-Taplow

At South End Yard there was a staff of four shunters under a Foreman; these shunters ate and rested in a grounded six-wheel coach body. My friend, the late Harry Keen, was a signal lampman at Oxford from 1909, later a guard and Travelling Ticket Collector. He had a wonderful memory and was sure that the railway at Oxford had its fair share of wonderfully eccentric characters. He knew the South End

shunters well: 'Old Mo', the Head Shunter; 'Old Coddy', the Transfer Porter; 'Bishop' Deacon; 'Jelly' Pill; the two Webb brothers, 'Spider' and 'Legs'; and another shunter called 'Sooty'.

'Old Mo' retired in 1910, but for years after came back to the coach for tea and a chat with his old mates. One day, soon after the end of the Great War, they were all sitting round at a break in the work; Mo was there, and someone said, 'I reckon you'll come back here and haunt this place when you're dead, Mo.'

Well, they all laughed and forgot the remark, then a couple of months later Mo died. A few months later again a new Foreman was posted to South End and the shunters, sitting round one evening, thought they ought to give him a welcome and decided to invoke for his entertainment the spirit of the greatest Foreman of the yard - 'Old Mo'.

They made their preparations carefully. A ouija board was made up, and 'Sooty' made up his face dead white and painted his shunting pole the same colour. The stove was 'roared up' until the top was red-hot, and a packet of detonating fog signals was placed handily nearby. The new Foreman was then invited in and they all sat round the table, touching the ouija board, their handlamps showing ghastly-green lights. Outside in the darkness lurked 'Sooty'.

'Bishop' Deacon did a good job of invoking the spirit, calling and calling and dropping a lurid groan now and then until everyone began to feel just a bit queer and shivery in spite of the roaring stove. Judging his moment, 'Sooty' opened the door and came in, wailing and white-faced, brandishing his dreadful shunting pole. Right on cue the man with the 'shots' lifted the lid of the stove, intending to throw a single 'banger' into the fire - but he tipped in the entire packet of 12. The shots exploded, the stove was shattered and the coach was filled with genuinely frightened, yelling men tumbling over benches in the dark towards the door pursued by flying coals, soot and shrapnel. The story of 'Old Mo' was still current when I came to work at Oxford in 1968, but Harry Keen was working there when the event took place.

Wartime improvements

Prior to 1900 the double track lines leading to Oxford from Banbury, Evesham and Didcot were very poorly equipped to accommodate goods trains. There were hardly any 'lay-by', or, as the railway called them, 'refuge' sidings to permit a

goods to be taken off the main line to allow a following passenger train to run past. Where refuge sidings did exist, they were always inconvenient, because trains had to reverse into them. A train might also be crossed from, say, the up to the down main line in a reversing movement, a time-consuming operation.

The more convenient goods loops - which freight trains entered 'head-first' through facing points in the main line - were then non-existent between Didcot, Banbury and Worcester, except for the up loop at the south end of Oxford station, which was really for use of trains calling at South End Yard. Down goods trains might be refuged off the main line by reversing on to sidings at the North End, but these were really for marshalling trains.

The siding at Wolvercot Siding box was installed perhaps as early as 1875, but it was short, for loading wagons with local produce, and was not intended for use as a through-freight refuge. Oxford station was always a severe bottleneck, even after the improvements of 1940-2, because the traffic developed along with the increased accommodation.

An Up Loop was installed from Wolvercot Junction to Oxford station, 3 miles, in June 1900. It was equipped with a 'Loop to Main' junction at Oxford North box, and south of that point, as far as Oxford Engine Shed box, it was known as 'Jericho Loop', and was specifically for the stabling of empty coaches or the Station Pilot and coaches.

From 1900 to 1940, north of Didcot North Junction (53 miles 74 chains - mileage from Paddington via Didcot station) the sequence of signal boxes was:

Appleford Crossing (down side, 54 m 64 ch)
Culham (up side, 56 m 10 ch)
Radley (up side, 58 m 25 ch)
Kennington Junction (up side, 60 m 75 ch)
Oxford South (down side, 63 m 1 ch)
Oxford Goods Shed (down side, 63 m 40 ch)
Oxford Engine Shed (up side, 63 m 49 ch)
Oxford North (up side, 63 m 73 ch)
Wolvercot Siding (up side, 65 m 47 ch)
Wolvercot Junction (down side, 66 m 31 ch)
Kidlington (Banbury line) (up side, 69 m 17 ch)
Yarnton Junction (Worcester line) (down side, 67 m 22 ch)

On 4 April 1910 the 'New Line' was opened from a new 'flying junction' at Aynho on the Oxford-Banbury line to the GW&GC Joint line at Ashendon Junction, thence to Old Oak Common, near Paddington. This provided a shorter and faster route from Paddington to Banbury and points north, and reduced the number of Paddington-Birmingham trains via Oxford. But the GCR-LSWR trains were running by then, and freight traffic still tended to go via Oxford, leaving the 'New Line' relatively free for the 'fasts'.

In 1912* an Up Goods Loop was laid from Aynho Junction to Aynho station, holding 145 wagons. Then in May 1915 the Down Refuge siding at Aynho station was converted to a Down Loop by being extended southwards 2 miles to an entrance at Fritwell & Somerton; it held 485 wagons. A Down Refuge was installed at Bletchington in 1901, holding 52 wagons*. Between 1900 and 1920*, probably during the Great War, Up and Down Refuge sidings were added at Heyford, holding 61 and 63 wagons respectively. The Up Refuge exit points were approximately 400 yards from Heyford signal box and were operated by a ground frame at the points, electrically released from the signal box. An Up Refuge was installed at Kidlington in 1901-3*, and from 1906 it was possible to use part of the Woodstock branch as a Down Goods Loop; trains entered the branch at the station and exited 166 yards further north.**

Getting goods trains through Oxford was very difficult. The station was occupied with the shunting of vehicles on and off passenger trains, and numerous 'trip' goods trains transferring wagons between the North End and South End Yards, while what loop accommodation there existed was usually occupied by trains awaiting their turn to detach and attach traffic in the Yards.

In the 1922 issue of 'Local Instructions' the guards of up fully loaded goods trains leaving Banbury, with no work to do at Oxford, told their drivers to 'blow up' two short whistles passing Bletchington signal box to signify that they were prepared to run through Oxford non-stop. The Bletchington signalman sent 'Train Entering Section' to Kidlington and followed this with the letters 'CR' (for 'Clear Run') on the box-to-box single-needle telegraph instrument. Kidlington would then ask 'Is Line Clear?' on the block bell to Wolvercot Junction and again follow it with 'CR' on the single-needle. If this fully loaded train wanted to run through Oxford but make a water stop (there was a water column at North box for up main-line trains), the driver blew up 'three short' and the single-needle code was 'WO' ('Water Only).

In either case the Wolvercot Junction signalman advised the North box signalman, who decided whether the train could 'come main line' or if it would have to be put in the loop at Wolvercot to allow a following passenger to pass. This would be likely if the following passenger was also non-stop through Oxford - but there were very few of them. If there was a train already in the loop waiting to get into the yard it would be a great shame to have to put

* R. A. Cooke, *Track Plans: Oxford*, Vol 27.

** See my *GWR Junction Stations*.

a through train in behind it, so the North box signalman would consult with the Engine Shed and Goods Shed boxes and try to get it through the station, either stopping it on the Up Middle or getting it through to Kennington Junction, where, if necessary, it could be reversed into the Up Refuge.

Accommodation for running freight traffic to the south of Oxford was woefully inadequate until 1940. The Up Goods Loop (known as 'the Old Main') was entered at the south end of the Up Platform at Oxford, and for practical purposes ended just north of the river bridge, 63 milepost. The loop did extend across the bridge to a final exit to the Up Main, but this length could not be used as a goods loop since it acted as a 'head-shunt' for South End Yard, as the exit road for trains starting from the yard, and as the only access to the gas works. There was an Up Refuge siding at Kennington from November 1900 and also a Down Loop*. Between Kennington and Didcot North Junction there was no refuge or loop on either road, and this situation existed until 1940/2.

The difficulties of running the goods trains between the passengers between Oxford and Didcot without delaying the latter are obvious. The Kennington and Didcot North signalmen had to 'margin' a train for a clear run to or from Oxford and consult with one another as to whether they would be able to 'take' the train. Thus they were thinking 20 or 30 minutes ahead - a crystal ball would have been very useful.

Accommodation for trains was increased between 1940 and 1942. Up and down goods loops were extended from Didcot North to Appleford Crossing in 1940. The line was also quadrupled from just north

* R. A. Cooke, op. cit.

of the Radley station overbridge, 58 m 46 ch, to the Isis river bridge, 63 miles; the new tracks were laid on each side of the old double tracks. Three new signal boxes were also built: Sandford, on the up side at the 59³/₄ milepost; Hinksey South, on the up side at the 61³/₄ milepost, just north of the Old Abingdon Road bridge; and Hinksey North, on the down side at 62 m 71 ch, just before the Isis bridge. The extra line on the down side from Radley was designated a Relief Line - it was permitted to carry passenger trains - as far as Sandford, and became a Goods Line thereafter through to Hinksey North.

In the up direction there were two Up Goods Loops between Hinksey North and South and one Up Loop from Hinksey South to Kennington Junction. Between Kennington and Sandford the Up Loop became the Up Relief Line and reverted to Goods Loop status from there to Radley. This quadrupling was part of a larger plan: the building of a marshalling yard on the down side of the line between Hinksey North and South, the latter divided into an up and a down yard; and the construction of a well-arranged double-track junction between the LMS and GWR at Oxford North, approximately the 63 m 65 ch point. The Down Loop, terminating at North box, was extended to Wolvercot Junction and an eight-road marshalling yard and turntable were constructed at Yarnton Junction, on the south side of the Fairford line. All this work was completed by 1942, while improvements at the locomotive shed yard and North End Yard were started in mid-1944 and completed in January 1945.

The new yard at Yarnton Junction under construction on 24 October 1940. The Fairford branch is on the extreme left, the signal box and station in the right distance. A large number of wagons stand in the old exchange sidings. *GWR*

Connected with these improvements was work further south. Between August 1942 and April 1943 the single-track line from Didcot East Junction to Newbury East Junction and from Newbury, Enborne Junction, to Woodhay was doubled and the marshalling yard at Moreton Cutting Yard, about 1½ miles east of Didcot was built. All these works were vital to enable the huge volume of wartime traffic to be handled.

There had been, before 1951, infrequent occasions when either the GWR or LMS (Rewley Road) turntable was out of action for maintenance or due to damage, and engines normally serviced on that shed had to go to the other shed 'to turn'. Prior to 1940 all these movements would have had to go through the exchange sidings lying between the GWR and LMS main lines at the north end, since there was no proper junction between the two routes*.

How the signalmen must have cursed all these very awkward shunting movements! Probably they reduced movements by coupling engines together. From an enthusiast's point of view the sight would have been magnificent, with ex-GER, Midland, GCR, GNR, LSWR and LNWR engines seen side by side or running in procession.

The ex-LMS engine shed closed on 3 December 1950 and thereafter all engines from the LMS turned on the ex-GWR turntable. From 1 October 1951 the passenger services from Bletchley and Cambridge

* In my library of photograph negatives I have a rather out-of-focus view, taken in 1929, of an ex-LSWR 'T9' 4-4-0 standing on Rewley Road turntable, with an ex-LNWR 4-6-0 alongside.

worked into the ex-GWR station. After the closure of the ex-LMS shed, there were some rare occasions when, the Western Region turntable being out of action, engines requiring to turn had to go to Yarnton Junction to use the one in the yard there. Some 'LMS' men were transferred to the WR shed, but a lot of the work fell to WR Oxford men using the LMS and LNER engines. They particularly enjoyed working the ex-Great Eastern 'Claud Hamilton' Class 4-4-0, but many of them disliked ex-LNWR engines, with the 0-8-0 'Super D' freight engines at the very bottom of the list. These engines had a different arrangement of the vacuum brake from that used on the GWR, which proved worrying to Western men, who were quite certain - and with good reason - that their system of brakes was the most perfect available. Their alarm was increased by what they saw as the curious methods of the signalmen on the 'Bletchley line'.

Doubtless the latter were following time-honoured instructions, but the Oxford men working 'Super Ds' with heavy trains behind were made nervous, on the approach to a Home signal at 'Danger', to see another train plainly in sight standing ahead of them on the same line. Morale and high confidence is (or was) everything on the railway, and the GWR men were quite justifiably proud and confident in the perfection of all things Great Western. Two Oxford locomen, George Field and Harry Yelland, got up a petition against the use of the 'Super D' and were suspended from duty for their cheek! And, of course, GWR Oxford men remembered the Rewley Road shunter - an ex-LNWR 0-6-0 with water-cooled *wooden* brake blocks. . .

COMPANY SERVANTS

Oxford locomotivemen

Oxford locomotive crews in the 1920s and '30s worked to Wolverhampton via Worcester and via Birmingham, and to Paddington three ways: via Didcot, via Thame and Northolt, and via Thame and Bourne End. They also worked some trips on the Fairford line, sharing the jobs with the Fairford men; sometimes the Oxford crews worked all the way to Fairford, sometimes only going as far as Witney and changing over there with the crew of a train out of Fairford. They worked the Woodstock branch 'push-pull' train with No 1473 *Fair Rosamund*. They also worked 'double-home' or 'lodging' turns - it was not distance that caused them to sleep in lodgings at the far end of the trip, but the length of time the job took; they had 'lodging' turns to places as near as Leamington and Worcester when they worked 'all stations' freight shunting trips. The variety of working gave the men a wide knowledge of roads and handling experience.

There was a constant circulation of engines and men, of work and conversation, as the daily 'diagrams' ticked over. For example, a set of Stourbridge men came into Oxford on an 'all stations' goods and were relieved by Oxford men who worked the train to Didcot, put the train off in the yard, took the engine to shed, then picked up another engine to work on. Later, a set of Oxford men, who had been shunting Milton depot all day, brought their engine on to Didcot shed about teatime, picked up the (now re-serviced) Stourbridge engine, went to the yard for their train and worked it to Oxford, where a set of Stourbridge men were waiting to work back 'all stations'.

The Newcastle-Bournemouth and Birkenhead-Deal trains worked into Oxford with 'GC' men on the former and GW Chester men on the latter, and changed engines and men at Oxford. The Edinburgh-Swindon (6.25 pm York) and the 10.13 pm York-Bristol, both off the Great Central, had Sheffield engines and men working through to Swindon, where the men lodged overnight to return next day.

Oxford men working the 7.10 am to Paddington ('all stations' to Reading, non-stop to Paddington) came back with the 10.15 'West Midland', arriving at 11.20. These men handed over to a Worcester or Wolverhampton crew, then went on shed to prepare an engine for Chester men to work home at the head of the 9.24 am Deal-Birkenhead, leaving at 1.44 pm. The Chester men would arrive at Oxford on the 8.00 am Birkenhead-Deal at 12.21 pm, and would hand over to an Oxford crew who, with an Oxford '51xx' 2-6-2 tank, took the train on at 2.25 pm to Basingtoke.

Iron ore trains from Irthlingborough to South Wales were worked by Oxford men from Yarnton to Gloucester via Honeybourne; they reversed a mile on to the Stratford-Cheltenham line, then away for Gloucester where they got relief. During the war, when iron ore was running in extra-large quantities and the usual routes were congested, they also worked these heavy trains from Yarnton to Gloucester via Kingham and Bourton-on-the-Water. This was about 22 miles of single track with corkscrew curves and mountainous gradients - 1 in 60 was normal. Trains were hauled by '28xx' or other powerful 2-8-0s, and were assisted by a pilot engine from Kingham. At Bourton-on-the-Water they stopped to put the pilot

Above Oxford engine shed (left), the office block (centre) and repair shops (right) in 1921. The wooden sheds opened in 1854 and remained continuously in use until 1 January 1966. No 1473 *Fair Rosamund* is 'on the vans'. *GWR*

Left Oxford drivers and firemen before the Great War. *Source unknown*

the dangerous descent into the Severn valley. There were 3 miles at 1 in 60 down to Andoversford Junction and a further 6½ miles at 1 in 60 to 1 in 90 down to the main line at Hatherly Junction. The highest standards of enginemanship were required to work heavy, unbraked trains over this section by day; on a moonless night the work required cool courage and a skill that seemed quite uncanny to an outsider.

on the back, thus becoming a bank engine for the 6-mile climb, most of it at 1 in 60, to the 'Stop Board' at Notgrove station. Initially the line fell leaving Bourton, giving them a chance to get going before the slog to the summit began. What a sight and sound they would have made!

Notgrove station was 760 feet above sea level, bleak and remote on the windswept Cotswolds. There was a passing loop, its western end at the very crest of the summit, under the high three-arch bridge that spanned the cutting. The train engine came to a stand at the loop starting signal and, while the guard pinned down wagon brakes, the banker came past on the other track to get on to front of the train engine as pilot again for

Sometimes all that was left was courage. My friend Len Wheeler, an Oxford driver who began in 1917, was one who worked over this line during the war. On one occasion he was coming back from Gloucester to Yarnton with a 'Yankee' 2-8-0 and a long train of iron ore empties. It was in the dead of night and he had a driver learning the road with him. They stopped at the top of Notgrove bank to pin down brakes for the drop into Bourton and set off again. The drag of the wagon brakes as the guard pinned them down was as great as it ever was, but for some reason there was not enough brake power to hold the train on the downgrade; it overpowered the brakes and Len realised that they were running away. He kept this information to himself and sat quietly, the steam brake on, as they rushed the bends, helter-skelter down the hill at up to 50 mph, hoping that the up-grade at Bourton would stop them. It did - and the first person beside himself to know the story was me, when Len told me, safe in his sitting-room, in 1970!

Another friend, Oxford driver Charlie Turner, recalls (although he never himself did this) that sometimes, working home from Gloucester, Oxford men would be booked over the LMS to Evesham. Passing Churchdown box, between Gloucester and Cheltenham, they blew '1 long, 2 short' to indicate to the signalman that they wanted to go 'left-handed' - on to the LMS at Cheltenham, Lansdown Junction. From there they went as far north as Ashchurch before turning right on to the branch to Evesham. At Evesham they gained access to the GWR Worcester line through the exchange sidings, which required a back-shunt. It was an awkward movement but, during the war, the congested tracks brought about all kinds of odd workings.

Before the war Oxford men worked excursion trains as far afield as Leicester, Nottingham, Sheffield and Weymouth via Swindon. In order not to take on the hard, northern coal, the Oxford engine's tender was piled and packed with coal, the firebox well filled, then the tender topped up again. No Oxford men worked Southern engines between Oxford and Basingstoke until after 1947.

Among the locomotivemen working on Oxford shed in the period 1910-40 there was the very much respected Driver Peter Young, who was killed at Reading in 1914* on No 3816 *County of Leicester*, and his fireman Frank Wheeler; Driver 'Agony' Richardson, who was 'agony' to work with because he rarely spoke to his fireman but made gestures to indicate what he wanted done; Fireman 'Black Dick' Copson, who achieved his nickname because of his large family (think about it); Driver Bill 'Bristol Bill' Lintern, a very cheery, rough diamond of a Bristolian with a 'Brissall' accent, whose every third word was unpublishable.

Algy Hunt and his close friend Albert King were tutors in the shed's 'Mutual Improvement Class' between 1924 and 1948 along with George Wall. Footplate work drew the men close together; most but not all were staunch trade unionists, some, like Albert King and Arthur Rhymes, were devoutly Socialist. Algy and Albert, Arthur and Jim Honey formed a close group - Jim and Albert made a very venturesome walking holiday together to San Sebastian in Spain in the early 1930s - no package tours, except the pack on your back. There were so many good men and keen young lads. There were also some 'rough

ones', men who had a 'report' to answer every week. As an outsider I did not get to meet them, but I heard about them. The men who were willing to talk at length about their work were the keenest, the best of them. I would like to pass on their stories, starting with Reg Hanks, General Manager of the Western Region 1954-62, who lived in a large and beautiful Victorian house in Belbroughton Road, near to my lodgings in Polstead Road, Oxford.

Reggie began his railway career as a Swindon Works apprentice in 1912. He recalled the high morale of Swindon New Town, which was entirely railway orientated. If one man asked another where he worked, the answer would be 'R' Shop or 'G' Shop - it was automatically assumed that everyone worked 'Inside', in the railway factory. The working day began by being woken up by the Works hooter at 5.20 am, to enable everyone to be at his place, 'Inside', at 6 am. They worked 54 hours in a six-day week.

Reg remembered starting work in freezing temperature and pitch darkness at 6 am, outside 'A' Shop inside the smokebox of an engine, with an acetylene lamp for lighting, trying to split nuts with a hammer and an icy chisel. He recalled the labour involved in fitting axle boxes into their guides - an apprentice job. Each heavy, cast iron and brass box, its white metal rubbing surfaces coated with marking blue, was placed on a pad of sacking on the apprentice's back. He then raised himself to push the box up into the guides. The box had then to be dropped, and the 'high spots', as indicated by the rubbing of the 'blue', scraped down. The box was then offered up again until it was a perfect, sliding fit. He said they worked to 1/64 of an inch - the thickness of a sharply inscribed line - which was far superior to any other Works' practise.

The worst part of the axle box job was when the boy had lifted it into position, on his back, trying to hold it still while his mate was poking about with a bar trying to locate adjacent holes so as to slip a bolt through. Sometimes the man grew impatient with the bar and put his finger in the hole - just as the lad grew tired and relaxed, dropping the heavy box half an inch. There were quite a lot of fitters with the tips of their fingers missing.

Reg's indentures were signed by G. J. Churchward. Churchward's presence in the Works was something close to that of God, Reggie assured me; the great man was held in complete awe by everyone. He could recall no friendly stories about him - except that the rabbits that he shot on the Downs above Ogbourne St George were given to railwaymen. Just once Reggie thought he would take a photograph of Churchward. He took a camera to work intending to 'snap' the great man as he strode to his office. He saw him coming in the distance, then the thought of a young

* See my *Grime and Glory*, page 69.

apprentice standing in front of 'The Chief' and pointing a camera at him produced an overwhelming feeling of panic. Instead he hid behind the corner of the office building and only stepped out to photograph the man's back - and, Reg said, he felt extremely daring in doing that.

Reg was taught technical drawing by F. W. Hawksworth, and was a personal friend of O. V. Bulleid. 'One did not mention the "Leader" tank when at dinner with O. V.,' said Reggie, and added, 'The "Leader" didn't work because it had far too many innovations, a stupid boiler and sleeve valves.'

Reg served in the Royal Engineers, Railway Operating Division (ROD), during the Great War, and after the war, 'to avoid being conscripted into the trade union' as he put it, he joined up with a man called William Morris who was making bicycles in Longwall Street, Oxford. Morris went into motor car building out at Cowley and became the very rich, very modest and very generous Lord Nuffield, while Reg Hanks became his Works Manager. When Reg became General Manager of the Western Region in 1954 he re-introduced something like a Great Western standard of speed and appearance. He ordered the return to cream and brown coaches and introduced the handsome headboards for locomotives working the named expresses. He also had No 5066 *Wardour Castle* re-named *Sir Felix Pole*, and No 7005 *Lamphey Castle* re-named *Sir Edward Elgar*. The enthusiasm he unleashed caused Swindon to start painting certain engines in GWR express passenger livery to which, according to the British Railways scheme of things, they were not entitled.

Hanks went to his office at Paddington on the 8.55 am Oxford, but he rarely rode in the train - he usually fired the 'Castle' on the 60-minute non-stop gallop to London. He is also known to have missed Board meetings because he was firing the 'Cornish Riviera'! Almost certainly very bad form in the eyes of all the stuffed shirts, but a terrific morale raiser as the story got around - 'we've got a REAL railwayman for a Boss!'.

Reggie Hanks raised morale, but there was no one to follow him, so the 1955-62 period on the Western Region was an 'Indian', or more properly a 'Hanksian', Summer for which those of us who experienced it are eternally grateful. Reg had come up through the ranks, he was a skilled engineer and understood what made railwaymen tick. He built and ran 3½-inch gauge locomotives on his garden railway, and in good weather, right up until the time of his death, he would hold steaming weekends to which he invited Oxford enginemen, including Bill Wall, who also built miniature locomotives. What a sight! All these men who spent all week driving or firing big engines sitting on tiny engines going round and round the garden - the General Manager of the Region in the lead! They did not think of themselves as 'enthusiasts', that was for the laymen - they were 'Railwaymen' and they lived and breathed locomotives.

To keep the account true to life I have to record that Hanks suffered the theft of all his engines while he was away on holiday. The shock was great and some say that his death a few months later was brought forward as a result.

'Gentleman' Jim Honey was 73 when I first met him. Honey the engine driver and Hanks the General Manager of the Region had certain ideas in common: a great respect for each other and for all conscientious railwaymen, and a belief in 'pride in the job' and 'service to the public'*. This morale, on which the functioning of a difficult job depended, did not come about as a result of exhortations on 'Victorian values' from hypocritical politicians peddling some Disneyland fantasy of history, but grew up out of the hard work and commitment of generations of railwaymen and women.

Jim Honey's garden came down to the lineside at Kennington Junction and sometimes he used to come through the fence and into the box of an evening - he liked to be in touch with the railway. During several visits he told me about his life. He had joined the GWR as an engine cleaner at Oxford in March 1911, aged 16, and, apart from voluntary service in the Great War, spent his entire working life on the railway. Even then he had not had enough of it, and came to the signal box. His life as a loco-man had not been easy by our 'Health & Safety' standards, designed for robot factories and 'push-button' offices. He had worked hard at a job where all the human spirit was used. The whole job was a lifetime *challenge* to be overcome by good will, personal skill, courage and determination. In fact, any railway worker had to be 'in training', so to speak - then he knew he was good at his job. There was satisfaction in his difficult work and companionship from his mates.

I recall Jim saying to me one day, in reply to a question about the amount of work involved in firing an Oxford-London non-stop express: 'Your idea of firing is a bit out. Going up on a "City" or one of Churchward's "Counties" with 10 "eights", you put away 56 pounds to the mile from Kennington here, and you kept at it all the way to Southall before you could put the shovel away and wash up.' It was exactly this hard work that developed the 'pride in the job' that kept the railway running. Some men left their

---

* The Stockton & Darlington Railway had embossed on its Seal the motto 'At Private Risk - for Public Service'.

work behind them when they went home, others lived and breathed railways on and off duty.

Jim joined the GWR at Oxford and got his first firing job in 1913 at Llantrisant. That was normal in those days; young firemen were usually 'made' in the South Wales area, then looked for a 'mutual swap' to get themselves home. Jim got home in 1915 when Colonel Hammersley was in Oxford to raise men for four batteries of heavy howitzers - the 128th, 132nd, 135th and 156th. Jim volunteered for the 135th*. The recruits were billeted in Exeter College while they did their basic training in drill and small arms before moving under canvas in Port Meadow where they learned how to operate their howitzers. From there they went to Larkhill for live firing practise, then across to Le Havre and marched to the Somme front in time to take part in the legendary week-long barrage. Jim was transferred to the ROD, and after the Armistice he worked freight and 'leave' trains from Boulogne to Hervestal. This was the best period of his career to date - driving French express engines over relatively undamaged tracks through Liege and

Namur. Jim stayed as an army driver until 1919, by which time his knowledge of engine working was encyclopaedic. He worked all kinds of French and British locomotives under conditions of the worst maintenance coupled with the threat of instant death, not to mention cold, constant hunger and lack of sleep. Thousands more men did likewise.

On demobilisation he went back to Llantrisant as a fireman 'on the goods' and managed a transfer home to Oxford in 1922 as a passenger fireman.

'I must have been mad!' he said. 'I shovelled more coal in a day at Oxford than in a week at Llantrisant - 56 lbs to the mile on a "fast" to "Padd" wi' a 4-4-0 - and even more on a "stopper" down the Worcester road.'

Jim drove a Royal Train twice, in September 1957 and January 1958. One of the two absolutely standard letters he received on these occasions is reproduced here. Readers will note that while he was considered

* See my *Grime and Glory*, page 65 et seq.

Jim Honey as a Sapper driver in the Royal Engineers during the Great War. *Courtesy the late Jim Honey*

The standard letter of thanks for a Royal Train driver. *Courtesy the late Jim Honey*

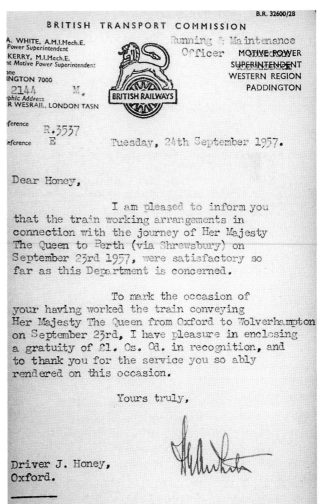

skilful enough to be placed in charge of the Queen's Majesty, he was not sufficiently elevated to be given a handle to his name by the Locomotive Superintendent, Mr H. E. A White. The result is a curious greeting - 'Dear Honey' - and one can only be glad that Jim's name was not 'Darling'.

Jim retired at his own request on 30 August 1958

after 47 years' service, and the valedictory letter is also reproduced here. Note that now that Jim has retired, the Superintendent feels it safe to give him a 'Mr'! The 'note of appreciation' from the General Manager is a standard message on a printed card with the date and Jim's length of service typed in. Reggie Hanks's improvements never reached this department.

After 47 years of brilliant and blameless service as a locomotiveman - in war as a soldier/driver under fire, and as a driver/civilian in peacetime, Jim received a pre-printed card of 'congratulations'. *Courtesy the late Jim Honey*

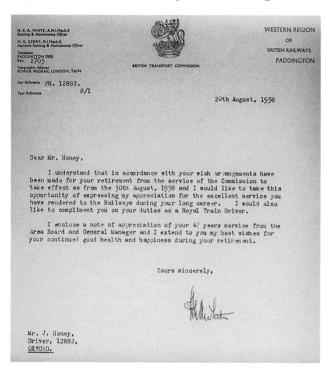

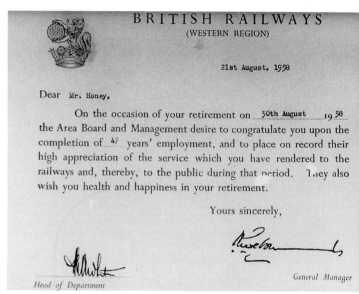

Arthur Rhymes

I visited Arthur Rhymes and his wife Hilary at their home in Summertown, Oxford, during 1969 and 1970. We sat on each side of the fire in his living-room, waited on by Hilary. I noticed that the mantelpiece was worn away at one end from scores of years of Arthur's boots resting on it as he reclined in his armchair, and at the centre of the same mantelpiece, in pride of place, was a clock that measured the length of my visits with very musical 'Westminster' chimes. Below the clock face was a silver plate, engraved with a presentation legend, the words of which I did not write down but were to this effect: 'Presented to Arthur Rhymes by his driver, Edgar Ponting, in recognition of (?) happy years on the footplate. 1926.' In the corner by the door was a barometer with a brass plate recording its presentation to Arthur by his mates on Oxford shed at the time of his retirement in 1962.

Arthur was 16 when he started on the GWR as a cleaner at the already ancient Oxford shed in June 1913, earning 2s 2d per 12-hour day, which included many a turn in the notoriously antiquated coaling stage described on pages 20-21. Arthur was concerned to look smart on duty, and recollected a lot about the etiquette and upkeep of what might nowadays be thought of as very mundane garments - his overall jacket and trousers. To him they were as important as a uniform to a soldier, they marked him out as an employee of the GWR, heading towards a career as an engine driver.

The GWR did not issue overalls to its locomotive staff until 1924, thus the men and boys had to supply their own. Arthur's mother bought him his from a certain shop in Wolverhampton, which sold extra-thick cloth, unobtainable anywhere closer to home. 'They were as thick as boards, so they'd almost stand

No 3837 *County of Stafford* alongside Oxford's ancient and dreadful coaling stage *circa* 1928. If a boy could survive this, he had the courage to become an engine driver - working express trains at 70 mph, in the dark, through busy junctions, driving on steel nerves and with a faith in the little green lights of the signals. AVC

up on their own,' said Arthur. These overalls became exceptionally dirty when worn by a cleaner-lad, and Arthur recalled, with some regret, how red his mother's hands - and later on his wife's hands - became when they had to scrub the denim clean. They used very hot water, yellow soap and a hard-bristled scrubbing brush and the ribbed washboard. 'My poor mother's hands was the colour of boiled crabs,' he said.

The colour of new overalls was dark blue. After a hot wash some Wolverhampton overalls went purple - which was something like a personal disaster for the wearer, because there were plenty of excuses for teasing young hands without the excuse of *purple* overalls! On most sheds there was the so-called 'practical joking', which, if there was some sadist* in the ranks, could degenerate into downright bullying if some young lad was small or in some other way did not come up to the scratch that was expected of him.

I have not been told of any bullying on Oxford shed. Arthur recalled tearing his trousers and being told, 'Go and see ol' George - he'll mend 'em for you.' 'Ol' George' was a bit crusty at the best of times, and young Arthur got the benefit of his caustic tongue for being such a simpleton.

Some overalls held their colour very well, which was regarded as a nuisance. What was required was a gentle fading of the colour to pale blue with the white cotton in the seams standing out well. After washing, the hard-working mother/landlady/wife would iron them and send her son/lodger/husband out in smart order to the engine shed.

Each birthday Arthur's pay went up by sixpence a week. On his 18th birthday, in March 1915, he was sent to Tyseley as a fireman and remained there until March 1920. In 1970 he still referred to the Churchward standard engines as 'the new engines' when he said to me: 'We used to have card games in

the tenders and fireboxes - you could have had a Union meeting in the fireboxes of the *new engines*.'

The engines were cleaned *thoroughly*; this was normal practise on all railways before the Great War. There were four boys to an engine, the two most junior doing the engine's wheels, rods and all the tender, the senior pair doing the boiler, bright metal and the valve gear. When the job was finished the work was inspected by the Chargeman, the test being a clean cloth on the back of a side rod or spoke of a driving wheel.

Probably the cleanest engine on Oxford shed was not a GWR locomotive but a Great Central 'Single' or an 'Atlantic'. The 'GC' kept one engine, a driver, a fireman and a guard at Oxford to work the 7.45 am Southampton forward to Nottingham. One of the 'Singles' shedded at Oxford before 1914 was No 968*; an 'Atlantic' from this period was No 264*. In Arthur Rhymes's time as a cleaner on the shed the GCR driver was a Mr Booth, and the cleaner called Lennard. In 1913 Lennard moved away with promotion and his place was taken by Reg Drinkwater.

This GC engine had to be the most polished engine on the shed because it was a 'foreigner', and all the crew, not just the cleaner, felt that they had to 'show the flag', so you can imagine the elbow grease that went into it. And, of course, the GWR was not going to be beaten by the GC! Both Arthur Rhymes and Jim Honey recalled the presence on the shed of the GC 'Single' and, alongside, equally burnished, the GWR 'Single' No 3050 *Royal Sovereign*, which was driven by Ted Shewell.

Besides this regular GC engine there were others that came in on the York-South Coast services,

* Cruel acts of bullying are recorded in GWR Company records and are hinted at on page 11 of Driver Street's book *I Drove the Cheltenham Flyer*. There was severe bullying on Reading shed as late as 1955.

* Information from ex-GCR/LNER Loco Inspector Percy Banyard.

The original of this has written on the back 'Oxford shed cleaners 1914'. Nearest the cab is Arthur Perks, and under the safety valve cover are Fred Coleman (left) and Arthur Rhymes (right). Next to Arthur, by the chimney, in Basil Cox. By the smokebox, gripping the hand-rail, is Ern Knight. In civilian clothes is an off-duty cleaner, Cyril Taylor. All of them became engine drivers. It would be nice to be able to identify the others. *AVC*

turned, coaled and watered on the shed and sent out again, and others again that ran through to Swindon on services from York, their crews on 'double home' from Sheffield. These 'old hand' friends of mine particularly recalled (how could they forget?) a GC 'Director' Class 4-4-0 - No 429 *Sir Alexander Henderson* - in all its Indian Red and green finery, which was sent to Oxford brand new from Gorton in 1913*. This was because King George V was, in a couple of weeks time, to travel from Windsor to York, via Oxford, and the GCR wanted him to have the best engine they could muster.

But there was more to being a cleaner than cleaning

* Information from ex-GCR/LNER Loco Inspector Percy Banyard.

engines. Arthur did every labouring job on the shed, but because he was a stranger to the district, he did not act as 'call-boy', going out in the small hours to wake drivers up for their turn of duty. He acted as boiler-washer's mate, fitter's mate, fire-dropper and coaler. To drop an engine's fire, the locomotive was positioned over a pit by the 'Shed Turner' (Foreman's Assistant). In the cab Arthur used an 11-foot-long iron bar, the 'pricker', to lift some firebars away to create a space through which he could push the fire into the ashpan.

Then he got down into the pit, bent double, and with the fire rake dragged the red-hot and sulphurous contents of the ash pan towards himself, on to the floor of the pit, surrounding himself with swirling clouds of scorching dust and choking fumes in that confined space, and building a pile of red-hot ashes all around his feet. It was a strange way to run a railway! But that is how it had always been done and how it would continue to be done until the end of steam.

Arthur mentioned how, during these cramped operations under the engine, he might get a dribble of very hot water on to bare skin, and in the reflex action - the jerk of a hand - he would give himself a bad knock. 'But it was no good swearing - you just had to learn to be patient and get on with it.'

Arthur also worked as a 'steam raiser'. To do this he used a very heavy iron scoop, the metal of which was thick to prevent fire burning through it, so it was heavy even before it took its load of coal. The sides of the scoop were perforated and at the closed end there was an air-spaced heat shield, to which was attached the 2-foot-long carrying handle.

Arthur shovelled the scoop into the furnace of the sand drier and withdrew it, laden with blazing coal. He put a thick leather pad on his shoulder and placed the carrying handle on that. He then walked to the engine, with red-hot coals within 3 inches of his head, and thus laden climbed the vertical steps of the engine, making sure that he held the scoop horizontal. The burning coals of two or three such journeys were tipped into the firebox and fresh coal added. Arthur's job required him to perform this function for several engines. By day or by night, 12 hours a shift until the 8-hour shift was introduced in November 1918*, this is the sort of dangerous work that all the men undertook in loco depots all over Britain, to keep the railway rolling.

Only the best men could survive such tests of their patience and determination week after week, and that is why steam railwaymen were, without any doubt, 'the salt of the earth'**.

Arthur spent days and nights, 12 hours at a stretch, on the coaling stage, shovelling coal from the big wagons to the trams, wheeling them across and tipping the contents on to the tenders below as clouds of coal dust covered him from head to foot. Arthur told me that he and his mates went at this work 'hammer and tongs' because, shifting 40 tons with a bonus of 2¼d a ton, he could earn two days' pay in one, including the shilling he got for using his own overalls for the especially dirty work - I hope he paid his mother the shilling extra.

He went to Banbury as a fireman in March 1920 after a very thorough five-year apprenticeship in engine maintenance. His character had been tested to the limit and he had come out with his cheerful good humour intact. There were thousands more like him - no wonder I found such pleasure in the company of such men - and from their ranks were found the Foremen and the Superintendents. No wonder also that the railway worked so well. Everyone - even management - was tried, tested and proved in the hardest possible school.

* The 12-hour day continued to be worked for some years, but overtime was paid after 8 hours.

** P. S. A. Berridge MBE FICE, Assistant Chief Civil Engineer (Bridges), Western Region.

Of his move to Banbury, Arthur said: 'I got 21 shillings a week and my lodgings was 14 shillings - and I got my meals for that too. I was brought up strict Chapel so that 7 bob was enough to spend, not that I couldn't have done with more - but I didn't drink or smoke so I got by OK. I was working on the footplate now and I was looking forward to being a driver - but th' ol' GWR was still getting their labour on the cheap.'

Arthur recalled how, when he arrived on a 'foreign' shed, the men on the depot would not know his name, but would know which shed he had come from and would greet him with 'How's it going then, "Banbury"?'. This was standard practise - men were 'Worcester' or 'Oxford' or 'Swindon' unless you knew their actual name.

Arthur lost two friends in the Astrop crash when they lost their way on the down goods loop, failed to stop and went through the buffers into the river. The engine and tender were 'jack-knifed' across the river's banks and the men were crushed.

Standard Rates of Pay for Cleaners and Footplatemen, 1919-39

Cleaner's age	Rate per day
16 and under	4s 0d
17	5s 0d
18/19	6s 0d
20 and over	7s 0d
Firemen (year)	
1st/2nd	9s 6d
3rd/4th	10s 6d
5th onwards	11s 0d
Drivers (year)	
1st/2nd	12s 0d
3rd/4th	13s 0d
5th-7th	14s 0d
8th onwards	15s 0d

These rates of pay were subject to a reduction of 2½% from August 1928 until 1934, when the reduction was 1%. During this period and until July 1937 'enhanced' overtime rates (such as 'time and a quarter') were abolished. In July 1937 the 'enhanced' overtime rate was restored along with 1928 wage levels for all railway workers whose basic wage in 1928 did not exceed 45 shillings a week. Thus it was not until July 1939 that any engine drivers and most firemen got a pay rise.

What the boys aspired to be - a top-link Great Western footplate crew. Mr Churchward provided a beautifully simple, straightforward cab layout (for a steam engine). See how the men have kept it not just clean and tidy but burnished as well. The general feeling conveyed by this is of quiet confidence, a dignified pride in oneself and one's job. The engine is an express type, a 'Saint' or 'Star', and is on the up main on the 'Duke's Cut' bridge, chimney facing Banbury. *W. L. Kenning/AVC*

Like every old-hand Oxford driver, he recollected the skill and confidence that all drivers required in driving at certain places or under difficult conditions. An undulating road and a loose-coupled goods train required great skill on the part of the driver - and the guard, too, if he was to assist in keeping the couplings taut. Working over such a road in darkness made the job doubly difficult - in fog you would need nerves of steel to trust your judgement with your life. An example was the drop from Moreton-in-Marsh summit, going north-west, down to the sharp curve at Aston Magna, around which the line rose for a short way before falling again, past Blockley level crossing Distant signal, to the actual gates at the foot of the hill. One had to keep the couplings taut to avoid a coupling snatch and possible break-away on the curve, but yet be going steadily enough to stop at the gates if required.

The Kingham-Cheltenham and Thame lines were similarly difficult. The latter was a challenge that the local Oxford drivers learned to conquer, but it was always a tricky road to work over and was most feared by the 'Cockneys' (the Old Oak men) who were said to fear nothing. It had several very awkward gradient changes, which with passenger trains - never mind loose-coupled goods trains - made running and stopping difficult.

Coming from Princes Risborough the approach to Wheatley station was down hill, over the A40 road bridge and up steeply into the station. The way to tackle it with a stopping passenger train was to have steam on all down the hill and over the bridge, and not shut off and brake until you were in sight of the

platforms. The gradient was so steep that what seemed like an impossible stop was then made perfectly. If you approached the station in a conventional or respectful sort of way, you would brake too soon and would find yourself at a stand, short of the platform, with an embarrassing struggle to start on the steep gradient and pull forward into the station.

At the Risborough end of the Thame platform there was a nasty little dip, not marked on the charts, which was awkward if you had a loose-coupled freight. The wagons would accelerate down into the dip on their own and slacken their couplings, which might then snap when they became suddenly taut on the rise out of the dip. When Arthur was working a freight non-stop through Thame he would remember to keep the engine pulling so that all the couplings were drawn out tight and snatches were avoided.

The approach to Birmingham Snow Hill from the south was through a 596-yard tunnel whose northern mouth terminated right on the platform ends. Here the down main line forked to a platform loop, and there was a 15 mph restriction over the diverging route. The gradient through the tunnel was 'U'-shaped, each incline being a very steep - 1 in 45. The tunnel was equipped with a row of electric lights so that the driver could judge his speed, but usually the air was so full of smoke that the lights were little more than a blur. In addition, a 'clanger' was fitted near the station end of the tunnel so that drivers of down trains were warned that they were near the exit - it was so dark and smoky that they could not see.

Some drivers developed the skill of freewheeling a down passenger train through the tunnel so fast that the up-grade slowed them to the 15 mph required for the points to the platform, and they would roll to a stand with a gentle touch of the brakes. Arthur told me how he fired to a driver who could perform this feat: 'It was downhill after Knowle an' if you 'ad the back-boards orf you'd let 'em run and really get 'em going through Tyseley. The art was to judge the point where you'd shut th' reggerlater.'

But it was not given to everyone to accomplish it, and most drivers treated the gradients in the tunnel with respect. My friend Don Kingdom, when he was a fireman at Oxford during the war, fired to Dick Burden, an ex-Pontypool man. Dick was 'ace' at knowing precisely when to close the regulator in order to make the longest free-wheeling run-in to a station without sacrificing time. He had the knack, and when Don became a driver - a good, keen one, too - he tried without success to copy the finesse of his old mate, including the fast 'run-in' into Snow Hill.

But everything was road knowledge on the footplate when you were hauling 700 tons in loose-coupled tubs over a road designed to save the shareholders' money rather than make driving easy, or running at 60 mph with a small tank engine on a train stopping at every little wayside station over the same undulating road. Driving the 'Bristolian' over Brunel's 'billiard table' would have been a 'cake-walk' for any Oxford man used to humping a train of iron ore over Brunel's less well-known and not always well-designed road from Yarnton to Honeybourne.

To unwind after the hours of hard work and concentration Arthur kept a splendid garden where he grew 'enough vegetables to feed the street'. The feeling of satisfaction these men possessed as a result of their confident mastery of a difficult job came out in all the interviews. They had a justifiable pride in their years of achievement - proud in a proper way. Arthur and the other retired men I met mentioned that 'no decent locoman would smoke a "fag" on the footplate'. There was no logic to it - it was a matter of aesthetics. A 'fag' looked like bad form, a pipe did not.

During the Second World War Arthur spent some time on the Honeybourne banker-cum-yard pilots. Sometimes these were GWR engines, sometimes a 'foreigner'. No engine will steam with a clogged-up boiler, not even a GWR one, but it was the 'foreigners' that Arthur recalled as being 'useless' - and in particular a

'J39' that Arthur referred to contemptuously as 'one of those LNER *things*'.

Honeybourne bank was a 4-mile, 1 in 100 gradient out of the Vale of Evesham, climbing the Cotswold escarpment and piercing the ridge through the 887-yard Campden Tunnel, terminating at a point 1,144 yards on the Honeybourne side of Campden station. Arthur described the working: 'We'd go up behind a train to bank it. There'd be one of "our" engines on the front and we'd have this LNER *thing* - we didn't have enough steam to keep up with the train, never mind help push it, and we'd be left behind.'

The safest thing to do then was to keep away (not difficult) in case the train ahead stalled. 'It would be ages before we got to Campden and the bobby'd be looking out for us, all worried and anxious, 'cos o'course we was holding up the traffic.'

Arthur was working a train up the bank one day and saw a man lying inside the Company's fence with a gun beside him. It looked bad. He couldn't stop on the hill, but shortly he came across the permanent way gang and shouted a message. One of the men ran back along the line, and Arthur heard later that the platelayer found the man dead. Knowing who he was, he ran all the way to the house where he lived to tell his widow, hammered on the door and dropped dead on the doorstep. The woman was confronted with a dead body when she opened the door.

When Arthur spoke to me in 1970 about his life on the GWR he concluded by mentioning how nice it was - 'steam days' - when retired drivers would come to the engine shed to collect their pension. They would take the opportunity to walk round the shed and gossip with their one-time firemen, now promoted to drivers. When he was at work he was always pleased to see his old mates, and when he retired he liked to opportunity to get around amongst the engines and his friends. The feeling of 'family', of comradeship, was kept going in this way, but as Arthur observed to me, 'I get my pension paid by a computer up in Darlington now and I don't often see anyone from the old days.'

Bert Bourton and Jack Ody

Bert 'Babs' Bourton began his career as a cleaner on Oxford shed in January 1914, aged 17. He had taken the vacancy left when a cleaner called 'Babs' had been promoted to fireman, thus he inherited the

nickname, which remained with him all his working life. Anything less like a 'Babs' than gaunt, angular Bert Bourton would be hard to imagine.

On 17 June 1914 Bert was cleaning an engine

alongside Driver Peter Young's *County of Leicester*. He saw Young and Frank Wheeler climb aboard and go off shed to work a Worcester-Paddington 'runner', and at lunchtime he heard that Peter Young was dead, the only fatality in a high-speed collision at Reading in which he was entirely blameless. Bert said: 'Peter Young was a smallish man to look at. He was one of the finest drivers on Oxford shed, highly respected, conscientious and capable. Frank Wheeler was so shocked that he never worked on the "runners" again.'

Bert was fireman to Jack Gardener for many years. Jack and his wife and children were the proud possessors (or that is how they saw it) of 'Bulldog' Class No 3399 *Ottawa*. Should it so happen that there was a Sunday when Jack and the engine were off duty, the whole family made a picnic in the shed yard, husband, wife and children cleaning their pride and joy - No 3399. I learned this from Jack's daughter, Edna Reeves.

In 1929 Bert married Violet Axford, the daughter of an engine driver. Where Bert was tall and somewhat bony, 'Vi' was a slip of a thing. She was born in Swindon in 1901, the eldest of the family, and shortly afterwards her father was promoted, which involved a move to Wolverhampton. Her sister, Olive, was born in Wolverhampton but died six weeks later. Mrs Axford had four more children after that, Emily, Lily, Arthur and Doris.

The Axford family moved to Oxford into 'Class 1' (express passenger) work in 1908, and the children grew up with the children of other railwaymen and formed their friendships within the railway circle -

Violet met Bert when he became her father's fireman!

Bert spent 19 years as a fireman, some of them at Reading, where he worked freight transfer trips on to the SE&CR 'through the tunnel', as well as at Oxford, and was 11 years 'on the goods' before he got into the passenger links - although of course there were times when, as a senior goods fireman, he had to stand in on a passenger turn. As a young-hand driver he was first posted to Exeter for the summer season, and from there to Banbury as his regular posting. He was there by 1934 when he received John Drayton as his fireman. In his book *On the Footplate* Drayton characterised Bert as 'a kind and conscientious man, ever ready to lend a helping hand'.

Just about everyone took their railway work very seriously - they took a pride in doing it well. Bert recalled Driver Fred Potter ('He married Minnie Rolt,' chimed in Violet) being known for always filling his tender or tank to the very brim, and those standing around would call out: 'Make sure you stamp it down well, Fred - make sure you've got enough.'

The names and numbers of the passenger engines were also important to the old-hand drivers, and their conversation was sprinkled with these references. When Bert spoke about the engines he had worked, recalling some rough trip, fast run or particular driver, he would give engine name and number - and he'd be right, even though he was speaking 50 years after the event and through years of painful arthritis.

'We wuz goin' down wi' th' Mail, 12.10 Padd, 2928 *Saint Sebastian*, an' it had a leaky tube plate. . . That "Durban" - 37-hundred - always had a bad name for steamin'*, but one day Walt Turner an' me had it on the 5.55 branch - Risboro' an' Padd, back empty stock. Well normally we'd have had to put a jimmy in the blastpipe, but that perticuller day the engine did wonderful well. . . The best "City" we had wuz 3702 *Halifax* - although 3714 *City o' Gloucester* wuz good too - but 3702 wuz a marvellous engine, an' her driver wuz a real gent too, Frank Russell - he 'ad a big, black beard. . . Now, them "Dukes" wuz tricky things to fire, you didn't waunt ter put too much on, keep a thin, bright fire. . .

* I spoke to several Oxford locomen of Bert's generation and they all held the same opinion of Nos 3700, 3702 and 3714.

Bert Bourton, left, talks to his Foreman, Len Brown, on 6 May 1959. *Courtesy Albert Bourton*

but wi' 3702 we used to build the fire deep and then pull it through with the pricker and feed it to the back corners and under the door and let the front be fed from the back. Then she'd steam all day.'

During the Second World War footplatemen's wives kept their men 'coaled up' and 'turned round', always ready for the road. Without their wives locomen all over Britain would never have been able to work as they did, and the war effort would have suffered. Frequently Bert - and thousands like him - went out for an 8-hour job and were away for days on end. Those thousands of wives never knew when their men would come home when they said goodbye at the front door. They might be away for three or even four days sometimes - without proper meals, just a few biscuits and some cheese that was made available at the loco sheds.

Bert told me: 'You couldn't really refuse to work an ammo train or an ambulance train when you wuz asked so we used to go on. I've bin from Oxford to Padd, up to Brum, down to Southampton and back to Oxford again and get 'ome at three in the mornin' three days after I'd left 'ome for an ordinary 8-hour turn.'

Vi told me how she would be woken by the sound of Bert's key in the door and get quickly out of bed to hurry down the stairs to meet him. She recalled how exhausted he would be after days on the footplate without proper food. 'He'd be too tired to eat and only want to go to bed, but I'd say to him "You must be starving. I'll get you something before you go up." I saved a bottle of brandy, specially, you see, and I'd pour some and beat it up with a fresh egg from one of our chickens that we had in the back yard. Sometimes he'd go to sleep in the chair, sometimes he'd perk up and have a bit o' breakfast before he went upstairs.'

✳ ✳ ✳

I was taken to see Jack Ody by his old workmate, Oxford driver Charlie Turner. Jack and his wife Kathleen were spick and span - like a well-kept locomotive, everything well cared for and orderly, in their semi in a quiet road in Wolvercot. Jack had started his working life during the Great War at Wolvercot papermill, then went to work at Bicester Ordnance Depot. While he was there he saw reeling, shell-shocked soldiers who would throw themselves to the ground if they heard any sudden noise.

'They wuz a pitiful sight, Adren,' he said.

Jack had been a keen footballer and cricketer all his active life, and he and his wife kept a beautiful flower garden at home and grew vegetables on a council allotment. He had accepted the hardships of his job and found satisfaction in carrying out the skilful, difficult work. In that curious way of an old soldier, or a miner, he took a pride in his work scars. He told me how, in 1982, he had to go to the Radcliffe hospital in Oxford for medical attention, and the doctor commented on the scratched state of Jack's eyeballs. 'How did they get like that?' he asked. 'I was an *engine driver*,' Jack replied, and as he recounted the story to me, there was a hint of pride in his voice.

Jack got his job as an engine cleaner on the shed in 1919 through the influence and at the instigation of his brother who already worked there. 'That old shed! It was an old wooden place, I wonder it hadn't been burned down years before with all the hot cinder that got shovelled out of firegrates - it would have gone up like a torch.'

He said that there were 30 cleaners at the shed in those days - 'Some of them were ex-soldiers - Oh! the "Bull"!' Jack chuckled. 'The engines then had to be kept clean, especially underneath - the driver's didn't want their overalls messed up, their wives had put a lot of effort into scrubbing them.'

Jack remembered the rivalry between the drivers of the 'three Frenchmen'*.

'"The Frenchmen" used to come in on a Saturday night, and on Sunday Harry Goldsworthy, Jim Webb and Alf Hall would come in - unpaid, mind you - get their engines drawn up together and do little jobs on them, and made sure the cleaners did a proper job on them. "Jobber" Brown, the Foreman, would be there too, with his big beard, and maybe old Jack Gardener with his engine - there'd be a right-old conflab, I can tell you, criticising each other's engines and pulling each other's leg.'

For many years the Oxford drivers and firemen generally associated with them were: Alf Hall and J. New, No 102 *La France*; Harry Goldsworthy and J. Perks, No 103 *President*; and Jim Webb and J. Jones, No 104 *Alliance*. Jack Ody also fired these engines with Harry Goldsworthy and spoke highly of them, although he thought they had a tendency to slip on starting.

After a few months as a cleaner Jack was sent to Port Talbot as a fireman, working local coal trips up the valleys. He knew next to nothing about firing when he began and had the misfortune to be paired with a driver who not only refused to show him how to do the job, but took every opportunity to make fun of him and even went so far as to push him about. When the bullying got to the point of having an arm twisted up his back, Jack hit back and an uneasy truce existed. So he learned his firing the hard way. Jack worked at Port Talbot for 4½ years until six Old Oak

* The de Glehn 4-4-2 compound expansion engines, Nos 102/3/4, purchased by the GWR from the Chemin de Fer du Nord for comparative trials with GWR 4-4-2 'simple' expansion engines in 1903/5, were shedded at Oxford from 1913 until they were scrapped in 1926/7/8 respectively.

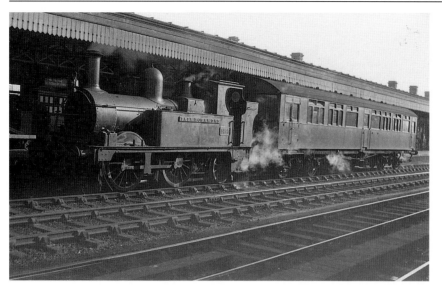

The Woodstock branch 'auto' at the up platform at Oxford on 6 November 1930 with the ultra-long-serving No 1473 *Fair Rosamund* propelling its coach. *Dr Jack Hollick/AVC*

retired driver, Ben Davies*, who referred to 'the squalor' of foot-plate life. Jack gave a dismissive sort of laugh. 'Footplate work was a rough ol' job - but there you are - it was what you were doing and if you didn't like it you could get out, like Ben did; he went down to Carterton as signalman - it takes all sorts and you 'ave to take the rough with the smooth.'

Jack fired to all sorts of drivers from Arthur Rhymes - 'a perfect gentleman, like Jim Honey' - to 'Agony' Richardson - who rarely spoke at work and was indeed 'agony' to work with. He indicated his wishes to his unfortunate fireman with a peremptory gesture - turn the feed on/off, water the coal, look out for a signal. Richardson was rough on the engine and hard on his fireman. Harry Goldsworthy was 'a bit of an old so-and-so, always ready to interfere with his fireman's work - he'd ask you to spot a signal and when you told him what was what he'd come across and look for himself - in the end the poor devil fireman didn't know what to do for the best.'

'Bangy' Wheeler got his nickname because he was rough on his engine and therefore rough on his fireman. Jack recalled going down to Worcester on a 'double home' goods as fireman to 'Bangy'. Afterwards they went back to his, 'Bangy's', usual lodge in Shrub Hill and after a bit of supper went to bed. They shared the same double bed and Jack could still recall the horror of it.

'Ol' Bangy was a dirty old sod. He never seemed to look clean. I washed before I went to bed but he didn't and I hated having to get in beside him - it wuz 'orrible, but I was tired so I got in and lay right on the edge as far away from him as I could get. That was the night I discovered he kept racing pigeons. How d'you think I found out? Well, after I'd got into this bed I lay there for some time wondering what the smell was and then I realised - he stank o' pigeon shit. What a night that was - what with the stink of 'is pigeon shit and the racket he made with 'is snoring, I don't think I slept at all. Next time I was booked on with him on this job I went sick and stayed home.'

Then there was Walt Turner, who would come to

Common men, sent to Oxford as firemen, returned to London, and six Oxford men, including Jack, were recalled. It seems that there was a chaotic state existing on the GWR just after the Great War as new entrants and returning soldiers were shunted into whatever job was available, and then had to sort themselves out into the postings they actually wanted.

Jack's first work was on the Woodstock branch, firing No 1473 *Fair Rosamund* with Driver Bill Pomeroy. 'Ol' Pom' was in charge of the engine shed at Woodstock and probably got half a crown a week extra for the paperwork. As branch driver he was well known in the little town and, indeed, might have been the unofficial Mayor of Woodstock. The 3³/₄-mile branch was his private fief, and he took his supervisory duties lightly. This may have been the reason why No 1473, for years the branch engine, was frequently brought to a stand owing to a lack of steam.

Jack, whose only experience up to then had been with heavy coal trains on steep gradients with unfriendly and unhelpful drivers, was glad to be with 'ol' Pom', but found firing the small fire of the very lightly laden *Fair Rosamund* a tricky business at first. The engine had a specially short-handled shovel, and only the tip of it was loaded with coal. The grate was small and had to be fired lightly to avoid 'blacking in' - if the firebed was getting clogged with ash, firing had to be done very sensitively to avoid a dead area of black coal.

Jack had not been working No 1473 for long when he ran short of steam, bringing the train to a stand, surrounded by fields, for a 'blow up'. He felt very silly and it must have showed as he fidgeted about, waiting for the pressure to rise, because a lady passenger who was also looking out called to him: 'Don't worry - you're not the first to run out of steam on this train!'

I mentioned to Jack the comment of another

work smelling of whisky. He was a 'heavy-handed' driver and pulled the fire off the grate with his clumsy driving methods. Jack recalled the famous evening in the later 1930s when Walt Turner and Harry Fudge worked an excursion with an Oxford engine through to Nottingham and back.

'He'd got at the whisky while they were waiting to come back, and on the way home he didn't stop where he should've and did stop where he shouldn't and he got back into Oxford with the fire piled up in the smokebox and the bottom of the door glowing in the dark. They took him off the main line after that and put 'im in the "Black Gang", shunting about around Swindon works.' Jack gave a dismissive wave of his hand. 'But there you are, it was a rough job and it takes all sorts.'

There were some 'awkward ol' devils', but most were good men and there were some 'real gentlemen' too: Reg Jones and Tom Breakspear were good drivers, considerate to their firemen. That was not to say that they allowed any sloppy work - they expected their fireman to be up to scratch - but at the same time they did all they could to make life easy by being friendly and using the steam, created by the fireman, wisely.

Frank Russell, Jack Gardener, Jim Honey and George Major were extra-special - this was generally agreed by all the old hands. 'If they'd been born 50 years later they would have been doctors or lawyers,' said Jack. 'Jim Honey could easily have been a University professor or a laywer, he was that sort of chap.'

Jack was an attender at the Oxford shed Mutual Improvement Class (MIC) and described himself in those days as 'a bit keen. I was young then and took an interest. We had a good time in the MIC with Albert King, Algy Hunt and George Level.'

Jack recalled his difficulties, as a driver, preparing an engine for the road - 'oiling round'. Each piston rod and valve spindle gland, the crossheads and slidebars, axle boxes, big-ends, little-ends, eccentric straps and the various rocking links and levers concerned with the valve gear had to be checked. Each one had an oil chamber sealed with a screw-in cork which had to be treated carefully if it was not to break off inside the hole.*

If any of these oiling points was missed there was a serious likelihood of destroying the bearing during the journey. Going round them all by day was difficult enough, but maybe it was pouring with rain, maybe the oil was like treacle because of the freezing temper-

ature. At night these same hazards were compounded by darkness and the so-called 'flare lamp', which often as not filled the driver's eyes with smoke.

Jack - and thousands of men like him - did the job faultlessly by day and night for decades. 'You had a system, Adren, a mental check list,' he said, 'and you 'ad to keep yer mind on what you was doing so's not to miss anything. 'Course, the worst wuz the four-cylinder ingins. To get at their valve gear you stood on the rear brake hanger and spread-eagled yourself over big-ends with yer back along the underside of the boiler and yer backside against the firebox. A chap at Didcot was crushed against the boiler by a "Castle's" crankshaft after the engine was moved when he was on top of the cranks, oiling. O'course it was the same if you was under one of the small tank engines with their inside cylinders - there was no room to get out of the way of the big-ends if they moved when you wuz oiling.

'I was underneath a "49" once, oiling, when someone nudged against it wi' another engine. There's no crankshaft to trap you but the eccentrics moved - just a bit. I was terrified for that moment and ducked down into the pit. So I was always nervous underneath a "Castle" or a "Small 40", but, mind you, I liked the "40s"* and many drivers preferred them to a "Castle".'

Jack particularly liked No 5063 *Thornbury Castle* (re-named *Earl Baldwin* in July 1937). Jack said of this engine: 'I fired to Fred Richards on that 'un. A good strong engine it wuz - and we worked it hard, too.'

Jack had married Kathleen in January 1940. He told me of his rather severe method of proposing to her: 'I told her - you won't just be marrying me, you'll be marrying the railway and working for the Company for nothing. You'll be scrubbing overalls, getting me meals at all hours and making up my box o' bait.' In spite of the job specification Kathleen took him on, and indeed, what she always recalls most readily is scrubbing his overalls on the concrete outside the kitchen door. Like thousands of wives she managed to keep her man cleaned, 'coaled and watered' in spite of rationing and his utterly ungodly hours of work, and they lived very happily together for many years.

Locomotivemen were particularly affected by food rationing. They very frequently worked for several days on end because there were so many trains to run, and no one felt like refusing to haul a troop, ambulance or ammunition train. Sleeping where they could, very often sleeping rough on some far-away shed, they stayed from home for three or four days at a time, finding food where they could and getting very

---

* My friend Driver Don Kingdom still has a set of five tools for digging out broken corks. An old driver had them made and when he retired passed them on to Don.

* A '40' or 'Small 40' was a 'Star' Class to the old hands.

hungry until in the end they had to refuse a job and ask to be sent home. All the old hands talked about this problem. They recalled how they would ask for food at the WVS or Salvation Army canteens set up to supply troops in transit, and the hurt they felt when the person in charge stupidly refused to give them 'tea and a wad'.

Jack recalled working troop trains and seeing the soldiers getting a hot meal while he and his mate on the engine had nothing but some tea and a lump of government-issue railwaymen's cheese. The risks to the life and limb of the enginemen and others by ill-treating them in this way was well demonstrated by an incident that happened to Jack one dark, winter evening in 1943. He was working a goods train home to Oxford, tired and hungry and even more chilled than usual because of his run-down state. The signal-man at Wolvercot Junction turned Jack's train into the up loop and warned him that there was a train ahead of him. Jack acknowledged the warning and let his train plod on at 5 mph.

'I must've dozed off for a half a minute, then I come to with an 'orrible shock - I realised I'd dozed off and that there was one ahead. I felt terrible, cold and shaky. My mate was fast asleep so I stepped across and screwed on the tender handbrake. Just as I'd done that we went over the "shot" that the guard of the one ahead had put down - that just about knocked my mate off his seat and we come to a stand right up behind him - buffers not quite touching. He was an Oxford guard and o'course he never knew how close a call he'd had. If something hadn't a' woken me up we'd've hit his van and he'd a' bin a goner.'

During the war civilians were under fire from the German Air Force, and many railwaymen who worked through that period had tales of narrow escapes from bombs. Jack recalled the night he worked a freight 'downhill' for Birmingham on 14 November 1940 and never got beyond the goods loop at Leamington. He and his mate sat on their engine and watched the sky to the north-east become fiery red and a mass of flying sparks like the tail of a comet - and realised that all of Coventry, 8 miles away, was going up in flames. So great was the fire that 42 miles to the south, at Oxford, the station staff watched the same sight. Stan Worsfold, then at Oxford South box, said the sky was fiery and a pencil-thin trail of rising sparks 'was as if a factory chimney was on fire, throw-ing fire into the air.'

Jack recalled another wartime incident when dis-cussing the relative merits of the engine drivers he had worked with. Old Fred Potter was made driver in 1914. 'He was a good old boy,' said Jack, 'but of course you had to have things right for him. When you was on Ranelagh Bridge yard, waiting to back into "Padd"

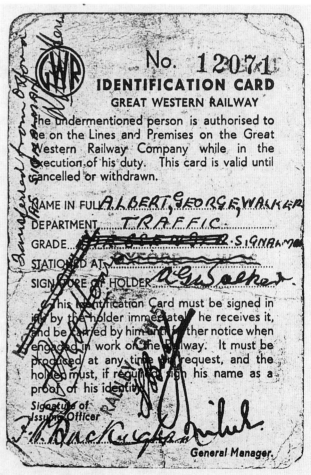

The wartime lapel badge, and the pass that went with it, to enable railway staff to walk about the railway while on duty - or when going to their duty - without being arrested as a spy. *Courtesy Albert Stanley and Albert Walker*

for a passenger, you couldn't make too much smoke and you couldn't let the engine blow off because of the houses so close - and because you'd have "ol' Ginger" the Foreman after you - but at the same time, Fred'd expect you to organise things so's we'd back into the station with a good fire in the box, all ready for the trip home, and have her close to the mark - not far off blowing off. And talking of "blowing off" - me and Fred Potter had worked the 4.30 Up during the war and we wuz on Ranelagh yard when one o' them bloody "doodlebug" things dropped just across the track, on Royal Oak station. That put the wind up us, I can tell you!'

Before the advent of the vacuum brake in 1875 there were no brakes on carriages or wagons. The normal way to stop a passenger train was to screw on the tender hand brake, put the engine into reverse and put on steam while the guard screwed on his brake. This method of braking must have been fairly uncomfortable for the passengers as the coaches jostled up against the engine and rebounded, and much more so for the enginemen as the engine's wheels turned backwards while the engine went forwards.

None of the old hand drivers I knew were alive when passenger trains had no brakes, but I asked several of them if they had ever been obliged, in an emergency, to put their engine into reverse, while going forwards, to assist braking. Jack Ody admitted to doing it - once. He had a '72xx' 2-8-2 tank engine with a load of iron ore from Irthlingborough to South Wales. He had picked the train up at Yarnton

Junction and was working it to Honeybourne. The journey to Chipping Campden was a 'steady old slog', but nothing untoward. At Campden they stopped to allow their guard to alight from his van and walk forward to pin down brakes for the descent of the 4-mile, 1 in 100 Campden bank.

As brakes were put down Jack drove the train forward slowly, and when he felt that there was enough drag against his engine he whistled up and the guard returned to his van. Down the bank they went, gingerly, engine hand brake on, and into the tunnel. Inside, on the wet rails, the unbraked portion of the train overpowered the braked part, and the engine's wheels began to slide.

'We wuz away! Things wuz looking bad,' said Jack, 'and that wuz when I thought I'd try reversing her. I shut orf, pulled the lever over an' put on steam.' He chuckled at the memory, but it wasn't funny at the time. 'That old engine jumped and jarred and shook. I put 'er in fore gear an' let 'er go - it wuz less worryin' to let 'er run away. We kept pumping the brakes and did what we could to hold 'em. Passing Honeybourne South box we blew crows on the brake whistle. He saw we wuz running away and warned the station. 'Course, once we got on to the level we soon stopped 'em - but I'd never bother to reverse an engine again.'

Albert King and Algy Hunt

Jack Ody mentioned the fun he had attending the Oxford 'Class' with instructors - fellow enginemen - George Wall, Algy Hunt and Albert King. Many others I met agreed.

Oxford engine shed was small enough to have a village atmosphere, compared to, say, Old Oak Common or Ebbw Junction sheds, which were more like towns. On a medium-sized shed like Oxford everyone knew everyone else, their likes and dislikes, hobbies, opinions - even where they went on holiday - and 'the Class' was part of the engine shed social life. It is natural to want to be good at your job, footplate work was their whole way of life and most locomotivemen took a keen interest in 'The Rules' and 'The Engine'.

Algy and Albert were born in Oxford. Algy Hunt started on Oxford shed in 1911 and in 1925 moved to Oswestry for his first driving job. Footplate crews who were required on duty between midnight and 6 am were given an 'early call' by a 'call boy' from the engine shed so as to be sure the men were woken.

This was often a thankless task. The boy could incur the wrath of the neighbours as he hammered on the engineman's door to get him to wake up and, having woken him, might be greeted with abuse for the noise he made in the process! But when the call-boy went to knock up Algy, the lad would find the front door ajar and Algy, ready for work, standing by with a cup of tea and a piece of cake for the youngster.

In 1940 Algy received a serious leg injury that brought him back to Oxford for treatment. Both he and Albert were clever, inquisitive and keen on any kind of engine - petrol, diesel or steam - and both found the money to buy and run a car in the 1930s. Algy, living at No 15 Abbey Road, with a back yard going down to the river, kept a motor boat as well. Its name was *Lavengro*, carried on each side at the prow, on brass plates cast at Swindon in return for some cigarettes. Legend has it that the foundryman was expecting rather more than 20 Player's and was justifiably annoyed at Algy's tight-fistedness.

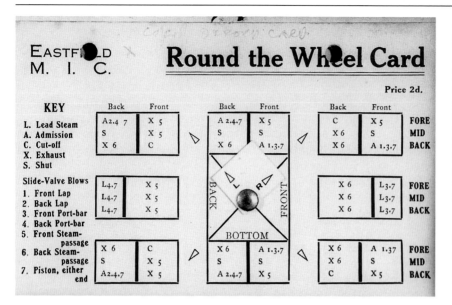

Albert and Algy's 'Round the Wheel' card was pirated and sold to raise funds by several classes. It was a 19th-century practice that drivers were expected to know the relative position of the piston and its valve at any part of the crank's revolution. In the case of a breakage in the valve or piston, such knowledge would enable the driver to know what had gone wrong. The central, moving, piece of card represents the left-hand and right-hand cranks, and by turning this one can read off the relative position of the valve and piston.

When Algy Hunt came back to Oxford, he and Albert used to travel by car or by train to visit out-stations like Honeybourne and Kingham and even further afield into LMS and LNER territory, giving classes on circuit, 'taking the word' like a pair of Methodist lay preachers. Albert described himself and Algy as 'Tweedledum and Tweedledee' squeezed into an Austin 7 - Algy being a big, bulky man, Albert the skinny one.

Algy kept the boat under the Thames bridge by Oxford South End Yard. Every spring and autumn he recruited the MIC to help him either haul it up or down the slip-way and bed it down for the winter or prepare it for the season. A certain amount of rowing and 'messing about in boats' was indulged in and, had the occasion demanded, there were several handy boatmen amongst the footplate staff of Oxford shed.

Algy's car was only a little Austin 7, but Albert - who must have had access to some money beyond his railway wages - owned a Standard, and, indeed, Charlie Turner recollects Albert garaging a red, MG sports car in the street where he, Charlie, lived as a boy. Albert took his interest in engines even further, taking flying lessons and obtaining his pilot's license*. He flew from the now defunct Witney airfield until the outbreak of war.

Albert and Algy were good enginemen, enthusiastic teachers and very able organisers; Albert had been a member of the Oxford Strike Committee during the Great Strike of 1926**, while Algy ran the MIC at Oswestry and Albert and George Wall gave weekly classes at Oxford shed attended by the engine cleaners, firemen and, indeed, drivers. George and Albert, although far apart until 1940, co-operated in the writing of instructional booklets on locomotives and worked together to establish a 'Federation of Mutual Improvement Classes'. They travelled together widely to organise this, even as far away as Newcastle, bringing about the 'Federation' in 1937 with the idea of forming a nationwide network of assistance for individual classes, and to distribute instructional booklets, teaching-aids and lecturers.

* Information from Mrs Zöe King.

** See my Great Western at Work 1921-29.

They had a friend called Horace Tolley, an 'outside' engineer (there was also a fireman called Tolley) who lived in Oxford and who, at their instigation, made to order all-metal, instructional model valve gears for any MIC at £4 each (in 1937); he sold them to Oxford, Old Oak Common amongst other sheds*. Albert and Algy also organised outings to Swindon Works, to Gresham & Craven's brake and injector factory in Manchester, or some other place where the class could improve their knowledge of the working of their engines - and have a few pints together afterwards.

Don Kingdom went on those trips and recalled them for me, with relish, 60 years after the event. There were enough men on the trip to warrant an extra coach on the back of the regular train. Not only did the Company supply the coach, but they also gave the group a free ticket so that they should not have to use their rather meagre annual ration of three free tickets.

They caught the Paddington-Chester Mail at 2 o'clock in the morning, and spent the day together -

* These were small beer compared to the instructional 'model' at Wolverhampton Stafford Road. The Class there had a good, brick classroom on the end of the Stores in No 1 Roundhouse, and in a pit in the classroom resided 'The Model'. This comprised the wheels, frames, valve gear and sectioned cylinders of an E. B. Wilson 0-6-0 for the Oxford, Worcester & Wolverhampton Railway, built in 1854 and withdrawn in 1904. By means of a handle and a very low-geared drive, the machinery could be turned to show the young cleaners and firemen the relationship of the valves to the wheel cranks at all positions of the wheels.

first in pursuit of knowledge, then in pursuit of ale - and arrived back at Oxford, via the GC, on the York-Swindon passenger, feeling decidedly convivial at 10 o'clock at night.

* * *

Albert King was born in 1899. Like all the old hands, he lived through and experienced gigantic upheavals and social change. In 1914 he became an engine cleaner on Oxford shed, and looked forward to a career in an industrial life with gritty, smoky locomotives, the best of them being at the forefront of technology at that time. Not long afterwards he took part in the Great War - the most bloody and destructive war in history up to that time. He was very impressed with the changes that had taken place in his lifetime, and compared his life's experiences to the peace and quiet enjoyed by his grandparents who had been born in the pre-railway age; his maternal grandfather had been the miller at Arncott, 4 miles south of Bicester, while his maternal grandfather had been a shepherd on the Quantock Hills.

As an engine cleaner in 1914 he worked a minimum of 12 hours a day or night, and was paid 12 shillings for a theoretical 72-hour week. His very first cleaning job was steam railmotor No 54, whose driver, Reg Jones, used to come to work an hour before time to assist in polishing the bodywork. Young Albert was full of questions regarding the machinery and Reg took pains to answer all his queries and show him round the engines.

Albert said that there were four cleaners to a gang and they were given an hour to clean an engine as a group. Particular engines were not allocated to particular gangs (as is said to have been the case 15 years earlier), but they moved around the shed cleaning the engines as required. He recalled the pride that the GC men took in their engine's appearance as the sole representative of the Great Central on the Western shed, and also remarked that 'The Frenchmen' had a lighter shade of red on their inside frames compared to that used on the 'Cities' and other outside-framed passenger classes.

The work on shed, including the dreadful coaling stage, was very wearing, and he began to think that it would be a better life in the war, in France. 'That was the impression I got from reading the newspapers,' he told me. So in October 1915 Albert volunteered and was accepted for the Oxford & Buckinghamshire Light Infantry. He was only just 16, and a rather skinny 16-year-old at that. The man who swore him in must have known he was under age but, as the old hands used to say, 'So long as you were warm, they'd take you', and a year later, amid the muddy, cold and hungry trenches of the Somme, Albert realised that 'truth was the first casualty in war', that newspaper reporting left a lot to be desired, and he yearned for 'a comfy 12-hour turn on the coaling stage at friendly old Oxford shed.'

He was wounded, struck by a bullet that travelled the length of his arm, and it was the much sought-after 'Blighty one'. He walked on his own, back to the field dressing station, losing a lot of blood and feeling very faint. They asked him where he lived so he could be put into a hospital close to home. He told them 'Oxford' and all the way back to Blighty imagined how he was going to end up in the Radcliffe Infirmary. He reckoned without the Army. They sent him to Glasgow.

After the war was over he returned to Oxford as a fireman and was promoted to driver, at Banbury, in 1935; then, by a mutual swap, he was able to return to Oxford before 1939. His working nickname was 'Notcher', from the habit he had, when working an engine with a 'pole' reverser, of making chalk marks at three places along the quadrant so as to show clearly the cut-off positions he was going to use. Albert was full of little 'aids' like that - everything to do with the engine was thought out beforehand. He had a sharp brain and took a great deal of notice of every aspect of locomotive work, the theory of the machine and the actual practise of driving it.

He fired on the French compounds and found the complication of working them most interesting. Of all the old-hand Oxford men who experienced these engines, he was the most enlightening on this subject. There were two sets of reversing screws, one for the high-pressure and one for the low-pressure engines (cylinders), and these could be worked independently or locked together and turned with one handle. Steam from the boiler entered the 13-inch (high-pressure) cylinders and was exhausted to the 22-inch (low-pressure) cylinders, where it did more work before being exhausted through the blastpipe and up the chimney.

To start a train, all four cylinders worked in 'simple' expansion with both valve gears in 75% cut-off. After a few turns of the wheels, compound working was brought in. The cut-off for the high- and low-pressure engines was set at a differential of 30%, the two control wheels were locked together and thereafter all adjustments of the valve travel remained in that relation to each other. When they were running fast on level track the best way of working them was to have the regulator wide open and the cut-offs at 35% high-pressure and 65% low-pressure. The blast from the chimney, and therefore on the fire, was much softer than on the 'simple' engines because steam was going to exhaust at a much lower pressure - so the fireman used a much thinner bed of coal in the furnace than was the case with any other GWR passenger engine.

Albert's personal preference as a fireman was the 'City' Class; they were a neat little engine to fire, and were free-running. The worst, by far the worst, was the '38xx' 'County' - 'Churchward's Rough Riders'. Firing a 'City' on a 'hard hitter' to London, Worcester or Birmingham, the fireman (and Jim Honey and Jack Ody agreed) built up a good thick fire before leaving the shed. When they 'set sail', the long pricker was rammed into the fire, the furnace doors closed on it and the fire pulled back and lifted. When the black smoke had cleared from the chimney, the engine was barking well and the fireman would start plying his shovel - 57 lbs of coal to the mile! All they asked was a smoothish ride and plenty of steam.

The fireman's job was made easier or more difficult by the driver - the driver was King of the Footplate. It was impossible for a mere fireman to interfere with his judgement of how the job ought to be done - indeed, a Locomotive Superintendent would have found it very difficult to alter a driver's method. The Locomotive Department gave some mild instructions on how to drive high-pressure, piston-valve engines, but some of the old-hand drivers could not be told. If the Company had taken the matter of instruction seriously it could have saved itself thousands of pounds in coal, or so Albert said, and also made life easier for the fireman.

This is why he was so keen on the MIC. Proper instruction was vital, not only for the Company's coal bill, but also for the good of the locomotivemen. But on the engine, the driver's word was Law. The Churchward engines - known as 'the new engines' to everyone - should have been driven, once they were properly under way, on full regulator and a relatively short cut-off, but many of the old boys to whom Albert fired insisted on the old slide-valve, low-pressure, non-superheated ways - a half-open regulator and a long cut-off.

For freight work, Albert considered that the GWR '28xx' 2-8-0 was *par excellence*, while the Dean 'Standard Goods' 0-6-0 was remarkably powerful for such a modestly proportioned machine, but had its limitations. Going down from Yarnton to Campden with a 'Standard Goods' and 60 empty coal tubs, running on axles lubricated with yellow fat, could find the engine and train at a stand at Moreton-in-Marsh with the regulator wide open and 50 lbs of steam on the clock; the drag of the primitive bearings and the drag of the wind in the open wagons was 'a killer' on the steady uphill grade. Three yellow-fat-lubricated coal tubs were officially reckoned to be equal to four oil-lubricated wagons, but Albert was quite sure that this was an under-estimate even in warm weather. In

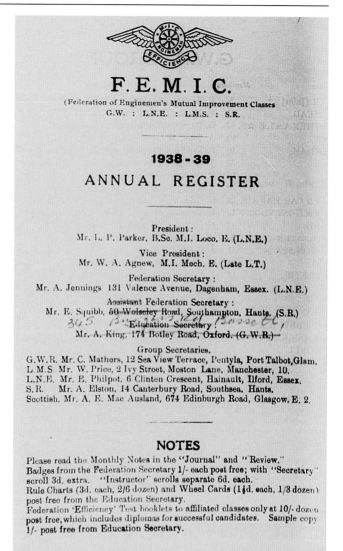

Albert King as 'Education Secretary' to the newly formed Federation of Enginemen's Mutual Improvement Classes.

cold or freezing conditions the thick fat became very stiff and made haulage even more difficult.

Albert as a fireman also thought highly of the Churchward 'Mogul'. He recalled an occasion when an Oxford driver was carpeted for bringing a semi-fast up the Worcester road and touching speeds of 80 mph on the downhill between the Kingham stop and passing Handborough. There were 'Halls' and 'Granges' on Oxford shed for passenger and fully vacuum-braked freights, but Albert preferred the 'Moguls' to these.

The worst freight engines Oxford men had to handle were, in his opinion, the ex-GCR ex-ROD 2-8-0s*,

---

* Albert had left the railway before Oxford men had regular turns over the LMS to Bletchley using the ex-LNWR 0-8-0 'Super D' freight engines. These were very powerful machines but they were

numbered in the '30xx' series on the GWR, but other Oxford men disagreed with him on this. Albert's opinion was coloured by an unpleasant experience he had when firing on one of these engines. He and his driver were working an iron ore train of '20 = 37 Class 1' (20 wagons equal in weight to 37 of coal). The locomotive's only power brake was the steam brake; there was no vacuum brake. Coming downhill towards Aston Magna from Moreton, the main steam pipe carrying power from the boiler to the brake blew out, leaving them with a cab full of scalding steam and only the tender hand brake and the guard's brake. Albert screwed on the former and his mate blew the whistle for the guard to apply the latter and they both got outside on the cab footsteps.

The guard's brake had no effect and there was no appreciable slackening of speed. Luckily for the wooden gates at Blockley, they were out of the way and the down Distant was 'off'. They roared through, steam billowing from the cab, pushed by 500 tons of train, much to the alarm of the ancient, white-bearded signalman, and with not a little fear on their own part that they would be pushed up the 1½ miles of 1 in 160 to Campden and from there down the 4-mile bank to Honeybourne. However, the rising gradient from Blockley to Campden station was sufficient, together with the guard's brake and the tender hand brake, to bring the train to a stand.

The Home signals at Blockley were close to the gates and the signal box. The firemen of trains delayed by either of these signals did not usually go to the signal box to carry out the provisions of Rule 55 but would yell to the signalman from the footplate - 'Sign us in mate!'. Thus very few footplatemen were aware, because they only ever saw the top half of the signalman at the window, that he had a wooden leg of the kind once much in vogue for pirates.

Albert told me of an incident that happened at Budbrooke Crossing box. The signalman had given Hatton (not quite 2 miles away) 'Line Clear' for the 12.2 am Birmingham-Paddington express at about 12.15 am, but then had rather succumbed to sleep. He never heard the 'On Line' from Hatton and was woken by the sound of an express train going through at around 80 mph down the 1 in 110 gradient. Feeling awful after the rude awakening from sleep, the signalman saw the train's tail lamp and staggered across to the up line levers to replace them to Danger behind the train.

The levers were nowhere to be seen. The signal-

man stared - and then saw that they had not been pulled over. They were still 'Normal' in the frame. The express had passed the whole lot at Danger without faltering for a moment! What became of the enginemen, whether the matter was even reported, Albert did not know, but he assured me that the incident took place.

Albert was full of anecdotes that popped out when something in the conversation reminded him of an incident. Like the time during the bitterly cold winter of 1947 when a train was stopped at facing points because, as the signalman explained to the driver, the facing point bolt was caked in ice and the lever in the signal box could not be moved.

'Don't worry,' said the helpful driver, 'I'll soon shift that for you.'

He collected the coal 'peck' from his engine, smashed the bolt free of ice, went back to the signal box and marched in.

'Which lever is it?' he asked.

'No 18 - the blue one,' replied the signalman.

The driver grabbed hold of it and with a triumphant sort of heave pushed it over. But he did not know how facing point bolts, with their fouling bars attached, react to the lever - they go heavily to begin with, then fly over easily. A signalman would control his effort accordingly. The helpful driver, still grasping the lever, was flung against the instrument shelf above the levers and gave himself a lovely black eye. He went home with his cap tilted over his face as a rakish angle.

During the Second World War Albert got back into uniform again as 'Sergeant King' i/c Oxford station Home Guard, which consisted of 130 men (in theory) and two rifles - and later on a third. The HQ of the unit was a coach parked on the West Midland sidings, right outside the staff canteen and its bar. Albert was retained on day work around the shed, acting as Foreman's Assistant, or 'Shed Turner' - moving engines about the shed and taking them to the turntable - because he had to spend each night on Home Guard duty. The most immediate recollection of those who knew him at this time is of him striding around the shed with his home-made 'pedometer' strapped to his leg to measure how many miles a day he walked in connection with these duties.

Thus Albert worked an early or late turn and spent a large part of each night in charge of the Home Guard unit. He would not like me to make his job sound too grand - he was at pains to impress upon me that only a handful of the 130 official strength ever turned up regularly, and sometimes no one came in at all. The men's job was to patrol and look out for characters dangling on parachutes or otherwise acting suspiciously.

crude - 'pigs to work' - and equipped with a braking system that left everything to be desired, according to the GWR men. Rewley Road men had a 'double home' job to Nuneaton with a 'Super D', leaving at 11 pm, and were much pitied by the GWR men.

One member of the unit was Driver Ern Gable, a good-natured 'rough old bird' by all accounts. He was on patrol with his rifle on Walton Well bridge when out of the darkness a figure approached and asked for a light for his cigarette. The person was quite unknown to Ern and it was in the wee small hours, but Ern was equal to the occasion. 'Yes, of course, mate. Here, hold me gun while I find them,' he said, and trustingly handed over his weapon to the stranger to rummage for his matches.

Regarding the third rifle, this was seen lying in a truck of rubbish on a southbound goods train by the signalman at Heyford. He reported it to Oxford and the Home Guard retrieved it. It was found to be a Canadian-issue .300 calibre Lee-Enfield with a British .303 bullet jammed in the barrel. Albert gave it to Horace Tolley who contrived to drill the bullet out. The rifle was then added to the 'strength' and, being issued with the correct ammunition, it was taken by the railwaymen-soldiers to the rifle ranges at Churn on the DN&S line.

More exciting than mere rifles were the four Spanish-made 20mm cannon that were sited at Oxford as anti-aircraft defence for the use of Albert's men. One of these was in South End Yard, another was outside the HQ coach, another by the locomotive turntable - Albert (in 1970) could not remember where they put the fourth gun, and wondered if maybe it was still there, lost in undergrowth. Chosen members of the Home Guard Company went down to

Poole Harbour occasionally to have firing practice on these rather nice heavy machine guns. Albert told me: 'We went down in a lorry. Some of us got on the lorry at our coach, others we'd meet as we went out of the town, cycling in. They'd chuck their bikes in the hedge and climb aboard. Wonderful booze-ups those trips were, on the way home.'

I do not think the guns were ever fired in anger. Albert told me that once a German plane crashed near the one at the north end of the station. 'Was it one you'd shot down?' I asked. 'No!' he laughed. 'I think it was lost and just ran out of petrol!'

Don Kingdom fired to Albert. He was a good mate to work with because he was skilful and careful of his demands on his fireman and because he was always good company. He carried with him a recorder, on which he played the hymn tunes he had learned as a boy in the Salvation Army, and a chess set for when he got tired of Sankey & Moody. Don recalled the otherwise tedious hours passed pleasantly, stuck in a wartime goods loop, talking about everything to

Albert King, holding the shield, and Algy Hunt with watch chain and engine driver's trousers. It is 1948 and Albert had just retired and the shield was presented to him by the men in the picture, all members of the Oxford engine shed Mutual Improvement Class, for his services to them over many years. Foreman Reg Jones has adopted a foreman's pose - thumb in waistcoat - and is wearing a trilby, and Jack Ody is the third face from the left. Identification of all these men would be most welcome. *AVC*

Albert, listening to his playing or playing chess. One night, playing chess by the light of the fire, the board on the up-turned bucket, they dropped a pawn and had to dig up the wooden floor with the coal 'peck' to retrieve it.

On the 'passengers' up to 'Padd', Oxford men backed their engine out to Ranelagh Bridge yard, where they turned it, cleaned its fire, took water, then waited two or three hours 'under the bridge' until it was time to go into the station for their return working. There, Albert and Don would have a bit to eat and pass the time with their usual pursuits - Sankey & Moody or chess to a background of the whistles, the barking exhausts and the clanging wheels of the passing trains. One morning Albert settled down to read a book and became absorbed, head bent. When it came time to move off into Paddington, the draught had frozen his neck in the reading position and he drove all the way back to Oxford looking at the floor!

Any work to do with steam engines was difficult, hot or cold and often dirty, and carried out in any weather at any time of the day or night. The men who did the job were tough without being 'tough', they were self-disciplined rather than 'hard men', and there were many men amongst them who, had they been born in a later generation, would have become a doctor or lawyer or gone into some other 'professional' job. This was typical of any grade of railwayman. But Albert King was always thought of as 'special' or 'different' - he had a 'boffin's' eccentricity that went with his legendary shyness where women were concerned.

One day in 1935, after Albert had been promoted from fireman to driver, the driver to whom he had regularly fired received Len Wheeler as fireman. Len told me how, soon after the change was made, he and his mate were 'up at Padd', waiting to work back to Oxford. The driver was down on the track checking the engine and Len, alone in the cab, was leaning over the cabside, being entertained by two attractive women. When his driver climbed up from the trackside, all he saw was Len's two legs and backside. They started their train and the driver said to Len: 'Easy to see I've got a new mate. If them two had come up like that and spoken to Albert, he'd a' bin over the side and down with me on the track in a flash.'

Algy Hunt returned to Oxford in 1940, for treatment for his leg injury, which treatment he received at the Radcliffe Infirmary. When the job was complete he invited two nurses he had become acquainted with for a river trip in *Lavengro*, and invited Albert along too. Albert was like 'a fish out of water'; he sat up at the pointed end and barely spoke throughout the trip.

Albert had a half a dozen hobbies from hill-walking (he even walked to work with his knapsack on his back) to piloting a plane, painting and, in the last few years of his railway career, making pottery. He had a workshop in the back yard of Marjorie Hopkins's 'East Gate Gallery', in The High, opposite the junction of Longwall Street. Here she sold very fine, antique oriental porcelain - upon which subject she was a great expert - to the dons and their wives. Through his connection with Marjorie and the Gallery he met his wife to be, Zöe.

Albert resigned from the railway in March 1948 at about the time he got married. He did not leave the railway because the GWR had ceased to exist. As a convinced Socialist he was pleased with Nationalisation, but, as he told me, 'I was just tired of the job and wanted to do something new.' That was one way of putting it. He had been developing himself as an artist and a craftsman for years, and now, with an encouraging partner, it was time to change. He became a teacher of pottery at Ruskin College, just up the hill from where he lived. He never lost his interest in railways, however, and was always pleased to talk about the old days.

Charlie Turner: 'young-hand fireman'

I met Charlie Turner in 1970 when became Class 1 signalman at Hinksey North. He had been an Oxford top-link express driver in steam days, but under dieselisation there were no 'links', and on some days he found himself driving an '08' shunter on the yard pilot and was not best pleased. In his book shunting turns were either for 'young hands' or 'cripples'. He had 36 years' service and would have preferred to have taken redundancy pay than soil his hands on diesels. During breaks in the shunting he came into the box with me and talked of the old days, I visited him at home and he wrote long letters in response to my questions.

He drove his last steam engine on 2 October 1971.

Preserved No 6000 *King George V* worked a special from Oxford to Stratford-upon-Avon and Charlie was booked as driver. When the train arrived from Didcot the platform was packed with sightseers. Charlie and his fireman, Terry Monk, forced their way through the throng and climbed aboard, and the man from Radio Oxford thrust a microphone over the cabside to ask: 'Have you done any practice runs to prepare yourself for this?' It was a mere six years since he had last driven a steam engine. Charlie replied: 'I don't need practice - I do this in my sleep!'

Charlie began his service on the GWR as a Carriage & Wagon Examiner's boy, aged 15, at Oxford in 1934. He was impatient to get into the engine shed, but he had to be 16 to start there. With the C&W man he walked around each goods train that stopped for 'exam'. The C&W man checked the state of lubrication on each axle bearing and marked those that needed oil or grease.

In 1934 there were still a lot of freight wagons still running on bearings lubricated with a heavy grease known as 'yellow fat', and this was particularly true of the coal tubs, many of which were privately owned. The axle box for this type of bearing had a lid at the top into which the 'fat' was pushed with a flat stick. The hardest job of the day was the 11.30 am Bordesley-Southall 'Long Tom'. This comprised 100 wagons - all coal. It came up the goods line from Wolvercot Junction and stopped at Oxford North at 4.30 pm - if it was on time.

The train was about 650 yards long, so with the engine at the loop exit signal at North box, the brake van was near the Hayfield Road bridge. In hot summer weather, the yellow fat got very warm and ran out of the bearings, so just about all the 400 bearings needed grease; the timetable allowed an optimistic 30 minutes for this. Charlie carried a can of grease and refilled it from large drums of grease placed at intervals so as to save some walking time.

When he was 16 he followed in the footsteps of thousands of aspiring engine drivers and took the train (and 5 shillings) to Swindon to be medically examined by Doctor Bennet at Park House. Charlie reckoned that waiting for the test inside the great, gloomy house was a very nerve-racking experience with nothing to distract his nervousness. The inside was depressingly Victorian, dim and dull, brown and beige, with ceilings 'a mile' above his head. 'It was worse than a dentist's waiting room because there wasn't anything at all to read and when I tried to looking out of the waiting room window all I could see was a public lavatory.'

Amongst the tests carried out was one requiring him to walk through a tray of smoothly raked sand in his bare feet. The impressions left by his feet were then examined to make sure he did not suffer from flat feet. He took two eyesight tests, one with a reading card, the other where he had to sort out a tangled bundle of coloured wools into separate piles of green, red and yellow.

He was passed as fit and was accepted by the Company - whereupon he paid over his 5 shillings as the '2nd class' membership fee to the 'Enginemen's and Firemen's Mutual Assurance Society' (MAS). He began as an engine cleaner in 1936 earning 24 shillings a week, looking forward to reaching the top rate after five years of 42 shillings. 'I knew chaps that got married on the strength of that 24 bob a week,' said Charlie.

Like all cleaners he took his turn on the ancient coaling stage, and it is from him that I got my description of the ghastly old contraption and the badly arranged layout of the engine shed. Not that Charlie was one to complain. He took conditions as he found them and tried his best to make them work - but he did have a special problem when working on the coaling stage. When he was shovelling out of the bottom of a 12-tonner whose door could not be fully opened, he was too short to see over the wagon side. He therefore had to throw the coal up and over the wagon side, in the general direction of the waiting tram, and to get a better aim he made two chalk marks on the wagon coinciding with the position of the tram on the other side. This was the way that the Great Western was kept running!

The Chargeman Cleaner at Oxford in 1935 was Arthur ('Domino') Watts. He had been a driver at Westbury and had lost an arm. so ended up in this job at Oxford. Charlie said of him: 'I suppose now, looking back, that he was about 55, but to us boys at that time he seemed very old. He worked from a little cabin at the bottom of the shed where he sat in an old leather armchair or doled out oil and waste to us cleaners and told us the numbers of the engines to be cleaned. He was never really strict - I can't say that he ever raised his voice, and he certainly never lost his temper with us - but he didn't need to because it was the aim of all of us to send our engines off the shed looking as smart as possible.'

Cleaners were expected to learn about the mechanics of the engines, how to run them and the rules governing safety on the line. When extra trains drew away all fully qualified staff - and there were always extra trains - the less qualified moved up, for the day, into the next step above, replacing the missing men. The most senior cleaner nearest the booking-on time of the vacant firing job was posted to that job; he was paid a fireman's wages for that turn and was formally credited with that day's experience as a fireman. If, after 300 firing turns, he still had not been promoted to fireman, he moved on to fireman's wages anyway.

At peak times even the youngest cleaner had to go out as a fireman - on the humblest of work - and Charlie's first ever firing turn was on the North End Pilot, No 1742. The first express engine he fired was No 5063 *Earl Baldwin*, driven by Fred Richards, an Oxford man. Charlie was still very young and the train was a passenger to Worcester, 60 miles away, but Fred was 'a gentleman' and looked after Charlie very kindly so that the young lad was able to complete a pretty heavy job to the satisfaction of his driver - and of the timetable.

He did not have to work 300 turns to get fireman's wages, but was promoted to fireman in May 1938, working in the Pilot Link and earning £2 17s per week basic, but with the inevitable overtime and regular night work his wages would be between £4 and £5 most weeks. After five years the fireman's basic pay was £3 6s per week. Charlie thought that relative to what a lot of ordinary work people were earning, the footplateman's lot was enviable - 'the children of railwaymen in our street were better dressed than the others - and they had holidays by the sea owing to their fathers having free tickets.'

There was no examination to pass to become what was, in effect, the old 'Class 3 Fireman', a goods fireman. Men in the Pilot Link worked the yard pilots and hauled 'trips' between the two yards, but did have some longer distance work to help both fireman and driver gain experience in the work. In this Link was the 3.25 pm passenger to Fairford and return, and on occasion they had a heavy goods to Honeybourne with Oxford's ex-GC ex-ROD 2-8-0 No 3031 working the 3.5 am from Oxford with empties for South Wales and return. This was a 'dead cert' for loads of overtime.

After the Pilot Link came the Goods Link, Spare Link, No 2 Passenger Link and No 1 Passenger, or Top, Link. To become what, on the GWR, was called a 'Passenger Fireman', and what the LMS and BR called a 'Passed Fireman', entailed passing a more or less difficult examination on the engine and the rules, depending on the severity of the Inspector. Having passed this exam, the newly made 'Passenger Fireman' was qualified to act as a driver. The six most senior 'Passenger Firemen' were kept 'in hand' on the shed, employed as suitably as possible, as substitutes for any driver who failed to come in for his turn. The 'Ordinary Fireman' worked goods and passenger trains, extending his knowledge of different routes as he moved up the Links.

On the subject of firing engines, Charlie told me: 'As to firing to "Padd" or to Worcester, there wasn't any difference - given a decent engine, proper coal and a good driver, of course. But there was nothing hard and fast with a steam engine. There were so many varying circumstances; the state of the engine, the state of the coal, the state of the weather, the weight of the train, the skill of the driver in running fast with a little steam or a lot of steam, whether the engine was working back to Oxford or going to drop its fire on Old Oak shed. All these factors, in all their permutations, would have an effect on the way the fireman worked.

'Going up to "Padd" with a passenger under ideal conditions - good engine, reasonable load, good train and fair weather - you'd fire her regularly as far as Maidenhead [24 miles from Paddington]. If the engine was going on shed at Old Oak you'd allow the fire to run down from there and the water to drop in the glass. If the engine was working back directly and you were going to take it on to Ranelagh yard you'd keep the fire in for a while longer before letting it run down because you'd need a fire to clean and rebuild for the return trip.

'If you were going down to Worcester with a "fast" you'd be firing with the engine "in the collar" almost all the way to Campden, but then you'd free-wheel from there, down the bank through Honeybourne and most of the way to Evesham. Coming back with a "fast" was no harder. You'd have the heavy climb 4 miles up Honeybourne bank and again the shorter bank from Blockley to just north of Moreton, but it was downhill from there for 30 miles to Oxford. But it all depended. We had 7008 and 7010 fresh from Swindon and on a "fast" down to Worcester 7010 regularly used half the coal that 7008 used.'

Firing a heavy loose-coupled goods from Oxford to Honeybourne had the extra complication of the wicked little 'hump' and sharp curve in the line going around the shoulder of a hill at Aston Magna. It curved sharply round the face of the hill, cutting between the village church and a brickworks on the right and the village on the left, then there was the sudden, short uphill piece right on the curve, followed by the continuing drop to Blockley. Negotiating the Aston Magna curve was something all steam age Oxford drivers mentioned - we have already heard Arthur Rhymes on the subject - when they talked about their work. If the driver shut off completely on the downhill the wagon buffers would close up together and there would be snatch as they ran back on the chains at the change of gradient and maybe bang the guard's head on the side of his van.

Finesse was required in handling hundreds of tons of train. The trick was to keep some small pull on the train, but this meant *steaming* downhill with a heavy load behind - and just around the sharp bend was the Blockley level crossing Distant. As we have seen, some drivers were nervous that, if they 'steamed' their train around the bend and then came upon the distant at 'Caution', they would not be able to pull up at the gates. Charlie would start to ease the regulator down as he passed Moreton and go over the summit and down the hill with the exhaust just lifting off the chimney. The art of driving was knowing the road, knowing distances, knowing where to let them run and at what point to apply the brakes given the circumstance of wind and rain and speed and weight of train. You began your manoeuvre a mile or more before the obstacle you were anticipating.

On the Fairford line, Charlie recalled that in 1938 he fired the ex-M&SW 2-4-0 and the two survivors of the once very numerous 'Metro' Class 2-4-0 tanks - Nos 3587/88/89 - which had the luxury of 'all over'

cabs. They always steamed well and steamed best running bunker first. The 21¾-mile branch from Yarnton Junction to Fairford was laid over the top of the land with nothing very much by way of earthworks, so the line was a switch-back of steep but relatively short gradients. There were also nine intermediate stops in those 21¾ miles.

The firegrate on the 'Metros' was square and deep and very effective for that class of engine. With the usual load of three bogies it was possible to fill the box with large lumps at the commencement, either Fairford or Oxford, and not put anything else on throughout the entire run! Even with a heavy-handed driver, or on the Sunday 5.10 pm down when the load was six or even eight eight-wheelers, they were relatively light on coal. Charlie believed that these 19th-century engines were better machines than the '74xx' 0-6-0 Pannier tanks that superseded them in about 1938. He also thought that the firegrate design on the '74s' was poor, far too shallow at the back end with a steep slope to the front where it was not productive to have a lot of coal.

The '37xx' class 0-6-0 pannier tank had the old-style grate and these were also very successful engines. Not that they 'flew' everywhere. Charlie worked them as fireman and driver over the long and steep gradients between Kennington Junction and Princes Risborough. The climb from the main line at Kennington over the river and up to Littlemore and Morris Cowley, about 2½ miles, had stretches of 1 in 93 and 1 in 82.

'Going up the hill from Kennington with a "37" and five bogies, you could feel her strug-

Above left 'Metro' tank No 3589, the Oxford Station Pilot, was also a frequent performer on the Fairford branch. It has an ex-LSWR coach at the south end of the station on the Up Middle road on 29 June 1935. *Dr Jack Hollick/AVC*

Left Less popular with Charlie were the '74xx' Panniers. This is No 7411 on the 2.2 pm to Oxford; at this time, 2 June 1954, it was still in (very oil-stained) GWR green and had the grand initials in gold and red on its tank sides. *Hugh Ballantyne*

gling 'til you'd tip over the first summit at Littlemore, just like a child scrambling up and over a steep bank.'

Charlie fired over the line on through passenger trains to Paddington. He recalled a trip on No 4903 with eight bogies and milk tanks behind - something like 'a full digger', especially as the line was steeply graded throughout. They were booked to stop at all stations from Littlemore to Greenford, then fast to Paddington. The return was down the main - fast to Slough, 'all stations' to Reading, then non-stop to Oxford. The engine, being Oxford-based, had a small tender and the entire supply of coal was used on that run of 119 miles.

A fireman's job would be hot, sweaty and tiring on a run such as this, but it would be acceptable if the engine was responding to the hard work by making plenty of steam and the driver was being friendly and considerate - the hard work was part of the skilful job. What made the fireman's job actually miserable was a bad driver.

One bitterly cold day, late in 1939, Charlie was put on a special passenger - eight bogies from Oxford to Paddington, calling at Reading only. The engine was a '63xx' Class 2-6-0 and the driver was Ern Gable. His regular fireman had gone sick - with an illness or just sick of Gable was a moot point. Ern welcomed Charlie on to his footplate with silence. They brought the stock into the up platform and without a word Gable got off the engine and walked across to the South box. Charlie guessed from his driver's attitude what he was doing. He was phoning the Shed Foreman to complain about having a 'young-hand fireman' on his engine. Gable was told that Charlie was the only man available, and that was that.

While this altercation was going on over the phone, the South box signalman had 'pulled off' for the train and Charlie, who had not planned his fire with a view to a long wait at Oxford, could not stop the engine ramping away at the safety valves. Eventually Gable strode along the platform, swung up on to the engine and, without a word to Charlie, tugged open the regulator and off they went, the engine in full gear, rolling under the piston strokes, artillery crashing from the chimney and Charlie's fire rapidly disappearing in the same direction. Gable, meanwhile, had his back to the road, rummaging in his box for pipe and tobacco.

Charlie dared not go across and adjust the reversing lever, but eventually Gable pulled it back somewhat - although not enough - and Charlie steeled himself to keep steam and water in the boiler while Gable deliberately made life as difficult as possible. He had one live steam injector working and also the exhaust steam injector to maintain the water level. Then the exhaust injector froze, or the water pipe leading to it. Charlie went across to Gable's side of the cab to start the other live steam injector, but the driver pushed him away.

'That's no use - use the exhaust,' he shouted above the noise of the engine.

'I can't - it's frozen!' shouted back Charlie.

On they went, 'thrash-thrash-thrash', making no great speed for the expenditure of steam and coal, the lever too far down, the fire dancing on the bars and only a quarter of a glass of water. At the Reading stop Charlie decided to spend the time thawing the exhaust steam injector rather than building up his fire. He got down on to the track with a shovelful of fire and managed to do it, then they were off again, 'thrash-thrash-thrash', but at least he could maintain a safe amount of water in the boiler.

They came back 'on the cushions', 'riding passenger'. Gable led the way along the corridor and chose a compartment, occupied by two soldiers. 'I've got a boy in the Army,' said Ern. 'Do you know him?' When the young men confessed that they did not, Ern Gable went into a long description. 'You must've met him, surely?'

Charlie sat in the corner feeling pretty tired. He closed his eyes, partly from tiredness and partly to cut out his embarrassment with Gable. When they got back to Oxford, Ern Gable clasped one arm around Charlie's shoulder and said: 'There you are - no one can say I won't take a young-hand fireman!'

Charlie Turner: ROD experiences

On 15 February 1940 Charlie reported to the Royal Engineers at Martinique Barracks, near Longmoor. This was a hutted camp, built by Canadians, and here he fell in with all the other recruits, including a fireman from Reading (GW), Vic Cripps. They went through their course of 'square bashing' and basic small-arms training. Charlie got through it patiently, looking forward to going on to the Railway Operating Division (ROD) at Longmoor. After the Passing Out parade came the names of those posted to the ROD - 'Cripps, V.' was on it, but not 'Turner, C.'.

Charlie was very keen on locomotive work - keen enough to overcome his awe of the Regimental Sergeant-Major and complain! The RSM was, in fact, very understanding of a keen young Great Western fireman who did not want to be separated from his locomotives, and added his name to the list.

Longmoor barracks was an old Victorian place with all the barrack blocks and roads named after Boer War battles or Generals - Spion Kop Road, Baden-Powell Barracks. Here he and the others of his intake, from all four railway companies, did classroom lessons on locomotive mechanisms, with an exam to sit at the end of it. The exam papers came at two levels - questions designed for those thought suitable as drivers, and those who would start as firemen. All the ex-GWR firemen were given 'driver's papers'. He passed his exam, but could not be appointed as a driver until he was 21, six months away.

After this he and Vic Cripps were posted to 191 Transportation Company, Royal Engineers, at Louisburgh Barracks. When the full strength of 360 men had been reached they were given seven days' embarkation leave prior to going to France. Charlie said to me: 'We set off for home on 10 May 1940, but never got further than Liss station when the MPs [Military Police] turned us back - Hitler had invaded Belgium. How it was the Army did not know about this and let us set off is one of those great military mysteries - anyhow, back we went to Louisburgh Barracks and spent the time in weapon training and bayonet practice, with the invasion likely at any time.

'We were living in tents the whole time until September when my Section was sent to Crewe, where the townspeople made a great fuss of us as we were the only soldiers for miles around. After a fortnight of this we were all sent to Inverness for route-learning purposes. This was another idyllic time. All I had to do every day was ride the footplate of whatever engine I chose! I rode on the "Lochs" and the "Bens" and on one of the new "Black Five" Class that they were very proud of.

'The longest run I used to do was the 5.40 am Inverness to Wick, a "double home" job for the Inverness crew, but we used to ride as far as a place called Helmsdale, then come back on a southbound train at about 2.15 pm. The round trip was about 102 miles, all on single track with, if I remember right, 41 [single-line] staff changes.'

Charlie spent his 21st birthday at Inverness. He is not likely to forget it because he was caught smoking

in his sentry box and was put on a charge! Luckily for him, his Commanding Officer was an ex-GWR Traffic Department person, called up for the duration (and who returned to the GWR and became Divisional Superintendent of the Chester Division). This excellent man took the very unmilitary view that, as it was Charlie's 21st, he ought not to have been on sentry duty at all, and that therefore his smoking on duty was understandable. To placate the NCO who had put Charlie on the 'fizzer', the CO took away Charlie's 'going out' pass for 14 days.

A couple of days later some of the Company was told to pack everything and head for Spencers Wood camp, Reading. They all went up on the night train and next morning came to a grinding stop outside Crewe. There they stood for 2 hours. Charlie and some others climbed down on to the track and went to view the engine - *Duchess of Buccleuch*. The driver was pleased with his uniformed audience, invited them on to the footplate and showed off the tender's coal pusher to them!

After a week at the Spencers Wood camp 191 Company ROD was sent to Ashford, Kent. On the platform there they were told that their destination was Hythe on the Sandling Junction-Sandgate branch. Charlie was to be a fireman, working the locomotive hauling a 9.2-inch rail-mounted gun of the 4th (Super Heavy) Battery, Royal Artillery. The RE detachment lived in continental ferry vans for a while before moving into Hythe Golf Club clubhouse, which overlooked Hythe railway station.

The Battle of Britain was in full swing and there was a great deal of fighting overhead. Charlie recalled one of the many 'incidents': 'Behind the clubhouse there was a gun pit with a Lewis light machine gun in it. Some German bombers were flying over and the duty machine gunner decided he'd have a go at them. He fired off this little pop-gun thing and he must have hit something because one of these Jerry planes dropped a bomb. I was in a slit trench watching all this. The bomb came whistling down and hit the station - which was made of timber - fair and square. When the dust had settled all that was left of the station was the brick chimney - and out of the fireplace came the booking clerk choking and coughing, smothered in soot and dust. He'd taken refuge up the chimney when the firing started.'

At this time, with invasion an imminent prospect, all soldiers carried their rifles with them, even when off duty. Charlie recalls taking his rifle and gas mask with him to the cinema; in the middle of a film the show was stopped while a message was projected on to the screen: 'We are now being shelled. You may leave if you wish.'

Charlie's engine at this time was an ex-GWR

'Dean Goods', ROD No 195, GWR 2531. The load it hauled was around 800 tons: the First World War naval-type gun on a massive, multi-wheeled chassis, together with its train of radio wagons, ammunition wagons, and military personnel quarters. Other detachments of 195 Company were attached to Super Heavy Batteries on the Elham Valley line, near Shorncliffe, and on the Kent & East Sussex line.

The gun was pushed and pulled along the branch, intended to defend against warships and troopships in case of a German invasion, and the locomotive was kept in steam 24 hours a day while attached to the train, normally for 5½ days at a time before being changed for another loco. At lunchtime on Saturdays Charlie and his mate took No 195 into Ashford for 'wash-out' and any other servicing on the Southern shed. He and the driver put on their best 'BD' (battle-dress uniform) and army rations to last the weekend in separate bags in the engine's toolbox, hung their gas masks in the cab and set off for Ashford. The engine's fire was dropped on the shed and the engine left to cool. Charlie changed into his best uniform and with his gas mask over his shoulder set off into Ashford for relaxation in a cinema and perhaps a pub.

On the third weekend of this routine he was fortunate enough to meet an 18-year-old girl called Kathy as she came out of the cinema with her friend. Coming back from their night out, the soldiers slept in a camping coach, stabled at the back of Ashford shed. In the morning they washed-out 195's boiler, cleaned her tubes, re-lit her fire and left it to raise steam while he and his mate retired to the Alfred Arms, near the shed, for a very well-earned pint or two.

All this time everyone in England was under threat of invasion. They seem to have taken the knowledge with tremendous unconcern. However, Charlie recalls feeling somewhat shivery, just for a moment, reading the last line of the Orders for Christmas Day 1940: 'You are the first line of defence. There will be no retreat.' The difficulty with being threatened with invasion was that you had to go everywhere with your large and clumsy rifle. It was, Charlie recalled, very difficult sitting in a cinema with Kathy on one side, and a gas mask on your lap.

In 1941 the Battery moved to Rolvenden on the Kent & East Sussex Railway (K&ESR). The K&ESR line was very lightly laid - the rails were held to the sleepers with spikes and were awash with weeds and grass. Down this incredible backwater normally operated by tiny 'Terrier' tanks - and a railcar formed by two Ford buses fixed back-to-back on railway wheels - the Army now intended to work a heavy 0-6-0 goods engine and a far heavier naval gun. The 7½-mile journey from Headcorn Junction to Rolvenden was

uneventful, but at Rolvenden (which was closer to Tenterden than Rolvenden) the 'Dean Goods' spread the track and was derailed. The Royal Engineers re-railed the engine and re-laid the rails on good sleepers with chairs. They also laid a chaired-track siding on which the gun was parked.

Charlie recalled how the gun train became part of the neighbourhood, the local people taking an interest in their welfare and little boys looking for rides on the engine. The locals got more of the gun than they wanted on the one occasion when it was fired. The Royal Artillery decided to practise and fired three rounds from the Rolvenden siding towards the marshes. By the third blast, a party of aggrieved locals arrived on the scene to draw the gunners' attention to the fact that the gun blast had broken all the windows in nearby houses and also that the carriage shed at the station had collapsed like the proverbial pack of cards. Charlie never saw the gun fired again.

The Germans were only a few miles away across the Channel and throughout 1940-42 they raided daily into Kent. The rail-mounted guns were an obvious target for the 'tip and run' raid - a couple of bombs and a machine gun strafing from a Messerschmidt 110 - and for that reason Charlie did not carry boys on his engine. He was wise to act so. The Elham Valley line, from the coast at Shorncliffe to Canterbury, was closed to the public in 1940 and used for rail-mounted guns. An ROD driver had a 10-year-old boy on his footplate on 6 October 1942 when a German bombing raid took place on Canterbury. The engine was attacked and the driver shielded the boy with his own body, but the bullet, coming down at a steep angle, passed over the driver's shoulder and hit the boy in the head, killing him.

Ashford railway works and engine sheds were also targets, as were the factories in the town. It was usual for the German raiders to come over and machine gun the crowds cycling to work. One moment the street would be full of purposeful people, cycling, walking or on buses, going to work or coming back off night shift, the next there would be a snarling roar and the street would be full of over-turned bicycles, running figures, men cowering under walls - and the insane cacophony of machine guns. Charlie was working on 195 in Ashford shed when the Fokker-Wolfs came over at rooftop level, strafing the works and bombing.

Kathy took her turn at fire-watching at the factory at night and, in common with the rest of Ashford, was regularly machine gunned in the street on her way to work. One morning her factory was bombed a couple of minutes after she had clocked on; she and all the rest were sent home. At about noon on 11 December 1942, Charlie and Kathy were walking back from Ashford to her parents' house when the street was machine gunned. 'The planes came so low down the street that they may as well have parked up and shot us all,' said Kathy. The following day Charlie and Kathy were married at St Mary's church, Ashford, and are still happily together in 1994.

Charlie and his engine did not leave the K&ESR line except to go to Ashford for servicing and the one time that the big gun had to be taken to Grateley for practice firing. The little 'Dean Goods' hauled the gun and its supporting train the whole way to Bulford and back without any particular difficulty.

Charlie was promoted to driver in 1943 (although his military rank was still 'Sapper'). Prior to the invasion of Europe, in June 1944, he was posted to 164 Transportation Company and, in a wonderfully typical piece of military nonsense, was sent back to school to learn the complicated system of signalling on French railways. It was a very thorough course.

Meanwhile the RAF was making a very thorough job of smashing up the French railways in northern France. When 164 Company landed in France they were very glad to find that the rapidly re-laid tracks were signalled under the simple military system with which Charlie was very well acquainted. There was now no time for 'courses' - there was a very furious shooting war going on. He had no idea of 'the road' - where the gradients and curves were - as he took an American Baldwin 2-8-0 out of Liseux, at midnight in pouring rain, with a 1,500-ton train of tanks - 'armoured fighting vehicles' - *en route* for Caen.

'There's a tunnel somewhere along the line,' he was told before he left! He shot through the tunnel, and the gradient dropping into Caen was a great surprise, but thanks to the Westinghouse air brake he brought the train safely to a stand at the appointed spot.

The American 2-8-0s were fine engines, and their brake - a matter of immense concern to a crew who frequently did not know the road while travelling over it in pitch darkness. Charlie often had cause to be grateful to the Westinghouse. Also at work in France in 1944 were the British 2-8-0 'Austerity' locomotives, but these were crude, uncomfortable things compared to their American counterparts. When US Army crews found themselves working a British 2-8-0 they either 'lost' it and found themselves a Baldwin - or blew up the British loco.

This was the spectacular difference between British and American railroad practice in wartime - or so I am informed by Charlie Turner, and also by the late Col D. S. Hart RE ROD, who was Bristol Divisional Superintendent when I was signalman at Challow. The British ran a loaded train outwards, and if the vehicles could not be returned loaded they would go back empty. If the Americans thought that an empty

train back to base would be a nuisance, they were very likely to remove the nuisance by running it off an embankment - or, failing that, applying a little dynamite to the problem.

Not until he got to Belgium did Charlie work the British 2-10-0 'Austerity' types. These were very fine machines. Charlie's unit was part of the 21st Army Group and all the engines carried the Group's badge stencilled on the cabside. He worked day and night out of Caen depot to begin with. The engines were coaled and serviced by German PoWs, captured SS men and airborne troops. These men lived in a hutted camp within a wire cage, but those German prisoners who would not work for the Allies slept on the ground, without shelter. The town had been very severely damaged in the D Day assault, and Charlie walked through and over piles of rubble to go between his billet, near the cathedral, and the locomotive depot.

The depot 'Foreman' was an RSM. He ran the shed as neatly as he could and took especial care to give his crews as much rest between trips as possible. Having booked on duty, a crew might be 8 hours just getting off the shed and arriving at their train. They could then be two or three days on the round trip. When a crew booked off duty at Caen in the morning, or evening, they could see from the book how many had booked off ahead of them and thus had some idea of how long they would have for rest before being called back on duty. Six hours off was a luxury.

In October 1944 Charlie and the rest of his unit were posted to Antwerp loco depot. They arrived just as the German bombardment of the city began. On 16 December his mate 'Jock' Dewar was killed as he was watching a film in the packed Rex cinema, which took a direct hit from a V2 rocket; 567 people were killed, including 296 soldiers. On 14 February - St Valentine's Day - his friend Lance-Corporal Charlie Nott, along with Sappers Bisacre and Wood, all GWR men, were killed by a V1 flying bomb that exploded alongside their billet, an SNCF ferry wagon. Charlie and the rest of the Company had moved into a substantial building, a disused police station, but Charlie Nott with three others asked to stay in the ferry wagon. The German bombardment ended in March 1945, by which time 4,248 V1 flying bombs and 1,712 V2 rockets had exploded on the city, killing 731 soldiers and 3,752 civilians, men, women and children.

In March 1945 Charlie and his Company were sent to Nijmegen. One of their first jobs here was to open the line to Roosendaal, which was reputed to have been heavily mined. The technique was to take a Dutch 2-10-0 and propel six wagons ahead to explode any mines in the track. On the first day Lance Corporal (Driver) Haines had the job and exploded one mine halfway along the route. The next day Charlie had the job but found no mines and arrived safely at Roosendaal. While on the subject of mines, Charlie recalled a curious event when a horse became very excited by a passing train and galloped along with it, level with the engine - in wartime the maximum speed allowed was 25 mph. The galloping horse had the great misfortune to tread on a mine, which exploded, killing the horse and sending out shrapnel that smashed the locomotive's cylinder. The engine was repaired but could always be recognised by its scars.

From Nijmegen Charlie's Company was sent to Wuppertal inside Germany. From here he drove troop trains and rode shotgun with German locomotive crews when they were working British locomotives, such as the 2-10-0 'Austerity' Class. He was supposed to keep his loaded rifle at the ready while the Germans worked, but he very quickly became impressed with their professionalism and skilful enginemanship. 'They were railwaymen the same as me, and it didn't seem right to point a gun at them,' he said. He put his Lee Enfield away and took a hand at firing and driving.

Charlie would spent days with a single crew. They saw he could handle their engine, which was literally foreign to him, and they respected him for it. He in turn respected their skill and they became good friends. The German loco crews were issued with army rations, but they gave them to their half-starved families and Charlie shared his rations with them; many other ROD men did the same.

Charlie worked into Hamm, Dusseldorf and Cologne and his German crew would look after him when they entered the locomen's huts in the devastated and roughly repaired German yards. He felt very awkward walking, armed and in uniform - if somewhat sooty - into these grimy dens, filled with dishevelled and for ought he knew resentful, defeated Germans. Then he was glad of his two friends - the men he was supposed to be policing! They would show he was in their care, and find him somewhere to lie out, usually nothing more than along the tops of some lockers. Charlie would pretend to sleep amidst the clatter and hear the surprise in the voices of the men as they came into the hut and saw him, uniformed, lying there: 'Was ist - Englander?'

Charlie came back from Europe in May 1946 and, after taking all the leave due to him, started work at Oxford shed in August. After seven years' intense experience in locomotive work and three years as a driver under the most testing conditions, he could only work as a 'kind of floating fireman', to use his words, 'on all sorts of odd jobs, the Fairford goods, South End Yard Pilot.'

Out on a goods to Moreton-in-Marsh one day, they passed Kingham and in the sidings north of the Banbury line flyover was a regiment of ex-WD 2-8-0 locos, and among them was one with the 21st Army Group badge stencilled on its cab and a heavily scored and dented cylinder - the same engine Charlie had seen in Holland, blown up by the galloping horse!

In December 1946 a passenger fireman was very badly injured on the shed when his engine ran him down and dragged him. Charlie stepped into this vacancy and worked all kinds of passenger trains through the epically ferocious winter of 1947. This was when fires of blazing coal were lit, 100 yards long, between the tracks in the shed yard to prevent injectors from freezing. He was put on the shed as a Senior Fireman in 1948 and made Driver in 1951. So the years passed, through the different jobs in peaceful England - on local 'Fly' goods, on long-distance goods, parcels trains to Worcester and 'vacuums' to 'Brum' until in 1957 he finally got into the Passenger Link.

Great Western Railway
Private and not for publication
Notice No 175/5

2-8-0 Austerity Engines to Kingham
All concerned to note that it is anticipated that several batches of these engines, dead-own-wheels, will be exchanged to this Company at Acton, Yarnton or Reading for stabling at Kingham.

These locomotives may work forward, four at one time, subject to the following restrictions:

1. Must not work chimney to chimney
2. Speed not to exceed 20 mph
3. Care to be exercised working into sidings
4. All usual service restrictions to be observed

Reading Control to make all necessary arrangements when these locomotive pass. This Notice is to be retained for future reference.

(Unfortunately the original notice from which this was copied had no date because it was the second sheet of a pair; the front one, lost, presumably had the date. In all, 79 'Austerity' Class 2-8-0 locomotives were stabled at Kingham. They took time to accumulate, but it is known that the movements took place starting in March 1946 and going on into 1947.)

There were several keen young firemen from Plymouth Laira on Oxford shed from 1946, all of whom fired to Charlie. He recalled Brian Horton who wanted very much to be a steam engine driver but who 'packed the job in' about 1959 when he saw drivers being 'put back' to firemen and realised that he would never be able to realise his ambition. Diesels held no charms for these young men.

Charlie had just moved into the Oxford 'Top Link' jobs in 1961 when he had to 'learn the diesels', something he detested. For him the only way to run an express train was with a 'Castle': 'I always ran them with full regulator and 15% cut off - always supposing that the engine was a good one. On a fast to "Padd" you set off out of Oxford in the 45% just to start and screwed it back to 35% at the cemetery and gave her some more regulator. Passing Hinksey South you'd be on full regulator and 25%, and by Radley you'd be on 15%. You'd go through Culham at 70 or more, shut off at Appleford's Distant and put her into the 45% for drifting and let her roll around the Avoiding Line. 40 mph over the junctions at East Junction and then you was on the "Silver Road". Full regulator and start to notch up. 25% at Moreton and you'd be flying at Cholsey. . .'

'. . .then you was on the "Silver Road". Full regulator and start to notch up. 25% at Moreton and you'd be flying at Cholsey. . .' An up express on the troughs at Goring in about 1954. *AVC*

'Cheddar' Wilson

No account of Oxford engine shed and its locomotivemen would be complete without some mention of 'Cheddar' Wilson. 'Cheddar' was not a West Countryman, he was born Frank Wilson in Oxford in July 1900 and picked up the nickname at his school, St Frideswide's. He could never be still, indeed he was hyperactive, a bundle of energy, always 'on the go'. He loved to walk for miles with his black labrador - he was mad on swimming and on speeding with the most inappropriate trains. If he could he would stop a man in the shed path, or out in the yard, hold him by the button of his overalls and recite a verse of 'The Walrus and the Carpenter':

> 'The time has come,' the Walrus said,
> 'To talk of many things:
> Of shoes - and ships - and sealing wax -
> Of cabbages - and kings - . . .'

To 'Cheddar' a 'king' must be a 'King' Class engine, and the verse fascinated him. He was known to all signalmen as 'that mad bugger Cheddar'. As a fireman, one of his regular drivers was Fred Slatford, and when they got together they were 'a pair of mad buggers'. Signalmen said that he never worried much about signals at 'Danger'; according to them his attitude was 'Never mind, kid (or 'my duck') - he'll pull it orf just before we gets there.'

Jack Ody told me how, one day in 1942, he was with his fireman on the up platform at Moreton-in-Marsh in company with 'Cheddar' and Fred Slatford. They had worked trains down to Moreton where they had been relieved by Worcester men, and they were now waiting for a train home. An up freight arrived, hauled by one of the 'Yankee' 2-8-0 locos that would later go to Europe with the army. Fred Slatford and 'Cheddar' asked if they could drive it to Oxford. The crew, knowing not what they did, were happy enough to hand over and went back to the brake van to join Jack Ody and his mate.

Jack was aghast at this turn of events and informed the train crew of their lack of wisdom in handing over 'to that mad pair'. 'All they wants to know is how fast it'll go - now we're for it.'

Jack said that the 'Yankee' engine and its long train of loose-coupled unbraked trucks went up to Yarnton 'like a passenger train. Gawd knows what Slatford and Wilson would have done if they'd had the Distant "on" for Wolvercot. It's downhill all the way and they wouldn't have been able to stop.'

On Ranelagh Bridge locomotive yard, having sorted out the fire on his own engine, he would not rest but would offer to clean the fires of other engines - 'Do your fire for you mate?'. He was known far and wide over the system for this. Those who knew of his reputation - or those who had been caught before - would refuse the kind offer, but there was often some innocent to be caught, someone who did not know who 'Cheddar' was. Those that gladly accepted would come back from their tea-break to find their firebox filled with black coal to the brick arch and not a flame - or a 'Cheddar' - to be seen.

'Cheddar', even as a fireman, loved speed; he loved to hear the exhaust crackling from the chimney and to see the sparks fly at night. As a driver he could indulge himself to his (but perhaps not his mate's) heart's content. The trouble was that he cared nothing for danger or 'the Regulations'. It was part and parcel of his desire for constant action.

Campden Tunnel and the severe incline were his playground. One day, perhaps on more than one occasion, they were approaching Campden with a down goods train. Instead of stopping to pin down brakes, 'Cheddar' said to his fireman: 'I've always wanted to "do the ton" down here - and today's the day!' And down the bank they went, no brakes.

Going down through Campden Tunnel with a fireman he had not had with him before, he left the footplate secretly, under cover of the noise and the dark, walked along the footplating, around the front of the engine and back along to the fireman's window. With a torch shining up from his chin he pushed his face against the fireman's lookout glass and gave his new mate a terrific fright. Several old-hand Oxford men have recounted this 'Cheddar' story.

Working a diesel railcar one day, he put his labrador in the driving seat, put his engine driver's cap on his head, then crouched down so that, from the platform, it looked as if the dog was driving. He set up this charade one morning running into Evesham. That was the day that the Worcester Divisional Superintendent and his staff were waiting on Evesham platform! He 'got a rocket', but was not removed from driving duties.

He gave no consideration to scientific driving methods - the engine was there to have fun with. Basil Marchant, signalman at Sandford during the war, told me that 'you could usually tell if "Cheddar" was driving because of the noise and the fire from the chimney. I saw him go by me one day with a goods, regulator wide open, fire going all ways and him sat up on the coal on the tender.'

'Cheddar' was finally obliged to leave the railway. No matter of safety was involved, although some of those who worked with him said that, the way he did his driving, it would not have been too long before he was taken off the footplate. His love of speed and sparks did not make for a good driving technique. He remained as mad on engines as ever and went to work as the shunting engine driver at Morris Cowley. This was only a diesel and incredibly slow, but better than nothing. Curiously enough, after he arrived the diesel failed and they had to borrow, for a while, No 1444, loaned from Oxford - you can imagine 'Cheddar's' joy at this*.

His love of the water was legendary. He is said to have swum in the locomotive water tank at Worcester, and it is said that he has changed into his

---

* The locomotive is shown in Lawrence Waters's *Rail Centres: Oxford*, page 33. Cheddar Wilson is not in sight.

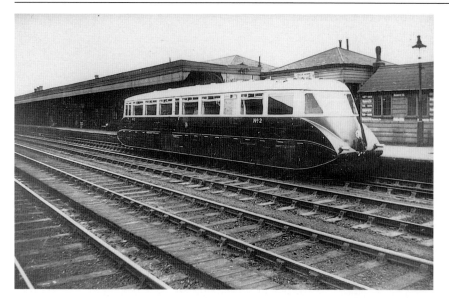

The Princes Risborough railcar leaves Oxford on 20 July 1935. The reflection in the front window prevents us from seeing whether 'Cheddar's' labrador is driving! *Dr Jack Hollick/AVC*

from the engine shed to his house in the Iffley Road he would be on the look-out for a game. No matter that he'd spent a long shift on the footplate, he was still full of energy. The game was 'Run a Policeman'. If he saw a constable he would start to act 'in a suspicious manner'. Having aroused the policeman's professional interest, he would set off at a criminal gallop, drawing the suspicious but unsuspecting policemen after him. Around the block, down alleyways, he would run him off his feet and thoroughly enjoy the exercise!

He became a kind of mascot for the Oxford City Police and each year they invited him to join them in their annual 1½-mile swim from the Folly Bridge down to Iffley Lock. 'Cheddar' swam this each year and encouraged the youngsters to take part. He swam, as near as possible, every day of his life until he died, well into his 70s.

swimming trunks on the footplate and jumped from his engine - stationary on the Avon bridge near Evesham - into the river. Everything he said was punctuated with 'my duck' - perhaps because he was mad on water. When he was asked why he swam so much and whether he would ever give up, he said: 'Well, my duck, old Father Thames is my doctor and cures all my pains.'

He was well known to the police. Walking home

Stan Worsfold

Stan's mother came from Buscot near Lechlade, on the Berkshire side of the River Thames, where her father worked on a farm rented by Mr Gillett from the Buscot Estate. She moved to Surrey to be 'in domestic service' and there she met the young man who became her husband. Stan's father served in the Great War in 1915, and Stan was their fourth child, born on 1 November of that year, after his father had arrived in France. Stan's mother now went to live with or near her parents, who had moved to Fairford. His father survived the war and in the end Stan was the middle of seven children.

He went to school at Fairford and entered the service of the GWR at Bampton (Oxon) station on 30 June 1930 as a Lad Porter. He was made redundant there in 1931 and moved to Oxford station as a messenger at the Telegraph Office. Here he worked here with Molly Eagle and Don Watson, a telegraph clerk, under the Chief Clerk, Freddy Palfry. Freddy

had lost a leg in the Great War and had a wooden replacement. He was a very likeable character and liked to sit with his wooden leg propped up on the table and 'delegate' responsibility - if there was anyone else at all who could do a job for Freddy, that person did it.

Stan travelled in from Fairford for a permanent late turn, 1.30 pm until 9.30 pm. Cecil Guy was the early turn messenger, 7 am to 3 pm, and Stan and Cecil's overlap covered the time that the clerks were having their meal break every day. The male clerks worked a 9-hour night shift, a 7-hour early and an 8-hour late turn. This was to enable the clerks on early turn to start work at 7 am rather then 6, and thus find a train that could get them to work on time. It was a mutual agreement, not an official one.

Stan, being a Messenger, was not required to learn morse or the single-needle, but Molly was a Trainee Telegraph Clerk and had to learn. Freddy Palfry

Stanley John Worsfold as a Telegraph Messenger Lad at Oxford station about 1931. *Courtesy S. J. Worsfold*

should have taught her, but he was busy with weighty matters - in particular getting the paybill together each week - and did not want to be bothered. The ordinary clerks were also usually too busy with the day's work to be able to teach her, so Stan and Molly taught each other. In later years, as a signalman and relief signalman, he found the skill of 'reading the needle' simply by listening to its 'tick-tick' useful. He recalled working at Wolvercot Junction in the 1950s, the last signal box to own a single-needle instrument, listening to the Banbury-Oxford circuit as the needle flickered left and right, ticking away, spelling out some brief train running message prefix: 'TM - 5.40 pm Birmingham 10 late'.

Many of the platform and locomotive staff at Oxford, even in Great Western days, liked to have a drink - both on and off duty. So important was this in the life of the station that some facts should be recorded. From 1850, Oxford GWR railwaymen of all ranks - Porters, Chief Clerks, District Inspectors - had

sunk their pints or their brandies at 'The Old Gate House'*.

They used the place for their social gatherings, 'glee nights' and presentation evenings. From July 1913 it came under GWR management (of a sort). In that month the then publican, Oxford City Councillor Mr Twine, retired with his wife from keeping the pub. Their place was taken by the retiring Platform Inspector Robbins. He had been at Oxford for the previous 15 years, so was well versed in how to run 'The Old Gate'. Mr F. Smith's short speech of thanks to the Twines betrays (reading between the lines) the importance of the pub in the lives of the GWR staff. He said that 'we could not let you leave without some mark of our esteem and respect. You carry with you the best wishes of everyone of the GWR staff that has ever come into contact with you.' To loud applause he then presented them with a large Crown Worcester china bowl. (*Oxford Times*)

Even closer to the station was the Railway Club, just behind Goods Shed (later Station South) signal box. It might once have been a 'Temperance' club, to compete with the fermented attractions of the Old Gate, but in oldest living memory it was selling beer and spirits, at almost wholesale prices.

Charlie Turner's father was a porter at Oxford in the 1920s; he drank there, and bought there young Charlie's ticket for the annual GWR children's Christmas party. Don Watson used to send young Stan Worsfold across to the Club with an empty beer bottle to be filled; 'And be sure to say who it's for,' he would say, to make sure he got a completely full bottle. (It was impossible to send Molly; no female entered the Club before the war.)

There was a saying in the Oxford shed Foreman's domain: 'Don't book anyone on the Pilot if they can't hold their beer'. The Pilot engine's normal stabling was West Midland sidings - right outside the Club - and any of the men liked to have a pint or three. Working on a steam engine after a few pints of beer did not have the same stupefying effect on the loco-man's brain as it would on his latter-day counterpart in the warm, enclosed cab of a diesel or electric loco. The steam engine's open cab and fresh air, and, for the fireman, the physical effort required, enabled the men to have some beer without devastating effect.

The trouble with the Club was that the few really boozy ones would actually get drunk, then someone else had to do their work, while covering up the fact of the man's incapacity if at all possible. This was by no means a rare occurrence, nor was the Oxford Club

* The name commemorated the fact that this was once the first toll gate of the 18th-century Besselsleigh turnpike road to Faringdon and Wantage.

Welford Park signal box, looking towards Newbury, on 3 August 1953. The signal box still had its original frame and interlocking at this time; new interlocking was installed one month after the picture was taken. The GWR bracket signal was replaced with a BR(WR) tubular steel straight post, perhaps when the frame was re-locked. The box was closed 3 July 1962. *AVC*

Great Shefford halt looking towards Lambourn, *circa* 1955. Beyond the 'pagoda' hut waiting shelter is a prettily made hut to house the booking office, and allotments surround the permanent way gang's cabin on the right. Wagons stand on a loop siding off the 'main line'; the connections to the running line at each end of the loop were operated by a ground frame lever unlocked by the single-line token carried by the train driver. *H. C. Casserley*

Hermitage signal box was designed by the Gloucester Carriage & Wagon Company (GCWCo). During Stan's tenancy the route was a single track and the signal box housed about 16 levers. The porch was not there when he left in 1939. The door opened directly on to the top step of the stairs - there was no 'landing'. None of the GCWCo boxes on this line were built with landings or porches, but they had them when they closed. Stan Worsfold suggests that the facility was provided to improve safety for the signalmen under blackout conditions, so that he did not step out direct on to a staircase in total darkness. The box was closed 10 August 1964; this photograph dates from 28 February of that year. *Roger Webster/AVC*

an isolated example; there was an equally accessible club at Worcester. There the Yard Inspector used to unofficially relieve the Goods Yard signalman at 10 am each day, so the latter could go for his first pint of the day. It might be that some men were so dependent that it was safer if they had a pint or two inside them.

For Stan Worsfold to get to work from Fairford to Oxford meant a very long day, so when, in about 1933, a weighbridge lad's job came up at Witney goods station, Stan applied and got it. Stan's recollection of Witney Goods was that it was 'a very industrious station', thanks largely to Messrs Smith & Marriot's blanket mills. Raw materials and coal came in and the finished products went out, sometimes by the trainload. All coal and other merchandise leaving the yard was weighed on the weighbridge to keep a tally of what left the yard and therefore what ought to arrive at the consignee's premises. A horse-drawn cart was charged 2d per weigh, a motor-lorry 3d.

When he became 20 Stan was classed as an 'adult' for wages, and therefore had to find an 'adult' job. He 'fell on his feet' as a porter's job came up at Fairford in November 1935 and he got it. Part of the staff establishment at Fairford consisted on two guards and a porter-guard, and as additional 'back-up' the porters were also required to pass out on the guards' rules.

This Stan did - and the memory of this made him chuckle when he was speaking to me, because Great Western passenger guards had to be 5 ft 8 in in their socks, of smart appearance, able to write with a good hand and have a St John's Ambulance, or Red Cross, first aid certificate. Stan was always 'of smart appearance', but he admitted to me that, had he actually applied to be a passenger guard, he would have failed on the other specifications. But he was passed on the rules and when the occasion arose he went as a passenger train guard. During the war this specification had to be scrapped because it was not possible to keep it up. In any case, it was bit academic because even before the war there were workings where goods guards, who did not have to be 5 ft 8 in tall, were officially rostered to work local passenger trains.

But Stan had always wanted to be a signalman, and on his 22nd birthday in November 1937 he was promoted to signal-porter at Welford Park, 6 m 19 ch from Newbury on the Lambourn branch, and began a somewhat meteoric rise through the signalling grades.

He did 4 hours as a signalman at Welford Park, which was a crossing station on the single line, and 4 hours as a porter, working at Welford and Great Shefford (at 8 m 14 ch). After six months he got a Class 5 post as signalman at Hermitage, a station and crossing loop on the single-track DN&S, and in March 1939 he went to Class 4 at Yarnton Junction.

Looking back, Stan reckons that this was his favourite box. The work was very interesting - working with the tablet instrument to Eynsham, Double Line Absolute Block to Handborough and Wolvercot Junction, and by telephone over the double-track goods lines to the LMS at Oxford Road Junction. The views, perched high above an embankment, were good. He could see over the countryside and over the surrounding railways: the Birmingham line trains could be seen from just north of Wolvercot Junction until they passed the Grapes pub at Yarnton Lane, and the LMS trains on the hillside, across the valley just north of Wolvercot Tunnel. If the morning was clear, bright and frosty, from his high vantage he could see the trail of steam from the first up Fairford train as it ran between South Leigh and Eynsham. When it left Eynsham at 7.53 - 3 miles away as the crow flies - he saw each pure white, sunlit blossom of steam rise as the train started. At Eynsham the signalman was the only person on duty at the station, so he was on the platform when the train left and Stan saw the train leave half a minute before he got 'Train Entering Section'. Yarnton was a perfect signal box indeed; peaceful countryside, an interesting layout and a busy train service.

Occasionally life was not so peaceful. One night in the late 1920s the signalman at Yarnton, Alfred

Stan Worsfold happy at his work in his (and my) favourite signal box - Yarnton Junction - in 1954. *Courtesy S. J. Worsfold*

Stan Worsfold looks out from his lofty viewpoint in Yarnton Junction box to enjoy and admire No 7007 *Great Western* on an up Worcester express in 1955. *Peter Barlow/AVC*

Knott, had to cope with an unusual emergency. A man came into the signal box and confessed that he had just murdered his wife. He and his wife were servants in a big house nearby, perhaps Yarnton Manor. The man was not threatening and Alf took the incident in his stride. He telephoned to Oxford station, told them what had happened and in due course a light engine arrived with police on board and the man was taken away on the footplate.

In 1940 everyone's peace was shattered, even at Yarnton. Stan was there throughout the building of the new yard when additional traffic had to be handled in spite of the engineering work going on all around. Just as the work was complete he moved to Class 3, Oxford South, in September 1940. He was one of the first signalman to work the new Hinksey North box in March 1942, the other two men being George Mundy and Arthur Lane.

Another duty that came upon Stan - and many others - from 1940 was that of 'fire watching'. In each street a group of able-bodied men and women was organised into a roster so that a different pair each night did their shift. They all received training in the use of the sand bucket, sand thrower and the stirrup pump. Had one fallen, they could have extinguished a phosphorous incendiary bomb and raised the alarm to save lives. In fact, the only bomb to fall on Oxford was an accidental one on the Co-Op, down the Botley Road.

Stan's post, twice a week, after he had finished his late shift at 10 pm, was at the station. A billet was prepared in a hut inside the big iron gates of South End Yard, alongside the GWR stables. The hut was equipped with bunks, chairs, table and a kettle, and in this pungent home-from-home he and five others spent the night, playing cards and sleeping. At 6 am they all went home to a proper bed. Stan, with his usual cheerfulness, said that it was a very useful duty because he was able, each morning, to carry home a sack of horse manure for his vegetable garden. It is worth remembering that all these people were working harder than ever before, with less food due to rationing and with less sleep due to these other duties; other men were in the Home Guard.

Stan worked Oxford South/Hinksey North until 1944 when he moved to Class 1 at Station South, then in 1945 'went out on the relief'. He was under the Didcot District Inspector and passed the rules to work all the boxes from Cholsey & Moulsford to Milton, Didcot North Junction to Kidlington, Yarnton Junction and the Fairford branch. It was an interesting life because he was posted to work in such diverse surroundings and with such a variety of operational experience.

He lived in Jericho, one of the poorer districts of Oxford, known then as 'the railwaymen's dust hole', not at all the smart, professional ghetto that it is today. His transport was bicycle or bicycle and train, later substituting a little NSU motor cycle for the pushbike. The train service was such that he could usually get a train to work, even when booked on duty at 6 am at Yarnton, in that case catching the 5.40 parcels. If he was working at Radley or Culham, there was another early morning parcels.

On Sundays, booked a long bicycle ride from home, he could perhaps get a lift on a light engine, put his bicycle up on the tender and thus ride to work. He recalled once that he had a ride home from Didcot, Foxhall Junction, to Oxford on the footplate of 'the GC engine'. It was a bitterly cold night and Stan recalled the delicious tea he was given - the driver squeezed some fresh lemon juice into the cup. Now that was travelling in style, lemon tea on the footplate!

On the Fairford branch, as on the Lambourn, Stan - or any signalman - had to know how to carry out the station office work for the times when he was the only person on duty at the station, such as early in the morning before the porter came on duty and after 6 pm when he had gone home, handing the key of the till and the safe to the signalman before he left. He issued tickets to passengers, took in parcels and livestock and did the paper work for them. Then of course there was the recording of all traffic arriving, freight into the yard by road, wagons by rail, and parcels arriving in the passenger trains. Besides this clerical work, if the station had no mains water, and many did not, he pumped water by hand into a roof tank to supply the lavatory cisterns.

Each evening he attended to the station lamps and the signal lamps. These would be a mixture of plain old 'wick' lamps and the paraffin pressure 'Tilley' lamps, along the platform, in the office and in the waiting room. The furthest lamp might be 200 yards away, at the entrance to the station - and it would be a crime if this was not lit or it went out.

A country branch-line signalman, on the Fairford or other line, might well also have the duty of cleaning, trimming and filling the signal lamps around the station, but for the Distant signal lamps, perhaps a long way down the line, some other arrangement might be made. Of course, on the Fairford line, thanks to the Automatic Train Control ramps, there were no Distant signals to attend to.

Stan Worsfold spent 28 years 'on the relief', working all sorts of boxes from Fairford to Oxford Station North and Didcot, Foxhall Junction. I had the great pleasure of working with him from 1968 to 1973 when the Oxford boxes were closed. He was the most cheerful and even-tempered of all the many delightful men I worked with. He then spent another seven years working the Oxford Panel. This was a console bearing a diagram of the layout, dotted with push-buttons and turn-switches in a room about the size of a 40-lever signal box. With this console, or 'panel', the signalman took over the signalling from Ascot-under-Wychwood (exclusive) and Tackley and Bicester through Oxford to Radley. The layout was of course very drastically reduced from steam days.

Stan wrote to me: 'It was a revelation to see such a change-over take place, and perhaps a bit sad to see the old signal boxes done away with. Of all the boxes I worked in, Yarnton Junction box gives me the most happy memories of them all.'

Molly Eagle: Oxford Telegraph Office, 1932-49

The Chief Clerk at Oxford in 1913 and in 1926 was Arthur Hurrell. Hurrell was the deputy Station Master, second-in-command and directly responsible for all money matters at the passenger station. Under his supervision were the up side and down side booking offices with perhaps 10 clerks; he may have supervised the parcels department too. He had nothing to do with the Goods Department, which was a completely separate organisation all the way up to the Chief Goods Manager at Paddington.

Arthur Hurrell had a niece, Molly, who lived with him and his wife at their house in Cripley Road, next to the station. Thanks to his influence she began as a learner in the Telegraph Office in September 1926, one month before her 16th birthday. The telegraph office was on the up side, the door just on the Banbury side of the subway steps. The gents toilet was at the London end of the building, the last to be under the canopy. South of this there was a square building with a pointed roof where the shunters lived, next to that was the guards' room and, after a gap of 4 feet, the GPO men's hut. After that came the water tank.

Young Molly Hurrell, accustomed to the quietly genteel surroundings of her aunt and uncle's home, found being outside in the world very strange, and the first thing she had to learn was 'to become accustomed to being amongst so many people in such strange surroundings'*. Then she had to learn the Byzantine intricacies of the single-needle telegraph** and morse sounder instruments. These were the main means of railway communication in those days between Oxford and the rest of the system. Molly learned quickly, with her supportive uncle close by to keep an eye on her, and was very happy at her work. She left to get married in 1937.

Molly Eagle was born in Oxford in 1916. She came from a railway family - her grandfather had been Station Master at Shrivenham in the 1890s, and he saw to it that his son, Joseph, or Joe, also entered

* Her letter to me of 11 August 1994. Molly Hurrell's instant recollection of her uncle Arthur was his total dedication to 'The Job'.

** The single-needle telegraph instrument was invented in 1869 by Mr C. E. Spagnoletti, Telegraph Engineer of the GWR. The system remained unchanged for 100 years.

GWR service. Joe started as a Lad at Basingstoke in 1897 and arrived in a clerk's job at Oxford in 1903. Another young clerk just arrived at the station was Frank Buckingham, of whom more in the next section. Oxford suited Joe Eagle very well - he never wanted to move on and was happy to await promotion there. When Arthur Hurrell retired in 1928, Joe got his job. Joe was a convivial, popular sort of person, a supporter of the Established Church as Churchwarden, and a great supporter of the Railwaymen's Club behind the Goods Shed signal box. Chief Clerk though he was, 'he would buy anyone a drink'. Hence his popularity! Molly remarked to me, as an afterthought - 'the only person he didn't "treat" was Mother - although he couldn't boil an egg and was dependent on her for everything.'

Some of Molly Eagle's earliest contact with the railway was when her father delivered the weekly wages on the Fairford branch and took her and her sister with him. They went by train, of course, handing out the wage bag at each station, and at Fairford they had a picnic and 'sometimes the Station Master let me pick some of the station flowers to take home to mother,' said Molly.

Molly Eagle began her career on the GWR in 1932, as a Telegraphist at Oxford; Molly Hurrell did what she could to help her learn. As, in this book, I am recording the way things were once done, it is also worth remembering how different every aspect of life was in those days. Molly recollected that when she began work, over 60 years ago, the Botley Road, the main road to Bristol, was a leafy lane with over-arching trees. A mile or so west along the road her uncle lived in a 16th-century farmhouse and farmed the land around with horses. In the 1950s his house became a 'listed' building - listed as worthy of preservation. It was demolished in a single night to make way for the Southern bypass and the monstrously brutal building alongside.

But to return to Oxford in 1932, the Telegraph Office contained a small switchboard by which telephone calls from the GPO 'outside' could be diverted to a few main offices around the station, and the offices could 'ring outside' through the switchboard. There was also a GPO morse sounder. This had a different tone from the GWR sounders, and by this the

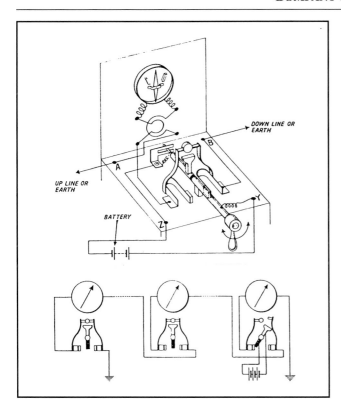

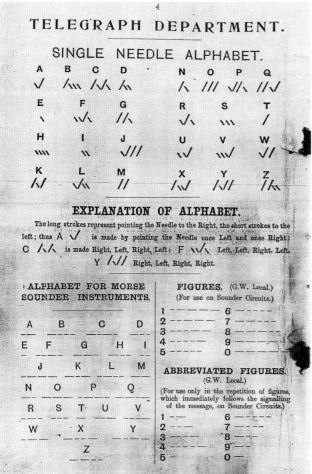

TELEGRAPH DEPARTMENT.

SINGLE NEEDLE ALPHABET.

A	B	C	D		N	O	P	Q
√	/ııı	/ı/ı	/ıı		/ı	///	√/ı	//√

E	F	G			R	S	T
\	ıı√ı	//ı			√/ı	ııı\	/

H	I	J			U		W
ıııı	ıı	√///			ı√	ıı√/	√/

K	L	M			X	Y	Z
/ı/	√/ı	//			/ı√	/ı/ı	//ıı

EXPLANATION OF ALPHABET.

The long strokes represent pointing the Needle to the Right, the short strokes to the left; thus A √ is made by pointing the Needle once Left and once Right; C /ı/ı is made Right, Left, Right, Left; F \\\ı Left, Left, Right, Left; Y /ı// Right, Left, Right, Right.

ALPHABET FOR MORSE SOUNDER INSTRUMENTS.						
A	B	C	D			
E	F	G	H	I		
J	K	L	M			
N	O	P	Q			
R	S	T	U	V		
W	X	Y				
Z						

FIGURES. (G.W. Local.)
(For use on Sounder Circuits.)

1	— — — — —	6	— — — — —
2	— — — — —	7	— — — — —
3	— — — — —	8	— — — — —
4	— — — — —	9	— — — — —
5	— — — — —	0	— — — — —

ABBREVIATED FIGURES.
(G.W. Local.)
(For use only in the repetition of figures, which immediately follows the signalling of the message, on Sounder Circuits.)

1	— —	6	— —
2	— — —	7	— —
3	— — —	8	— —
4	— — —	9	— —
5	— — —	0	—

Left The workings of the single-needle telegraph instrument.

Below left The alphabet for the single-needle instrument and the morse sounder.

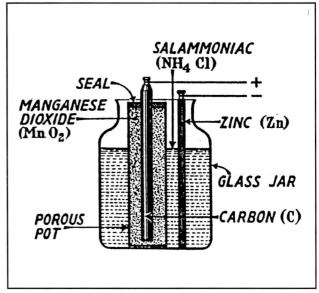

Above 'The Leclanché cell consists of a glass jar containing an electrolyte of salammoniac surrounding the positive and negative plates. The former is a carbon rod encased in a mixture of manganese and crushed carbon in a porous earthenware container. The negative plate is a zinc rod in direct contact with the electrolyte. The top of the glass jar is sealed. No chemical action takes place until the cell is placed on a closed circuit, then the zinc and ammonium in the salammoniac solution change places and a part of the zinc is converted to zinc chloride, ammonia gas (which combines with water to form ammonium hydrate) and hydrogen, which is set free. This hydrogen must be removed in order that it does not give rise to polarisation, which reduces the voltage output of the cell, eventually to zero. Immediately the hydrogen is released it combines with the manganese to form water. If the current drain is continuous the voltage falls off because the hydrogen is not oxidised as fast as it is produced, but on the current flow ceasing the oxidisation has time to complete and the cell regains it original voltage. It is on account of this regenerative property that the Leclanché cell is widely used on circuits where the drain 1s intermittent, such as single-needle telegraph, telephone and signal bell circuits.' (Adapted from *Railway Signalling and Communications*, page 110, an LNER text book for S&T technicians published by St Margaret's Technical Press, undated.)

The conversion of the hydrogen into water diluted the electrolyte, which, if left unchecked, would have stopped the cell working. The electrolyte had to be replenished with fresh salammoniac crystals at certain periods depending on the amount of work the cells performed. This work might be done by the lineman or his assistant, or in some cases by 'battery boys' whose sole job it was to go from location to location, feeding the cells with the salammoniac. The Fairford branch, with its ATC ramps as well as its single-needle and signalling circuits, had rather more than the usual complement of cells. Joe Lambert began his career in the GWR S&T Department as a battery boy, solely to look after the Leclanché cells. He went on to spend 50 years as the Fairford branch lineman.

railway and GPO sent telegrams to each other - using each other's lines for passing messages from the public.

There was no 'exchange' for internal railway circuits. Internal telephone and single-needle circuits entered the room on separate instruments; a message from one would be written down and transmitted onwards on the relevant circuit.

There would be a dozen or more single-needle telegraph instruments or telephones on one line, which was known as an 'omnibus' circuit - because everyone was on it - but always called the 'bus line'. Each instrument on the circuit had its own call sign: the initials of the signal box spelled out on the needle or a number of rings on the telephone bell. The single-needle instrument's needle was deflected to left or right; the left-hand deflection was the visual equivalent of the morse code 'dot', therefore a right deflection represented the morse 'dash'. The-single needle instruments' circuit was over a single wire with a common earth, so when one instrument's needle deflected, so did all the others in the circuit. (The morse sounders could not be on a 'bus line', but were on a dedicated wire to their single destination.)

The current to operate the instruments and telephones came from Leclanché cells until dry batteries began to replace them perhaps in the 1930s. The Leclanché generated hydrogen gas and had to be kept outside in a well ventilated place.

Long-distance single-needle or morse sounder circuits connected Oxford with the following places by separate lines: Banbury, Leamington, Birmingham, Worcester, Gloucester, Didcot, Reading and Paddington. Messages were sent to one of these main centres, then relayed on. There was no direct line from Oxford to anywhere to the west or south of Didcot: for stations on the Berks & Hants line as far as Westbury, Oxford sent to Reading; a message for any station on the Weymouth line south of Castle Cary was sent to Paddington; for anywhere along the DN&S line or for any station between Didcot and Bristol, and Swindon to Stoke Gifford, the message was sent to Didcot and sent on from there. Some messages might have to be relayed by three Telegraph Offices.

Oxford's local circuits connected it to all stations and signal boxes on the Fairford branch, the Thame and Princes Risborough line, and those to Didcot and Reading and Banbury to Kingham. Messages for Abingdon, Wallingford and Woodstock were sent to Radley, Cholsey and Kidlington respectively and relayed on by the signalman or clerk at those places. Those 'local' messages for beyond Kingham went direct to Worcester for action.* A message for High Wycombe had to be sent to Paddington.

* These details from the GWR Book of Regulations, 1933.

Within the Oxford station area, local communications between signal boxes, stations and offices were by single-needle supplemented by the telephone 'bus lines', installed in recent years ('recent' in the context of 1932). Oxford Telegraph Office had an instrument for each of the various local 'bus lines' and the clerk had to keep an ear cocked to the particular rhythm of his/her call sign. This was difficult given the noise in the office, from out on the platform and the fact that the 'bus line' single-needle instruments would be ticking more or less continuously as up and down the line people queued for their turn to use the wire - but a call sign would be repeated until the required clerk answered it.

In theory the needle was read visually, any noise it made in operation being incidental, but in fact really skilful operators read it aurally. To improve the sound it made, little tin 'sounders' were fitted to the left- and right-hand needle wire stops to create a 'tink-tonk' sound equivalent to a morse sounder. These 'sounders' are mentioned in the GWR Regulations for Telegraph Operators. Also mentioned is the paper 'butterfly' that was fixed to the needle by piercing the paper with the needle. Each 'wing' of the 'butterfly' carried a very slim strip of metal, bent around and pinching the paper to act as a hammer to hit the stops and thus beat out the code. A packet of 'butterflies' was kept in a drawer in the office.

Thus all long-distance communications were carried out - important messages regarding trains or passengers, everything we would now send down the fax line, was sent by these, to us, fragile means. In becoming used to this way of going on, the operators became highly trained and highly skilful - once again it was the actual difficulties of the job that made them so good at what they did!

In the case of the telephone 'bus line' instruments in the Telegraph Office, the clerks were spared the otherwise constant ringing of bells as people all along the line rang each other's call signs; the remote phones had a separate call button to press in order to ring the Telegraph Office. There was a Fairford-Oxford South box telephone 'bus line', each station or signal box with its own call sign. Another line connected Yarnton Junction to Moreton-in-Marsh; at the latter box the signalman could turn a switch to connect this line to the Moreton-Worcester 'bus'. A separate circuit connected Oxford South to Princes Risborough, all stations, and another went to Didcot. There was also an Oxford-Banbury line.

If, say, a person at Witney Goods wanted to send a message to anywhere beyond Oxford, he called the Telegraph Office by single-needle, gave his message, using the correct code words - which he or she also did even if speaking on the telephone - and the Oxford clerk passed it on. Perhaps it was concerning a consignment of blankets leaving Witney for Maple's store in London. The Witney telegraph clerk would call Oxford with the call sign 'OXF' until Oxford answered, also with 'OXF'. The Witney clerk would then send the prefix to denote what sort of message was to be sent - 'DB' for an ordinary traffic message. At Oxford the clerk would then send 'G' for 'Go on with the entire message without further delay', or 'T', 'Understand so far, give me the message word by word'. An operator sending 'T' would be one not skilful enough to take the whole message 'on the run', so to speak. He or she would take one word at a time and send 'T' when each word had been deciphered. This was when old-hand telegraph operators would become decidedly 'shirty' and tell the inexperienced operator to fetch an experienced person.

Assuming it was 'G', the Witney operator would follow on with the time of day and the number of words that were to be sent, these in code, then the identity of the sender and the recipient of the message spelled out in full. The message might read something like:

'WTNY - OXF. 2 pm. 6 words. Avon, blankets, PDN 3.40 pm WTNY. Ohio. SN.'

The telegraphic code words used are 'Avon' - 'Following traffic for undermentioned station will travel as under. Arrange forward first means'; 'Ohio' - 'Send on all speed'; 'PDN' - Paddington; 'SN' - End of message.

It was important to say how many words were to be transmitted so that the receiving clerk would know that he/she had received the complete message. After each message the sender would transmit 'SN' and the receiver would count up the words and wire back how many he or she had got; the telegram message form had a box at the top for 'No of words'. If it was correct the telegraph clerk would start the next message.

Witney's message would then be relayed to Paddington, signalling 'PDN' until that station acknowledged. The reply might come back 'MQ' - 'Busy, will re-call'.

As much as possible of the daily eventualities of railway work were covered by code words, a selection of which are given in the accompanying table. For example, 'COW PACO 2.40 pm OXF' sent to a station meant 'Be prepared to detach from the rear (COW) of the 2.40 pm Oxford a horse box (PACO)'. The single-needle and morse code alphabets, the abbreviations and the system for sending messages had to be learned to automatic perfection, and all this Molly Eagle and Stan Worsfold taught each other, with a bit of help here and there from sympathetic clerks like Molly Hurrell.

A selection of telegraphic code words

ASMO Covered goods motor-car truck, 32 ft 8 in long, fitted to run in passenger trains.
BANDON Return bank engine immediately upon its arrival at your station.
BOVINE Empties waiting power at undermentioned station. Arrange to clear at once. Special if necessary. Wire what done.
CHOPPER Weather foggy here. Instruct Drivers and Guards of following trains to light their head and tail lamps.
CIRCUMA Trains must be diverted in accordance with instructions shown in Notice of Diversion of Trains to Alternative Routes.
COLUMBIA No extra engine power required (as in 'Columbia 10.30 am Paddington').
DAMO A Covered goods motor-car truck, 30 feet long, to carry two motors.
DAMO B Covered goods motor-car truck, 20 feet long to carry one motor.
DONKEY We are now asked to deliver following traffic to firm named. Wire if we may do so.
ELK We sent you in error on date named the following. Forward with all speed to the following station.
GAZEL Your enquiry respecting following. Correct as received. You may deliver.
GUM. FALCON Your message of today. No trace.
HEBREW Following train is leaving here with assistant engine (as in 'Hebrew 10.30 am Paddington').
PRUNE Bank engine required to assist following train (as in 'Prune 1.10 Pontypool').
RELOCO Engineman does not know the road beyond your station. Provide engineman forward.
WALNUT. REDE Please make all necessary arrangements as far as you are concerned. Arrange and advise all concerned.
STRONGBOW Two locomotives required for this train.

The latter would ask them to do simple jobs on the morse sounder or single-needle instrument, and in this way their confidence grew. Molly needed confidence - the system was very complicated, and working with a highly competent - and impatient - telegraph clerk at the other end of the wire, she would stumble and the other clerk would send her 'GT CK' ('Get clerk'). She would wait for a few seconds, then send 'CK HR' ('Clerk here').

Molly said, 'I'd been in the office a year and had

just about got the hang of the system when Mr Buckingham called me into his office and said, "Molly, I'm terribly sorry but I've got to let you go."' It was 1933 and the GWR was laying off staff owing to the Depression. In June 1932 the Company told 300 senior engine drivers to retire on their pensions*. Molly was on the dole for a year, then came back to take the place of the female switchboard operator who had given up her job to marry.

The men in the office worked a fairly normal three-shift pattern. Officially each shift, 'early', 'late' and 'nights', lasted 8 hours straight through, but in reality the night shift did 9 hours, the early shift 7 and the late turn 8, so that people could get to work in the morning when they lived so far away. The women's shift times were more awkward. Molly worked shifts of 8 am to 1 pm and 2 pm to 5 pm; 10 am to 2 pm and 4 pm to 8 pm (split shift); and 2 pm to 10 pm straight through. They had half days off when they worked 8 am to 1 pm, 3 pm to 7 pm or 6 pm to 10 pm.

'There would be as many as 20 messages to send off to Worcester or Paddington,' remembered Molly. 'You'd be there for an hour. We used to get "telegraphist's cramp" and sometimes the older people would have to ask the younger ones to operate the keys for them because their arm had very painfully seized up. You couldn't lift your arm. I've had to go to the Radcliffe sometimes.' She said that it was the morse key that did this; 'Agony it was,' she said.

'Outside' people also used the railway telegraph for their messages instead of going up the town. There would be piles of them. Molly recalled the smell of bitter oranges on the employees from Cooper's Oxford Marmalade works who brought over their works messages for transmission on the railway telegraph because it was close by, rather than a long walk to the GPO, and the smell of the brewery when the man from Morrell's office came across with messages to send.

Oxford Goods Department also brought in their messages to be sent. Each department brought them in in bulk to be transmitted; it was rather like the office routine of 'going to the post' in mid-afternoon. There was, for instance, 'the Big 5' at 5 pm when Morris Cowley brought in their 'train loads' messages for dispatch, with each truck's number, type (ASMO, DAMO) and contents.

Cecil Guy was a great joker in the office; 'Always acting about,' said Molly. 'More than once he threw me off my seat while I was dealing with someone on the switchboard and had his foot on my neck and I still had my head-set on answering this inquiry. "I'm sorry, I'd didn't quite hear that."' Molly told this fearsome story with an affectionate laugh!

* See my *Great Western at Work 1921-1939*, page 155.

When the war came, 12-hour shifts became normal and half days off were a thing of the past. In fact, hours of duty simply had to be 'as long is necessary', according to circumstances. The wooden walls of the station were sandbagged and Molly recalled the smell of the wet, earth-filled bags piled against the windows of the office. A larger switchboard was installed in 1940, requiring two operators. These were both female and were 'directed' labour, and Molly felt that they were resentful of being pushed into the work. They stuck rigidly to working the switchboard and refused all efforts to get them to learn morse code and the way to send messages with the morse sounder keys.

Ken Smewin arrived in the Telegraph Office as a Messenger in 1940 and offset any conscript resentfulness with his 'larking about'. In the office at that time there was a very precise and - to Ken - ancient bachelor, Ted. Ken was young and full of fun and at once latched on to Ted's precise correctness - it was irresistible. Ken would throw himself in Ted's lap, put his arms around him and say 'Come on then, give us a cuddle, darling!'

'Get off, you stupid great fool!' Ted would bellow.

But Ken would keep it up: 'Come on, darling - give us a cuddle!'

During the last week of May 1940 came the drama of the evacuation of the British Expeditionary Force off the beaches at Dunkirk. Molly was present in the Telegraph Office when the message came through from the War Office in London asking that anyone who had a boat, even a rowing boat, should be contacted, and told to bring it to the station to be railed to Dover. These boats were tied together with rope and towed across the Channel to help bring the soldiers home.

She was also on duty when train loads of soldiers, evacuated from Dunkirk*, came through Oxford. The dishevelled - and in many cases, unarmed - soldiers threw messages on to the track as they went through. The station staff, including Molly, collected all the bits of paper, messages to be sent to the families of the men to say that they were safe.

When the German bombers flew towards Oxford the air raid sirens howled their frightening 'up and down' wail (once heard, never forgotten - it still puts shivers up my spine). After dark the station was lit with dim electric lights, some of these being painted blue. If the sirens went after dark, while Molly was on duty, it was her job - 'It was my *favourite* job,' she told me - to go along the platform to a special switch and turn it to extinguish every

* There is a short account of the GWR's maritime contribution to the evacuation on pages 145-47 of my *Grime and Glory*.

light on the station, then to turn them on again when the steady howl of the 'All Clear' siren signified the end of the raid.

Twice a week she was rostered to act as her street's firewatcher when the awful sirens howled their undulating wail and the 'Red Alert' was on. After a long day and another long day to follow, to spend half the night out in the street under the drone of German bombers was somewhat wearing. Molly said: 'We'd hear the planes going over, the sirens wailing and the searchlights swinging about and we'd wonder if the bombs were going to fall. In the first half of the war we'd sometimes see the red in the sky to the north if Coventry or Birmingham were getting it.'

After the war Oxford station was considerably run down and the staff were tired; some of them were not as keen as they should have been. 'They'd only come into the job because of the war and they weren't very interested,' said Molly, 'and I got a bit miserable at the station. The hours were long and the pay wasn't so good.' Molly was fairly exhausted after the hard

years, and the hours in 1947 could not have been longer than those she had worked in wartime.

In 1949 the Government started to recruit 'mature students' to become teachers, and Molly's sister volunteered her for teacher training. Molly was aghast - 'I couldn't be a teacher' - but she was persuaded and went before a selection committee. And who should be on it but her old headmistress and a school inspector who had known her father when they were churchwardens together.

Her headmistress was pleased to see her and said that she would do very well, and there was Molly saying 'No, no, I can't do it', but they took her on and she went to college at Wimpole Park in 1949. She subsequently became an infant school teacher at SS Mary & John.

But she has never lost her pride in having been a Great Western employee; she can still beat out the morse on the table-top with her finger and thumb, and she still remembers how to send a telegraph message. The loyalty to 'The Job' of all these railway people is something of a marvel.

Mr Buckingham

The man in charge of the station from 1927 until 1941 was Mr Frank Buckingham. He was born in the village of Ramsden, near Charlbury, in 1881. His father was a builder and stonemason, a well-known craftsman of his time who spent a lifetime repairing and restoring stonework in houses and churches. Frank won a scholarship to Burford Grammar School, and it seems likely that he had determined on a railway career before he left school.

In 1897, aged 16, he entered Great Western service at Buildwas as a Lad Clerk. This was a long way from home - as if, on leaving school, he was impatient to get on to the railway, and rather than wait for something closer to home took the very first clerical vacancy that arose. From Buildwas he went to Hartlebury for his first 'adult' job, then to Moreton-in-Marsh, arriving as a clerk in the Parcels Department at Oxford in January 1903.

Frank was a real 'live wire'. The Company was the centre of his life and while in the Parcels Office he undertook the GWR Correspondence Course on Rules & Regulations for Train Signalling and sat the examination. This took the form of a day's work, 2 hours in the morning, 2 hours in the afternoon, answering a total of 20 questions. There would be a

question on the operation of temporary single-line working; how to set it up, and how trains were accepted by the different signal boxes involved under varying conditions. There might be a question 'What is "detection"?' - that is 'detection' of the positions of railway points and signals, not of criminals. A short essay on the purposes and mechanisms would be required, and the more information you gave the more marks you got up to a maximum of 500. Frank Buckingham scored 408 to gain an 'Honours' pass.

Frank's hobby was singing. He had a very good baritone voice and sang with the Oxford Choral Society as well as the Oxford Glee Singers, and organised some very popular concerts for Oxford station staff. By July 1913 life was going swimmingly for Frank. He was very happy at work, a very popular Chief Clerk in the Parcels Office, and he was very happy at home, married to Mary Elsden. All four of her brothers were salaried railwaymen; three were with the LNWR, while the fourth, Arthur, was with the Great Western and became Station Master of Birmingham Snow Hill. Frank's managerial and leadership qualities were recognised early by the GWR and by the wider bourgeois community - he had received and accepted the invitation to join the Bertie Lodge of the

Freemasons*. His daughter, Mrs Betty Cole wrote to me: 'My father was such a happy person - he got up in the morning singing.'

In July 1913 came his promotion to the Divisional Superintendent's Office (DSO) at Paddington. This was a sure sign that his exceptional capabilities had been recognised. He was to be brought closer under the watchful eye of top management and given greater responsibilities. He had been at Oxford for 10½ happy years, so his departure had to be signalled by a convivial presentation evening at The Old Gate House. The station staff had made a collection, a watch had been purchased and inscribed, and it was presented to him by Chief Clerk Arthur Hurrell.

After three years at Paddington he was experienced

* It was common for GWR employees reaching the rank of Station Master, District Inspector or Shed Master to have previously joined a Freemasonic Lodge. It was good insurance if nothing else. Swindon station at one time had a Freemasonic temple upstairs at the western end of the up platform building.

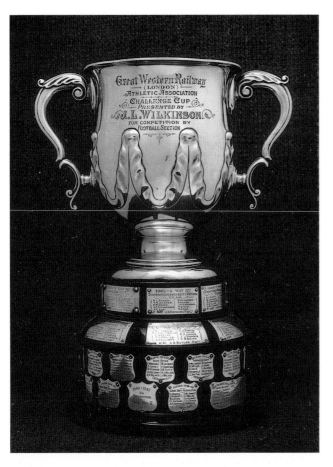

Frank Buckingham formed the Reading Branch of the GWR Athletic Association. This is the General Manager's Football Challenge Cup. At the base, amongst all the plaques commemorating the winning teams, one shows commendable stiff upper lip, viz: '1940-1947. No Competition. World War II'.

enough to be sent out into the London Division as a Relief Station Master, to go to any station and stand in for the regular incumbent. This was also very good training for him. In 1922 he was sent to Reading as Assistant Station Master to Mr Knutton; both men had worked together at Oxford. Once more in a settled posting, Frank started his concert parties - 'The Minster Gleemen' - and not only formed the Reading Branch of the GWR Athletic Club, but also found the club its own playing field. All this he did for the staff, and for the fun of the railway life, incidental to his main concerns which were, of course, the safe and efficient working of the station. He was a very popular Officer.

Mr Knutton died 'in harness' in October 1924 and Frank Buckingham became Acting SM. On 29 December an odd incident happened, as they do on the railway from time to time. At Paddington a family was seeing off relatives who had been staying with them over Christmas. The visitors were catching the 2.45 pm Down and the whole party boarded the train. Among the 'platform party' was a young mother with a babe in arms. The baby was put down on the seat while the mother did the hugs and kisses routine with aunt and uncle. There was the usual excited pandemonium, the party divided as the guard blew his whistle and off went the train with aunt and uncle, waving from the window, backs to the seats. No sooner had the train cleared the platform than the baby was missed.

The distraught mother rushed to the Station Master's office, a telephone call was made to Frank Buckingham at Reading and the baby was collected from the compartment. Frank took the little bundle back to his office by the fire, had it properly addressed and labelled and placed it in the charge of the guard on the very next express train back to Paddington, where it was re-united with its tearful mother.

Frank remained Acting SM until Norman Mansfield was posted to the job early in 1925, and in 1926 Frank became Station Master at Didcot. Here he and his family lived in a good, large railway-owned house, one of a pair fronting the Kynaston Road, their gardens running back to the railway embankment; the other house was occupied by the Didcot District Inspector.

Frank was promoted to Oxford in April 1927. There was no GWR-owned 'Station Master's house' at Oxford (indeed, there were no 'railway' houses for any station staff), and the Buckinghams lived in a non-GWR-owned house on the Cowley Road, which he took over from the previous Station Master, A. C. Foster. Mary Buckingham liked to move, so they changed houses several times in the eight years up to 1933. In that year Frank was handed the additional responsibility of the LMS station*. The Rewley Road station house was refurbished, being equipped with hot running water amongst other improvements, and into this house he moved with his family.

There was no particular advantage to living in a 'Company' house - the occupant paid rent just as he would have done to a 'private' landlord. However, railway rent was deducted from wages and one had no choice as to the type of house or the amount of rent, whereas if one rented 'privately' the cost of the rent and the type of house was open to choice. There was quite a 'colony' of railway families in the Abbey Road, Cripley Road and the streets of Osney Town.

Frank Buckingham is remembered by his daughter, Mrs Betty Cole, and by railway people who worked under him, as a man of great energy who moved quickly, darting into the offices to see what was going on and putting right anything that was wrong with good-humoured firmness.

Smoking on duty was forbidden. Going into the Parcels Office he just missed the man putting his lighted cigarette into a drawer, but the smell was in the air.

* This was a result of the GWR/LMS/LNER policy of co-operation and pooling of resources, which was close to amalgamation. See my *Great Western at Work 1921-1939*, page 34 et seq.

Smart and trim, Station Master Buckingham (right) congratulates guard John Jarvis on his retirement after 49 years' service on the railway, as featured in the local paper.

'Changed to Navy Cut today, then, Ernie?'

When the Buckingham and Elsden families met, the talk between the brothers-in-law was, of course, railway 'shop'. Each year both families went to Cornwall for their holiday; St Ives was a popular destination. They went in a GWR 'Family Saloon' attached to the rear of a Wolverhampton-Weymouth from Oxford to Swindon, where it was attached to a West Country train and shunted again at St Erth for St Ives. There were four-, six- and eight-wheel Open Saloons for family parties. It seems likely that a two-family party would have required an eight-wheeler. What a way to go on holiday!

Mrs Mary Buckingham insisted that, for this time at least, there should be no railway 'shop' talked, and if a railway discussion appeared to be breaking out she and the children chorused their boredom with 'BAS-INGSTOKE! BASINGSTOKE!'. This was indeed a most effective in cutting 'shop' talk short since Frank knew full well that this was a reference to Gilbert & Sullivan's 'Ruddigore', when the word was used as a tranquilliser to calm 'Mad Margaret'.

At Oxford a Remembrance Day service was held annually on the up platform at 11 am on 11 November. These were obligatory under a Royal Proclamation from 1920* until the last in 1938. By order of the Proclamation it was obligatory that trains that were booked to leave a station at 11 am or close to that time were held for the 2 minutes' silence. The Vicar of St Aldate's used to conduct the service, gathered around the Roll of Honour with Frank Buckingham, the Goods Agent and as many Inspectors and staff as could be mustered. If a passenger train or trains were held at the station, the passengers lined the corridors or got out on to the platform to stand bareheaded for the period of silence, and without doubt had tears in their eyes when the Oxford & Buckinghamshire Light Infantry bugler played 'Last Post' and 'Reveille'.

The railway station before the rise of road transport, prior to the Great War, was a very important part of the life of the City of Oxford (and indeed of any town or city), since it provided the only long-distance transport. Anyone coming to Oxford came by train. With the rise of road transport, the importance lessened, but only gradually, and the conception of the station as an important place remained and the figure of its Station Master was well known - especially such a 'high-profile' man as Frank Buckingham.

Soon after he arrived as Station Master a character sketch of him was published in an Oxford newspaper: 'A Station Master spends his time conciliating the different grades of railwaymen and, more important,

* See my *Grime and Glory*, page 34.

That 'genial, obliging little man', 'Ambassador Buckingham', became something of a celebrity in the columns and cartoons of the *Oxford Mail*. Here he contemplates what was presumably a proposal to modernise the station.

explaining away the lateness of a train to an irate passenger who is going to lose everything by being five minutes late. I love the trains to be late at Oxford, I love to lose my ticket or my luggage - and I get my chances of all this at Oxford - but then I get the chance of a talk with the Station Master. Three minutes talk with this genial, obliging little man and I am *ever so glad* I lost my luggage - in fact, I learn that it was *good* for me to lose my luggage. What would the Great Western do at Oxford - with its strange population of impossibles and improbables, if it had not got Ambassador Buckingham?'

When I first arrived at Oxford in 1968 there were vague stories still lingering on at the station concerning certain sorts of arrogant undergraduates, whose fathers or uncles might have been Directors of the GWR. These young men were said to have asked Mr Buckingham to 'lend me a fiver', and, when politely refused, expressed their surprise at the outcome - 'After all, what else are Station Masters for?'

He was out on the platform amongst his passengers, he was around the Departments, keeping people up to the mark, he was in his office dealing with correspondence, he was out amongst the factories and shops meeting business people, helping to get traffic. His popularity as a 'jolly good sort' would have been as helpful in gathering business as in keeping up the morale of his staff. His diplomacy helped to negotiate with William Morris (later Lord Nuffield) to arrive at terms that would bring motor car traffic to the railways. He ordered the creation of the first car park at the station, and got cheap, evening tickets to London

on any train starting with the 4.30 pm up express.

Six months after his return to Oxford - in the 'driving seat', so to speak - the GWR inaugurated its Oxford-Witney-Burford-Cheltenham (and back) bus services connecting these important market towns with the best express trains*. It would be nice to think that the energetic move was initiated by Frank Buckingham.

The University provided the station with a continuous stream of eccentric academics plus visiting Bishops, Princes, Princesses, Politicians, Dukes and Duchesses and tourists from the USA. Like any GWR Station Master, Frank made it his business to get to know as many of his passengers, humble or exalted, as possible. He first made the acquaintance of Stanley Baldwin in 1901, when he sold him train tickets at Hartlebury, junction for Bewdley, Baldwin's home town. When Baldwin became Prime Minister he wrote personally to Frank to reserve a compartment for himself. As can be seen from the accompanying note, Baldwin used the train to make a lunchtime engagement at Worcester. The directness, the commonplace lack of fuss of this method of proceeding is admirable, and leaves me wondering how many people would be involved today should the Prime Minister take the novel step of travelling anywhere by train.

The railway in those days *wanted* traffic. Nothing was too much trouble. At 4 pm on Saturday 13 August 1928 the local agent for a motor-bus company telephoned Mr Buckingham for assistance. He had a party of 150 motor-bus passengers booked to travel by of his coaches from Oxford to Birmingham, but owing to road traffic congestion, the necessary conveyances had not arrived in Oxford from Birmingham - could the GWR carry the people?

'Send them along directly!' said Mr Buckingham, and while the travellers were walking through the town, he telephoned the Goods Shed signal box.

'What's the next train coming down for Birmingham?'

A Portsmouth-Birmingham empty pigeon special had just passed Radley.

* See my *Great Western at Work 1921-1939*, page 47.

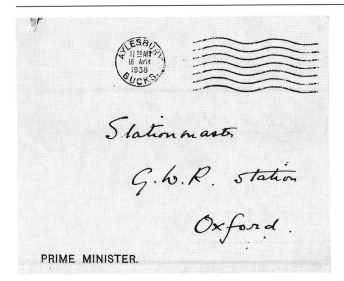

Stationmaster

G.W.R. station

Oxford.

PRIME MINISTER.

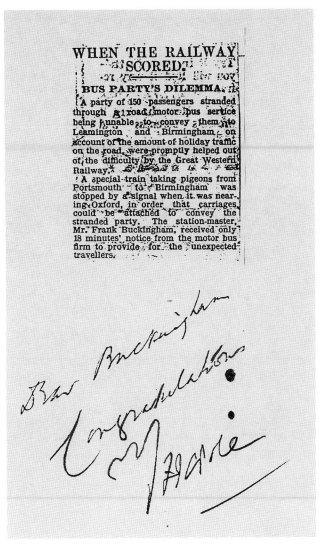

GWR, sent the press cutting to Frank Buckingham with a message hand-written in ordinary pencil (the great men of those days did not stand on ceremony): 'Dear Buckingham, Congratulations. F. J. C. Pole.' The message has been preserved by Frank Buckingham's daughter, Betty Cole.

WHEN THE RAILWAY SCORED.

BUS PARTY'S DILEMMA.

A party of 150 passengers stranded through a road motor bus service being unable to convey them to Leamington and Birmingham on account of the amount of holiday traffic on the road, were promptly helped out of the difficulty by the Great Western Railway.

A special train taking pigeons from Portsmouth to Birmingham was stopped by a signal when it was nearing Oxford, in order that carriages could be attached to convey the stranded party. The station-master, Mr. Frank Buckingham, received only 18 minutes' notice from the motor bus firm to provide for the unexpected travellers.

Chequers
Butler's Cross
10, Downing Street,
Whitehall.
Aylesbury
Bucks.

Please have compart-
-ment reserved for me
on Saturday.

11. 24 A.M. Oxford
to Worcester.

4. 10 p.m. Worcester
to Oxford.

Stanley Baldwin

'Put that in the platform and put three coaches on the back.'

Eighteen minutes later the crowd of refugees from the buses arrived at the station to find their train formed and awaiting their pleasure. We know about this example of GWR efficiency because someone (perhaps Mr Buckingham?) reported it to the national press. Sir Felix Pole, the General Manager of the

In 1931 Frank was invited to dinner by the new General Manager, Sir James Milne, and offered the 'Station Mastership' of Taunton. The next step after this would probably have been to become Station Master at Paddington; there were several men who had followed this line, from Reading and Taunton to Paddington. But Frank was an Oxfordshire man and very happy where he was. He declined the promotion.

Frank Buckingham wanted courtesy and smartness from his staff, and he set the example. Ken Smewin, a new arrival in the year Buckingham retired, remembers well the sharp rebuke he got from his Station Master who saw him wearing his uniform cap on the

'Oxford's popular Station Master', Frank Buckingham, 'misses' the train to Taunton, much to the relief of grieving railway staff (and milk churns), not to mention presumably the city at large. The cartoon emphasises the position an SM of those days held in the local community.

back of his head. 'Put you cap on properly - have respect for your cap.'

Not long before he retired, Princess Maud, who was a regular traveller from the station, moved to another part of the country, but before she left she came to the station to give Frank Buckingham a silver cigarette case 'in appreciation of the many kindnesses shown to her at the station'. This was the sort of status and respect that many people gave to the gentlemanly and public-spirited Great Western.

Frank Buckingham retired on 2 October 1941, aged 60, after 44 years' service with the Great Western. He had already taken on the voluntary job as Chief Clerk to the Civil Defence Department in Oxford and now gave his entire time to that work. He survived barely a year and died at the end of September 1942.

Like many railwaymen before and since, he lived for the railway. His daughter feels sure that his salary was not a large one, especially when his wide responsibilities are considered and the importance of the railway station(s) to Oxford in those days. She is equally sure that his pension was very small. In this regard, Molly Eagle remarked that her father, as Chief Clerk, retired to a very small pension.

The loyalty all these railwaymen had to the job did not come from high pay, because there was no high pay, but from being involved as part of a team running a serious, honourable, public service. The Station Masters of Oxford after Frank Buckingham were Mr Price, with Jim Miller as his assistant, then Mr Miller as Station Master, and Mr Swancote was the last.

To regard the railway in the same light as a hamburger joint rather than a national transport system will not produce the essential loyalty and commitment described above - neither will it produce a satisfactory transport system.

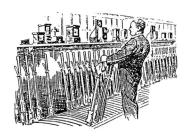

EAST OF DIDCOT

The following sections will look at all the signal boxes in and around Oxford, their history, the men who worked them, the layouts they controlled and how the traffic was dealt with.

The sequence of signal boxes between Reading and Wantage Road in 1885 was Reading West Main, Cow Lane, Reading West Junction, Scours Lane, Tilehurst, Pangbourne, Goring & Streatley, Moulsford, South Moreton, Fulscote Crossing, Didcot East Junction, Didcot East End, Didcot West End, Foxhall Junction, Milton Crossing, Steventon Station, Steventon Causeway Crossing, and Wantage Road.

Most, but not all, signal boxes were permanently fitted with a 'block switch' so that they could be switched out of circuit; this was quite irrespective of whether or not they were scheduled to be open continuously. It is doubtful if any level crossing box was ever provided with a switch (although I suppose anything is possible). Some of the larger boxes not provided with a switch included Paddington Arrival and Departure, Reading West Main, and Didcot East Junction, East End, West End and

Foxhall. Didcot North Junction was provided with a switch.

On Sundays in 1885 the following boxes were switched out, all being switched in again at 7 am on Monday: Reading West Junction (10.30 am), Tilehurst (11.40 am), Goring & Streatley (11.00 am), South Moreton (7.00 am), Steventon Station (7.00 am) and Wantage Road (9.00 am).

When all these boxes were switched out the block sections were Reading West Main-Pangbourne-Moulsford-Fulscote Crossing-Didcot boxes-Steventon Causeway-Uffington. In 1892 Moulsford was abolished and two boxes, Cholsey & Moulsford East and Cholsey & Moulsford West, opened; the West box switched out at 6 am Sunday to 8 am Monday. In 1905 the same arrangements applied except that Reading West Junction did not switch out and the other boxes were switched out for a hour longer than previously.

Up until the outbreak of the Great War the GWR was able to maintain the economy of switching out boxes on Sundays. After the war Sunday switching-out was re-introduced, but fewer boxes were involved.

Pangbourne

In April 1865 the up line only between Goring and Pangbourne was chosen for a trial of 'block working' using C. E. Spagnoletti's instruments. Between 1870 and 1872 the 'block system' of train control was extended to cover all 'running lines' from Paddington to Goring, and by Christmas 1873 the lines west to Bristol and as far north as Oxford were thus signalled.

The 1872 Pangbourne signal box was replaced in 1893 and this lasted until the abolition of block sig-

nalling in 1965. It was what the Signalling Record Society terms a 'Type 5', and stood at approximately 41 m 43 ch (from Paddington) on the down side. It had a floor area 30 ft 5 in by 12 feet housing a 'double twist' pattern frame of 45 levers at $5^{1}/_{4}$-inch centres. Every lever was in use and there were no spaces in the frame. In June 1952 a new 'vertical tappet' frame of 59 levers at 4-inch centres was installed.

From 1893 the signalman controlled four running

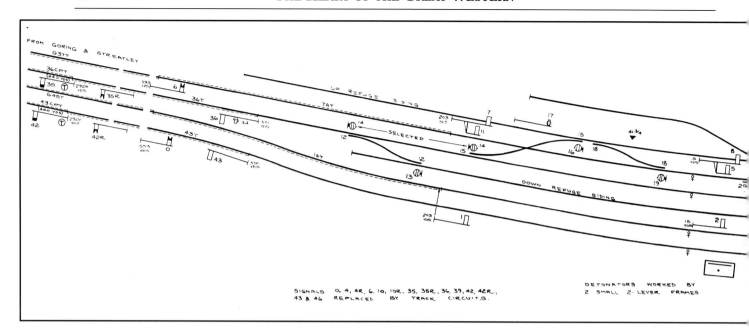

SIGNALS 0, 4, 4R, 6, 10, 10R, 35, 35R, 36, 39, 42, 42R, 43 & 46 REPLACED BY TRACK CIRCUITS.

DETONATORS WORKED BY 2 SMALL 2-LEVER FRAMES

Left Pangbourne signal box, 29 September 1963. *Roger Webster/AVC*

Below left Looking west from the down main platform, *circa* 1960. The signal box is obscured behind the post of signals 44 (off) and 40, controlling the Down Main/Down Relief junction. *AVC*

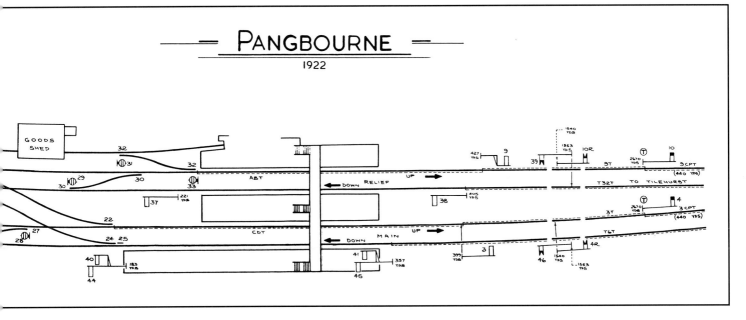

PANGBOURNE
1922

The 'block system'

Originally under this system the line was considered to be clear unless stated otherwise. Signals were maintained in the 'off' position (arms lowered) and the block signalling instruments were normally 'pegged' to 'Line Clear'. After a train passed a signal box the signals were placed to 'Danger' behind the train and 'Train Entering Section' was sent to the signal box in advance. When the train cleared the Home signal of the box in advance, complete with tail lamp, the signalman there sent 'Line Clear', whereupon the first signalman lowered his signals once more to 'All Right'.

In November 1883 this system was altered to the one in use today - that the line is considered to be *blocked* until the signalman says it is clear, and signals normally remain at 'Danger' except when they have to be lowered for the passage of a train and the line is clear.

lines - the newly installed Up and Down Relief lines running parallel to and on the north side of the Up and Down Mains - and junctions from Down Main to Down Relief and Up Main to Up Relief. He was not permitted to use the 'Warning Acceptance', although it would have been a useful facility if he was using the junction from Down Main to Down Relief when a train was 'asked' on the Up Main. It was a Class 2 box for pay in 1922 and 1938, working at 247 marks per hour (see the table on page 80).

From 1907 he also worked two 'intermediate block sections' (IBS): Basildon, on the down lines, 1 m 53 ch west, brought into use on 11 August 1907; and Purley on the up lines, 1 m 33 ch east, brought into use on 7 August 1908. These IBSs roughly halved the distance between Pangbourne and Goring to the west and Tilehurst to the east.

Each IBS consisted of a Home and a Distant signal for each line, and levers in Pangbourne box operated both signals simultaneously (4 and 10 on the up lines and 35 and 42 on the down - see the accompanying diagram); these levers were electrically locked in the frame until the box in advance (Goring on the down lines and Tilehurst on the up lines) had given the Pangbourne signalman 'Line Clear' on the block instrument. The effect of the IBS system was to create a new block section, enabling trains to run closer together without the need for a new signal box and extra staff to operate it.

The line was track circuited from Pangbourne's advanced starting signals through to Goring's home signals on the down line and to Tilehurst's homes on the up. The levers operating the Advanced Starting signals for the up and down roads were free to be pulled provided the track circuits were cleared for 440 yards beyond the appropriate IBS Home.

After the Advanced Starting signal had been lowered, the arm was automatically replaced to 'Danger' behind the train by 'Hall's Signal Replacer', an electro-mechanical device known locally as the 'mouse trap'. This was an excellent safety device, since the signal levers were not interlocked 'sequentially'; without the device, if the Starting signal was left 'off' by a forgetful signalman he could lower the rest of the signals for that line, Distant included, even though a train was occupying the line ahead.

Rates of Pay for Signalmen, 1914

Paddington Arrival and Departure boxes were classified as 'Extra Special A' under the GWR system, one below the highest grade. In 1923 the marks per hour worked at Departure only amounted to 266 - Class 1 - but it was given 'Special Class' status because it was Paddington Departure. Paddington Arrival box worked at 452 marks per hour in 1923 and was easily 'Special Class'.

The GWR system of signal box classification for pay was complicated and finely tuned. The signal boxes were broken down thus: London; Principal Main Line (PML); Secondary Main Line (SML); and Light, Cross-country and Branch Lines (LCC).

In 1914 the rates of pay (in shillings - 20s = £1) were as follows (I am indebted to Larry Crosier for this research):

London boxes:		SML boxes:	
Special	35	Third A	24
Special A	37	Third B	24s 6d
Extra Special	38	Second A	26s 6d
Extra Special A	39	Second B	27
		First	29
PML boxes:		Special	31
Third class	25s 6d		
Second A	28s 6d	LCC boxes:	
Second B	29	Third	23
First	32	Second A	25s 6d
Special	34	Second B	26
Extra Special	36	First	28
Extra Special A	38		

National Rates of Pay for Signalmen, 1921

There was a 2½% reduction in wages (5% for the higher-paid grades) between August 1928 and July 1937, and there was no improvement on the 1921 wages until July 1939.

Class	Wages per week (shillings)	Min marks to obtain Class
Special	75	375
1st	70	300-374
2nd	65	255-299
3rd	60	150-224
4th	55	75-149
5th	50	30-74
6th	48	1-29

From The Railwaymen by Prof P. Bagwell, Vol 1, page 432.

The device was incorporated in the signal wire and was situated below the operating floor. The electric part of the mechanism was triggered when the train passed over a track circuit; at that moment the device operated to release the signal wire, producing a loud 'crash' or 'bang' under the box. Given that there were four of these under Pangbourne box and the trains were passing on average one every 5 minutes, it seems that the signal box was a noisy place to work. 'Hall's Signal Replacers' were also installed on the down roads at Tilehurst on the approach to Purley IBS. These devices were abolished with the installation of the new frame; the 'sequential' locking between signal levers removed the need for the automatic replacer.

The IBS Distant signals, which were operated by electric motors, were also replaced automatically to 'Caution' behind the train by the simple expedient of cutting off the current to the motor.

Another feature of the Reading-Didcot line (as far as the signalmen were concerned at any rate) was the Signal & Telegraph Department 'accumulator train', which was scheduled to occupy the Down Relief line on Mondays only. This train had started running in 1936 - if the non-appearance of its path in any Working Time Table (WTT) earlier than 1936 is a guide - and ran for many years after that. It was described in the WTT as 'Signal Department Equipment Train', and ran as a 'K' headcode - '3 bells' - through the block sections. It left Reading on the Down Relief line at 7.40 am and consisted of a small locomotive and an S&T Department brake van fitted up to carry 'cells' (batteries to non-S&T Department persons). Apart from stopping at each station along the line between Reading and Didcot, it called at 21 intermediate locations, and must have been a bit of a nuisance to the signalmen. Its purpose was to carry fresh batteries to the location boxes - where S&T staff changed old cells for new.

In the 1936 WTT it was booked to return non-stop, as empty stock, from Didcot at 11.40 am. However, locomen who worked this train in the 1940s recall that, on the return trip, they backed into the Up Refuge at Cholsey and awaited the arrival of the branch train. The engine off this was removed and came on to the accumulator van while the engine off the van, fresh from wash-out, went on to the branch coach. The 'stale' branch engine could then return to Reading for boiler wash-out and any other servicing. This train was still running in 1947.

Pangbourne signal box was taken out of use under the multiple aspect signalling scheme (MAS) controlled from a new 'Panel Signal Box' at Reading on 9 May 1965.

Above 2-2-2 No 1132 *Prince of Wales* on the Down Relief passing Basildon troughs between Pangbourne and Goring on 27 May 1905. Note the early-pattern trough without the water-retaining 'lip'. *GWR/AVC*

Below Basildon troughs looking west *circa* 1954. A Worcester-Paddington express on the Up Main behind No 5952 *Cogan Hall* passes the Up Basildon IBS Distant signal (controlled from Goring). The water storage tank for the troughs is on the extreme right. *AVC*

Goring & Streatley

The next signal box westwards from Pangbourne was Goring & Streatley. The box stood at approximately 44 m 60 ch, between the Up Main and Down Relief lines.

There was a box here from 1872, which was replaced in 1893 by the wooden version of 'Type 5', raised on a narrow brick plinth. The floor space was 33 ft 1 in by 12 feet, and was 13 feet above rail level. It housed a 49-lever 'double twist' frame, with one empty space, No 44. The detonator placer levers for the four tracks were a pair of the specially designed, two-lever frames, which were bolted to the upper surface of the operating floor. It was a Class 2 box for pay in 1923 and still in 1938, working at 251 marks per hour.

The signalman here controlled Basildon IBS on the up roads (levers 37 and 45), and the signal box had a pair of 'Hall's Signal Replacers' under the box attached to the Up Relief and Up Main Advanced Starting signal wires.

Below Goring's Up Relief Advanced Starting signal, No 38, was the Distant signal for Gatehampton ground frame Home signal. This ground frame operated a single trailing connection from the Up Relief line down to the locomotive water softening plant on the east bank of the Thames. Sludge removed from the river water was taken away in wagon loads, and the water was fed to the locomotive water troughs close by. When the 'pick up' goods had to call at the siding, a porter from Goring station obtained the key to the ground frame from the signalman and accompanied the train to Gatehampton. On arrival at the ground frame he replaced the Home and Distant signals to 'Danger', then 'reversed the road' to allow the train into the siding. Because the Up Relief Line was track circuited from Goring's No 38 through to Pangbourne's Home signal, it was not possible for the Goring signalman to lower No 38 so long as a vehicle was standing on the line at Gatehampton.

When the train's work was done and it had gone away towards Basildon IBS signals and the siding points were set once more for the straight run, the porter informed the signalman by telephone and the latter could then 'get the road' for the goods train to go to Pangbourne. The porter lowered the Gatehampton signals, walked about three-quarters of a mile back to the station and returned the ground frame key to the signalman. This account is taken from the 1922 GWR No 1 Sectional Appendix (Local Instructions). The instructions were unchanged in the 1938 Appendix.

When South Stoke signal box (see below) was abolished in favour of an IBS, the ex-South Stoke down line signals were controlled by 'turn-switches' mounted on the instrument shelf.

The Goring diagram shows the Down Main to

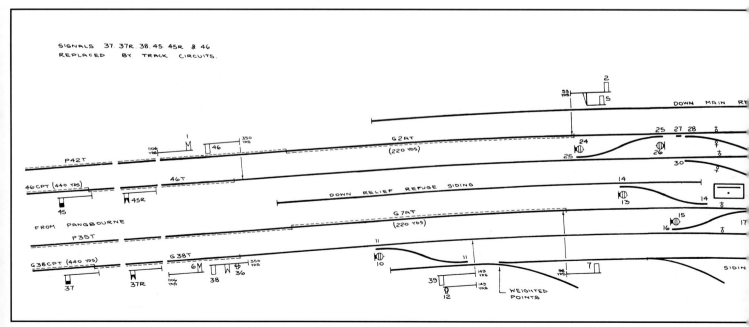

Goring & Streatley signal box on 13 July 1963. *Roger Webster/AVC*

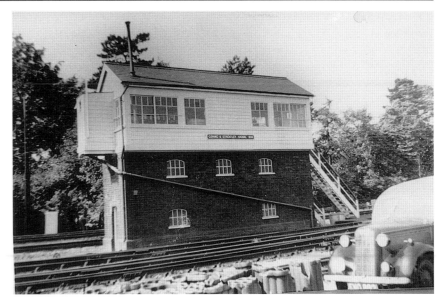

Goring & Streatley station looking west from the up sidings on 13 July 1963. Note that the splitting Homes on the 1918 diagram have been replaced by a single arm following the reversal of direction of the Main to Relief junctions. *Roger Webster/AVC*

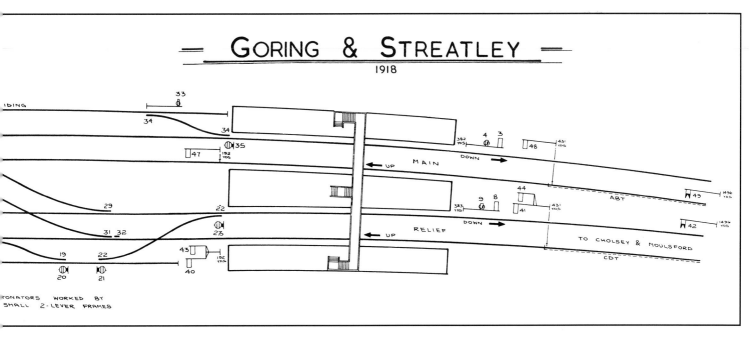

Down Relief/Up Relief to Up Main junctions. These were taken out of use 6 December 1936 and relaid in the reverse direction. The new junctions - Up Main to Up Relief/Down Relief to Down Main - were brought into use on 2 May 1937*.

In April 1960 a standard vertical tappet frame of levers numbered to 65 - with 10 spaces - was installed. The new frame departed from GWR convention and took on an LMS flavour as the signal levers were in the middle, more or less below the block instruments, with the levers controlling points and their signal discs at the outer ends. This arrangement saved the signalman a lot of walking since he could attend to his bells and indicators, then put his hand almost directly on to the relevant signal levers. The new frame had four detonator-placer levers in the frame, and two levers in the frame to work the Down IBS at South Stoke - replacing the turn-switches on the instrument shelf.

In accordance with the 1955 Instructions for the signal box, the signalman did not ask 'Is Line Clear?' and 'pull off' for any up or down train until he received the 1-2-1 'Train Approaching' signal; he then sent the 1-2-1 ahead as the train was passing his box. There was an exception to this for the up 'Bristolian'; for this train (and in 1960 for the up 12.10 Taunton as well) the 1-2-1 was sent to Pangbourne when the 'Train Entering Section' signal was received from Cholsey - which meant that the train was passing South Stoke Up IBS Home signal. The Goring signalman was not permitted to allow the 'Bristolian' (and later the 12.10 Taunton) into the Basildon IBS if he had not lowered the IB Distant and Home signals. The reason for this was that there was insufficient braking distance between the Distant and Home signals to enable the driver of this high-speed train to stop before IBS Home having passed the Distant at 'Caution'. Whether this instruction applied in GWR days to the 'Bristolian' and its older sister - the 'Cheltenham Flyer' - is not known.

The 1955 Instructions laid down that the Up Main Inner Home, No 47, 192 yards from the box, was the fog marking point. When this was obscured the signalman called out his fogmen and, until they were on duty, worked 'long block'. In addition to this he was forbidden to allow any up train to pass Goring until 'Line Clear' had been received from Pangbourne. The authorities seem to have been very nervous of braking distances for Basildon IBS on the up roads.

Goring was not authorised to use the 'Warning Acceptance' (3-5-5) on the bell. If he was crossing a train from Down Main to Down Relief, or from Up Relief to Up Main (before the junctions were altered) he could still give 'Line Clear' for a train on the Up

Main because the Up Main Home signal, No 48, was more than 440 yards to the rear of the junction, and thus he had his 'clearing point'. If he was making the above-mentioned junction movement when Pangbourne asked 'Is Line Clear?' for a train on the Down Relief, he would be obliged to 'refuse the road' because the junction lay within the clearing point of his Down Relief Line Home signal, No 7. Had the signal box been authorised to accept trains 'under the warning', that would have been an occasion when it would have used.

Up express trains bound for Basingstoke were belled from Cholsey to Goring in the usual way - 4 beats - but the Goring signalman 'asked on' using a local routing code: 2-5-1.

Goring & Streatley signal box was abolished on 9 May 1965.

✳   ✳   ✳

The history of signal boxes west of Goring is complicated. In the 1872 scheme for block signalling between Paddington and Bristol, the next signal box west of Goring was at Moulsford station; this was part of the original GWR and was called Wallingford Road until 2 July 1866 when the Wallingford-Wallingford Road branch was opened; the latter then became Moulsford. This station lay at the 47½ milepost, immediately below the road bridge carrying the Reading-Wallingford road. The platforms extended east and west of the bridge above. The one-time hotel, part of this station, still stands on the up side of the line, to the east of the road bridge.

The original double-track railway west of Reading was quadrupled, not in geographical progression, but according to the works involved. The first four-track section to be opened was from a new station called Cholsey & Moulsford, 48 m 37 ch, to Didcot on 27 December 1892*. At or before that date the old Moulsford station and the signal box were closed** and the Wallingford branch was brought to a termination in a bay at the new station.

From 11 October 1892 until 27 March 1893 a signal box existed called 'Moulsford River Bridge' where the four tracks were reduced to two to cross the bridge until the widened bridge was ready. From 28 March 1893 until 23 July 1908 the next signal box west of Goring & Streatley was Cholsey & Moulsford East, making a block section about 2¾ miles long; the latter was abolished on that date.

* See MacDermot Vol 2, page 205.

** The Signalling Record Society, which draws its information from GWR Signal Department records, gives 29 February 1892 as closure date for Moulsford signal box.

On 5 May 1916 an 8 by 6 feet, 6-lever, wooden, ground-level box called 'South Stoke' was opened at approximately the 46½ milepost; the signalman operated a block post for the up and down main lines only. This little box was abolished around 1920, and Goring was again in contact with Cholsey & Moulsford.

On 11 February 1940 a second South Stoke box was opened at 46 m 41 ch; this was 14 by 11 feet in timber, with plain gables, the floor 8 feet above rail level. It contained a 14-lever frame and controlled signals on all four roads. This box was taken out of use 16 August 1953 when its function was taken over by IBS signals worked from Goring and Cholsey. Relief Signalmen Harry Englefield and Charlie Pavey (both to become District Inspectors) worked this lonely place.

Cholsey & Moulsford

We have now reached the territory of the Didcot District Inspector. In 1923 this was Inspector A. Kirby, in 1944 Inspector Tom Stacey. Their District was from here to Wallingford, westwards to Milton, and northwards from Didcot through Oxford to Woodstock, and westwards again to Fairford. The Reading DI covered to Goring, Newbury DI covered as far north as Upton & Blewbury, and the Swindon DI came up as far as Steventon. These men were long-service signalmen, highly experienced in heavy signal boxes and finally promoted to their position of great responsibility.

They had responsibility for the proper working of the signal boxes, the rostering of signalmen, relief signalmen and relief porters, and the issue of uniforms to all Traffic Department staff. They were mature and experienced as people and knew well how to handle men. It is extremely unlikely that any of these men attended any higher grade school than the primary and secondary school, therefore they had all left school by the age of 15. It is also very unlikely that they were sent on any 'courses' by the GWR. They learned their skills from the older men and from years of experience. Many highly skilled signalmen could have become a District Inspector, but of course there were very few vacancies, and then again many men were quite happy to remain where they were, with the responsibilities that they had.

Cholsey & Moulsford station is situated at the 48½ milepost. There were two signal boxes there from 29 February 1892 until 23 July 1908 - the East and the West boxes. East box had a 37-lever frame in a floor 25 ft 6 in by 12 feet, raised 12 feet above rail level. Whether it was built in brick or timber is not known. The West box, between the Up Main and Down Relief lines, just beyond the west end of the station, was a 'Type 5' with a floor of the same dimensions as East, raised 7 feet above the rail and containing a 39-lever frame. Both these were abolished on 23 July 1908 in favour of a new, centrally located signal box called simply Cholsey & Moulsford. This box was a 'Type 7', 46 ft by 16 ft with a 75-lever frame including six spaces. The levers were at 5¼-inch centres, interlocked by a GWR horizontal tappet machine. The fog marking point was signal No 68, the Down Relief Inner Home.

The 1840 hotel designed by I. K. Brunel for the original 'Wallingford Road' station, seen in about 1960. *AVC*

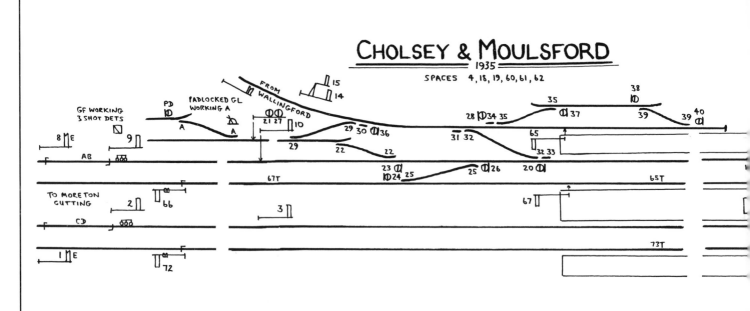

Looking west from the Down Main in about 1900, with the old West box in the distance. *AVC*

The new Cholsey & Moulsford signal box from the Up Relief line platform on 13 July 1963. *Roger Webster/AVC*

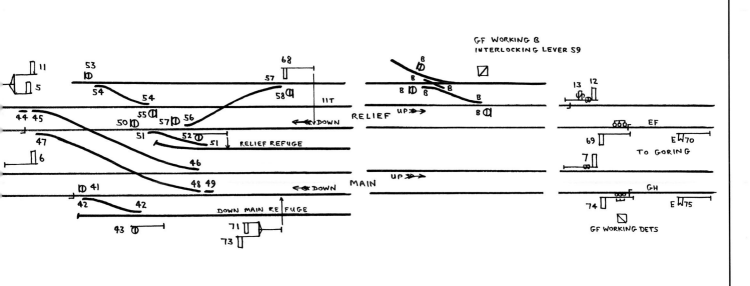

The 12.45 pm Paddington to Oxford stopping train pulls into the Down Relief platform on 6 June 1959 behind Didcot's No 6996 *Blackwell Hall*. *Hugh Ballantyne*

The Cholsey signalman was not authorised to use the 'Warning Acceptance', '3-5-5', because his signals were so spaced as to make its use unnecessary. Before a route was set from Down Main to Down Relief, or while a train was standing on the Down Main in advance of the junction, siding points 42 had to be set as a trap from Down Main to Siding. Similarly on the Up Relief Line, siding points 54 had to be set to the sidings as a trap when the junction was reversed.

All the boxes between Didcot and Reading were very busy, but those who worked them say unanimously that Cholsey was the hardest - because the frame was so long. When the IBSs were installed on each side - South Stoke on the up roads from 16 August 1953 and, from 1954, Aston Tirrold on the down roads, the signalman's life was exceptionally hectic, and from 1954 he was relieved of the obligation of maintaining a full train register but to record only the time that the 'Train out of Section' was received and any emergency bell codes or other unusual events.

The signalman 'asked on' for trains on the Down Main and Down Relief lines when he received 'Train Approaching', '1-2-1', from Goring, but for up trains he 'asked on' as soon as he had 'given the road' to the box in rear. Without the IBSs the signalman could have had a maximum of eight trains to think about simultaneously, with the IBSs added he could have had 16 trains 'on the go'- for instance, on the Up

Relief Line he could have one between the IBS Home signal and Goring, one waiting 'Line Clear' from Goring at the IBS Home, one moving up to his Advanced Starter and another approaching from Moreton Cutting, and similar situations on the other three roads. The situation was unlikely, but it gives an idea of what he had to contend with.

Harold Gasson, who worked there, said: 'You really could have done with roller-skates. You'd have trains coming at you all ways, you'd rush up and down the frame and sometimes a train missed the Distant [passed the distant at 'Caution'] simply because I just couldn't get to the lever in time to pull it; it was mainly the length of the frame that was the killer.'

The box was in Class 2 at 229 marks per hour in 1923, Class 2, 271 marks, in 1938, and Class 1, 285 marks, in 1951 - before the IBSs were established. Cholsey & Moulsford signal box was abolished on 9 May 1965.

Wallingford branch

The branch line to Wallingford was 2 miles 52 chains long according to the GWR Working Time Table. The line was worked without block telegraph equip-

No 5064 *Bishop's Castle* arrives on the Down Relief line on 27 September 1958 with a stopping train; the Wallingford branch train waits in the bay platform. *R. M. Casserley*

A closer view of the Wallingford branch train at Cholsey & Moulsford, an 'auto car' or 'push-pull' set, waiting to connect with the Paddington-Oxford stopping train arriving on the Down Relief line *circa* 1957. AVC

ment on the 'Wooden Train Staff and only One Engine in Steam' principle. The signalman gave the wooden Train Staff to the driver of the first branch train and took it in again from the last train - except when it had to be retrieved from the passenger train to be given to the driver of the branch goods.

The 'signal box' at Wallingford was more correctly a 'ground frame', since there was no block telegraph working over the line. It was opened in 1892, a wooden 'Type 5', 16 ft 1 in by 11 feet, and housed a 13-lever frame. The passenger trains were scheduled to be operated by 'auto car' (locomotive-hauled push-pull carriage), so the Cholsey signalman did not have as much work to do on the branch as he might have done if the engine had been obliged to 'run round' its coach at the end of each journey. Under normal cir-

cumstances of 'auto car' working he would have lowered No 14 signal (No 34 reversed all the while to bolt No 35 'Normal') at the time the train was to leave Wallingford. When the train arrived he would replace 14, then lower 65 a few minutes before departure time. There was also some shunting to do with freight at times during each day.

Wallingford ground frame was abolished on 19 January 1964.

Aston Tirrold

During the Great War a small signal box was installed at Aston Tirrold at the 50 milepost; this was probably very similar to that erected at South Stoke during the same period, and was abolished at around the same time. A second Aston Tirrold was established on 28 January 1940. This was a timber building, 14 by 11 feet, the floor raised 8 feet above rail level. It contained a 14-lever frame and was abolished on 25 April 1954.

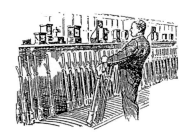

THE DIDCOT AREA

Moreton Cutting

There was a signal box called 'South Moreton' in the vicinity of the 50 milepost in 1884, if not earlier, which was abolished in about 1892.

The first signal box to be called 'Moreton Cutting' was ordered from the GWR's Reading Signal Works in 1891. It was 15 by 12 feet with a 17-lever frame and was abolished about 1907. The second 'Moreton Cutting' box was ordered from the Works in April 1907 and had a 36-lever frame (two spares). It stood on the north side of the Up Relief line at 51 m 38 ch and was a 'Type 7', and the floor was 13 feet from the front to the back wall. This box worked at 179 marks per hour in 1923 and was Class 3; it became Class 2, 226 marks, in September 1936. In August 1943 the box was extended at the east end to have a floor 33 ft 6 in long to accommodate a 90-lever frame (11 spaces). This was in connection with the construction of the marshalling yard north of the box. The additional work generated by the yard made it a Class 1, 309 marks, in April 1945.

In the 1956 Instructions the signalman did not 'ask the road' ahead for a down train until he received 'Train Approaching', 1-2-1, from Cholsey &

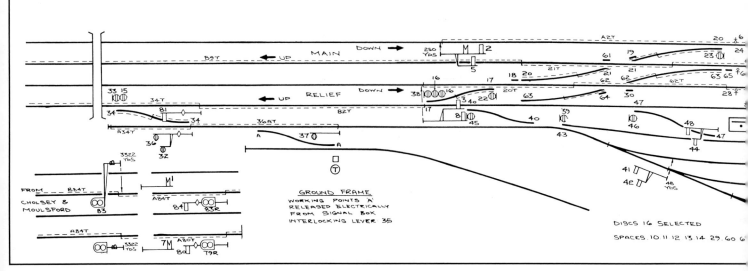

MORETON CUTTING

GROUND FRAME
WORKING POINTS 'A'
RELEASED ELECTRICALLY
FROM SIGNAL BOX
INTERLOCKING LEVER 35

DISCS 16 SELECTED
SPACES 10.11 12 13 14 29 60 6

Moreton Cutting signal box on 13 July 1963. The 1943 extension can clearly be seen. *Roger Webster/AVC*

No 5044 *Earl of Dunraven* on the Down Main passes Moreton Cutting's Down Main Advanced Starting signal *circa* 1955, with Didcot East Junction's Down Main Inner Distant below, also 'off'. The central arm is Didcot East Junction's 'routing' Distant for Down Main to Down Relief, and the left-hand arm as we look at it routes Down Main to Down Avoiding Line. Moreton Yard can be seen in the left background. *Les Reason*

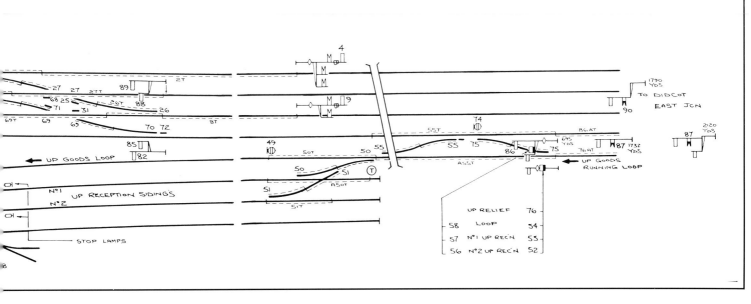

Moulsford; he did not send the 1-2-1 forward but sent 'Train Entering Section' (TES) as the train passed by. On the up roads he 'asked on' as soon as he had 'given the road' to the box in rear, and sent 1-2-1 to Cholsey as the train was passing him, sending TES as the train passed the up IBS Home signal.

The fog marking point was signal No 82, the Up Relief line Inner Home. The signalman was permitted to use the 'Warning Acceptance' on the Down Relief line only provided that there was not a train carrying passengers to the rear of the clearing point. Under standard regulations, after 'Line Clear' has been given for a train to approach, it was forbidden to alter facing points in the path of the train until that train was at a stand at the Home signal; at Moreton Cutting, however, the box Instructions permitted the signalman to alter facing points after he had given 'Line Clear' provided that (a) he had not yet received TES for the train, (b) he had not yet lowered his signals for the train, and (c) he had obtained 'Line Clear' for the train over the new route. This permission was not available during fog or falling snow (see the section on Didcot North).

The Up Goods line (know locally as 'the Up Gully') was worked under Permissive Block regulations, which allowed more than one train to occupy the section between Didcot East Junction and Moreton Cutting.

Moreton Cutting signal box was abolished on 17 May 1965.

Didcot East Junction

There had been a signal box called 'Fulscot Crossing' to the west of the Moreton cutting where a lane crossed the track to Fulscot Farm. The signal box was there in 1874, at 51 m 60 ch, but was abolished in 1892 when the line was quadrupled and the present bridge at the western extremity of the cutting erected.

The Didcot, Newbury & Southampton Railway

The opening of the Didcot, Newbury & Southampton Railway (DN&S) from Didcot to Newbury via Upton & Blewbury took place on 13 April 1882. From Newbury Greenham (later Enborne) Junction to Winchester (Chesil) opened on 4 May 1885, and from there to the LSWR main line, for Southampton, at Shawford Junction on 1 October 1891. This railway was the property of the DN&S company, which was attempting to 'short circuit' the GWR route to the south, the latter going via Goring, Reading West and Basingstoke. The DN&S line had the use of a bay platform at Didcot, on the down side at the east end. Connection to the GWR was restricted to a single set of points from the branch to the Down Main, and from there to the Oxford line; thus northbound trains from the DN&S could run directly to the Oxford line through Didcot station, but there was no southbound 'facing' connection between the two. Through trains from Oxford to Southampton could only gain DN&S metals by reversing from the Up Main to the down side at Didcot station.

These 'through' trains did run but they were tediously slow, with lengthy station time booked at Didcot and Oxford, then calling at every village station along the way and labouring over the steep gradients of the DN&S, a task made even more onerous through the necessity of slowing to 10 mph to exchanging by hand the single-line wooden Train Staff or the electric staff/token.

From the opening of the line in 1882 until at least 1901, the DN&S was worked under the Train Staff & Ticket system. Between Didcot East Junction and Upton & Blewbury the wooden Train Staff was of circular cross-section, painted bright red, and the Ticket was also red. Each succeeding section had its own distinctive Staff and, for when all these boxes were switched out, there was a 'long section' wooden Train Staff for the section Didcot East Junction to Newbury East Junction; this was of half-round cross-section and was painted buff; the Ticket was also buff. By 1907 the Webb-Thompson 'Electric Train Staff' had superseded the old system over the DN&S.

On 4 August 1942 passenger and goods train services over the DN&S line were suspended (except for one or two essential freights) while the single track route was improved to carry the heavy traffic resulting from the war.

Right A sketch to show the connections between the Oxford and Newbury lines at Didcot station prior to 1933.

Below Looking west along the Down Relief Line from outside Didcot East Junction signal box on 17 March 1934. The token set-down 'cow's horn' and net and the signalman's footway in foreground were for receiving the token from DN&S trains, as described in the text. Just beyond the Down Relief to Down Avoiding Line junction signal are the facing points, and beside them the three-'doll' routing signal for trains coming off the Up Avoiding Line. In descending order of height they route to the Up Relief, Up Main and Newbury Line. The Down Main Starting signal in the left background is lowered, and to its left is the Newbury branch signal with route indicator to Bay or Down Main. The Distant signals belong to West End signal box, beyond the station in the distance. *GWR*

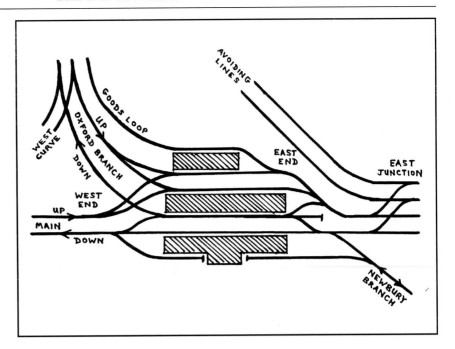

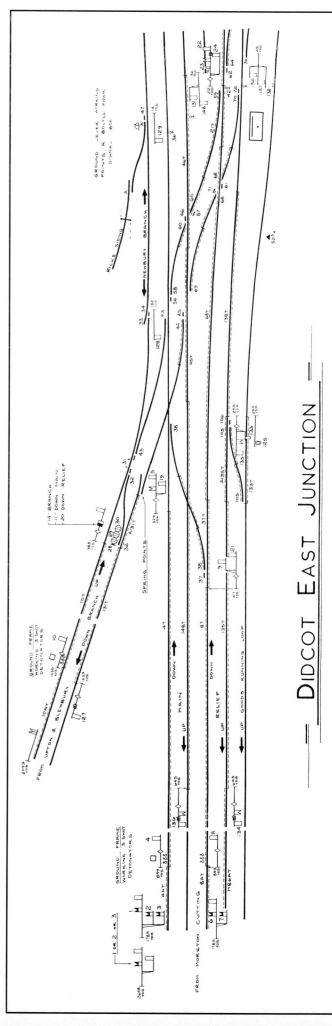

— DIDCOT EAST JUNCTION —

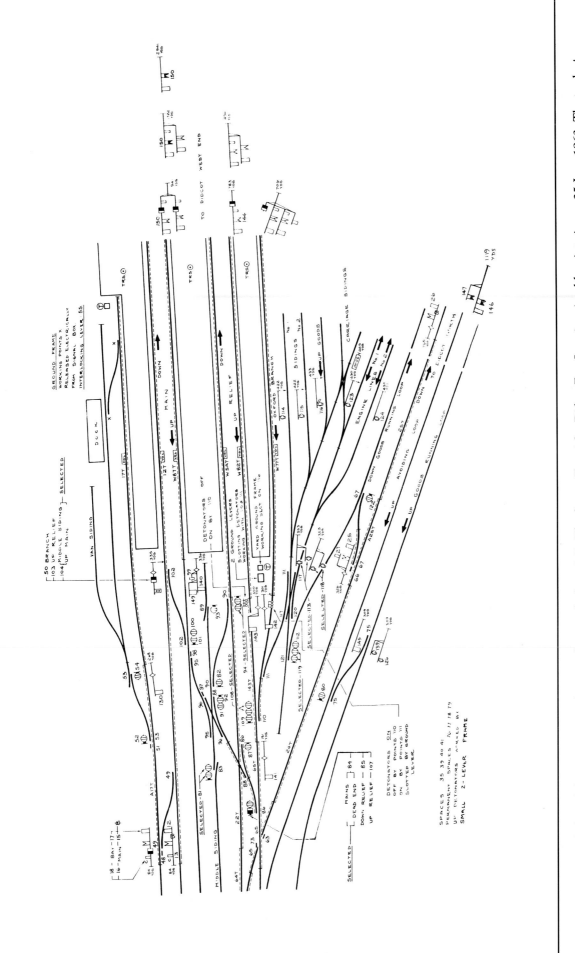

Top left 'Tom', father of the East Junction kittens, photographed in 1963. The diagram of tracks above him shows the Avoiding line at the bottom, connections to the loco shed and shunting yard in the centre, and the station at the top. *AVC*

Top right Didcot East Junction signal box interior on 25 June 1963. The track circuit and lamp repeaters are on the upper shelf, with the block bells and instruments at eye level. Signalman Freddie Sugar is leaning forward. At far end, in the left-hand corner, is a large sack containing waste paper for mother cat and kittens. *Roger Webster/AVC*

The first 'Didcot East Junction' signal box was abolished about April 1890, to be replaced by a 45-lever box at 52 m 68 ch. This was required because of the quadrupling of the tracks from Reading, which were opened on 11 November 1892 for goods and 27 December 1892 for passenger trains. However, the quadrupled tracks terminated at East Junction, the Relief lines merging into the Didcot Avoiding Line. Didcot station track layout remained an antique shambles; unchanged by the quadrupling, it was, if not the original 1844 layout, very much influenced by it, and remained unchanged in essence until 1932, a tribute to the traditionalism of the GWR!

In 1923 Didcot East Junction signalmen were Class 2, working at 260 marks per hour, then on 23 October 1932 the 1890 signal box was abolished to be replaced by a new building on the up side of the Up Relief line, at 52 m 68 ch. It was made of concrete blocks in a steel frame under a hip gable roof (SRS Type 9) and housed a 150-lever frame (number of spaces unknown). This new box was to work an enlarged and vastly improved layout and to take over the functions of the old East End box.

The new layout was beautifully engineered, a triumph of orderly planning over the ancient layout of three years earlier. The quadruple tracks were extended from East Junction through the station to be merged with the Up and Down Main lines at Foxhall Junction, and the Newbury branch was connected with the Main, Relief and Avoiding lines by a series of well-laid-out double junctions; this particular

---

Didcot East End

Didcot East End box was in existence in 1874, and at that time was situated on the down side of the line about 100 yards east of the present-day entrance to Didcot station. It was re-sited when the DN&S was built in 1880/1 because it stood in the way of the new DN&S bay. The new East End box was probably a 'Type 3' and was situated on the north side of the Up Main, at the east end of the up platform at about 53 m 5 ch. It housed a 45-lever frame interlocked with the GWR 'double twist' and levers at 5¼-inch centres. In about 1905, GWR records show, a frame of 57 levers was installed at East End, but whether this entailed the construction of a new signal box is not known; with the levers at the new spacing of 4-inch centres, the old box would have sufficed. This new East End box was busier than the old one and was Class 1 in 1923, working at 308 marks per hour.

---

improvement was brought into use on 18 December 1932. The new box was worked by two men and a boy on each shift. Their work was assessed in September 1933 and they were awarded 'Special Class' pay, working at 427 marks per hour.

The Newbury branch remained a single track and thus there was still the need to deliver and collect the staff to and from the trains. This was easier than might appear at first glance, and there was no need for an auxiliary token instrument on the station, released from the signal box, as I had at first imagined. All goods trains and light engines to and from the branch and all engines going to the Newbury bay to pick up a train came past the token pick-up/set-down posts on the Up and Down Relief Lines respectively, so the signalman - or the booking lad - had not too far to walk, over a wooden 'cat-walk', to collect/deliver the tokens.

There were seven up passenger trains and six down branch passenger trains each day in 1936/7. Only two up passengers ran to the bay, and only one down passenger left from it; the engine for the latter picked up the token as just described. In the case of the two up passenger trains, the signalmen were content to wait for the token until the engine off the train ran past the box on its way to the shed. If there was another unscheduled up branch train coming along behind, which required the Upton-Didcot token to be replaced in the token machine during the next 10 minutes, the Didcot signalmen would send the booking lad across the tracks - a dangerous job because there was no 'cat-walk' to the branch.

The only scheduled 'through' trains on the DN&S in the winter/spring of 1936/37 were the 7.33 am Southampton-Newcastle (10.06 to 10.15 am at Didcot station), and the 2.50 pm from Oxford (3.12 to 3.35 pm at Didcot). The latter train provided a connection to the heart of the Berkshire Downs for passengers off a Manchester and Birkenhead to Bournemouth express, although they had a 25-minute wait at Oxford after their express had steamed away for Bournemouth via Reading West; a very similar train had been running in 1907. There was another 'through' train - the 6.45 am Newbury to Steventon - which enabled people from Lambourn and the other villages to take jobs in the military depots at Didcot and Milton. There was also the remarkable Sundays-only 6.55 pm Lambourn-Oxford, hauled very often by one of the ex-M&SW 2-4-0s.

For down trains Didcot East Junction asked 'Is Line Clear?' as soon as it was received from Moreton Cutting. The same applied on the up roads provided that the train concerned was not stopping at Didcot. For trains starting from Didcot, 'Is Line Clear?' was asked on when the train was 'rung out' by the platform staff. This working also applied to trains leaving Didcot for Newbury.

East Junction was authorised to use the 'Warning Acceptance' for any train or light engine approaching on the Up Main, Up Relief and No 7 Platform (up Oxford branch) lines, and this regulation could also be used for freight trains on the Up Avoiding Line provided that there was no train conveying passengers within the clearing point. East Junction was also permitted to alter facing points from Up Relief to Up Main under the same conditions imposed at Moreton Cutting (see also the section on Didcot North Junction).

The greatest number of levers to be moved to set up one route was 26. This was to set the road for a train to run from the up Newbury line (the 'Gold Coast') to the Down Avoiding Line Goods Loop ('Down Gully'). Consult the signalling plan on pages 92-3 to follow the sequence. First *push back* to 'Normal' in the frame the following blue-painted 'bolt levers', which, by being pushed back, remove the safety bolts from the facing points and 'switch diamonds' (better known to railwaymen as 'elbows'): 31, Up Branch facing; 46, Up Main 'elbows'; 56, Down Main facing; 57, Up Main 'elbows'; 62, Down Relief line facing; 63, Down Avoiding line 'elbows'; 66, Down Avoiding line to Down Goods Running Loop facing; 73, Up Relief 'elbows'. Eight lever movements so far.

Now *pull over* the following levers - some work points, others work the safety bolts: 74, Up Avoiding trailers (to protect the

movement from a wrong-direction runaway on the Up Relief); 67, Down Avoiding to Goods Loop facers; 66, bolt for 67; 64, Down Relief facers; 65, Down Relief 'elbows'; 62, Down Relief facers bolt; 73, Down Relief 'elbows' bolt; 58, Down Main facing; 60, Up Main 'elbows'; 57, Up Main 'elbows' bolt; 59, trailing end of Down Main to Down Relief junction; 56, Down Main facing point bolt; 43, Up Branch to Down Main facing; 31, bolt for 43; 27, Down Avoiding Line to Goods Loop signal; 24, Down Relief to Down Avoiding Line signal; 20, Up Branch to Down Relief signal; 10, Up Branch Home signal. 18 lever movements.* And of course, once the train - or light engine going to shed - had come over this route, it had to be 'dismantled' for the straight run! I have had the privilege of making this route and found the experience quite breath-taking. This was why the regular signalmen were quite happy to let me do it for them.

---

* Each set of 'elbows' had two bolts, and both had to be withdrawn in order that the 'elbow' points could be moved. However, both bolts did not have to be replaced for this particular movement - only the bolt for the facing direction.

Above right Didcot station from the footplate of a 'Castle' on the 9.15 am Paddington-Worcester in April 1964. The train is taking the Down Avoiding Line, and the signal ahead, just visible beside the firebox, has a diverging arm for the Down Goods Loop, the termination of the long route across from the DN&S described in the text. *E. J. Nutty/James Nutty*

Right Part of the pre-1934 layout at Didcot seen from the up main platform on 26 October 1930. No 6367 with empty stock is masking the short Up Branch platform, and has been signalled into the head-shunt by Didcot East End. The Up Branch platform line merges into the Up Main beneath the engine, and the upper arms of the signal route from the Branch platform to the Up Main. *Dr Jack Hollick/AVC*

Between Didcot East Junction and Didcot West End signal boxes trains were permitted to run in the wrong direction over any of the four main lines - after the signalman's permission had been obtained through the use of the bell code 2-3-3. If it was safe for the movement to take place, the signalman towards whom the train was to run acknowledged the 2-3-3 and placed his block instrument at 'Train on Line'. When the train had passed in the wrong direction through the section (for example up the Down Main), and the section was again clear, the signalman who had 'cleared away' the train sent 'Train Clear of Section', 5-2 on the bell, to the box from whence the movement began, and took off the 'Train on Line' indication.

If the wrong direction movement did not go right through, but returned to its starting point to clear the section, the latter signalman sent 'Train Withdrawn', 2-5 on the bell, to the box in rear. The signalman there acknowledged and again took off the 'Train on Line' indication.

Didcot East Junction signal box was abolished 17 May 1965.

Upton & Blewbury

The signal box was opened with the single-track Didcot, Newbury & Southampton line from Didcot to Newbury on 1 January 1891. It was supplied by the Railway Signal Company of Liverpool and was situated on the up (west) side of the line, 2 m 75 ch from Didcot East Junction, close to the 14¾ milepost. In 1923 it was a sleepy little place, working at 40 marks per hour, making the signalmen Class 5 on the branch line scale of pay.

Didcot station lies on the 200-foot contour above sea level, and running parallel to the south of the GWR main line the Berkshire Downs rise to 400 feet. The line south to Newbury must cross this high ground and the Didcot-Newbury line rose at 1 in 106 for the most part of 4 miles, starting almost as soon as it left Didcot East Junction, easing through Upton & Blewbury.

The box survived the doubling of the line between 4 August 1942 and April 1943, and, after the doubling, held a 25-lever frame (three spaces). An Intermediate Block Section (IBS), known as 'Ilsley signals', was installed approximately 1¾ miles south of Upton & Blewbury; lever No 5 operated the Down IBS, while lever No 5 in Compton signal box operated the Up IBS. This broke up the relatively long block section on the steep gradient and enabled more trains to be worked across the line.

The signalman's working life was transformed by the war as the line took on a vital strategic importance to the war effort, its civilian traffic outnumbered by the troop, ambulance and munition trains.

The 1957 box Instructions permitted the use of the 'Warning Acceptance' on the down (southbound) line provided that there was no passenger train within

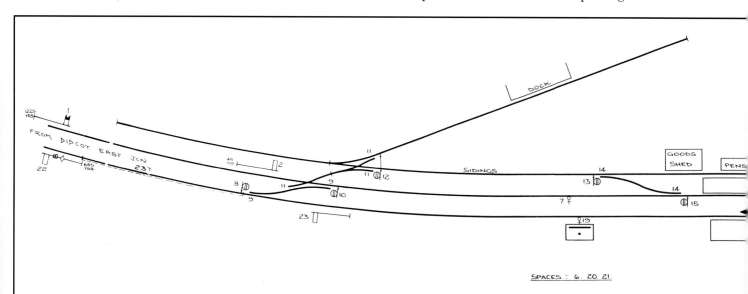

The signal box, photographed on 28 February 1964. It was constructed for the original DN&S Company by the Railway Signal Co. *Roger Webster/AVC*

The signal box diagram, 1960. *AVC*

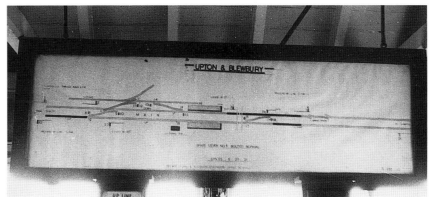

the clearing point. Because of the steep gradient falling back to Didcot, the signalman was ordered to keep points 14 open for the siding to act as a trap (a) before he accepted a train from Didcot under the 'Warning' and (b) before any wagon was detached from a train standing at the down platform.

Perhaps this was an instruction born of bitter experience. On 24 March 1943, while the line was still

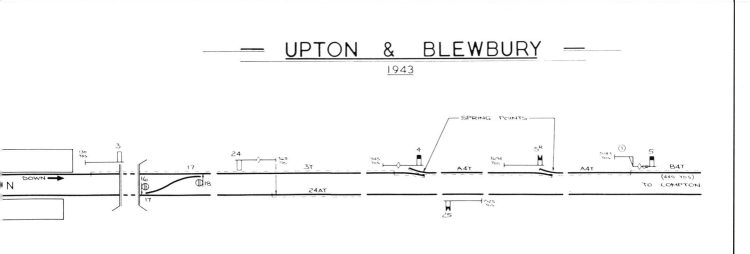

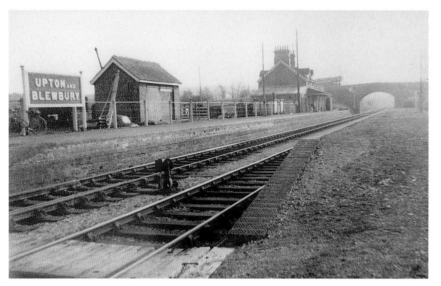

virtually closed to civilian traffic, engine No 3293 was standing at the down platform, the engine nearest Newbury; behind it was a goods brake van and, at the Didcot end, a MacAlpine's workmen's coach, No 1362. The train had to go back to Newbury, so the brake van had to be placed at the rear of the train. The coach was uncoupled from the brake van, perhaps with the intention of running it through points 14 into the yard in order to get the brake van past it. Whatever the thought behind the uncoupling, the person doing it had failed to ask the signalman to reverse points 14, so they were still set for the straight run - and he was also unaware that the coach had no brakes.

Having been uncoupled it at once began to roll downhill. The military guard that was with the train ran after the coach and placed pieces of wood in front of its wheels - which the coach very sportingly jumped over - while the signalman sent 2-5-5, 'Train running away in wrong direction', to Didcot East Junction.

Luckily for the main line, there was a catch point at 15 m 24 ch (half a mile north of Upton station), and here the old carriage's bid for freedom was brought to an end, becoming derailed all wheels at 11.45 am. Single-line working was instituted at 12.25 pm and the breakdown vans got out there at 1.25. The men had the coach back on the rails, hauling it up re-railing ramps with No 3283, at 2.58 pm. Single-line working was dispensed with at 4.25 pm.

The Ilsley IBS was taken out of use in 1949, and Upton & Blewbury signal box was abolished on 10 August 1964.

Didcot West End

There was a signal box here by 1874, which was replaced, about 1904, by a wooden hip-gabled building housing a 51-lever frame. This box survived until September 1932, when it was replaced by a 'Type 9' signal box holding an 88-lever frame (two spares, five spaces), which stood in the 'V' of the junction between the Oxford line and the Up Relief line at 53 m 22 ch. During the Second World War a brick blast-protection wall was added.

The signal box was manned by a single signalman without a booking lad. In 1923 he worked at 265 marks per hour and was Class 2, but in October 1936 it was reassessed at 304 marks, Class 1. The 1962 'footnotes' for the box state that on the Down Relief line the clearing point was reduced to 178 yards for trains that were booked to stop at Didcot. Under these circumstances the signalman could give 'Line Clear' to Didcot East Junction for a train on the

Above The old layout at Didcot station, seen from West End box in May 1904. The Down Main is far right; the train is leaving the Down Main Loop platform to return to the Down Main. The Up Main runs straight through the centre of view with the loop to the Up Branch platform forking left. The Oxford branch is on the left, with connection to the Up Main Platform and the Branch platform. *Science Museum, 7579*

Below The view from the new West End box on 29 March 1933. The old central platform has been greatly extended and the Oxford Branch platform demolished. The Down Main is still far right, but the Down Main Loop is now part of the Up Main, the old Up Main is now the Down Relief and the old Up Main Loop is part of the Up Relief. A clerestory coach and some wagons stand in the down bay on the right, used by Didcot-Swindon stopping trains. *GWR*

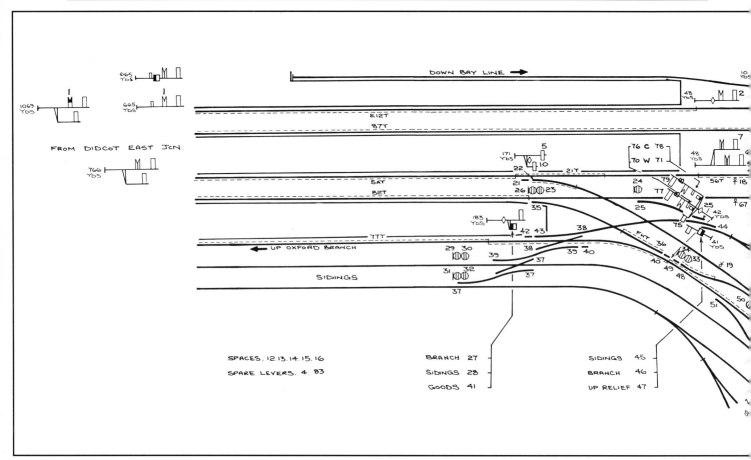

Down Relief when the line was clear only as far as his Inner Home signal, No 6. Thus he would be able to have an up train crossing from Up Main to Up Relief Line at the same time as giving 'Line Clear' to East Junction for a down train on the Down Relief.

Trains running on the Down Relief line that were not booked to stop at Didcot were never permitted to

run through under clear signals. When 'Is Line Clear?' was asked by East Junction to West End for such a train, the West End signalman was bound by the box Instructions to answer with the 'Line Clear to Clearing Point Only', 2-2-2 on the bell. This then ensured that Didcot East Junction maintained its Distant signals at 'Caution' against the train. It was a lack of this working

Left Looking at this I might be forgiven for thinking that my railway would go on, unchanged, for ever. 2-6-2 No 4148, fresh from Swindon, is held at West End's Up Relief Home signal while No 6023 *King Edward II* crosses from the Down Relief to the Down Main, prior to reversing to the down bay to couple to two coaches forming a Didcot-Swindon stopping train *circa* 1960. *David Anderson*

Right West End signal box on 12 July 1963 with the Relief lines running in front. *Roger Webster/AVC*

Far right No 6021 *King Richard II* on the 1.30 pm Paddington-Bristol parcels stands at Didcot West End's Down Relief line Home signals, GWR symmetrically balanced arms, *circa* 1960; the lower arm routes to Oxford. *David Anderson*

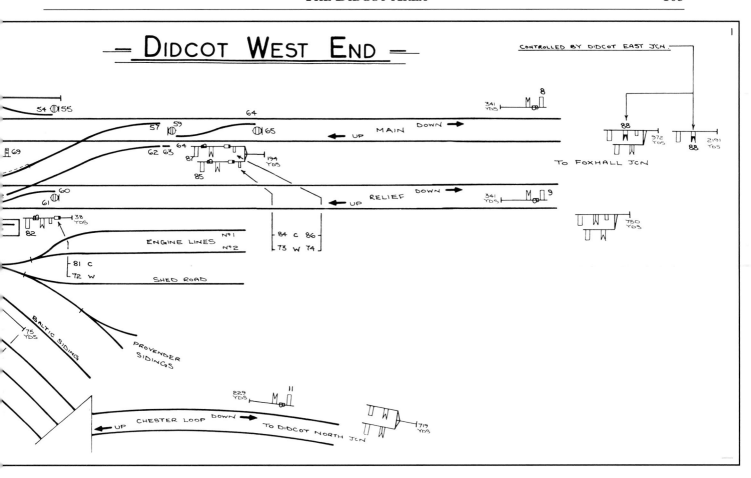

— DIDCOT WEST END —

CONTROLLED BY DIDCOT EAST JCN

TO FOXHALL JCN

UP MAIN DOWN

UP RELIEF DOWN

ENGINE LINES Nº1 / Nº2

SHED ROAD

BALTIC SIDING

PROVENDER SIDINGS

UP CHESTER LOOP DOWN TO DIDCOT NORTH JCN

in 1967, after the boxes had been abolished to make way for colour-light signalling, that allowed a fatal passenger train derailment to take place on the 20 mph Relief to Main junction at Foxhall Junction.

The West End signalman was authorised to use the 'Warning Acceptance' against any train approaching him on the Main, Relief or Branch lines, even if there was a passenger train within the clearing point. However, the 'footnotes' did not permit altering the facing points after giving 'Line Clear' as was the case for the other Didcot boxes.

For trains not stopping at Didcot, the West End signalman asked 'Is Line Clear?' to the box in advance as soon as he had given 'Line Clear' to the box in rear.

For trains starting from Didcot he 'got the road ahead' when the train was 'rung out' by the platform staff.

In clear weather only, trains were allowed to run in the wrong direction over any running lines between West End and East Junction. The movement known as 'Shunting into forward section' was also permitted. The fog marking point was the Up Main Home signal, No 87, 194 yards from the box.

Didcot West End signal box was abolished on 17 May 1965.

Foxhall Junction

Foxhall Junction came into being on 15 February 1886 when the 'West Curve' was opened from the Bristol to the Oxford lines. The 1886 signal box was probably the one replaced on 27 November 1915 with an all-timber 'Type 7' box, 33 ft 10 in by 11 ft 2 in, the floor 11 feet above rail level, housing a 45-lever frame. According to the GWR Working Time Table (WTT) this box stood in the 'V' of the junction, east of the West Curve, facing the Up Main at 53 m 56 ch. In 1923 the signalmen there were Class 3, working at 157 marks per hour.

This box was replaced on 13 October 1931 with a 'Type 9' housing a 76-lever frame with eight spaces when it was fully operational. When it was assessed in March 1933 it registered 236 marks and was raised to Class 2. It was still a Class 2 in 1956, although the marks rate had risen to 254.

The new box stood on the up side of the line, perhaps 25 yards west of the West Curve junction, but still, according to the GWR WTT, at 53 m 56 ch. This was part of the Didcot improvements mentioned in the section on East Junction.

Such a large job had to be brought in by stages, and at the date of the interior view opposite, 2 December 1931, certain parts of the layout are not yet installed; see the accompanying caption.

The photograph also shows the 'three-decker' 'Slot on/Slot off' repeater behind lever No 1. There was insufficient braking distance between Didcot West End's and Foxhall Junction's Distant and Home signals; however, Didcot East Junction's Down Outer Distant signal was 1,799 yards from its Home signal, so could provide braking distance for all of Didcot on the Down Main. Therefore all the Distant signals through Didcot on the Down Main were 'slotted' electrically. This means that although the East Junction and West End signalmen could pull off their Down Main Distant signal levers, the arms would not lower until Foxhall Junction's Distant signals had cleared. This triggered West End's Distants, which in turn triggered those for East Junction. As each set of arms lowered, eastwards along the Down Main, the red 'Slot on' indication in the Foxhall Junction repeater changed to a green 'Slot off'. The Down Relief Line Outer Distant signal was fixed at 'Caution' below West End's Starting signal. Only the Down Relief Inner Distant was workable.

The photograph also shows three track circuit repeaters on the shelf, two brass-cased and one with a wooden case. The centrally pivoted indicator, a red bar, is lying diagonally to indicate 'Track Circuit Clear'. When a train or vehicle occupies that particular section of track the diagonal bar drops to the horizontal to show 'Track Occupied'.

Foxhall Junction signal box from the Down Main on 12 July 1963. The Down Relief Line Starting signal has a bracketed arm routing to the RAF Depot. The West Curve forks left and Didcot's Provender Stores are on the skyline. *Roger Webster/AVC*

The interior of Foxhall Junction signal box on 2 December 1931. The Down Relief Line has not yet been extended to Foxhall, as can just be seen from the diagram. Also some signals are not yet in use - Nos 3, 4, 6 and 57, to name a few (the brass plate for 57, a ground disc, is lying on the window sill, together with some others). The Down Goods Loop is in use, the exit points at the far end being operated by hand-generated current from the Westinghouse machine seen at the far end of the frame.

The lever brass on the West Curve Up Distant signal, No 5, states that this signal is worked by an electric motor ('Electric Switch'), but the lever handle is full length. With the loop exit points being power-operated, one would expect to see a shortened handle on that operating lever too, but there are no cut-down levers in the frame. Obviously the policy of shortening the handles of levers that did not have to be pulled with any strength had yet to be introduced at that time.

This frame must have been subsequently re-locked, because on the SRS diagram overleaf, accurate for 1960, Foxhall's Up West Curve Distant signal is 'fixed', and No 5 lever operates the Up Home signal on the West Curve. No 3 signal lever, missing from the 1931 frame, was put in later and operated the Down Relief Line Inner Distant signal. There are several other alterations that can be traced by comparing the 1931 lever brass legends with the numbering given on the track diagram.

The legends that are legible on the photograph read as follows (lever number followed by description and the numbers of the levers that must be 'reversed' - pulled over - in the frame before that particular lever can be reversed):

1	Down Main Distant 54 10 9 8 2
2	Down Main Home 54
3	(Temporary space - will become Down Relief Distant)
4	(Not yet in use - will become Down Relief Home)
5	West Curve to Down Main Distant [Electric Switch] 54 48 42 * 31 21 10 9 8 7 6
6	West Curve Home 31 21
7	West Curve Outer Home 55 54 48 42
8	Down Main Starter 54
9	Down Main Advanced Starter
10	Down Main Outer Advanced Starter
11	Down Main to Goods Loop Starter
12	West Curve to Sidings Home 25 23 22 21
13-18	(Spaces)
19	Down Main Detonators
20	Up Main Detonators

* A blaze of light on the polished brass obscures the number.

Note the 'three-decker' 'slot' repeater behind lever No 1, the Down Distant signal lever, and the two kinds of track circuit repeaters on the shelf, above levers 6-10 (both described in the text).

Note also that, although this large frame of levers has only just been installed at the time of the photograph, all the lever handles are polished smooth as silver. *GWR*

The 1949 'footnotes' ordered the signalman to ask 'Is Line Clear?' for down trains to the box in advance as soon as he received that signal from West End. The 'Is Line Clear?' signal for an up express passenger train was sent on as soon as it was received, but if the up express was one that called at Didcot the Foxhall signalman 'asked the road ahead' when he received 'Train Approaching', 1-2-1, from Milton - ie it was 'off Stivvy' (Steventon).

In clear weather, or during fog or falling snow when the fogsignalmen were on duty at Didcot North's Up Distant and Foxhall Junction's Up West Curve Home signals, Foxhall could give 'Line Clear' to Didcot North on the up West Curve when that line was clear to the Inner Home signal, No 6, or when the road was set towards the RAF Depot and permission had been obtained for the train to enter the Depot. Having given 'Line Clear' to Didcot North, with the line clear up to No 6 signal, the Foxhall signalman was not permitted to lower his West Curve Home signal, No 5, until the line was clear for 440 yards in advance of No 6 (these lever numbers are those shown on the track diagram).

The 'Warning Acceptance' could be used against freight trains and light engines on the Down Relief line when freight trains or light engines were crossing to or from the West Curve and Main lines.

In the 1949 Instructions the Foxhall Junction signalman was permitted to alter the position of facing points after he had received 'Train Entering Section' provided that he had not lowered his signals and that the train concerned had not passed his Distant signal. These were special instructions dating back to GWR days - and a little bit 'iffy' in my opinion. BR(WR) later altered the provisions, as described in the section on Moreton Cutting.

The Up Goods Running Loop from Steventon and Milton Crossing had existed since 1915. From October 1931, on the south side of the Down Main, there was a new Down Goods Loop, the exit from which was through electrically operated points driven by a Westinghouse hand generator in Foxhall Junction. This loop was converted to a Running Loop to Milton in May 1942, and the exit from the loop at Foxhall was taken out.

The West Curve was laid to a tight radius, and the track rose towards the main-line junction. Steam locomotives on up freights, heading westwards off the

Right Looking west from Foxhall bridge *circa* 1960. No 4703 is on the Up Main with the 11.45 am Dr Day's parcels, while in the distance a '72xx' trudges from the Up Goods Loop to the Up Relief line with an 'H' headcode goods. Foxhall Junction signal box is behind the goods train, and the West Curve is on the right, passing the sheds of the RAF Depot. *David Anderson.*

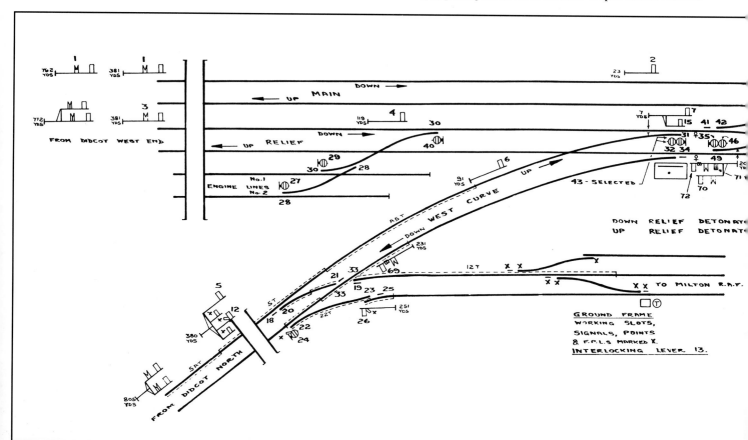

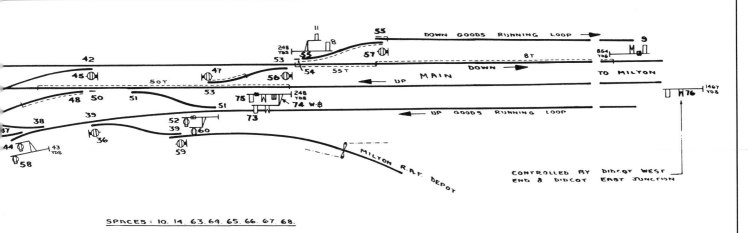

SPACES : 10. 14. 63. 64. 65. 66. 67. 68.

DIDCOT FOXHALL JUNCTION

Left Looking north towards Foxhall Junction's West Curve Up Outer Home signal from the points into the RAF Depot *circa* 1954 - note the 'switch diamonds', or 'elbows', where the Depot line crosses the down line. *Peter Barlow/AVC*

Below left Looking south from about the same spot, looking towards the main line with the line into the RAF Depot on the right. *Peter Barlow/AVC*

diamonds' ('elbows' in railway slang) was installed. The 'elbows' were required, not because the junction was crossed at high speed, but for added safety in negotiating the points, which made an even tighter curve within the West Curve. It was probably at this time that the track layout within the Depot gates was enlarged, necessitating operation from a ground frame; the Foxhall signalman reversed lever 13 to release the levers in the ground frame.

Inside the Depot gate the line ran directly alongside a lengthy platform, or a train could be diverted, by the ground frame operator, 'right-handed' to the 'Out-going Road', or 'left-handed' to the 'Hump Siding Road'. The two lower arms to the left and right of Foxhall's West Curve Up Home were 'slotted' by lever No 12 in Foxhall Junction; the man at the ground frame set his points according to the track he wanted the incoming train to occupy and pulled the relevant lever to lower the correct signal on the big bracket signal, but the arm would not clear until the signalman at Foxhall had pulled his No 12 lever.

The Foxhall signalman had a hard pull when setting the route from the West Curve to Milton Depot. The rodding followed the tight curve for 300 yards, which would have been a long pull even on a straight run. Sometimes an accumulation of sand prevented the blades of the points from closing tight against the stock rail, so that the point bolt would not locate its port. Then the signalman would be faced with a 600-yard walk there and back to put matters right.

A workmen's train worked in and out of the Depot each weekday morning and evening, to and from Oxford, calling at Radley. It left Oxford at 7.23 am and was worked by the engine booked as Depot Pilot

Curve, often slipped and struggled as the curve itself, then the reverse curves over the points to the Down Main line, accentuated the gradient. Trains westbound on the Curve were considered to be travelling 'up' as far as No 6 signal protecting the main line; conversely, up trains became 'down' trains on the West Curve.

Southern Railway engines that had brought freights into Moreton Cutting yard came to Didcot to turn on the triangular junction, using the West Curve, so that they were chimney-leading on the journey home.

In November 1931 the junction into the RAF depot off the West Curve was a single facing lead from the westbound track of the Curve, with a trailing 'slip' connection from that single line to the northbound, or down, line. There was no ground frame within the gates of the Depot at that stage. Later a proper double junction complete with 'switch

A '28xx' 2-8-0 struggles off the West Curve with a heavy rake of coal. It is easy to appreciate the extra friction involved in dragging this dead-weight uphill off the sharp curve and across the junctions to the Down Main. This picture was taken about 1960, but the Churchward 2-8-0 design had been blasting off the Curve at Foxhall Junction since 1906. *David Anderson*

for the day. It returned each evening at 5.15, arriving in Oxford at 5.33. This was the working in 1936 and the same schedule was still in use in 1953-54.

There was a lot of shunting and 'trip' work in connection with the RAF Depot. The Foxhall signalman was permitted to set a train back in the wrong direction towards Didcot North Junction - that is to say, to reverse a train down the up road on the West Curve - always provided that the leading vehicle of the reversing train was a brake van that was occupied by a competent man, and the 'Blocking back' signal had been acknowledged by North Junction.

Long trains for the Depot from the Swindon direction would require to draw up past the Down West Curve Starting signal, prior to setting back into the Depot. In this case the Foxhall signalman asked 1-3-1*, 'May a train shunt towards your Home signal?', to Didcot North. If the line was clear to Didcot North's Home signal the bell code was acknowledged, whereupon Foxhall pulled off the Starting signal, then sent 'Train Entering Section' to Didcot North so that the block indicator could be placed at 'Train on Line'. When the train was withdrawn from Didcot North's section, into the Depot or back inside Foxhall's Starter, Foxhall sent Didcot North 8 beats on the bell - 'Shunt Withdrawn'.

Foxhall Junction was worked by one man, without assistance. It was abolished on 17 May 1965.

* 1949 Instructions. The Code was changed in May 1950 when 1-3-1 became the code for a 'parcels, fish, fruit, horse, livestock, meat, milk, pigeon or perishable train'.

Milton

Prior to the opening of Foxhall Junction, the next box west of Didcot was 'Milton Crossing', with 11 levers, in existence in 1874 at 55 m 70 ch on the up side. On 16 September 1907* an Up Goods Running Loop was laid along the north side of the Up Main

* R. A. Cooke, *Track Plans: Berkshire*, Vol 23.

line from Steventon to Foxhall Junction. It ran behind Milton Crossing box which appears* to have had no control over it.

A new box, called 'Milton', a timber 'Type 7' structure at 55 m 67 ch, still on the up side, was opened on 18 October 1915. This was the first stage of work in connection with a manufactory for military aircraft

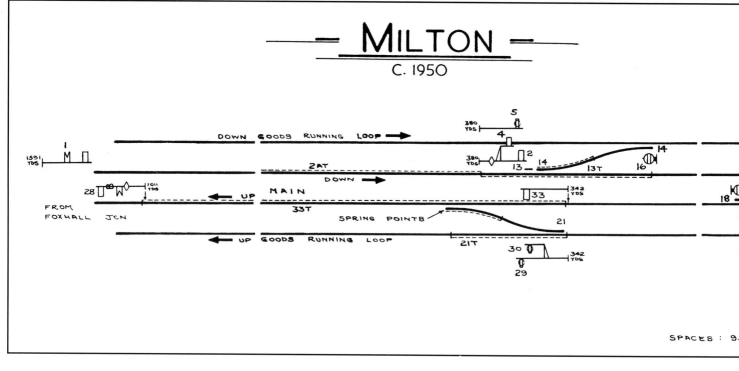

on the up side of the line and the enlarged railway layout required as a consequence of the factory. The new box was 25 by 11 ft, 11 feet from rails to floor, with a 27-lever frame, the levers at $5\frac{1}{4}$-inch centres being interlocked by horizontal tappets. In June 1916 a new frame of 46 levers was brought into use, which were interlocked with a vertical tappet machine bringing the levers to 4-inch centres, thus not requiring a larger signal box to house the larger frame.

A Down Goods Running Loop from Milton to Steventon was laid and an extra, short, Up Loop was provided, inlet and exit controlled by Milton. From this a single track led through gates into the factory.

This short loop made a 'Reception Line' to enable traffic for the factory to clear the main Goods Loop while it waited acceptance into the works complex.

By June 1916 there were five parallel tracks at Milton connected by a 'ladder' crossover consisting of four double compound points. In 1923 the box was a Class 4, 119 marks per hour, but became Class 3, 160 marks, in May 1937.

On 12 April 1942 this signal box was taken out of use and by the 15th had been dismantled and sent to Exeter East. The factory connection, the short loops and 'ladder' crossover were abolished and a new system was installed three-quarters of a mile further east.

This was brought into use over 12-15 April 1942. The new signal box was again on the up side, at 55 m 7 ch, and was built in brick, categorised as 'Type 13' by the SRS. It had a floor 30 ft 2 in by 13 feet, 11 feet from rail to floor, and housed a 35-lever frame with six spaces.

This was in connection with the improvement in goods train accommodation by the extension of the Down Goods Loop from Foxhall Junction to give a continuous Down Goods Running Loop from Foxhall to Steventon, and to

The wartime signal box at Milton, photographed on 3 October 1962. *Roger Webster/AVC*

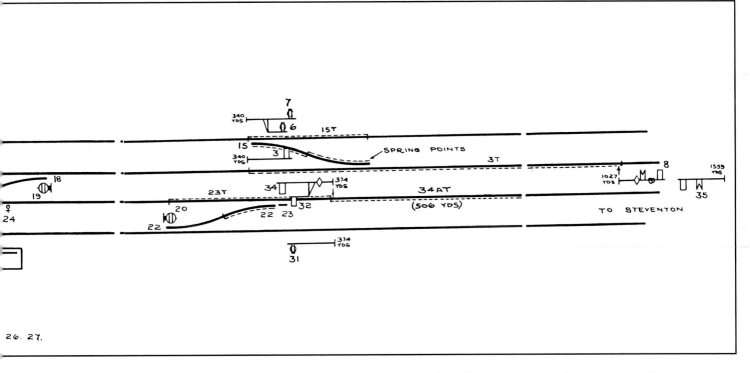

26. 27.

give junctions at Milton from Main to Goods and vice versa.

In the very busy war years Milton was an important place for 'margining' goods trains, and a place for relieving crews when Didcot was jammed. Its importance waned gradually in the 1950s as freight traffic was slowly reduced.

For both up and down trains the signalman 'asked the road ahead' as soon as he had returned 'Line Clear' to the box in rear. He sent 'Train Approaching', 1-2-1, to Steventon when Foxhall Junction sent 'TES', and 1-2-1 to Foxhall for up 'A' to 'D' headcode trains, but 'E' to 'J' he 'asked on' when he received 'TES' from Steventon.

Milton signal box was abolished on 1 December 1963.

WEST OF DIDCOT

Steventon

The history of the signal boxes at Steventon is complicated. There was a signal box at the west end of the up platfrom by 1874 and until 1 April 1928. This was a brick building with a pitched, slated roof, plain gables and small, house-style windows; this style is termed 'Type 1' by the Signalling Record Society. It housed a 27-lever frame.

Stocks Lane crossed the railway a little way west of the station at about 55 m 52 ch. From 1840 until about 1965 there was a long row of workmen's cottages, designed by Brunel in decorated red brick, parallel with the Down Main line, the west end of the row close to Stocks Lane. A 'Type 3' wooden signal box-type building existed on the east side of the lane, on the down side of the line, from at least 1884 until

March 1928. This housed levers and a gate wheel necessary to operate the level crossing gates across Stocks Lane. During the period mentioned this was not a block post but merely a ground frame, and was called 'Stocks Lane'.

West of Stocks Lane, 'Causeway Crossing Signal Box' existed from 1874, named after an early medieval causeway through which the railway passed. This causeway was raised through the village of Steventon 'so that folk might come and go clere' of the swampy ground that then existed. The medieval causeway still exists, but unfortunately the signal boxes have gone.

Causeway Crossing signal box would probably have been a 'Type 1'. On 26 July 1921 it was demolished

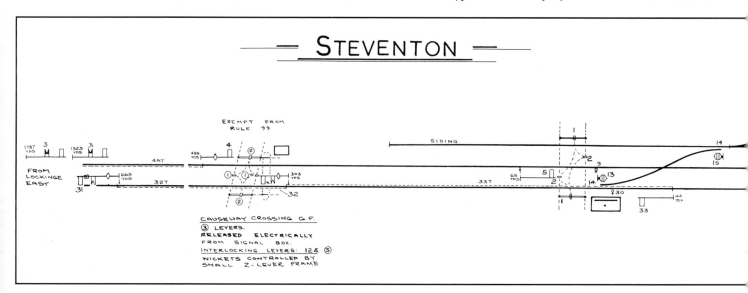

The timber Steventon (Stocks Lane) signal box in 1962 - with apologies for the poor quality. *AVC*

Causeway Crossing Ground Frame, with the medieval causeway visible on the left. The building dates from *circa* 1884 and was moved here from Stocks Lane in 1928 in exchange for the 1921 Causeway Crossing signal box, which went to Stocks Lane. *AVC*

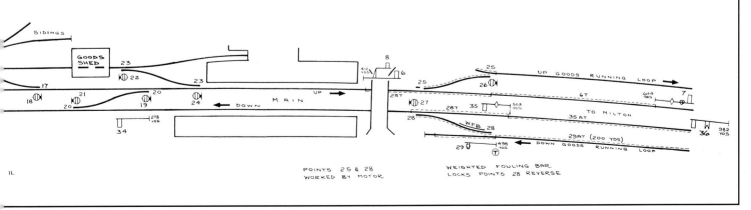

The normal position of Causeway gates was across the road, and a code of bells between the Causeway and Stocks Lane boxes was as follows:

May the crossing be used?	1-4-1
Crossing clear, gates in normal position	1-2
Train Approaching	1-2-1
Close gates - train signalled	3-2-1
Obstruction Danger	6
Cancel last signal sent	3-5

In response to 1-4-1, the Stocks Lane signalman would, if it was safe to do so, reverse the interlocking lever 12, which released Causeway's levers and locked Stocks Lane's signals. If Causeway did not close the gates when he saw the repeater instrument move to 'Line Clear', indicating that Stocks Lane had 'given the road' for a train, the Stocks Lane man would give him a minute or two, then send 3-2-1. When the gates were shut across the road, Causeway sent 1-2. He did not lock his pedestrian wicket gates until Stocks Lane sent 1-2-1 to indicate that the train was 'getting handy' - perhaps on the outermost track circuit of his layout.

The gates at Causeway, when closed across the rails, completely closed the line but at Stocks Lane when the gates were across the rails they did not reach across the Up Main. One day, a Pannier tank, running 'light' and very fast on the Up Main, arrived at Steventon before Stocks Lane gates were out of the way. The engine over-ran the signals and shot through the gap between the gates, doing no damage and providing everyone with a lot of laughter.

Note from the diagram that there are six signals on

and replaced by a 'Type 27' measuring 22 by 11 feet, 8 feet from rails to floor, housing a 17-lever frame and a gate wheel. In March 1928 the box at the station was abolished, and Causeway Crossing box was moved to Stocks Lane, which then became a block post; the 'Type 3' Stocks Lane building was moved to Causeway Crossing to become a ground frame controlled from Stocks Lane signal box, which now held a 36-lever frame (two spaces).

At an earlier period the gates at Causeway were bolted mechanically from Stocks Lane, but latterly the control of Causeway gates was by electric locks activated by a cut-down signal lever. Causeway Crossing ground frame had 'repeating' instruments to show the state of the block sections from the east and the west and had a single-strike bell to convey messages from the Stocks Lane signalman. In Stocks Lane box messages from Causeway were rung out on a 'gong' made of a coiled metal strip.

the Down Main worked from Stocks Lane, five stops and a Distant; Stock's Lane signals covered both crossings. The junctions to and from the goods loops were worked by electric motors running on hand-generated current. Stocks Lane in the 1930s was probably a Class 3, but I have no positive information on this.

Stocks Lane signal box was reduced to the status of a ground frame in about March 1965 when the Reading multiple-aspect signalling (MAS) scheme was extended to Wantage Road exclusive. The gates were still worked from the ex-signal box by the signal-man, now a crossing-keeper, but they were released by Reading Panel, and the controls at Causeway Crossing also 'slotted' the Stocks Lane controls. The fine old gates at Causeway and Stocks Lane remained in use until 11 November 1975 when the whole installation was abolished in favour of lifting barriers at both Stocks Lane and Causeway, worked from a new - and exceedingly ugly - building on the west side of the Causeway. The Stocks Lane gates were observed by the man at Causeway by means of closed circuit television (CCTV).

Lockinge

In the original scheme of things, the next box west of Steventon was Wantage Road, but a box called 'Lockinge' was introduced purely to break the long section between these two places. It was a 'Type 28', 12 ft 6 in by 10 feet, and had 4 levers, a Home and a Distant on each road, and stood at 58 m 51 ch. (An identical box, for break-section purposes, was built at Shottesbrook, 27 m 71 ch, and this is illustrated here in lieu of a photo of the original Lockinge.) The box was ordered from Reading Works in August 1903, a simple, wooden kit, and was probably in use by the end of that year.

This little box survived until 15 September 1940, when a military stores depot on the up side of the line was opened and connected to the railway. To serve this two signal boxes were required, Lockinge East and Lockinge West. Lockinge East was close enough to Steventon Stocks Lane to carry the latter's Distant signal below its Starting signal. It was a 'Type 13' - all brick, pitched roof, plain gables, concrete lintels over the locking-room windows - and stood on the down side at, approximately, 57 m 20 ch. It controlled access to a loop - or possibly two - extending westwards on the up side of the line; the loop(s) continued through gates into the military depot. The box was 25 by 12 feet, the floor 8 feet above rail level, and it housed a 35-lever frame - with many spares. It was brought into use on 25 August 1940.

Simultaneously a new box, Lockinge West, was brought into use on the down side at 57 m 77 ch to operate the western end of the new layout. This was a curiosity in so much as it was built to a design very similar to the pre-1914 'Type 7'. In the period of wartime austerity this was an expensive design, but there were few of them - the very big Taunton Silk Mill Crossing is an example, opened about five weeks earlier.

The original Lockinge signal box of 1904 would have looked very similar to this 'break section' box at Shottesbrooke. *Peter Barlow/AVC*

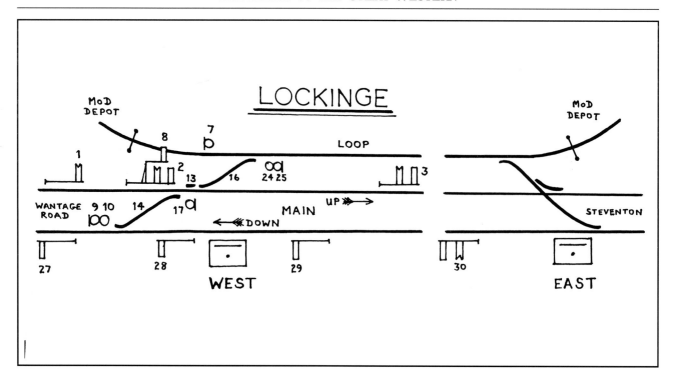

Lockinge West had the same floor dimensions as East, but housed a 36-lever frame, again with many spares.

The military depot ceased to be rail-connected and Lockinge East was taken out of use on 16 August 1950. The signalmen at Stocks Lane thereby lost a 'one Sunday in three' extra Sunday turn. With the loops no longer in use, Lockinge West changed its name to simply 'Lockinge' and remained purely as a 'break section' block post.

In the days when these boxes were in use, many signalmen got around by bicycle. East and West box could be reached by walking along the track from Steventon if the signalman lived in the Didcot/Steventon area, but even so the West box was a fair walk. If the signalman was coming from the Wantage area or beyond, to cycle to Steventon then back along the line 2 miles to Lockinge West was tedious - and even worse, going home tired in the morning after a night shift. The shortest route from the Wantage side was down a mile-long, muddy lane, to Smith's Farm, through the farmyard and across the fields. The West box was lonely and inaccessible - and *very* unpopular. There was many a dry eye when it was abolished at 6.50 am Sunday 20 August 1961.

The accompanying diagram is accurate in the details it gives, but is not complete.

Lockinge East box some years after closure with No 5954 *Faendre Hall* on a down 'D' headcode vacuum goods, *circa* 1958. Steventon's Up Distant signal is below the Starting signal. *Peter Barlow/AVC*

Lockinge West box on 25 May 1963.
Roger Webster/AVC

Wantage Road

Wantage Road station was not part of the original GWR, as planned by Brunel in 1835, but was an afterthought, opened in 1845. There was nothing 'Brunellian' about its appearance. The station entrance was on the road bridge, appearing from the road to be a two-storey, red-brick construction combining booking offices with the Station Master's family quarters; there was an awning over the public entrance, but from the platforms it rose, tower-like. In living memory the booking office and waiting rooms were at platform level.

Wantage Road signal box existed by 1874 and presumably was a little brick 'Type 1'. This was replaced on 5 December 1915 with a handsome 'Type 7' at 60 m 26 ch. This had a floor 25 by 11 feet, 6 feet above rail, and housed 35-

lever frame (four spaces and eight spares). This box was in turn abolished and replaced by a 'Type 9' box on 7 October 1932. The 1932 box was at 60 m 24 ch and held a 61-lever frame (13 spaces) to control the eastern end of the newly quadrupled layout from there

Some of the Wantage Road station crew in August 1964. From left to right: signalman Bill Windridge, lorry driver David Castle, station clerk Betty Goodenough, a daughter of Bill Orpin, a signalman at Wantage Road, relief porter Albert Stanley and signalman Wally Randall. *David Castle*

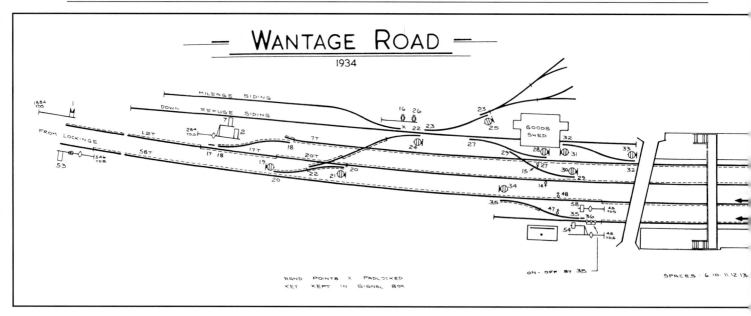

— WANTAGE ROAD —
1934

HAND POINTS X PADLOCKED
KEY KEPT IN SIGNAL BOX

ON - OFF BY 35

SPACES : 6. 10. 11. 12. 13

to Circourt and Challow, 64 milepost. The box was Class 3 in GWR days, but was raised to Class 2 in 1954 when Circourt box was abolished in favour of an IBS.

The signalman at Wantage Road was permitted to use the 'Warning Acceptance' for down freight trains provided that there was no passenger train within the clearing point.

Wantage Road signal box was abolished under the Reading MAS scheme on 30 May 1965.

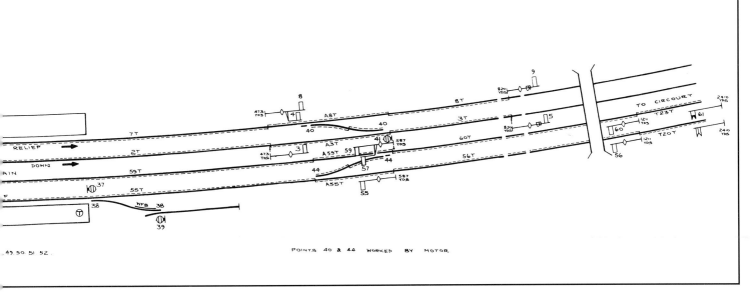

POINTS 40 & 44 WORKED BY MOTOR

Below left Wantage Road station on 5 April 1932, looking west. The main pedestrian entrance to the station was from the road, on the bridge, and the awning over this entrance can be seen. The booking office was just inside and the passenger then went down a long flight of narrow stairs to the platform. *GWR*

Below Looking east from the road bridge on the same day, showing the old and new signal boxes; the latter stands well back to make room for the new Up Main and Up Relief lines. The track nearest the locomotive water storage tank is the original Up Main, but when the works are completed this will be the Down Main and the existing Down Main will become the Down Relief line. *GWR*

No 6126 at the down platform *circa* 1960, showing the lofty entrance building from below. Note the Wantage Tramway Co locomotive No 5 on the platform. *Lens of Sutton*

The Wantage Tramway

No sketch of Wantage Road could ignore the famous tram - the first roadside tram in the world to use steam locomotives.

On 1 October 1876 the Wantage Tramway Company (WTC) opened for goods traffic its 2½-mile horse-drawn standard-gauge, tramway from the GWR station to the town; passenger traffic began on the 11th. Steam power was introduced in August 1879 and locomotives running on compressed air were given a trial in 1880.

The tramway passenger 'station' at Wantage Road was simply a length of line parallel with the eastern foot of the road embankment on the south side of the GWR. Goods traffic to and from the GWR ran into the GWR goods yard, and there were times when the tramway company's engine was used to shunt trucks on the GWR main line.

The GWR inaugurated a motor-bus service between Wantage and Swindon on 28 May 1925, with a shuttle of buses to meet the trains and connect Wantage Road station and the town. The GWR purchased the tramway as from 1 August of that year, and abolished the passenger service although retaining the tramway for the busy freight traffic.

The last passenger tram ran on 31 July 1925. The last 'down' goods train was the 4.30 pm Wantage Road-Wantage Town on 18 December 1945, and the last 'up' train ran on the 21st. After that only track-lifting trains ran, in May 1946. On 24 April 1946 the Great Western Railway, its own end in sight, most honourably purchased WTC No 5 from the Company for £100 with the intention of restoring it for static display at Wantage Road station, 'in view of the long association between ourselves and the tramway company'. The name *Shannon* was added during the restoration at Swindon*.

* Information taken from Canon S. H. Pearce-Higgins's *The Wantage Tramway*.

'Asking the road', Didcot-Wantage

The system of 'asking the road' through from Didcot to Wantage Road and Challow in GWR days is not known, but it was probably the same system used in 1960, with Lockinge West in circuit. For down trains from Class 'A' to 'D', Foxhall Junction sent 'Train Entering Section' to Milton, Milton sent 'Train Approaching', 1-2-1, to Steventon and Steventon then asked 'Is Line Clear?' to Lockinge, who 'gave the road' and 'asked on' to Wantage. Wantage 'gave the road' and 'asked on' to Challow; Challow 'gave the road' back, but did not 'ask on'. The signals were now lowered from Milton to Wantage Road inclusive.

If the down train was the 8.45 am Paddington, 'The Bristolian', Challow 'refused the road' to Wantage Road until he had 'got the road' from Uffington. Once he 'had the road' from Uffington he gave 'Line Clear' to Wantage and 'pulled off'; in that case the signals were then 'off' from Milton to Challow. Otherwise, on receipt of 'TES' from Steventon, Lockinge sent 1-2-1 to Wantage Road, who at once sent 1-2-1 to Challow. Challow then 'got the road' from Uffington and 'pulled off'.

On the up road, trains from Class 'A' to 'D' were 'asked on' by Challow to Wantage, and Challow 'pulled off'. When Uffington sent 'TES' to Challow, Challow sent 1-2-1 to Wantage, who then 'asked on' to Lockinge, and Lockinge to Steventon. Challow sent 'TES' to Wantage when the train passed the Home signal of Circourt IBS; Wantage then sent 1-2-1 forward to Lockinge, who passed it on to Steventon, who then asked 'Is Line Clear?' to Milton, and Milton to Foxhall Junction.

Drivers of up trains wishing to go via the West Curve at Foxhall Junction were supposed to 'whistle up' passing Wantage ('2 long, 1 crow') and the Wantage Road signalman would then advise Foxhall - or so the 'footnotes' directed. This would, however, only have been the case in some exceptional circumstances - for all scheduled services the signalmen were well aware of the route to be taken by a train.

DIDCOT TO OXFORD

Didcot North Junction

The first North Junction came into being on 22 December 1856 when the Didcot Avoiding Line opened on the north-east side of the station. Of course this was at first and until about 1874 operated by switchmen on the ground, manipulating hand-operated points and 'disc and crossbar' signals. The

Didcot North Junction looking south from between the Up and Down Main lines *circa* 1954. The Avoiding Line with its Up Goods Running Loop curves left, the line to the station and West Curve right; the Down Goods Running Loop is on the extreme right. *Peter Barlow/AVC*

first signal box at North Junction for which we have any details was a 'Type 3'* box situated on the up side, close to the facing points. GWR S&T Department records show that this box had a 26-lever frame. From October 1901** it also controlled the entrance to the Up Avoiding Line Goods Running Loop from the 'Up Northern' line (the line from Oxford) to Didcot East Junction.

* Photograph in *Railway Magazine*, November 1905.

** R. A. Cooke, *Track Plans: Berkshire*, Vol 23.

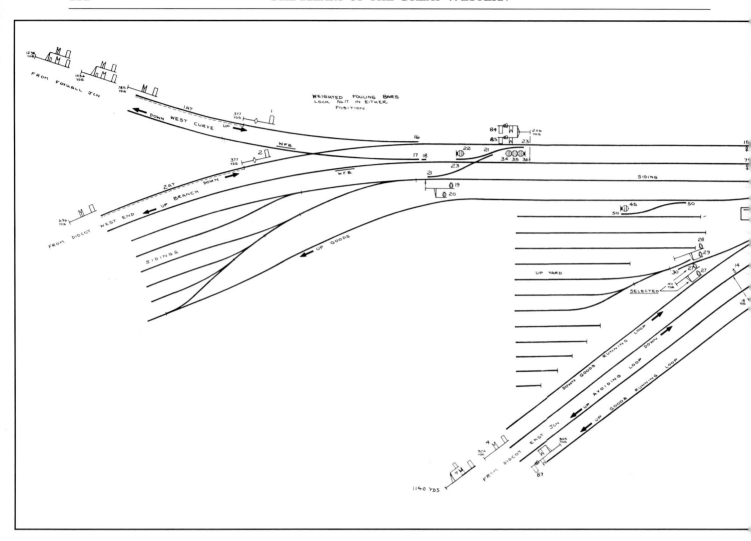

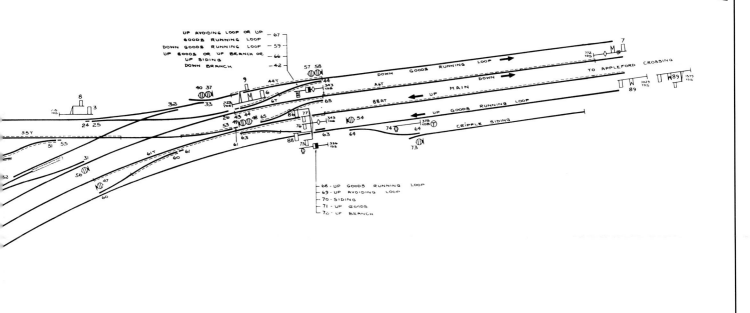

UP AVOIDING LOOP OR UP — 67
GOODS RUNNING LOOP
DOWN GOODS RUNNING LOOP — 59
UP GOODS OR UP BRANCH OR — 66
UP SIDING
DOWN BRANCH — 42

DOWN GOODS RUNNING LOOP
DOWN MAIN
UP MAIN
UP GOODS RUNNING LOOP
CRIPPLE SIDING
TO APPLEFORD CROSSING

68 - UP GOODS RUNNING LOOP
69 - UP AVOIDING LOOP
70 - SIDING
71 - UP GOODS
72 - UP BRANCH

DIDCOT NORTH
1957

SPACES 10 11 12 13 41 52 62 80 81 82 83

Left Looking north from between the Down and Up Main lines on 17 November 1942; the Avoiding Line comes from behind the signal box. The old power box is the further half of the building - with painted-on trees to fool the Luftwaffe or marauding German paratroopers - while the 1942 extension is clearly evident as the nearer half. Note the low building beyond the signal box - this used to be the battery room for the 1905 power box. The signal in the distance is 'off' for the Down Goods Running Loop. *GWR*

Right Looking north along the Down Goods Running Loop. No 30857 *Lord Howe* approaches with an 11-coach Newcastle-Bournemouth train, and signal 88 is 'off' for him to go round the Avoiding Line. On the extreme right the Up Goods Running Loop Starting signal has a route indicator for five routes, and the Backing signal from the Down Loop has an indicator for four routes. *David Anderson*

DIDCOT NORTH

The man with the responsibility for the decision-making and the safety of this complicated junction in 1964 - signalman Ron Almond. The three large, mahogany-cased instruments nearest the camera are Tyers/GWR Permissive Block instruments; the nearest works the Up Loop from Appleford, and the other two work with Didcot East Junction. There is a signal arm repeater and a 'block bell' between them. After the third instrument is the 'box to box' phone working solely with Appleford Crossing. After this come the instruments for working the Absolute Block lines to and from Appleford, East Junction and Foxhall Junction. *BR*

There was also, prior to 1905, a signal box to control 'West Curve Junction' at 53 m 50 ch, where the West Curve diverged from the main line into Didcot station. On 16 July 1907 North Junction and West Curve signal boxes were abolished and replaced by a new brick 'Type 7' box called Didcot North Junction, in the 'V' of the junction between the Avoiding Line and the Main Line at 53 m 64 ch (measured via Didcot station). The box floor was 25 feet long and the building had a tower-like appearance, tall and narrow, due to the height required to give the signalman a clear view northwards over the accumulator house sited at the foot of the box stairs.

The box housed a Siemens electric power frame of 38 miniature levers (seven spaces) in a raised console to control the North Junction and West Curve Junction layouts. The box worked at 148 marks per hour in 1923, Class 3. In 1927 the power frame was replaced by a conventional frame of 36 levers controlling the same layout.

At the outbreak of the Second World War the box was extended at the south end to accommodate a larger frame necessary for an enlarged layout. A Down Goods Running Loop (the 'Down Gully') was brought into use between Didcot East and Didcot North Junctions on 6 March 1940, the Up Goods Running Loop from Appleford Crossing to Didcot North Junction was brought into use 1 September 1941*, and from North Junction to Appleford Crossing a Down Goods Loop came into use 27 October 1941. In the latter month

* A GWR 'Notice to Enginemen' shows this loop being brought into use during the period 15-28 June 1941, but it seems that pressure of work prevented this. GWR Chief Civil Engineer's and Ministry of Transport records both give the later dates. See R. A. Cooke's *Track Plans: Berkshire*, Vol 23.

the Down Avoiding Line Goods Loop was extended across the junction to join the loop to Appleford. Other additions were made to the layout, mainly more connections between Didcot Yard and the running lines. The new works were fully brought into use on 27 October 1941 controlled by an 89-lever frame with 11 spaces. In August 1945 Didcot North Junction was working at 253 marks for Class 2, and in 1951, at 285 marks, the signalmen got into Class 1.

In accordance with the 1949 Instructions for the signal box, the signalman asked 'Is Line Clear?' to Appleford Crossing, the next box northwards, as soon as he had given 'Line Clear' to the box in rear. On the up road, he 'asked on' for 'A' or 'C' Class trains when he received 'Train Approaching', 1-2-1, from Appleford, while for other classes of up train he waited until he received 'Train Entering Section'. He was permitted to use the 'Warning Acceptance' against any train coming from Foxhall Junction, and was permitted to alter his facing points after he had given 'Line Clear' for a train to approach provided that (a) it had not passed his Distant signal, (b) he had not lowered any signals for it, and (c) he had obtained 'Line Clear' for it to travel over the revised route. In 1961 this permission was altered to conform to the conditions in force at Foxhall Junction.

'Shunting into forward section', 1-3-1 on the bell, was in use on the Up West Curve line to Foxhall. The signalman was also permitted to reverse a train from Didcot Yard, Reception line or Down Goods Running Loop, across, in the direction of Appleford, to the Up 'Northern' (Oxford) line or Up Goods Running Loop, going outside his Home signals in either case. Before he made this movement he 'put the block on' by sending 3-3 to Appleford. When Appleford acknowledged this code, the Didcot North signalman placed the relevant block instrument to 'Train on Line', then signalled the movement.

The box layout at Didcot North Junction was now very impressive, and of course it had a train service and shunting work to go with it. Here all the routes and all the traffic from east, west and south were gathered together and funnelled north, through a double-track bottleneck, to Oxford. Yet it was worked by a single signalman without a booking lad.

It is important to remember, when one thinks of 'double track', that this actually means only one down line and one up line. In this sense they are both 'single' lines, upon which everything must follow, one behind the other. That, of course, forms a great obstacle where you have a loose-coupled goods train running at 25 mph (more or less, depending on the length and weight of the train) with a fully braked 60 mph passenger trains coming along behind. For a 60-wagon freight train to clear a section of - say - 2½ miles of level track, from passing one signal box at 25 mph to diverging to the goods running loop at the next, would require about 8 minutes.

If it was not a *running* loop, but merely a loop, the entrance and exit being controlled from the same signal box and having a capacity of between 60 to 100 wagons, then the driver had to be even more cautious about running into it, because he must be able to stop a train weighing hundreds of tons at the far end. In this case the 2½ miles might take 10 minutes. Meanwhile the block instrument for that section is standing at 'Train on Line' and nothing can enter until the 'Train out of Section' has been sent from the box in advance.

The loose-coupled goods train driver's problem was not how to go fast - it was rather a matter of how to keep speed down, to go slow enough to be able to stop hundreds of tons of jostling, unbraked wagons neatly in the braking distances afforded by the positioning of the Distant signals relative to their Home signal.

Until 1940 there were no loops north of Didcot North until the short loop at Kennington Junction, a distance of about 7 miles, which required a lengthy 'margin' of time for an 'F', 'H' or 'J' headcode freight to cover. The signalman had to make this judgement and hold or let go the goods so as not to delay the following passenger trains. After 1940 trundling freights could be diverted on to the Relief line at Radley, 4½ miles away, and from June 1941 freight could be put into the goods loop to Appleford Crossing. Then the Appleford signalman could let them out on a 3½-mile trundle to Radley.

Didcot North Junction signal box was abolished on 17 May 1965.

Appleford Crossing

Appleford Crossing signal box was sited on the down side of the line at 54 m 64 ch. When the first signal box was erected is not known - but it had eight levers and a gate wheel to work the gates across a track to a farm. In 1923 it worked at 105 marks per hour and was Class 4.

In 1941 it seems likely (but is not known) that a new signal box was built to accommodate a 22-lever frame (five spaces) to operate the new layout to Didcot North Junction. This was a wooden signal box with a floor 19 ft by 11 ft 6 in. It was damaged in September 1942 when an express passenger train on the Down Main collided with a train emerging from the

Down Goods Running Loop. In October 1951 it was working at 153 marks as a Class 3.

The signal box on 3 October 1962. *Roger Webster/AVC*

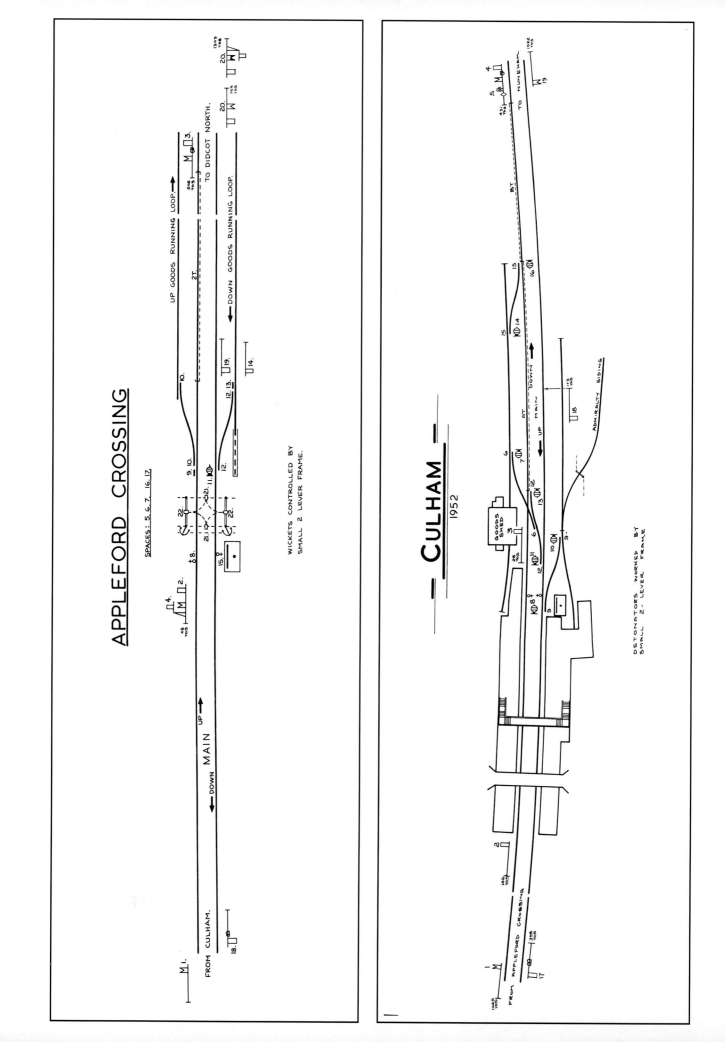

APPLEFORD CROSSING

SPACES: 5, 6, 7, 16, 17.

UP GOODS RUNNING LOOP.

TO DIDCOT NORTH.

DOWN GOODS RUNNING LOOP.

← DOWN   MAIN   UP →

FROM CULHAM.

WICKETS CONTROLLED BY
SMALL 2 LEVER FRAME.

— CULHAM —

1952

GOODS SHED

TO NUNEHAM.

← DOWN   MAIN   UP →

ADMIRALTY SIDING.

FROM APPLEFORD CROSSING.

FROM NUNEHAM.

DETONATORS WORKED BY
SMALL 2-LEVER FRAME.

Right Looking north over the lane crossing *circa* 1954. The signalman is returning to his box after passing a message to the driver of a local freight - the engine is a '15xx' 0-6-0PT signalled into the Up Goods Running Loop. *Peter Barlow/AVC*

Below right The scene from Appleford Crossing signal box on 13 November 1942. A down goods on the Down Goods Running Loop, hauled by 'Saint' 4-6-0 No 2975 *Lord Palmer,* was driven off the end of the loop because the driver, Charlie Forbes, had mistaken the main-line green lights for his own. The derailment happened in the small hours of the 13th just as the 12.45 am Paddington-Birkenhead was passing. Charlie Forbes and his regular fireman, both reliable and conscientious men, were killed. (See Harold Gasson's *Footplate Days*, page 35.) Signalman Jack Gough, with whom I once worked, was on duty in Didcot North Junction at the time; when he got home he found his wife had given birth to their first child at about the time of the crash. *GWR*

The box was completely demolished on 25 September 1952 when a down goods train driver mistook the main line signals for his own, accelerated along the loop and ran off the catch points to crash into the signal box. The box was then rebuilt.

The 1953 Instructions, the earliest surviving, show that the signalman asked 'Is Line Clear?' for all down trains as soon as he received the signal from Didcot North Junction. He 'asked on' for up expresses and all 'C', 'D' and 'E' headcode trains as soon as he received the code from Culham, and sent 'Train Approaching', 1-2-1, to Didcot North on receipt of 'Train Entering Section' from Culham.

The Reading 'Panel' signalling automation scheme made the box redundant as a block post on 17 May 1965, but it still exists today - April 1994 - as a ground frame to work the gates.

Culham

The next signal box north of Appleford was Culham, situated at the north end of the up platform. The station is marked in GWR Working Books as 56 m 17 ch from Paddington, measuring via Didcot Station. The signal box existing at Culham in 1951 was a 'Type 2' design - having a hip-gabled roof, which, in so small a box, would have made the roof pyramid shaped. It housed a 19-lever frame, with no spares or spaces. In 1923 the work was assessed at 96 marks per hour for Class 4,

floor 25 by 12 feet holding a 29-lever frame with nine spaces.

One man who worked here during the Second World War, Bill Culham, told me that his best memory of the place was watching Lord Harcourt's Suffolk Punch draught horses, four-in-hand, coming to the station yard hauling a 'timber-bob' loaded with tree trunks to be put on rail at the station.

but this had risen to 125 marks, Class 3, in November 1951.

This box was taken out of use on 18 November 1952 to be replaced on the same site (within a few feet) by the one shown in the photograph. This had a

The signal box was abolished on 12 February 1961, leaving the block section Appleford to Radley, a distance of 3 miles 52 chains.

Nuneham

During the rebuilding of the 99-yard-long river bridge over the Thames at Nuneham, 1,960 yards north of Culham station, the track was singled over the bridge, controlled by a pair of temporary signal boxes, 'Nuneham Viaduct South' and 'Nuneham Viaduct North'; both were abolished on 9 March 1930.

On 15 December 1940 a new signal box called Nuneham was established at 53 m 32 ch, on the down side immediately north of the river bridge. This was a wooden building 12 by 11 feet, the floor 8 feet above rail level, and containing a six-lever frame. The box was close enough in advance of Culham to have its

Down Distant signal placed below that box's Advanced Starting signal.

The purpose of the signal box was simply to break the section between Culham and Radley. The Didcot locomotiveman-turned-signalman-turned-author, Harold Gasson, sometimes worked this place when he was 'on the relief'.

Nuneham signal box was replaced on 18 October 1953 by an 'Intermediate Block Section' (IBS) worked from Culham on the down road and Radley on the up. This in turn was abolished on 25 January 1961, leaving the block section Culham to Radley, a distance of 2 miles 17 chains.

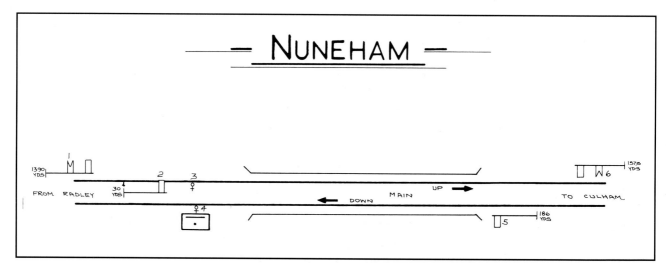

Radley

The branch line to Abingdon opened on 2 June 1856 as a broad gauge single track from a junction with the main line at 57 m 60 ch for a distance of 1 m 70 ch to the town. There was no proper station at the junction, merely wooden platforms to enable passengers to change trains - as at Kemble for Cirencester - but after 17 years of discomfort a substantial station was built, 61 chains further north, at 58 m 36 ch, called 'Radley'.

This station was opened on 8 September 1873, whereupon the old junction was abolished and the branch line extended, by 61 chains, parallel to the Down Main into the new station. The down main platform was an 'island' with the branch line on the west (down) side; this branch 'terminus' was self-contained, and branch trains could come and go without interfering with main-line trains. It seems likely that a signal box was part of the new station, but all that is known for certain is that there was a signal box at Radley by 1884, situated on the southern half of the down platform, between the Down Main line and the Abingdon branch.

Radley station looking north from the branch ci: ca 1914, with the signal box on the south end of the up platform. *W. L. Kenning/AVC*

This was replaced in 1896 by a new box, a brick 'Type 5', situated on the up platform at 58 m 36 ch. GWR S&T Department records show that an order for the box was placed with Reading Signal Works on 11 December 1895; it was then described as a 'Special signal box', although the design appears to have been the 'standard' of the period. The floor was 30 ft 5 in by 12 feet, for a 43-lever frame with 'double twist' interlocking, and levers at $5^1/4$-inch centres. On 28 April 1896 the same records note that 22,000 bricks had been ordered with which to build the box. The interlocking was converted to standard tappet locking in 1942 without affecting the appearance of the frame in the operating room.

Work to widen the line from Radley to Oxford began in December 1939. On 30 April 1940 a new Up Goods Running Loop from a new box at Sandford was brought into use, on the east of the Up Main, which loop terminated at 58 m 46 ch immediately north of the road bridge; the northern end of the station platforms terminated at 58 m 39 ch. A new Down Relief Line commenced at 58 m 46 ch and ran on the west side of the Down Main as far as Sandford.

The 1954 Instructions for the signal box ordered

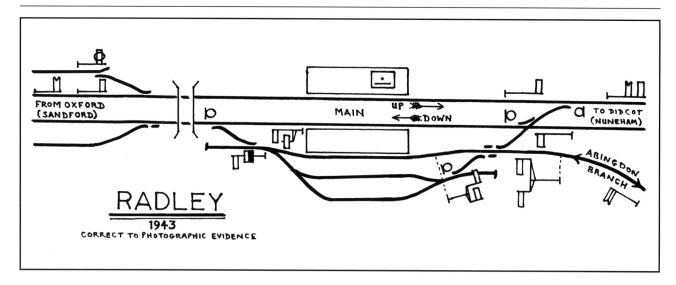

the signalman to ask 'Is Line Clear?' to Sandford for all down trains as soon as he received 'Train Approaching, 1-2-1, from Culham. When Nuneham

box was open, the signalman there would have sent 1-2-1 to Radley when he received 'Train Entering Section' from Culham. On the up line Radley 'asked on' to Culham when he received 1-2-1 from Sandford - ie the train was 'off Kennington'.

Signalman Bernard Smallbone leans from his box as an up fast comes by, *circa* 1914. *W. L. Kenning/AVC*

The signalman at Radley was permitted to use the

'Warning Acceptance' against all up and down non-passenger trains provided that there was not a passenger train within the clearing point.

In 1923 the box worked at 152 marks per hour, Class 3. It was taken out of use under the Reading MAS scheme on 23 May 1965.

The Abingdon branch

In 1876, and still in 1936, the branch line was worked by the Train Staff & Ticket system. The Train Staff was of varnished oak, square in cross-section, while the Ticket was square and pink. Under this system two or more trains could run from Radley to Abingdon (or vice versa); all but the last train to

Above No 5003 *Lulworth Castle* steps away from the branch to the Up Main at 9 pm with a return 'Riverside Excursion' from Abingdon to the Southern in 1954. The train consisted of 11 Bulleid and Maunsell coaches and was hauled to Abingdon by a '14xx' 0-4-2 tank. *Peter Barlow/AVC*

Right At the north end of the station No 5903 *Keele Hall* runs into Radley with an up stopping train in 1954, GWR 1940-style signalling in the foreground. Note that the entire signal is placed on one side of the main mast; BR(WR) used this design but placed the 'dolls' on each side of the mast. *Peter Barlow/AVC*

(say) Abingdon would carry a Ticket, and the last train in that direction would carry the Train Staff. Only when the Staff had arrived at Abingdon could any train leave that place for Radley.

In 1936 the weekday passenger service consisted of 18 trips each way, worked by an 'auto-train' that shuttled to and fro carrying the Train Staff, except once or twice a day when the Staff had to be left behind at Radley or Abingdon and the 'auto' go forward on a Ticket so that a goods train could follow with the Staff. On Saturdays the weekday passenger service ran, augmented with two late-night trips.

Because the branch was not a 'One engine in

steam' system, all trains had to be signalled with bells and instruments. As there were 40 trains over the line between 6.50 am and 10.15 pm, and as each train required three bell codes, the Radley signalman's instrument work and 'booking' for the branch was quite busy, together with, of course, shunting with the goods train to and from Abingdon. The 1936 GWR Working Time Table does not show a Sunday service on the branch.

The signal box at Abingdon was a 'Type 3', a design dating from the mid-1880s. It housed a 20-lever frame, with two spaces, the levers at 5$\frac{1}{4}$-inch centres interlocked, almost certainly, with GWR 'stud' locking.

In the 1950s the branch guard was an old GWR man, Reg Warrell, Oxford City Councillor, Sheriff of Oxford 1953-54 and long-time public house keeper.

Abingdon signal box, built about 1885, and quite unchanged in 1955. *Peter Barlow/AVC*

The ancient interior of the signal box, surviving to delight all-comers in 1955. At the left-hand end of the shelf is a lamp repeater instrument, next to it is a signal arm repeater, then the block bell working with Radley and an ordinary double-line Spagnoletti block indicator; the brass plate says 'RADLEY', and the 'Up Line' and 'Down Line' indications are just as relevant on a single line, with trains running in both directions. The signalman's handlamp is to the right of the block instrument.

Lever 18, on the extreme right, works the 'Up Main Platform Starting' signal, and cannot be pulled unless facing point bolt lever 13 is reversed; 13 is the pale (blue) lever seen 'reversed' (pulled) on the left. The plunger on the front of the shelf appears to operate a 'Platform bell' to warn the station of the approach of a train. *Peter Barlow/AVC*

Sandford

Sandford signal box stood on the up side at 59 m 59 ch. It was a plain-gabled, wooden box of 'Type 28' in the SRS notation, and was brought into use on 7 April 1940 with a floor 20 by 11 feet, 8 feet above rail level, housing a 34-lever frame with three spaces and two, separate, two-lever detonator-placer frames. The box finally controlled four running lines brought into use between May and August 1940. There was also a siding from a trailing connection in

Right Sandford signal box from the down side on 12 April 1963. *Roger Webster/AVC*

Below The view south at Sandford on 13 August 1940, the new Down Goods Running Loop on the right and points laid in on the left for the end of the Up Relief, which became the Up Goods Running Loop here. *GWR*

the Down Goods Running Loop to a Government refrigerated meat store, operated from a ground frame released electrically from the signal box; this was

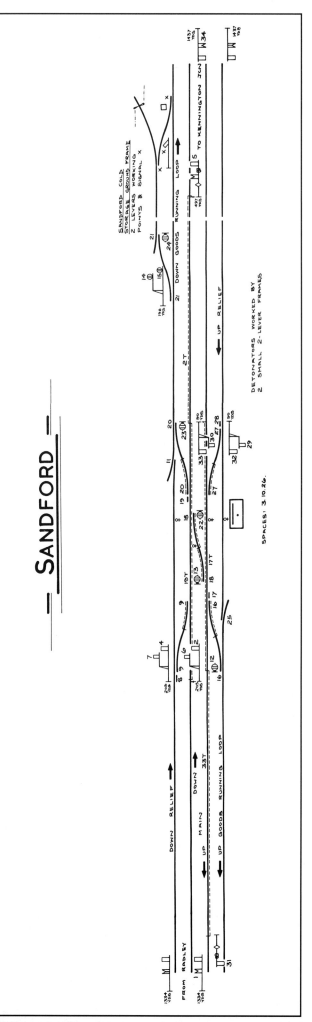

SANDFORD

SPACES: 3.10.26.

DETONATORS WORKED BY
2 SMALL 2-LEVER FRAMES

SANDFORD COLD
STORAGE GROUND FRAME
2 LEVERS WORKING
POINTS & SIGNAL X

TO KENNINGTON JCN

DOWN RELIEF

DOWN

UP MAIN

UP GOODS RUNNING LOOP

UP RELIEF

DOWN GOODS RUNNING LOOP

FROM RADLEY

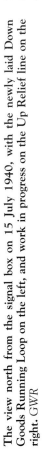

The view north from the signal box on 15 July 1940, with the newly laid Down Goods Running Loop on the left, and work in progress on the Up Relief line on the right. *GWR*

The same scene circa 1955 with the Up Relief in place; the Abingdon goods stands on this new line, its locomotive just returning from the down side after a visit to the cold store. *Peter Barlow/AVC*

brought into use on 10 July 1942.* It was served once or twice a day by the Abingdon branch goods.

The Down Relief line from Radley became a Down Goods Running Loop at Sandford, so passenger trains on the Down Relief had to re-join the Down Main here, through points 9. Conversely, the Up Relief line from Kennington became an Up Goods Running Loop from here to Radley, and up passenger trains put into the Up Relief Line at Kennington rejoined the Up Main here, through points 27.

* R. A. Cooke, *Track Plans: Oxford*, Vol 27.

The first signalman to work a shift at Sandford was Basil Marchant, promoted from Morris Cowley. The Sandford signalman was very much involved with 'margining' trains and storing goods trains at the behest of the signalmen at the larger boxes at Oxford or Didcot. The box was Class 3.

Sandford box was built to help cope with the greatly inflated freight traffic of the 1940-45 period, and traffic density only fell away gradually, the line being busy well into the 1950s. The box succumbed to the decline in traffic on 14 December 1964 when it was abolished.

Kennington Junction

There had been a small brick signal box at Kennington, controlling the junction to the Thame branch, as early as 1874. It stood on the up side of the line, hard by the facing points at about 61 m 15 ch. In November 1900* the layout was enlarged with a Down Goods Loop from 60 m 76 ch to 61 m 19 ch, a Main to Main crossover and a connection from the Up Branch siding to the Up Main to permit trains on the Up Main to reverse into the siding; prior to this trains had to occupy the single line before they could reverse into this refuge siding. Kennington Junction had existed since 1874 without such simple conveniences as these.

In 1901 a new signal box was

* R. A. Cooke, op. cit.

Above right GWR staff at Kennington *circa* 1914: George Blake under the bowler hat, and Bernard Smallbone, third from the left. Note the wicker lunch basket on the right and the GWR uniforms, good-quality cloth, well cut and, above all, dignified. *W. L. Kenning/AVC*

Right Lunchtime for platelayers in Kennington box *circa* 1914. The 'box to box' circuit and single-needle instruments are on the extreme left. *W. L. Kenning/AVC*

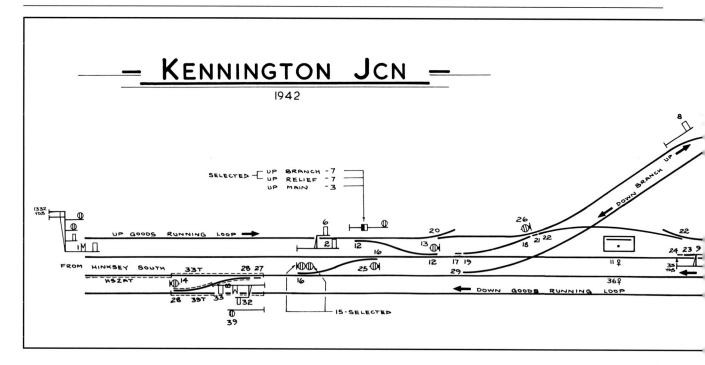

– KENNINGTON JCN –
1942

The signal box faced the Thame branch in readiness for its upgrading to main-line status, and the picture gives the illusion of a double-track line here, although the up and down branch tracks merge behind the camera. The 6.50 am Wolverhampton-Paddington (8.55 Worcester) express is passing on the Up Main *circa* 1955. Note the Up Goods Loop crossing the branch in the foreground. *Peter Barlow/AVC*

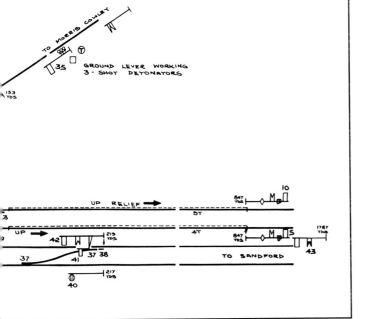

brought into use. It seems strange that the GWR should have increased the frame size of the old box just a few months before they knocked it down, rather than bringing the new layout into use with the new signal box. The new box was a brick 'Type 7' standing in the 'V' of the junction at 61 m 12 ch. This box had a floor 29 by 12 feet, 11 feet above rail level and housing a frame of 43 levers (41 working, two spare). The interlocking was by the GWR 'double twist' mechanism, spacing the levers at 5¼-inch centres. The old box was cut down to half-height and re-roofed to be used as a platelayers' cabin, in which form it survived the box that replaced it.

In 1923 the box was Class 4, working at 131 marks per hour, and this undoubtedly rose to Class 3 by the mid-1930s, although there is no record of the marks rate.

From 1902 single-needle telegraph instruments stood at the north end of the box on top of a locker by a window looking on to the main line; they had been removed by 1939.

The 6.50 am Wolverhampton passing the rear of Kennington box on the Up Main, again in 1955. In 1936 this train, 'Castle'- or 'Star'-hauled, was booked to leave Oxford at 10.10 and run the 63½ miles to Paddington non-stop in 60 minutes. It was booked 12 minutes for the 10¾ miles to Didcot East Junction, allowing for the coasting/braking period from Appleford to the 40 mph permanent restriction over the junction from the Avoiding Line to the Up Main at Didcot East Junction. From there to a stand at Paddington, almost 53 miles, was scheduled for 48 minutes. *Peter Barlow/AVC*

Of the three signalmen working at Kennington in 1913, two are known by name - Basil Smallbone and George Blake. They allowed interested boys into the box to watch the working, and my late friend Bill Kenning, a pupil at Radley College from 1913 to 1917, was a regular visitor to this and the Radley box. At weekends, with his mother's permission, he spent the time with George Blake and his family at home.

Mrs Kenning may have been a Christian Socialist - she named Bill 'William Lovett' after a well-known Christian Socialist reformer of the 19th century - and she had encouraged Bill to take an interest in railwaymen and their work. She brought him a camera and with this he recorded his railway friends. Bill's father died before 1913 and he was parted from his mother for long periods while at Radley College, so he was ever grateful to the railwaymen and their families for their kindness to him, and remained for the rest of his life a keen visitor in signal boxes and on locomotive footplates.

Kennington Junction signal box faced the Thame branch. This was because, in 1902, the GWR management intended to rebuild this very hilly and single-track branch as a high-speed double-track main line. This would have involved not only widening all bridges but also easing the fierce gradients and opening the 530-yard-long Wheatley Tunnel - all this to shorten the distance between Paddington and Kennington Junction from 61 m 12 ch to 53 m 31 ch, yet still leave the trains to squeeze through Oxford station.

It seems very likely that, if this scheme had been adopted, Oxford station would have been rebuilt with a better layout. In the end the GWR built (partly with the Great Central) a superb new route from Old Oak Common West to Aynho Junction, which cut 18½ miles off the distance between Paddington and Birmingham and avoided delays at Reading, Didcot and Oxford.

During November and December 1939 work was under way to create the extra running lines south of Kennington already mentioned in the sections on Sandford and Radley. On Saturday 30 December 1939* the first stage of the work was brought into use when what were to be the Up Relief line and Down Goods Running Loop were commissioned, with some signals, as 'Contractor's Sidings'. The former from Kennington to Sandford and the latter from Sandford to Kennington were brought into use on 28 August 1940**. The continuation of the Down Goods Loop to Hinksey South came into use on 16 June 1942, and

* GWR Signalling notice.

** R. A. Cooke, op. cit.

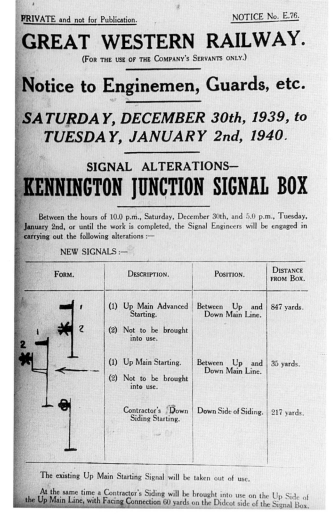

GREAT WESTERN RAILWAY.
(FOR THE USE OF THE COMPANY'S SERVANTS ONLY.)

Notice to Enginemen, Guards, etc.

SATURDAY, DECEMBER 30th, 1939, to TUESDAY, JANUARY 2nd, 1940.

SIGNAL ALTERATIONS—
KENNINGTON JUNCTION SIGNAL BOX

Between the hours of 10.0 p.m., Saturday, December 30th, and 5.0 p.m., Tuesday, January 2nd, or until the work is completed, the Signal Engineers will be engaged in carrying out the following alterations :—

NEW SIGNALS :—

FORM.	DESCRIPTION.	POSITION.	DISTANCE FROM BOX.
	(1) Up Main Advanced Starting.	Between Up and Down Main Line.	847 yards.
	(2) Not to be brought into use.		
	(1) Up Main Starting.	Between Up and Down Main Line.	35 yards.
	(2) Not to be brought into use.		
	Contractor's Down Siding Starting.	Down Side of Siding.	217 yards.

The existing Up Main Starting Signal will be taken out of use.

At the same time a Contractor's Siding will be brought into use on the Up Side of the Up Main Line, with Facing Connection 60 yards on the Didcot side of the Signal Box.

the Up Goods Running Loop from Hinksey South to Kennington and its continuation, across the branch line, into the Up Relief line was brought into use on 12 July of that year. The work here, and north and south, from Radley through to the new yards at Hinksey, the new junction to the LMS at Oxford North and on to Wolvercot Junction, was commissioned in many stages over those 2½ years.

In 1942 the 'double twist' interlocking mechanism was replaced by the standard vertical tappet mechanism as the layout reached its final form and the levers required more interlocking. The lever frame in the operating floor retained its original appearance, with levers standing almost upright at 5¼-inch centres between the original, 'flat' cast iron 'sweeps' (the metal floor plates in which the levers moved).

The Kennington signalman was very busy with trains, 'turning them out' and 'putting them in'. He used the telephone to make inquiries about 'margining' trains, or whether the yard wanted a particular train just then, but he did not have any formal function in the 'wiring' of train-running advices.

In a traffic census undertaken over 24 hours on 9/10 August 1949 to establish whether the signal box should be upgraded to give the signalman a higher rate of pay, it was found that 205 trains passed the box and the signalman made a total of 1,771 lever movements. His quietest daytime hour was from 10 am to 11 am, when he saw six trains and made 64 lever movements; his busiest daytime hour was 2 pm to 3 pm, when he signalled 12 trains and made 122 lever movements.

Between 6 pm and 6 am his busiest period was between 6 pm and 7 pm when he handled 13 trains and made 121 lever movements; his quietest period was from midnight to 1 am, with only three trains and 23 lever movements. He collected or delivered the electric train token on 46 occasions in 24 hours, usually two or three times an hour, during one hour five times, and between 1 am and 4 am not at all.

A census of the total number of trains passing the box taken over four weekly periods showed the following:

Weekending	Trains
14.8.48	1,043
16.10.48	1,179
12.2.49	1,235
9.4.49	1,226

When I was signalman at Kennington in 1968 there was a piece of mirror in the box engraved 'LNER', which came from the LNER passenger brake van that was destroyed in the rear-end collision of 1944. A goods train on the Down Goods Running Loop, hauled by No 2803, over-ran the signal at about 40 mph, the driver thinking that he was on the main line, and crashed into the back of a long train of 'Warwells', the engine of which was standing at the Red Bridge, outside Hinksey South. The rearmost vehicle was an LNER passenger brake, and No 2803 tunnelled into it, nearly halfway, and the last 'Warwell' came back into the front half of the brake, leaving the guard terrified but unharmed at the centre.

There was a curious inconsistency in the interlocking at Kennington Junction. It allowed the road to be set from the Thame branch to the Down Main without having the

Down Main to Down Goods Loop points, which were to the rear of the junction, set for the loop. Thus there was no 'trap' to protect the Thame branch in the event of a down train over-running at 'Danger' the Down Main Home signal, protecting the Thame line junction.

The correct method of dealing with this was that, if the signalman was asked 'Is Line Clear?' for a Down Main train after he had accepted a Down Branch train, he 'refused the road' because the branch junction into the Down Main was within the clearing point of the Down Main Home signal - the points lay within 440 yards of that signal. If, however, the signalman set the road for the loop he could accept the Down Main train if the loop was clear for 440 yards. But this was not forced on him by the interlocking - it was something he had to remember to do.

In British Railways days a 'County' Class engine hauling a Swindon-Longbridge 'C' Class vacuum goods on the Down Main was approaching Kennington's signals at 'Danger' when a passenger train was signalled off the branch. The signalman - who shall remain nameless - had forgotten to set the road for the loop, and this just happened to be the very day on which the 'gremlins' decided that the wheels of the goods train should skid. Its driver was unable to stop at the Home signal - the wheels had 'picked up' on the down-grade - and came on towards the junction as the passenger train came over the river bridge with the signals 'off'.

The 'County's' driver saw this, put his engine into reverse and managed to bring his train to a stand, the passenger train's coaches passing within inches of the 'County's' buffers. My friend, the railway photographer Ray Simpson, was indoors, 300 yards from the incident, but the peculiar and loud noise made by the 'County' running forward with the engine in reverse brought him out to see what was going on.

Another incident, not in GWR days but still worth recording, happened to Signalman Pete Hall, who

Right Low, summer evening light at Kennington throws the shadow of exhaust steam and the engine's cab and tender on the wall of the signal box as No 6902 *Butlers Hall* gallops down the hill from Sandford with an express in 1955. *Peter Barlow/AVC*

told me about it. He was on night shift when the door of the box burst open to admit a very agitated man, clad only in his vest and brandishing a carving knife. He had come from the Littlemore mental hospital and was demanding that a train be stopped in which he would melt into the crowd and make good his escape. Peter handled the very frightening situation with aplomb. He called for help without worrying his visitor further, and in due course the sick man was collected and taken back to the hospital.

Kennington Junction box was abolished under the Oxford MAS scheme on 15 December 1973.

The Thame branch

Nearly a mile east of Kennington Junction on the single-track line to Thame and Princes Risborough was Littlemore station, at 17 m 47 ch (from Princes Risborough) and built to serve the mental hospital there. The second signal box on the site came into use in 1892; this was a 'Type 5', 16 ft 1 in by 11 feet, the floor 7 feet above rail level, housing a 15-lever frame. It controlled access to the mental hospital siding and, from October 1928, a siding to the petrol storage depot owned by National Benzole*. It had been reduced to ground frame status by 1938 and was abolished altogether on 19 February 1951**.

* R. A. Cooke, op. cit.

** Signalling Record Society, *Signal Box Register*.

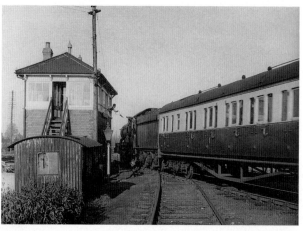

Access to the petrol depot was by levers standing in the open, locked by the single-line token.

The first signal box east of Kennington on the branch was at Morris Cowley (see the next section), 2½ miles away, all of it on steep gradients varying from 1 in 93 to 1 in 77. From 1902 until at least 1918 trains were regulated over the single line with the Electric Train Staff, but this heavy, clumsy device had been replaced by the lightweight Electric Key Token by 1935.

When a train was to pass through the single line to Morris Cowley, the Kennington signalman withdrew the key token from the instrument in his signal box - with the active co-operation of his counterpart at Morris Cowley - placed the token in its 'banjo' carrier, walked down his stairs and across the branch, and placed the token, in its pick-up hoop, on the pick-up post, then, of course, back into the box. There were about 14 steps to descend and ascend.

A 'cow's horn' set-down post was provided on which the locomen were supposed to place the token carrier as they came off the single line, but this was not often used, as the track passed close to the signal box at its north corner and the signalman, leaning out, could take the token carrier from the fireman of the passing train and save himself a journey outside.

From July 1935 streamlined diesel railcars were put to work on the Thame branch. The driver on one of these cars was alone and was unable to take up or set down the hooped token carrier in the usual way. Therefore the signalman had to go outside to hand up and retrieve the token, and to do this the token was offered up on an 18-inch or 2-foot-long rod.

Above left The guard of W15, just arrived from Morris Cowley, hands the token pick-up hoops to signalman Ron Almond in 1955. The flow of traffic was unequal - more up than down - so tokens and hoops gathered at Cowley, and Kennington had a shortage. The hoops could be returned easily enough, but the single-line tokens could only be removed from the Cowley instrument by the S&T lineman, and it was his duty to return them to Kennington. *Peter Barlow/AVC*

Left The usual way of delivering a used token at Kennington. The 'Castle's' fireman hands it up, in its hoop, to signalman Almond, again in 1955. *Peter Barlow/AVC*

Morris Cowley

Half a mile east of Littlemore, at 16 m 9 ch, the Garsington road passed under the Thame branch, and Garsington Bridge halt was opened on the west side of the bridge on 1 February 1908. The platform was closed on 22 March 1915*. This seems odd when a Government factory producing exploding mines was built to the east of the road, rail connected, and one would have thought that the platform would have been useful for the workers. These sidings and the factory had been abolished by 1922*.

In March 1926 the site was re-opened by the new Pressed Steel Co, which made the bodies for Morris cars. The Morris Motors factory was extended in 1927, running to the east of Pressed Steel and coming close to the railway line. Trains gained access through ground frames unlocked by the single-line token. The layout then lay mostly on the north side of the line between two road underbridges, covering from 16 m 6 ch to 15 m 62 ch.

The factory was turning out 55,000 cars a year, and the large traffic in materials and in the finished product demanded something better, and the signal box was opened on 24 October 1928. However, not until 1929* was the platform at Garsington road bridge re-instated. The platform was long enough to hold five or six coaches and was provided with a wooden building housing booking office, waiting room and lavatories.

The signal box was an all-timber building with a floor 25 ft 2 in by 12 ft 2 in; it was 8 feet above the rails and housed a 31-lever frame. In 1936 the box was switched out every night at 10.45 pm until 5.10 am the following day; when it switched out on Saturday night it did not come in again until 6.45 am on Monday. The single line on each side, to Kennington and Wheatley, was worked with the Electric Train Token. To switch the box out, the Cowley signalman sent 7-5-5, 'Closing signal box', to the box on each side and those signalmen replied, each holding down for several seconds their bell

key so as to release the Morris Cowley switching-out lever, No 22.

The cast iron 'sweeps' of the frame had two intermediate notches. Lever No 22 was first pulled out of the 'normal' notch to the second position, then, when an indicator on the shelf registered 'Lock Off', the signalman was able to bring the lever to the third position. Now the mechanical interlocking was disarranged so that he could lower both the up and the down direction stop signals along the single line; the Distant signals were permanently fixed at 'Caution' and could not be moved.

Having done this he brought the lever to the fourth position, fully reversed, and this action released the 'Long Section' instruments at Kennington Junction and Wheatley. These signalmen then tested bells - 16 beats - and, if all was in order, the Cowley signalman could go home. During the war the box was very rarely closed down - Albert Walker recalls doing it once only.

The layout of sidings, on both sides of the line, continued to grow, and in May 1943 a new frame of 43 levers was installed. At about this time the bomb splinter and brick blast-protection skirt was added. In 1946, on the down side at the Thame end of the layout, a siding was opened to serve a rubbish dump. Train-loads of refuse from London came here and gangs of men worked all day for years unloading the wagons.

There was a serious collision here on 12 January

R. A. Cooke, op. cit.

Morris Cowley signal box in 1968. *AVC*

1961. Hardly the GWR period, but the innocent drivers involved were GWR men. A Washwood Heath to Cowley goods had arrived behind No 48134, with my friend Driver Bill Whiter of Oxford in charge. The signalman, a fairly inexperienced man, allowed the train to come to a stand beyond the Starting signal, on the single line, at the Wheatley end of the layout. This was done in spite of the fact that he had given permission for the West London parcels train to leave Wheatley.

It was Bill's fireman who first saw the danger. He shouted to Bill, 'Blimey, Bill, here's the Parcels coming', to which Bill replied, 'Yeah! Pull the other one!'. The fireman yelled again, Bill looked up and saw the approaching train. His first thought was to run towards it waving a red light, so he looked for the gauge lamp - 'But, of course, we were on an LMS engine and they, unlike GWR engines, did not have a red glass in the gauge lamp,' Bill said disgustedly.

A moment later he realised that the situation had gone beyond waving red lights, and he jumped. He hit the ground, bounced, dived headfirst under a 'Bo-Car' on an adjacent siding, cracking his head painfully as he did so, and seconds later No 6979 Helperly Hall on the parcels crashed into the LMS engine with a quite terrifying, explosive wallop that ripped open the frames of the engines like so much banana-skin. No one was seriously injured, but the signalman resigned and the work was continued by more careful men.

The box continued to work as a block post with Oxford 'Panel' and was not closed until 28 January 1982.

Top left The diagram in 1968. AVC

Centre left Looking east towards the signal box (amongst the telegraph poles in the middle distance) from the Garsington road bridge in 1968. AVC

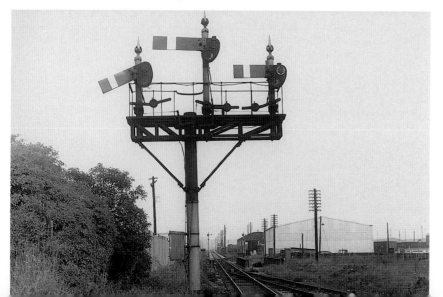

Left Looking east from remains of Morris Cowley station, again in 1968. Signal 11 is lowered, routing into the Up Siding; the centre arm is No 4, the right-hand arm No 12. AVC

OXFORD

Hinksey South

Between Kennington Junction and what was originally the next signal box north, Oxford South, at 61 m 51 ch, lay Abingdon Road Halt. The northern ends of its platforms butted against the brick arch bridge taking the said road over the railway. The halt was in use from 1 February 1908 until 22 March 1915*.

On 29 March 1942, about a mile further north, Hinksey South signal box was brought into use on the up side at 61 m 62 ch; at this stage it was called simply 'Hinksey'. It had a 72-lever frame with 11 spaces, but at that first stage only a few of its 61 levers were working. GWR Signalling Notices show that the full layout was not complete until September 1942 when the No 1 Up Goods Running Loop with its associated signals was brought into use.

The box was built of brick to the GWR's Air Raid Precautions (ARP) design (SRS designation 'Type

* R. A. Cooke, *Track Plans: Oxford*, Vol 27.

13'). The intention was to make the building, to some extent, resistant to blast and shrapnel damage, and to this end this type of box had 14-inch-thick walls and a 12-inch reinforced concrete roof*. The floor of the box was 43 ft 6 in by 13 feet, 11 feet above the rails. There was one signalman per shift without a booking lad and it opened as a Class 3 box.

An application for a re-assessment of the work was handwritten by Albert (Bert) Webb and also signed by F. G. (Fred) Weston and W. H. (Bill) Dale on 5 October 1942. The box had not been open a year, so the four-week census of trains could not be made and the marks could not be assessed - however, their strategy was that, when the census was made and the classification of the box was raised, the back pay owing to them would be calculated from the day they put in their application.

All three men were aged about 27/28 years. Bert Webb left the railway as soon as the war was over; Fred Weston went on to work Dolphin Junction, Slough, and became a Platform Inspector; and Bill Dale left the railway some time in the 1950s, lured by the double pay obtainable at Morris Motors, Cowley.

The 24-hour traffic census took place over 25/26 November 1943, and the salient points included 123 through trains and 70 starting or terminating. To handle these the signalmen made 2,362 lever movements; 23 trains were signalled then cancelled, and 19 'Shunting into forward section' movements were made and withdrawn. The box was working at

* Signalling Study Group, *The Signal Box*.

---

the Gas Works Sidings will be connected to the New Box.

Sunday, March 29th, 1942.

BRINGING INTO USE A NEW BLOCK POST BETWEEN
OXFORD SOUTH AND KENNINGTON JUNCTION SIGNAL BOXES
AT 61 m. 62 chs.

Commencing on Sunday, March 29th, a New Block Post will be brought into use between Oxford South and Kennington Junction Signal Boxes, and will be situated on the Up side of the Line at 61 m. 62 chs. The New Signal Box will be known as :—
HINKSEY SIGNAL BOX.

— HINKSEY SOUTH —

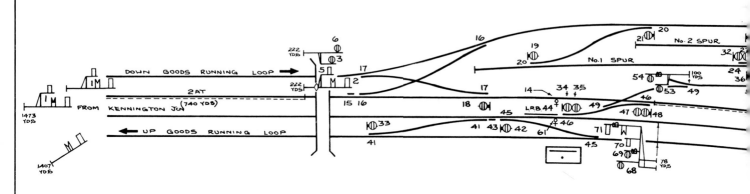

the rate of 244 marks per hour, so was upgraded to Class 2, the rise being back-dated to 29 March 1943.

Its name was changed to Hinksey South on 22 April 1944, according to a GWR memo that I have before me as I write*.

* This is hotly disputed by the signalmen; see the section on Hinksey North.

Naturally enough, once the war was over the box was less busy, but the wartime period was one where the whole railway was working at more than its full capacity, and there were enormous delays. Even in 1961, a normal eight-hour weekday shift would see the signalman dealing with 94 trains, from expresses to light engines and inter-yard 'trips'. This was very busy working.

A flavour of the sort of activity that went on can be gained from the following accident report (GWR internal report). The activity was typical, the contretemps was not. At 6.29 pm on 14 February 1947, engine No 5130, running 'light' for Banbury, was brought to a stand outside Hinksey South box, by order of Control, so that the men working it could change footplates with those working the 10.30 am (sic) Banbury-Reading goods, which was approaching on the No 1 Up Goods Running Loop.

Hinksey South box in 1955, with a '61xx' tank engine hauling a freight from the Yard to the Up Main. *Peter Barlow/AVC*

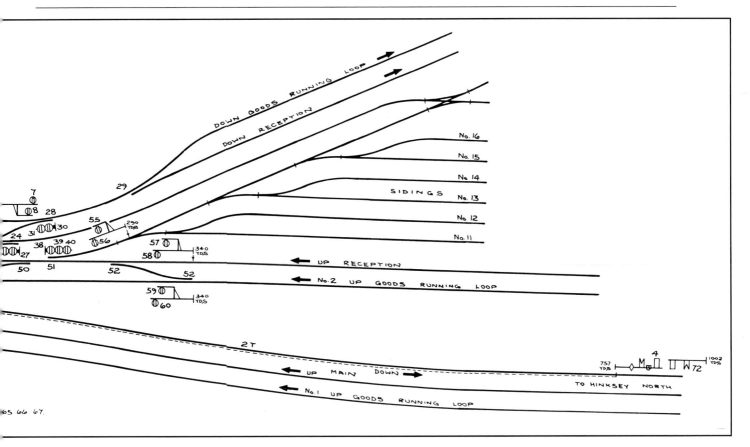

The block instrument for the Down Main was still pegged to 'Train on Line' because No 5130 was within the clearing point. At 6.34 pm Kennington phoned to say that he had a second engine waiting at his box, No 7240, also 'light for Banbury'. The two signalmen decided that they would couple the two together to save a 'path' through Oxford, so Hinksey South sent 'Train out of Section' to Kennington and accepted No 7240 under the 'Warning'. This he was perfectly entitled to do.

However, on the Down Goods Running Loop the 6.5 pm Abingdon goods was approaching, and when the Hinksey South signalman saw the headlamp of its engine at a stand at the Down Loop Home signal, he mistook it for No 7240 and lowered his Down Main home signal. A few moments later he saw the headlamp of No 7240 approaching and realised

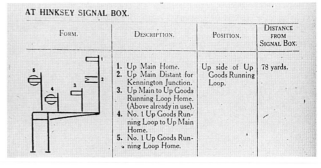

			DISTANCE
FORM.	DESCRIPTION.	POSITION.	FROM SIGNAL BOX.
	1. Up Main Home.	Up side of Up	78 yards.
	2. Up Main Distant for Kennington Junction.	Goods Running Loop.	
	3. Up Main to Up Goods Running Loop Home. (Above already in use).		
	4. No 1 Up Goods Running Loop to Up Main Home.		
	5. No 1 Up Goods Running Loop Home.		

AT HINKSEY SIGNAL BOX.

The same location looking south. The 1942 gantry is unchanged in 1970 except that the two left-hand arms have lost their 'goods line' rings. At the time that this picture was taken, the old ringed arms were lying underneath the signal box. AVC

Above Looking north towards Hinksey South along the Up Main on 15 May 1942. The Down Main to Down Goods Running Loop signal has an 'Out of Use' 'X' on the arm. It is interesting to note that this brand new signal has been constructed with timber posts when all the other signals erected in the area were in tubular steel. *GWR*

Below The dial phone on the locker top is a recent addition to an otherwise GWR scene on 12 April 1973. The working timetable and train register are open beside it, while above them on the wall is a GWR telephone call-code card in its glass and wood frame. On the wall at the extreme left of the view is the Hinksey North-Hinksey South 'box to box' phone, and above the modern dial phone is the 'Tannoy' loud-hailer to and from the shunting yard; the shunters' requests to the signalman for different routes screeched out of this. To the right of the calendar is a GWR 'eight-way' selector telephone; you turned the central black knob to the number indicated on the call-code card, then pressed the small button at the foot of the case the required number of times. *David Chipchase*

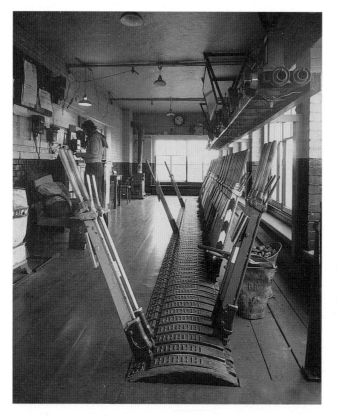

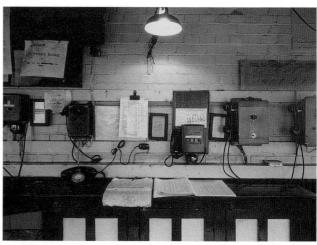

Left The spartan, 1942, interior of Hinksey South box unchanged on 12 April 1973. The author is on duty. *David Chipchase*

Above Interlocking between levers is essential to prevent conflicting routes being set up. This shows the GWR standard five-bar vertical tappet interlocking machine under the operating floor at Hinksey South in April 1973. The origin of the device dates from James Deakin's patent of 1870. Each lever has a cam plate, the ends of which are at the top of the picture. Attached to each of these is a vertical tappet blade that has notches or 'ports' cut out of it to accommodate the locks. When the lever is reversed the tappet blade will be driven downwards, displacing the locks laterally and locking adjacent tappet blades or, by means of the long horizontal bars, driving other locks into their ports in tappet blades further down the frame, locking those levers. *David Chipchase*

Right If the interlocking allowed the lever to be reversed, the drive was transmitted by a wire under and around pulleys to pull signal arms 'off', or through cranks and rodding to move the blades of points or their bolts. This is a typical scene in the locking room at Hinksey South. Nearest the camera (top right) is a long, vertical spring. When the lever is 'Normal' in the frame this spring is compressed, so when the signalman pulls the lever over, with the weight of the signal wire and signal arm balance weight attached to it, the energy stored in the compressed spring gives the lever a rapid start to build up the momentum of the pull. *David Chipchase*

that he had 'pulled off' too soon for the engine and threw the signal back to 'Danger'. The driver, however, was going too fast to stop, so fast in fact that he collided with No 5130 standing 222 yards ahead of the signal.

Stan Worsfold recalled how Hinksey South was given permission to alter its up facing points after 'Line Clear' had been given. The Chief Inspector asked him why there was so much delay to up through goods trains at Oxford. Stan reminded him that according to the standard regulations, facing points must not be altered once 'Line Clear' had been returned to the box in rear. Therefore the Hinksey South signalman, being asked 'Is Line Clear?' for an up goods train, would have to 'refuse the road' until he had decided whether to 'run it' or 'put it in'. To make this decision he had to make telephone inquiries about any following passenger train. While he was refusing the road to Hinksey North, that man had to send 2-2-2, 'Line clear to clearing point only',

to Station South, which was repeated to Station North and from the latter to North Junction. Thus the Distants were 'on' for that goods all the way from near Wolvercot Sidings.

Special dispensation was therefore given to Hinksey South to alter the up facers after 'Line Clear' had been given, provided that the train had not been 'sent on line' and Hinksey South had not pulled off for it.

As one by one the branch lines around Oxford were closed, then freight on rail generally began to go to the roads, Hinksey Yard became quieter and finally most of it was lifted - but Hinksey South was still very busy because of an increase in passenger trains. On 15 August 1973, on the 6 am to 2 pm shift, I dealt with 91 trains; between 7.23 am and 8.24 am 19 trains were dealt with, including those in and out of the yard.

The box was abolished by the Oxford MAS scheme on 15 December 1973.

Hinksey North

In 1941 work began on a new marshalling yard on the down side of the line between the old Abingdon Road and the River Thames bridge. This was a peaceful area of water meadow intersected with streams, but now the buttercups became the victims of war as the main contractor, MacAlpine, employed Italian prisoners of war to cover the area - to the depth of several feet - with cinders and other 'fill' to create a level space alongside, and to the west of, the existing railway.

Where streams crossed the site they were placed under long culverts. One of these could be seen as an concrete arch rising about 6 feet above the stream towards the north end of the site. I visited this when I was signalman at Hinksey North and saw that the Italians had signed their work. I made a note at the time, but unfortunately have since lost it. There was a man's name over the arch and below it 'Master Mason' (in English) and the name and number of the regiment to which the men belonged. The Italian PoWs were a feature of Oxford life in those days. A large number of them lived in a hutted camp on Cumnor Hill and cycled to the various railway construction sites each day, without guards, often singing snatches of opera.

Between 22 March and 5 April 1942 a new 'Oxford South' box was brought into use on the down side,

south of the river bridge at 62 m 71 ch*. It was to the GWR's 'ARP' design with a floor 43 ft 6 in by 13 feet and 11 feet above rail level. It was built by the Italians, employed, I think, by sub-contractor Hinkins & Frewin. Their bricklaying was somewhat eccentric in places; I was shown the non-bonded courses in the upper levels, above the stairwell, when I became a signalman there in 1969.

When the layout was finally complete on 30 September 1942, there were 58 working levers, two detonator-placer levers and nine spaces. It was manned by George Mundy (who retired from Station North box in the 1950s), Fred Wickson and Stanley John Worsfold.

The new box was Class 3 although it was easily worth Class 2. The signalmen did not apply for upgrading until 15 December 1942, but the letter never reached the District Inspector, and as a result of waiting for an answer and then re-applying, it was 30

---

* GWR inter-departmental letters state that the box was called 'Oxford South' until re-named 'Hinksey North' on 22 April 1944, but Stan Worsfold is adamant that the box was called 'Hinksey North' from the outset. 'If it had been called "Oxford South" to begin with they would have transferred the "Oxford South" plate, then taken it down in 1944 to replace it with a new one saying "Hinksey North" - but I've no recollection of that, and I'm sure that every time I answered the phone I said "Hinksey North".'

NOTICE No. E.20.

GREAT WESTERN RAILWAY.

(FOR THE USE OF THE COMPANY'S SERVANTS ONLY.)

Notice to Enginemen, Guards, etc.

Sunday, March 22nd to Sunday, April 5th, 1942.

OXFORD NEW YARD

Between the hours of 6.0 a.m. Sunday, March 22nd, and 6.0 p.m. Sunday, April 5th, or until the work is completed, the Signal Engineers will be engaged in carrying out the following work :—

NEW SIGNAL BOX AT OXFORD SOUTH.

Commencing at 6.0 a.m. on Sunday, March 22nd, and until the work is completed, a New Signal Box will be brought into use at Oxford South, situated on the Down side of the Line at 62 m. 71 chs.

The existing Signal Box will be taken out of use and the Block Telegraph Instruments, Telephones, etc. transferred to the New Signal Box.

New Signals will be brought into use, and Signals at present worked from the existing Signal Box will be connected to the New Signal Box as under :—

	FORM.	DESCRIPTION.	POSITION.	DISTANCE FROM NEW BOX.	REMARKS.
A		1. Up Main Starting for Oxford Goods Shed. 2. Up Main Distant. (A.T.C. Ramp at signal.)	Down side of Down Main Line.	652 yds.	Existing.
B		Up Main Home.	Down side of Down Main Line.	303 yds.	Existing.
C		1. Up Goods Running Loop Starting— Route Indicator. To Up Main. To Spur. 2. Not to be brought into use at present. 3. Up Main Starting. 4. Up Main Starting— Route Indicator. To Up Reception Road.	Gantry spanning the Up Goods Running Loop and Up Main Line.	89 yds.	New.
		1. Up Main Advanced Starting. 2. (To be brought into use after 29th March)	Down side of Down Main Line.	936 yds.	New.

August 1944 before a traffic census was undertaken.

In 24 hours, 30 August 1944, 180 trains were signalled through Hinksey North and 58 started or terminated, a total of 238 trains. There were nine pilot trips between Oxford's South End Yard and the 'New' Yard, and there were several trips in and out of Oxford gas works because, No 27 lever (see diagram), which operated three sets of point blades rather than the usual two, was moved eight times. None of these trips were, however, classed as 'trains'. The total number of lever movements was 3,659.

The bell code 2-3-3, 'Working in the wrong direction' (along the Up Goods Running Loop, known locally as the 'Old Main'), followed by 3-3-4, 'Wrong direction movement now at a stand', was used 12 times, and 'Shunting into forward section', 3-3-2, was used on the Up Goods Running Loop to Hinksey South 23 times - the loop was used as a head-shunt for the South End Yard and long rakes of wagons being drawn out required to pass the Up Loop Starting signal, No 29.

The signalmen responded on 57 occasions to a locomotive whistle code. There was also a great deal of telephone work; literally hundreds of calls had to

Looking south halfway between Hinksey North and Hinksey South on 14 May 1942. The Down Main Home signal for Hinksey North with Oxford Station South's Distant below it is on the extreme left. There is, as yet, no No 1 Up Goods Running Loop to the left of the main lines, but the No 2 Up Goods Running Loop and the Up Reception are in use, as is the Up Yard, worked from Hinksey South. The Down Yard has yet to be laid. *GWR*

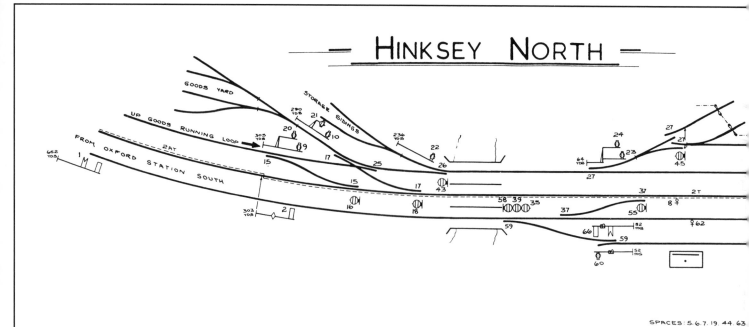

Left   Hinksey North box from the up side in 1969, together with the Down Main Starting signal above Oxford Station South's Distant. *AVC*

Right   The interior of Hinksey North box from lever 60 to lever 1. Seen in 1955, all the original instruments are still in place. *Peter Barlow/AVC*

Below   Hinksey Yard Ground Frame, working the points and signals marked 'x' on the Down Reception and Down Goods Running Loop between Hinksey North and Hinksey South.

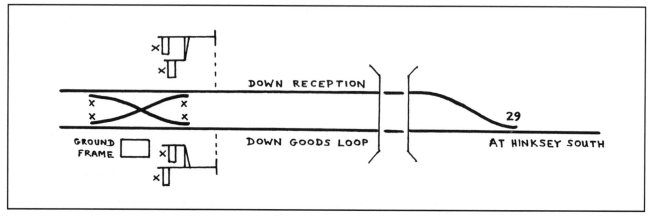

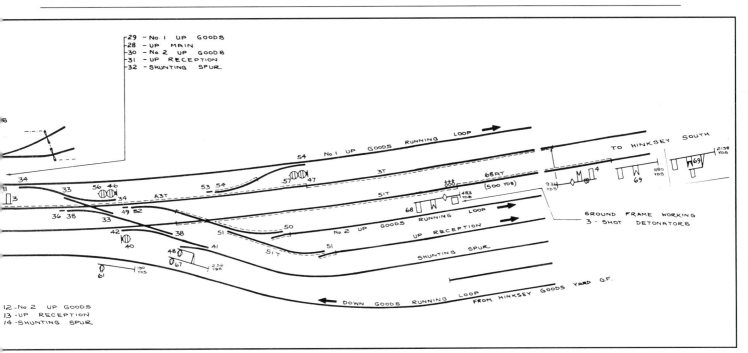

29 – No.1 UP GOODS
28 – UP MAIN
30 – No.2 UP GOODS
31 – UP RECEPTION
32 – SHUNTING SPUR

54 No 1 UP GOODS RUNNING LOOP

TO HINKSEY SOUTH

3T

68RT
(500 YDS)

No 2 UP GOODS RUNNING LOOP

UP RECEPTION

GROUND FRAME WORKING
3 – SHOT DETONATORS

SHUNTING SPUR

FROM HINKSEY GOODS YARD G.F.

DOWN GOODS RUNNING LOOP

12 – No 2 UP GOODS
13 – UP RECEPTION
14 – SHUNTING SPUR

GREAT WESTERN RAILWAY.

.(FOR THE USE OF THE COMPANY'S SERVANTS ONLY.)

Notice to Enginemen, Guards, etc.

SUNDAY, AUGUST 30th, to WEDNESDAY, SEPTEMBER 9th, 1942.

SIGNAL ALTERATIONS—

OXFORD NEW YARD

BRINGING INTO USE A NEW No. 1 UP GOODS RUNNING LOOP BETWEEN OXFORD SOUTH AND HINKSEY SIGNAL BOXES.

Between the hours of 6.0 a.m. Sunday, August 30th, and 5.0 p.m. Wednesday, September 9th, the Signal Engineers will be engaged in bringing into use a New No. 1 Up Goods Running Loop between Oxford South and Hinksey Signal Boxes.

The following New Signals will be brought into use :—

AT OXFORD SOUTH SIGNAL BOX.

FORM.	DESCRIPTION.	POSITION.	DISTANCE FROM SIGNAL BOX.
	1. Up Main Starting. (Already in use).	Gantry spanning Up Goods Running Loop and Up Main Line.	89 yards.
	2. Up Main Starting. Route Indicator. To No. 2 Up Goods Running Loop. To Up Reception Road. To Shunting Spur, (Above already in use).		
	3. Up Goods Running Loop Starting—Route Indicator : To Up Main. To No. 2 Up Goods Running Loop. To Up Reception Road. To Shunting Spur. (Above already in use). To No. 1 Up Goods Running Loop.		
	4. Up Main to No. 1 Up Goods Running Loop Starting.		

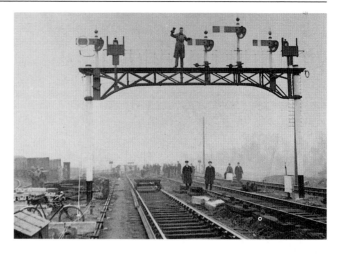

Left The 'New Works' notice for the new gantry, with Doug Constable's signature at the top.

Above Douglas Constable, New Works Inspector, waves from the newly erected gantry at Hinksey North in April 1942. *D. Constable*

be make or answered in connection with sending train running information to Reading Control, Didcot Yardmaster's office and the Traffic Regulators in Didcot East Junction and Oxford Station North.

There were in addition 99 telephone calls from the New Yard ground frame in connection with shunting movements and the release of trains from the Yard on to the Down Reception or Down Goods Running Loop. The latter, from Hinksey South to Hinksey North, was worked without bells or instruments - 'No block'. The Hinksey South signalman advised the ground frame operator what train was next, and the man at the ground frame allowed it to pass along to the exit at Hinksey North, or turned it on to the Down Reception line if it was carrying traffic for Hinksey Yard or South End Yard (see diagram).

Before a train left Hinksey Yard

Thanks to Stan Worsfold, all these men can be identified. From left to right they are Arthur Brown, Special Class Relief Signalman, Didcot; the very dignified Didcot/Oxford District Inspector, Tom Stacey; his Assistant, William (Bill) Smewin; Jack Allan, New Works Inspector from Reading Signal Works; Charlie Jarvis, Didcot Special Class Relief Signalman; and Douglas Constable, who donated the photograph. Jack Allan and Doug Constable were responsible for the signalling of new works at Oxford, Didcot-Winchester and in the Marlborough area of the M&SW section. *D. Constable*

the ground frame would identify to the Hinksey North signalman the train he was about to let go and the number of wagons it had on, so the signalman would know where it was going, and could send it onwards with the correct code. A goods train for the Banbury direction would be 'asked on' with its standard code - 3-2 for an 'E' headcode (GWR Regulations), or 1-4 for an 'H' - but a goods train for the Worcester or Fairford lines went forward as a 1-2 - 'Branch goods' - and a freight for the LMS went on as

a 3 bells. The same system applied to down freight trains not calling at Hinksey - Hinksey South signalled them forward with their 'routeing' codes.

Hinksey North was permitted to use the 'Warning Acceptance', 3-5-5, against any train, up or down, provided that there was not a passenger train inside the clearing point, and Oxford Station South was also permitted to use it - indeed, the latter had to use it so much that a large proportion of down trains would have been 'warned' into the station at Hinksey North

Right The view north from Hinksey North box in 1952. A '61xx' awaits its path on the Down Main to the station, while a 'County' has just rumbled over the river bridge. The ringed-arm signal on the right in front of the gas-holder is lowered to permit the shunters to use the No 1 Up Goods Running Loop as a 'shunting neck' for the South End Yard. The Down Goods Running Loop is nearest camera. *W. L. Kenning/AVC*

Below Oxford South End Yard from the river bridge in 1969. Hinksey North's Up Main Home signal (seen in the left distance on the 'wrong' side of the line to improve sighting on the curve) is lowered. Its Distant signal is 349 yards to the rear, just in sight a fraction to the left of the bracket signal on the Up Goods Running Loop. *AVC*

- a relatively lengthy process in the busy context of Hinksey North box.

The averages over the preceding year were as follows:

Weekending	No of trains dealt with including Sunday	Daily average
16.10.43	1,149	164
19.02.44	1,127	161
22.04.44	1,253	179
19.08.44	1,439	206

In spite of having some track circuiting to lock signals to the rear of an obstruction, the signalmen managed to find 551 occasions during the 24 hours when they put a lever collar over a lever to prevent it from being pulled. A lever collar was worth half a mark, so ingenuity was used to find every possible occasion on which to make use of one.

The result of the census was that the men were deemed to be working at 288 marks per hour, which only qualified them for Class 2 pay - as I wrote earlier, a signalman then worked hard for his wages. Hinksey North was upgraded to Class 2 as from 15 December 1943, the men receiving the back-pay.

Even in the early 1960s more down trains were accepted by Oxford Station South under the 'Warning' than under full 'Line Clear'. Although this had been the case for as far back as anyone could remember, no proper 'Warning' semaphore signal was provided in 1942 when the ideal opportunity arose. There was, however, a little wooden shelf fitted - by the GWR carpenter - to the corner post of the front window at the southern end of the box, and another such shelf was fitted on Station South box. These were to hold the signal box lamp at night. When not in use it faced the wall, but when the 'Warning' was accepted by Hinksey North (or Station South) the signalman went to the window, turned on the green aspect and faced it down the track. The train concerned was in any case 'hard checked' on its approach, and the driver well knew what to expect.

The block section from Hinksey North to Station South was only half a mile - which in theory could be passed through in 1 minute, but during the war and even into the 1950s there were periods lasting several days when the trains crept through from Hinksey North to Station South, and the next crept down from Hinksey South to Hinksey North. This was what the signalmen called 'block and block', when, as soon as 'Train out of Section' was received for the previous train, 'Is Line Clear?' had to be asked for the one standing at, or creeping down to, the Starting signal -

and almost inevitably Station South would reply with the 'Warning Acceptance', 3-5-5 on the bell.

When that train cleared Hinksey North complete with tail lamp, Hinksey North could 'knock out' to Hinksey South and at once would be 'asked' for another train. Hinksey North might well reply himself with 3-5-5 if he wanted to turn one out on to the Down Main from the Down Reception, or bring a 'trip' across all roads from South End Yard to the Up Reception, or turn a main-line freight from the Up Main to the Up Goods Running Loop No 2 or the Up Reception. To save time, it was permitted for two goods trains to run coupled, one behind the other, to a maximum of 70 wagons, from Hinksey to Wolvercot or Yarnton Junctions. The work required quick thinking and constant decision-making, upon which depended the lives of many people. And as I pointed out at the start, none of these men was what the world would have called 'educated'.

Hinksey North's Up Main Distant signal was 349 yards from its Home signal, and the intervening track was on a falling gradient of about 1 in 150 - the braking distance was practically nil. Therefore the Up Distant signal of Station South had to be recruited to act also for Hinksey's Up Home; this procedure was 'Regulation 4A'.

The system worked like this. When Hinksey North sent 'Train out of Section' to Station South for an up train, Station South might very well have another train coming up and would ask 'Is Line Clear?' to Hinksey North for it. Hinksey North now had two choices. He could 'refuse the road' to Station South until he had obtained 'Line Clear' from Hinksey South, which might mean a delay of a minute or two, or he could reply to Station South's question with the uniquely GWR code, 'Line Clear to clearing point only', 2-2-2 on the bell. If Station South acknowledged this code by repetition, Hinksey North would peg his up line instrument to 'Line Clear' and the Station South signalman would not lower his stop signals until the up train had passed his Distant signal at 'Caution'.

There was an added complication to this because Station South's Up Distant was not the full distance in rear of the Home, so if the signalman there received 2-2-2 from Hinksey North, he had to reply to Station North's 'Is Line Clear?' with 2-2-2 also, to get Station North to hold his Up Distant signal at 'Caution'. But again, Station North's Up Distant was not out at the full braking distance, so if he received 2-2-2 from Station South in reply to his 'Is Line Clear?', he had to give 2-2-2 back to North Junction, resulting in the latter holding his Up Distant at 'Caution'.

The 'bottom line' of all this was, therefore, that

when Station North was asked 'Is Line Clear?' by North Junction for an up 'runner', Station North had first to 'ask on' to Station South and Station South had to 'ask on' to Hinksey North. If the latter replied 'Line Clear', then 'Line Clear' could be returned back through the boxes, but if Hinksey North replied 2-2-2, this was repeated back to Oxford North Junction and the train had the Distants against it. This is how the cramped layout at Oxford created large delays.

Hinksey North remained a slightly busier place than Hinksey South because it dealt with the South End Yard, which remained open after Hinksey yard was all but shut. As late as 1971 it was still possible to work 100 trains (counting Yard 'trips') in an eight-hour weekday shift, with 16 trains passing the box in one hour.

The box was closed by the Oxford MAS scheme on 7 October 1973.

Oxford South

Coming from Didcot, prior to 1942, the first of the truly 'Oxford' signal boxes was 'Oxford D' (not 'A' as one might expect); it was certainly in use by 1884, and probably brought into use in 1874. It was a timber box standing on timber piles driven into the embankment and controlled access to the South End Yard.

On 31 October 1903 Reading Signal Works was ordered to provide a new signal box for this site, so I suppose that this was in operation by 1904. It was a wooden 'Type 7' box on the down side, just north of the river bridge at the 63rd milepost. It had a floor 25 by 12 feet, 8 feet above rail level, and housed a 25-lever frame, five of them spare.

The signalmen here in 1920 were A. E. Meads, W. West and J. Holland. They were paid Class 3 wages - £3 a week basic, plus a 'cost of living allowance' of 3s 6d. They felt that this was not enough for the work they did, and on 31 August 1922 they applied to have the work assessed with a view to a pay rise. The final part of their submission reads as follows: 'That as a large amount of work is mental, we are of the opinion that the system of marks does not record it. As example in the regulating of up goods trains through Oxford, the following boxes all look to us for advice or instructions: Wolvercot Junction, Oxford North, Oxford Engine Shed and Oxford Goods Shed. While ahead of us we have to keep continually in touch with Didcot North Junction, and Kennington Junction and in some cases Reading Control Office. In addition we have to consider the requirements of the yard shunting staff. It will be seen that we are called upon continually to make decisions and give definite replies over the telephone which carries as much importance and is as arduous as the plain routine of train signalling, but which is not recorded by the marks system.'

The letter finished by reminding the Company that it had agreed to take account of 'exceptional conditions affecting the responsibility of the signalman'.

The letter was a good try - and is also illuminating as to the work involved in trying to work a heavy traffic through a bottleneck. A memo from the Divisional Superintendent's Office to the Office of the Superintendent of the Line states that 'there are no exceptional circumstances requiring consideration at this box', and the application was refused. The men nagged away and their request for the marks to be taken was finally granted on 20 February 1920. Every lever movement, bell code and telephone call was counted for 24 hours and the result was a disaster - the box was found not to qualify for Class 3 pay, but only Class 4. The Superintendent's office asked the DSO's office if South box wages should therefore be reduced. The reply - 'Although on a marks basis the men do not qualify for Class 3 pay, I do not recommend any alteration in classification' - was signed personally by F. R. Potter, the Divisional Superintendent.

Traffic on the railway increased over the following decade, and on 28 September 1936 the Oxford South crew of signalmen - B. Howell, F. Tritton and G. W. (George) Mundy - applied for an upgrading. The census was taken over the 24 hours 17/18 November 1936, and showed that in that period 187 trains were signalled through and 53 goods trains started or terminated at the South End Yard. That was 240 trains, against an average, taken over the whole year, of 238.5 per day. The signalmen made 1,209 movements with their 15 working levers, they gave verbal messages in the course of their signalling duties to 18 engine drivers, and sent or received 455 train-running messages. They were working at 191 marks per hour, thus qualified for a rise from Class 4 to 3!

At some periods during the census the box was very busy. From 3 to 4 pm the signalman handled 15 trains with 96 lever movements, but the 24-hour average was let down by the very quiet period on nights from 1 to 6 am, with 29 trains requiring 146 lever movements.

Oxford Goods Shed/Station South

Oxford 'C', or 'Oxford Goods Shed', was in use by 1885 and controlled the entrance/exit to the south end of the station. In 1906/7 the GWR was planning to improve the station's accommodation, but there seem to have been some changes of plan and therefore some delay before it was finalised. The records are themselves confused. A new box was ordered for the site on 23 March 1907 and again on 5 May 1908 - or this might be the date that the new signal box came into use. It was a wooden 'Type 7' on the down side of the line, 28 chains north of Oxford South, at about 63 m 38 ch. The floor in this box measured 38 by 13 feet and was 11 feet above the rails. It housed a frame of 47 working levers plus two detonator levers and eight spares.

There was one signalman per shift and no booking lad. Only 'skeleton' booking was carried out - delays to passenger trains and times of goods trains putting off traffic. The three signalmen in 1923 were J. Gardener, W. Sweetzer and W. Phillpotts. The box was a Class 2, the signalmen receiving a basic wage of 65 shillings (£3 5s) a week in that year.

The period after 1918 was unsettled. The Great War had shaken the old ideas and changed outlooks, and after the 1919 strike a national wages structure for all grades of railwaymen and women had been instituted. Some signal boxes were at once reclassified, including Oxford Goods Shed. Then problems arose in the way the new marks system worked, and some re-negotiation had to take place. It was May 1922 before the standard national system for railway wages was finally agreed and from that date brought into use.

The marks system tried to take into account every possible action the signalmen would make and gave percentage allowances for things like telephone calls and carrying out the 'Warning' procedure. A certain discretion was also allowed in border-line cases or where there was an added mental strain; a box falling just short of the higher grade might be given it. The new arrangements gave less grand titles to signal boxes - 'Specials' became 'Class 1' and thus upset the old classifications of signal boxes and appeared to create inconsistencies. But there had been as much inconsistency under the old, purely GWR, system.

Each grade looked at rises granted to others, signalmen reckoned they were less well paid than other grades and also looked at the classification of the boxes on each side of them and thought they ought to be paid more. For several years after 1919/22 the argu-

ments went on between the signalmen at a box and the Management as to which class they should be in.

The system tried to be fair, but it was difficult to meet every curious eventuality amidst hundreds of very individualistic signal boxes. Under the GWR system of assessment, Wolvercot Sidings, a glorified 'passing' box, was on a par with the very much more responsible work done at Wolvercot Junction and Kennington Junction - they were all 'First Class'. Under the new national pay rates for signalmen, they were all 'Class 3'. This demonstrates the other difficulty with the new system - the men's status, 'First Class' in this instance, was reduced.

The Oxford Goods Shed signalmen in 1914 had been rated 'Special' Class at 34 shillings a week, but under the new system they were called 'Class 2' at 65 shillings a week. Whether 65 shillings would buy in 1920 what 34 shillings would have bought in 1914 is a moot point. The wages were the signalmen's prime concern, but the lack of the title 'First Class' I am sure had some irritant effect.

The Goods Shed signalmen expressed the prevalent feeling of the period 1919-26 and in their letter asking for a pay rise show how signalmen were less well paid than they had been. Part of this letter reads:

'We also consider that our position as (sic) deteriorated in comparison with other grades whereas our responsibility as (sic) not decreased.

'Comparisons: Drivers 6/- to 8/- a day of 10 hours in 1913, now 15/- a 8-hour day. 100% increase in pay for fewer hours.

'Firemen 4/- per day of 10 hours in 1913, now 11/- a day of 8 hours. Nearly 300% increase for fewer hours.

'Passenger guards 27/- to 30/- per week of 60 hours in 1913, now 65/- for 48 hours. Over 100% increase for fewer hours.

'Special Class Signalmen, 34/- per week of 48 hours in 1913, now 65/- for 48 hours. 90% increase and no reduction in hours. [Oxford Goods Shed had been rated 'Special' Class in 1913 and from 1919 was graded Class 2 for pay.]

'Hoping you will give our case favourable consideration,

'Yours respectfully. . .'

The men maintained that theirs was a particularly strenuous post because the single signalman on duty

Right Oxford Goods Shed box seen from the Osney Lane footbridge on 12 November 1929. No 418 of the Southern Railway's 'L12' Class is on a Newcastle-Bournemouth express; this engine had been a regular performer on this run since 1914. The three-'doll' signal routes, from the left, to the southern end of the down platform; to the northern end of the down platform through the 'scissors' crossing, and to the through Down Main line. *Dr Jack Hollick/AVC*

Below right Twenty years later in 1949, the scene shows carriages and the Station Pilot in West Midland sidings on the left, a Southern 'Pacific' and an ex-LNWR 0-8-0 on the No 1 Up Siding, otherwise known as 'Mark's Hole'. *R. H. G. Simpson*

had to marshal passenger train formations between the main lines and the sidings, and because they had to keep all their 'acceptances' and the progress of the train service in their memories - the box did not have a booking lad and the signalman was exempted from keeping a record because he was so busy. However, the DSO declined to raise their pay - they were 45 marks short of a Class 1 and there was in his opinion nothing extra-special about the place.

But of course the marks were finally taken and it was found that in the 24 hours of 26 September 1923 the box handled 210 through trains and another 114 that started or terminated at Oxford. Many of the through trains would have required 'tailing', or the train engine would have been uncoupled to go to a siding or Through line to attach or detach vehicles, and of course all the starting/terminating trains would have been shunted into sidings and re-marshalled. 3,393 lever movements were counted. Besides these the signalmen 'blocked back' 15 times to protect shunting movements, they used the special 'Running round train' bell signal six times and, of course, the 'Warning Acceptance' for many of the trains. They also dealt with 353 train reporting messages. In the whole of that week 1,889 trains passed the box.

On the early turn, 6 am to 2 pm, they handled 98 trains and made 1,192 lever movements, on late turn, 96 trains at 1,492 levers, but the average was affected by the relatively quite night shift - 80 trains for 727 levers. The box scored 281 marks, 19 below the minimum for Class 1.

It is worth mentioning here that the Starting signals, the signals giving access to the sections in advance, were not electrically locked with the 'Line Clear' indication on the instruments. This was also the case at the Engine Shed (later Oxford North) box, and this situation existed until 1972. The signalman had always to remember not to pull his Starter unless and until he had received 'Line Clear'.

The signalmen were disappointed, then realised that they had not been credited with any marks for the fact that they did *almost no booking*. Their point was that they had the extra mental responsibility of remembering what was happening, rather than being able to consult the train register - and this when they were running 'trips', empty carriages and light engines through the station over the 'wrong' road, for example down the up road.

Both Goods Shed and Engine Shed signalmen

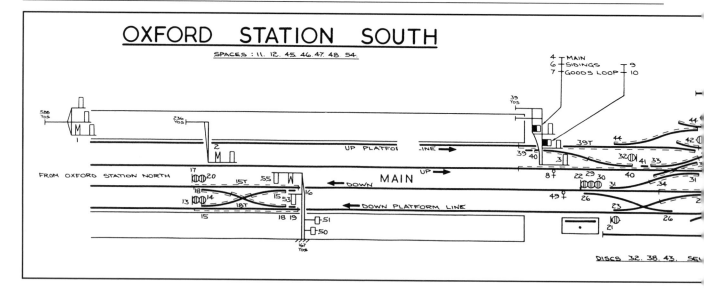

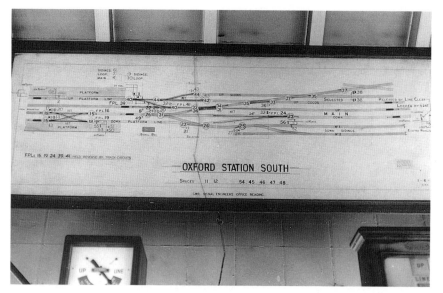

Left The diagram is dated 1.6.31 and was drawn and painted by 'D. M. C' - Donald Metford Clarke. It conforms to a style developed by Arthur Knight from 1899: main lines are coloured grey (track-circuited lengths of line have a red line within the grey), goods and platform lines are brown, and the signal box is represented by a red rectangle shaded on two sides with black. Points are marked by double black circles shaded in bright yellow, the number of the operating lever in black within the circle. The pre-1942 name of the signal box has been very skilfully changed without any damage to the paper. Photographed in 1966. *AVC*

Below Station South box in 1970, still with its 1942 brick 'skirt' and the splendid 'ladder' crossover leading towards it from No 1 Up Siding. *AVC*

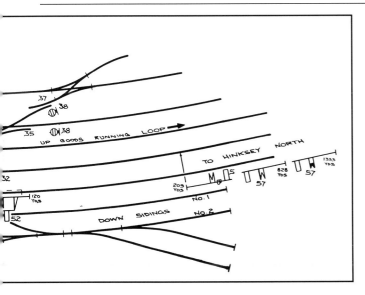

found occasions when they had to send the Station Pilot into the occupied section in advance in order to remove or attach vehicles from the rear of a stationary train. This movement had no bell code to signal it, nor was there any special signal to lower for the movement - one could not 'pull off' the Starter for a movement into an occupied section. The signalmen came to an understanding on the 'box to box' telephone as to what was to be done, and the man initiating the shunt went to the window and told the men to pass his Starter and go on to the back of the train. These movements were not recorded in writing and this working remained the practice until the end of

Oxford Station South in gleaming GWR trim - in 1970. The signalman is Arthur Lane, whose career spanned 50 years. AVC

semaphore signalling at Oxford. The Company argued, but finally accepted the 'mental strain' claim on 18 January 1924. The men were raised to Class 1 status - 70 shillings a week, back-dated to 1 May 1922. That settled matters for 50 years.

The layout controlled from the box was lacking one important set of points - from Up Main to Up Goods Running Loop or No 1 Siding. Trains calling at South End Yard could, if the southern part of the Up Platform line was unoccupied, be turned into that line at the central 'scissors' points and run through the platform directly to the Goods Loop/No 1 Siding. The only other way was to send the train 'up the main' to Oxford South and let it reverse into the yard there.

This was the mirror image of the situation on the down side at the north end of the station, where there was no access to the shed or Down Goods Running Loop from the Down Main direct, but only via the down 'scissors'. This parsimony wasted time and caused delays. At Oxford Goods Shed box the necessary connection was laid in on 4 May 1931*.

The box was given a brick skirt up to window sill level to protect the timber walls from bomb blast some time in 1942, and was also probably re-named Oxford Station South in that year.

The working at Station South was cramped. The distance from Station South's Down Home to the Down Starter was only 287 yards - thus Station South's clearing point lay 153 yards into Station North's section, so the former could not give 'Line Clear' to Hinksey North until he had received 'Train out of Section' from Station North, thereby proving that the down line for 440 yards ahead of Station South's Home signal was indeed clear.

Station North's Down Home signals were only 230 yards ahead of Station South's Down Starting signals, so if a train was standing at either of Station North's Down Home signals it might well extend into the clearing point of Station South's Home signal.

Suppose Hinksey North was 'asking on' a down train destined for the Down Platform line, which was occupied, but at the time of 'asking' the Down Main was clear through to Station North. Station South signalman would set the road for the Down Main and accept the train at 'Line Clear', and when it had come to a stand at his Down Home signal, reverse the road for the Platform line. There were many circumstances, many 'ifs' and 'buts'.

When Station North asked 'Is Line Clear?' to Station South on the Up Platform line for a passenger train that was booked to stop at Oxford, Station South could return 'Line Clear' if (a) the road was set

from Up Platform to Up Main and the Up Main was clear for 440 yards ahead of the Home signal, or (b) if the road was set for the Up Goods Running Loop and that line was clear for 440 yards ahead of the Up Platform Line Home signal. If he had no clearing point on either the Goods Loop or the Up Main, he replied to 'Is Line Clear?' with the 'Warning Acceptance' - provided that there was not a passenger train within the clearing point. If there *was* a passenger train within the clearing point he would 'refuse the road'.

It was permitted to admit a second train to an occupied platform, using the 2-4-2 acceptance code. But there was no point at all in admitting a 10-coach train into a platform already occupied by a 10-coach train when the whole platform could only hold 14 coaches.

The 2-4-2 bell code could be used by Station South or Station North for the Up and Down Platform lines respectively. As already mentioned, neither box was provided with 'Calling-on' or 'Warning' signals to provide a formal indication to the driver of the conditions under which he was to proceed. When Station South received 2-4-2 from Station North, the Station South man brought the train nearly to a stand at his Down Home signal, No 56, then lowered the arm. As the engine came past the box the signalman stood at the window, held up one finger and shouted 'In behind one'.

During fog or falling snow, when the approaching driver would not be able to get a good view of the rear of the train ahead, a competent man from the station who knew the position of the train at the platform was sent to signal 56. He boarded the engine and piloted the driver into the platform.

The procedures of Regulation 4A applied at Station South on the Up Main line and have already been described in the section on Hinksey North .

Station work was carried out on the main lines, which would frequently be occupied when Hinksey North or Station North 'asked the road' for a train, so Station South would be obliged to reply with the 'Warning Acceptance'. On the up side fresh engines for changing stood in 'Mark's Hole', the engine line next to the Up Goods Running Loop, but also on the Up Main or Up Goods Loop - wherever a space could be found. The Station Pilot worked out of West Midland Sidings on the down side by the signal box, where empty coaches were stabled.

Engines, with or without vehicles attached, were permitted to run in the wrong direction between Station South and Station North over any line, as well as running down the Up Goods Running Loop between Hinksey North and Station South. If either the Station North or Station South signalman

---

* R. A. Cooke, op. cit.

Right It was permitted to run transfer trips of unbraked wagons to and from North End and South End Yards without a brake van in the rear - but with a tail lamp on the draw-hook of the last vehicle. With the abolition of North End Yard there were fewer occasions when this permission was used, but it was useful when empty or loaded wagons of locomotive coal had to be worked to and from Hinksey Yard and the engine shed. Here in 1953, No 1935 and a '61xx', coupled together to save a 'path' through the busy station, are signalled 'up the Main', taking coal tubs to Hinksey North's Up Reception Line, whence they can be shunted into the Up or Down Yards. The engines will then go about their scheduled business. The middle signal arm routes from Up Main to Up Goods Running Loop or No 1 Up Siding, the lowest arm, with route indicator, from Up Platform to Up Main, Loop or No 1 Siding. *J. B. Snell*

Centre right Stepping back in time to Station South box as 'Oxford Goods Shed', on 14 February 1932. We are looking south from the up platform beside the locomotive water tower (in approximately the same position as the previous photograph), and single-line working is in progress as a 'Star' Class on a Paddington-Hereford express, having reversed from Down Main to Up Main, now runs 'down' the Up Main into the Up Platform. I believe single-line working was in progress because of laying a new connection from the Down Main to the engine shed. Note that access to the signal box was by an outside stair running up the rear wall of the box. *Dr Jack Hollick/AVC*

The view from Station South box in 1952: a 'Lord Nelson' in the up platform, 'Jubilee' No 45674 *Duncan* on the Up Main, and a 'Hall' on the Down Main. *W. L. Kenning/AVC*

required to make such a 'wrong direction' movement, he could send 1 beat for 'Call Attention' followed by either 1-6, 'May an engine or engine with vehicles attached run down the up line?', or 4-2, 'May an engine ditto up the down Line?'.

If the signalman receiving either of these codes was able to accept the movement towards his signals in the wrong direction, he repeated the bell code and went on the telephone to give his permission verbally. If he had already accepted a train from the rear on the same line of rails, he could not permit the wrong direction movement. In that case he did not acknowledge the bell code, but went on the phone to say 'No'. If, however, all was in order, the signalman initiating the movement placed his block instrument for the line to 'Train on Line'. The movement 'stopped the shop' at the signal box towards which it was running, until it came to a stand.

When the wrong direction movement arrived at the signal box at the other end of the station, the signalman there went on the phone and told the man from whom the movement had come: 'Train arrived'. With this the block instrument could be released from 'Train on Line'. These workings were not permitted during fog or falling snow. The signalmen had really to 'work' the station, to use their wits and experience, along with the rules and regulations, to do the best they could.

The 'scissors' crossovers at the centre of the down platform were worked from Station South, those at the up platform from Station North. The crossovers were not scheduled to be used by many trains - which was just as well, because when the points were operated they were so clogged with rubbish swept off the platform that they were heavy to pull and quite often could not be bolted owing to an obstruction between the blade and the stock rail. The down 'scissors' rodding was often clogged with soggy newspaper after the 3.25 am Paddington-Banbury 'Papers' had unloaded and the debris brushed on to the track.

Some down trains arrived at Oxford for two destinations - Birmingham and Hereford, for example - and were split at the down platform. The front half would normally leave first - maybe for Birmingham - then the engine for the second part would reverse along the Down Platform line. Station North would ask 4-2 to Station South, and telephone: 'That's the engine for the Hereford - give him the dummy' (the ground signal at the 'scissors').

If it was required to push some vehicles northwards out of the Down Platform line through the 'scissors' to the Down Main, this movement would pass beyond Station South's Starting signal, No 51, to enter Station North's section. The Station South signalman, being advised by the shunters what was required, would 'put a shunt on' - send 1-3-1, 'May a train shunt towards your Home Signal?', to Station North. Provided that Station North had not 'pulled off' for a train to leave the north end of the Down Platform, he could accept the 1-3-1 and 'peg up Line Clear' for the movement to take place. 'Train entering Section' was then sent. If the shunt went through to Station North, the latter sent 'Train out of Section'; if it returned, 'wrong road', along the Down Main to Station South, the latter sent 8 beats to Station North and the block instrument was then 'unpegged'.

When vehicles were moving about the station there was always danger for the passenger shunter(s) working with them. This came from other trains passing where the men were standing or coming out, almost on all fours, from between coaches where they had been coupling/uncoupling - or they were in danger from the train on which they were working.

The Passenger Yard Foreman in 1947 was George Greenaway. On 17 January 1947, a bitter cold day, the 6.20 am Paddington stopped at the down platform and, as there were no shunters available, George got down on the track intending to uncouple the usual two vehicles from the rear. He had therefore got down unseen and without telling anyone.

He had just got between the vehicles when - to use the words of his own report - 'to my astonishment the train began to move forward. I hung on to the drawbar hooks and vacuum pipes and I was carried to the north end of the down platform, a distance of approximately 200 yards, before the train came to a stand.

'I then ascertained that Shunter K. [Ken] Smewin, who was on the down platform, had noticed me between the vehicles as they passed him and had rushed into the brake van and stopped the train by applying the brake setter. Shunter Hill was the person responsible for giving authority for the train to draw out of the platform.'

Oxford Station South box was abolished by the Oxford MAS scheme on 7 October 1973.

Operating Oxford Station

The signalman operating a signal box was either 'regular' in the box or he was a 'relief' man. The latter was particularly skilled because he had to know the timetable for every box he was required to work. Culham was a simple box to work and any relief signalman new to that place would have picked up the working in a glance at the diagram and the lever badges. The complications were somewhat greater at Radley, greater still at Kennington Junction, far more so at the Hinksey boxes and very great at the three Oxford boxes - Station South, Station North and North Junction.

No signalman going to learn the latter boxes would be a beginner, but would have had some years of lesser experience elsewhere. He would feel the need to *learn* the new place. The lever frame appears to be the most complicated part of a signal box, but that is not what took the most time to learn. However complicated the frame was, the train service and the shunting movements took much more time to learn.

To work successfully at a busy place such as the area from Hinksey South to North Junction, the signalman had to think quickly, make quick decisions and only then move rapidly along his levers, pulling this one, putting that one back. The whole train service for the 24 hours was in his head, together with the shunting movements performed by each train. He had to remember what was going to be required in 10 or 20 minutes when he made a decision with a train now.

The greatest skill of a successful signalman was to learn to judge timings so as to be able to make correct decisions. He would learn how many minutes trains took to carry out movements - how long before they 'wanted' his Distant after being 'asked', how long to 'get across the road' with the Pilot. At Culham this skill was not much required, but at Hinksey North or Station South it was very important. In the end it became as automatic and instinctive as a car driver judging the width of his vehicle; then the signalman was settled comfortably into the job, knowing precisely how his operation fitted into the overall working of the route and having his own particular piece of it 'at his fingertips', always knowing what was coming next so as to be ready for anything.

The added skill for the relief man was to have all this 'un-bookable' knowledge in his head for maybe 20 signal boxes, and be able to take up the working of any of them as if he had been doing it daily for years,

when this shift might have been his first in that box for several weeks.

The routine of bell codes was basic. Apart from the obvious purpose of the codes - to ask 'Is Line Clear?' or send 'Train Entering Section', etc - they had an added purpose. On receipt of a bell code the signalman knew where the train was and, depending on the 'class' of train, how many minutes away it was. Thus the signalmen tried to send the bell codes promptly and always when the train was in the same position.

To take the down line as an example, the 'Is Line Clear?' code for a passenger train for Oxford stopping at Didcot was 'asked' from Moreton to Didcot West End, and the latter 'held' the code until the station staff 'rang the train out'. At that point Didcot West End 'asked on' to Didcot North, who 'gave the road' back to West End and 'asked on' to Appleford, who in turn at once 'asked on' to Culham; the latter 'held the block'. A passenger train for Oxford via the Didcot Avoiding Line was 'asked on' from Moreton through all the boxes as far as Culham.

When Appleford received 'Train Entering Section' ('TES') from Didcot North, he sent 'Train Approaching' ('TA') to Culham, who then 'got the road' from Radley and 'pulled off' his signals. Culham sent 'TES' to Radley, and Radley 'got the road' from Kennington Junction. When Radley sent 'TES' to Kennington, the latter 'asked on' to Oxford Station South, who 'asked on' to Station North. Therefore when a down train was 'asked' to Station South, the signalman there knew that it was 'just off Radley' - provided, of course, that the 'Is Line Clear?' was not asked the moment he gave 'Train out of Section' for the previous one. If that was the case the signalman could not be sure where the train was - it might have just passed Radley, or it might be waiting at Hinksey North. If Station South wanted to know he would have to telephone a box.

If the train was to run non-stop through Oxford, the 'Is Line Clear?' was sent through to Wolvercot Siding. If the train called at the station, the 'Is Line Clear?' was 'asked on' by Station North when the station staff 'rang the train out' - and again it went as far as Wolvercot Siding. When North Junction sent 'TES' to Wolvercot Siding, the latter 'asked on' to Wolvercot Junction, and the signalman there at once 'got the road' either from Yarnton Junction or Kidlington.

With the introduction of Sandford and the

No 2975 *Sir Ernest Palmer*, the 'Saint' Class engine involved in the unsaintly crash at Appleford in November 1942, seen here on the Up Middle road with a stopping train, apparently waiting to enter the Up Platform line via the 'scissors'. A Maunsell coach is alongside, so probably the train at the platform is a Birkenhead-Bournemouth; the date is 14 May 1932. *Dr Jack Hollick/AVC*

Hinksey boxes matters were so arranged that, when the train passed Radley, the 'Is Line Clear?' went through to Oxford station as before.

Oxford station was a great interchange point, for services (both GWR and 'foreign') coming in from eight main or branch lines, a fact belied by its apparently simple layout and few platforms. As we have seen, it was this frugality of accommodation that made the place such a delight for enthusiasts and such a difficult place to work for the staff. To increase their difficulties was that fact that it was a rural backwater as far as that most vital matter was concerned - communications.

Prior to 1924 all long-distance railway communications were by the single-needle telegraph instrument or the morse sounder. Local communication circuits between signal boxes were usually also by single-needle, although of course there would have been, by 1924, some provision of telephones; Paddington station had an internal telephone network, comprising a switchboard and satellite telephones, by 1910.

It was in 1924 that the GWR began to install its long-distance or 'trunk' telephone routes. By December 1930 the system extended from Paddington to Penzance via Newbury and via Bristol, to South Wales via Gloucester and Badminton, and Paddington to Chester via High Wycombe, Banbury, and Birmingham; Worcester was an exchange at the end of the trunk route from Birmingham.

Under this system people with a telephone connected to a trunk line exchange could ring through to an office somewhere else on the system. However, Newbury, for example, could not be reached directly from Paddington exchange but only through the agency of the switchboard at Reading; but there was a direct line from Paddington to Swindon. The trunk scheme, primitive though it seems now, was a large improvement on the morse sounder or single-needle system.

Like Newbury, Didcot and Oxford were not accessible by telephone from the rest of the railway except as extensions of Reading exchange. Oxford was one of the last important stations to be given its own exchange and thus become part of the trunk telephone system. The switchboard, with a single, female, operator, was installed during 1932; Stan Worsfold recalls holding the soldering iron or threading wires through holes for Jack Hall, one of the installers.

My friend the late Dr Jack Hollick attended Oxford University from 1928 to 1932, where he studied medicine - with railway operating as an important extracurricular subject, taken on the platforms of Oxford station and on the trains. How he graduated is a marvel, since he spent so much time with the station staff, the guards and Travelling Ticket Inspectors (TTIs) on the trains. Graduate he did, however, and became a well-loved General Practitioner in Derbyshire, generally known as 'Dr Jack'.

Jack frequently described trains as 'delightful', and the more eccentric they were, the more was the delight. He was fascinated with the complications of Oxford station's operation; the marshalling and re-marshalling of passenger trains, the way that the carriage sets were utilised for the different services and the complicated formations within certain trains. As has already been mentioned, Jack, travelling with the TTI, became very expert and produced a guide book for the use of the ticket staff on and off the trains! Given that Mr Buckingham was the most energetic Station Master, he must have had some idea of what was going on and must have given Jack's activities his tacit approval.

In a letter he wrote to me in 1975, Jack said of the station in 1930:

'The engine shed was the most primitive I ever saw at a station of the importance of Oxford, although Didcot ran it a close second. At Didcot, by the way, the Oxford branch platform could only hold three coaches and it was used by Swindon-line as well as Oxford-line stopping trains.

'But Oxford was *fun*! "Castles" were rare in my time - it was mostly "Stars", "Saints", "Halls" and 2-6-0s - but there was a "City" working to Wolverhampton each morning. I have delightful memories of the place. On a Saturday lunchtime there were crowds of football supporters wishing to be taken to Reading. One train they could catch was the 11.30 Malvern Wells. This was an express to Paddington, leaving Oxford at about 1.50 pm*, and slipping a coach at Reading at about 2.25. At about 1.40 the express would arrive, maybe behind a "Hall" or perhaps a "Star". It consisted of the Malvern portion - Brake 3rd next to the engine, Dining Car, Composite Class coach, Brake 3rd - the Stourbridge coach attached at Worcester, and the Cheltenham portion, which came across the Cotswolds through Bourton and Stow and consisted of a Brake Composite with a slip coach behind that. These two and maybe a horse box on the rear were attached at Kingham. The carriage roof-boards proclaimed "PADDINGTON, OXFORD, WORCESTER & MALVERN: PADDINGTON, OXFORD, WORCESTER, KIDDERMINSTER & STOURBRIDGE JUNCTION". I can't remember if the Cheltenham coaches had boards.

'Mr Buckingham and all his staff would be on the platform trying to tell everyone "Rear two coaches for Reading". When the train came to a stand the Pilot came on the back to pull off the horse box; the Carriage & Wagon man went between the slip and the main train to fit the adaptors to the vacuum pipes and to re-couple the coach to the train, using the hinged draw-hook on the slip coach; the guard changed his tail-lamps; and the mob of football fans surged forward on to the train. The station staff then had to get them out of the main train and into the Reading portion.

'Come 1.50, the driver is blowing his whistle and still the football people are arriving for the

* Actually due at Oxford from 1.44 to 1.52 pm in 1930.

An ex-Great Central 4-4-0, Class 'D9' under the LNER, hauling a varied assortment of coaches, stands at the up platform *circa* 1930. The two coaches next the engine might be ex-LNWR, followed by a Southern, followed by some Gresley stock. The train has come from Nottingham and, after an engine change, will go to the South Coast resorts. *Dr Jack Hollick/AVC*

train - these are early passengers for the 2.25, a Birkenhead to Bournemouth calling at Reading West, fairly close to the football ground - and the rear two coaches of the Malvern are crammed. Out beyond Engine Shed box the 1.5 pm Saturdays Only from Witney is blowing for the board, and the "SO" stopping train from Kingham is probably at North box with the Birkenhead to Bournemouth creeping up from Wolvercot Junction to Wolvercot Siding.

'Mr Buckingham decides he needs an extra coach for the Reading portion and sends the Pilot off to get it from the Up Sidings. The extra coach is attached at about 2 o'clock, and with the joyous football fans scattered throughout the length of the train - only the tail of which is going to stop at Reading - Buckingham decides to have the whole train stopped at Reading rather than make the slip*.

The 1.50 departure leaves at 2.5 and now they have the Witney, the Kingham and the Birkenhead queuing up to be dealt with. The Birkenhead would have that horse box attached at the rear while the engine that had brought it from Birmingham, a 2-6-2 tank, was changed for a Churchward 2-6-0.'

Jack saw the Michelin experimental road/railcar at Oxford on the afternoon of 24 April 1932; Michelin gave away tickets and he took a ride as far as Reading. The car did not operate the track circuits, nor was it fitted with the ATC, and travelled rather cautiously at 45 mph. The speed was known because there was a speedometer in the saloon for the benefit of the pas-

* Normally slipped at Reading, via the Platform line, at 2.24 pm. Mr Buckingham would write out and hand to the driver of the Malvern a 'Special Stop' order and would cause to be 'wired' to Reading the message 'SLIGO. 11.30 Malvern' ('The following train will stop instead of slipping at your station').

sengers. It seemed to be a less than serious train and Jack was not impressed.

Now, a 'delightful' train for Dr Jack was the 'Morris Cowley to Birmingham Workmen's' (unadvertised), passing Oxford non-stop on the Down Main at 5.20 pm, formed with a string of old Dean clerestories hauled by a 'Duke' or a 'Bulldog'. And a really 'grand' train was the 4.45 pm Paddington-Hereford; in 1930 this came into Oxford formed of two coaches for Hereford, two for Kidderminster, Restaurant Car for Worcester, a slip and Composite for Cheltenham via Honeybourne and Broadway, slipped at Moreton, and behind this an articulated set for the 'all stations' to Worcester.

The train was booked to arrive at Oxford at 5.55, and 5 minutes only was allowed to divide the train behind the Cheltenham portion and to load and unload; the express portion left at 6 pm. The engine for the stopping section backed on and left at 6.8 pm, and that was followed by the 6.15 pm to Fairford out of the Down Bay.

It was normal practise to run the trains combined in several sections to the point of junction, not just to Oxford but also to Swindon and elsewhere. On Sundays in 1930 there was the '10.10 Paddington, Shrewsbury and West Midlands' express. This arrived at Oxford at 11.34 with, for some unknown reason, the Shrewsbury portion on the rear - although it was booked to leave first, at 11.45. Therefore the train was divided at Oxford and the Worcester portion was drawn forward, leaving the 'scissors' crossing clear. An engine then ran from the shed, up the Down Main and on to the Shrewsbury part through the 'scissors'. The front part left at 11.45. The '12.45 Paddington, Banbury and Cheltenham' express was treated in the same way.

Inter-company trains were a great feature of Oxford. One of these was the 7.20 am Southampton-Newcastle/1.2 pm Newcastle- Southampton, carrying through coaches for Scarborough, Newcastle and Glasgow. Any Glaswegian sailors off some P&O steamer at Southampton, or other long-distance travellers, would have had a wonderful tour (which they may well have not appreciated) of the Hampshire and Berkshire Downs via Highclere and Compton, stopping at every station before arriving at Oxford - and only then did the famished travellers become supplied with a Dining Car.

At Oxford the Newcastle section was added: a Brake 3rd, 3rd and Dining Car. The formation of the train was GWR/LNER on alternate days. My friend the late Dennis Dawson, with whom I worked when he was a Relief Signalman, started his railway career as a boy on the 'Sheffield Diner'. He worked down on the 7.20 Southampton from Oxford to Sheffield and came back on the 1.2 Newcastle.

An example of the fiendishly complicated inter-company workings in 1930 was the 11.15 am Bournemouth-Newcastle, 2.30-2.36 pm at Oxford. The train worked into Oxford, northbound, behind a Southern engine, which came off there to be replaced by an LNER engine. The train thereafter had a remarkable itinerary. It ran via Banbury North Junction to Woodford Halse, Loughborough and Nottingham (Victoria) to Sheffield (reverse), then Rotherham, Doncaster and York. It was formed on alternate days with Southern Railway and LNER stock and ran in three sections: a Brake Composite, 3rd, Composite, Dining Car and Brake 3rd to Newcastle; a 3rd to Bradford (Exchange), detached at Sheffield and then via Penistone and Huddersfield; and a 3rd and Brake Composite to Leeds, detached at Nottingham then via Mansfield, Rotherham, Mexborough, Doncaster and Wakefield.

All these junction station calls *en route* gave passengers opportunities to reach yet more destinations by changing trains. Indeed, this train, like its brethren, gave connections between the South coast and coast to coast across the breadth of the North of England. The trick was to ensure that the passengers were in the right coach - and on weekdays connections were different from those obtaining on Saturdays. On a Saturday it was quicker to Bradford by travelling in the Leeds coach and changing at Wakefield than if you travelled in the Bradford (direct) coach.

In summer the train was packed with travellers, especially on Saturdays, extra coaches would be added and the GWR put in an extra TTI between Oxford and Banbury to help sort the passengers into their correct carriages. It is easy to imagine the struggling bodies, squeezing past each other, humping holiday suitcases and trailing unwilling children.

This was Oxford, handling trains from Abingdon and Aberdeen, Fairford and Folkestone, Weymouth and Woodstock.

Oxford Engine Shed/Station North

The signal box to command the north end of the station was originally called Oxford 'B'. It was in use by 1884, and probably in 1874. As already mentioned, GWR S&T records show that the GWR changed its mind several times over its plans for improving Oxford station. On 26 May 1896 an order was placed at Reading Signal Works for a 'Type 7' signal box requiring 40,000 bricks, with a floor 30 ft 5 in by 12 feet to house a 43-lever frame. This order was, however, cancelled in favour of a 69-lever box, then a 71-lever box, then a timber box for 97 levers and finally, on 16 September 1899, a 100-lever box with a floor 52 by 13 feet, 11 feet above rail level. These levers would have been interlocked with the 'double twist' mechanism, the levers set at $5^1/4$-inch centres.

In 1915 three-bar horizontal tappet locking, with levers at 4-inch centres, was installed. The 1919 traffic census for the box states that there were 86 working levers, including detonator-placer levers, and 14 spaces, making the levers number to 100.

A curiosity of the layout at this, the 'Engine Shed' box, was that access to the engine shed was not comprehensive - engines could not go on shed directly from the Down Main or the Up Platform line. There was also only a single siding leading off the shed, and Local Instructions until 1945 ordered that engines should normally leave the shed at Engine Shed box and go on to the shed at Oxford North box, thus avoiding collisions between 'in-going' and 'out-going' locomotives.

Probably since 1915 and definitely by 1919 the box was 'double handed' from 7 am to 11 pm. A 'Chargeman' signalman attended to the down trains with an 'Assistant' signalman to deal with up trains. Both men were the same grade and each took their turn on the down end; but if some train-regulating decision had to be made, the Chargeman was responsible. On 'nights' - 11 pm until 7 am - the box was worked by one man. There was no Lad Telegraphist on any shift and the only entries in the train register were to record delays. The Chargeman signalmen in 1919-23 were J. White, A. Lavington and A. G. Tritton. The box was a 'Special' under the GWR classification, but since 1919, with the national system of classifying all boxes, it had fallen into Class 1.

In April and again on 12 September 1922 the men asked for an upgrading. The letter they sent is headed - with inch-high letters - GREAT WESTERN RAILWAY. Below this, nearly as large is 'Oxford Engine Shed Box'. The letter reads:

'Dear Sir, We the under-signed respectfully make an appeal for our classification to be reviewed. Since the marks were last taken work at this box has increased considerably with additional trains involving large increases in coach shunting, tail traffic and engine changing. As you are aware a considerable number of trains change engines at Oxford and these engines must be dealt with promptly so as to be available for their return workings.

'In making this appeal we honestly believe we have a just causes and trust you will kindly consider same - thanking you in anticipation,

'Yours obediently. . .'

Oxford Engine Shed signal box on 1 May 1930, all but submerged beneath heavy shunting. No 2259, only one month old and shedded at Didcot, has placed a horse box on the Up Middle road and is waiting to reverse, but horse boxes and empty coaches are reversing from the Up Platform - probably into 'Jericho'. Note that the Down Main Starting signal is a straight post - there is no connection from the Down Main to the engine shed. The LMS engine shed is in the middle distance. *Dr Jack Hollick/AVC*

During the week ended 22 April 1923 a census of trains signalled by the box showed the following numbers of trains:

	Down	Up
Monday	185	154
Tuesday	205	174
Wednesday	210	178
Thursday	201	178
Friday	200	164
Saturday	216	185

From this the Divisional Superintendent decided that the marks could be taken on 6 July. The result of this showed:

Through trains	Starting/ terminating trains	Lever movements	Levers with 3 points
159	179	4,032*	169

* This total must be divided by two men between 7 am and 11 pm.

On 6 July 1923 the DSO, F. R. Potter, wrote: 'I note the new record gives an hourly average of 364 marks, 11 short of Special Class. I consider that the box should be advanced to Special Class. Oxford Engine Shed box is a difficult one and exceptionally heavy to work. Prior to the new classification it was "Special". Special Class would be more consistent and I recommend upgrading as from 6 April 1923.'

This settled matters for 22 years. Some comparison between Oxford Engine Shed box and others in the London Division is illuminating, as shown in the table below. All these boxes were 'single-handed', 'Special Class' and did no booking.

The interlocking was modernised in 1942 by the addition of five-bar vertical tappet interlocking to increase the amount of interlocking that could be placed on the levers. The appearance of the frame from the operating floor did not alter except that there were now four permanent spaces at the centre of the frame, and eventually there would be 96 working levers. The demand for extra levers and interlocking was in connection with the planned increase in the size of the layout to be controlled from the box. The levers in the frame operating detonator-placers became working levers, and a pair of two-lever detonator-placer frames were placed one at each end of the frame, each in its own raised quadrant. The box was probably re-named Oxford Station North in 1942 - although, as noted, the DSO and Superintendent of the Line's offices seemed to think it was called 'Engine Shed Signal Box' until 1944.

The Company's intention was to transfer all the work of the North End Yard to Hinksey Yard, then to redevelop the North End site so as to improve the locomotive shed's access at the station end, its facilities and to build carriage storage space. In fact, North End had to be kept working long after Hinksey Yard came into use, and even on 14 April 1943 the expenditure for the development of the North End site had not been authorised.

The work to clear North End Yard and re-lay it with the new layout was begun in late October or early November 1944 and the new work was brought into use on Sunday and Monday 12/13 November, and throughout the period 28 December 1944 and 5 January 1945. During the former period new signals were erected and minor layout alterations were made, preparatory to the big job, carried out over the New Year. During the latter period improvements to the shed inlet/outlet and to and from the carriage sidings were made, as shown in the accompanying extracts from the relevant Notice overleaf.

The division of the interlocking frame into an 'up' and a 'down' end by the four central permanent

Signal box	Shift	Levers in frame	Trains (total)	Lever movements
Slough Middle 19 June 1930	10 pm-6 am	113	159	1,587
West Drayton West 22 Jan 1925	6 am-2 pm	101	186	1,573
	2 pm-10 pm		198	1,700
Hayes Station 24 July 1925	6 am-2 pm	74	173	1,884
6 June 1923 Oxford Engine Shed Chargeman's work, down side only	6 am-2 pm	50	144	1,634
Oxford Engine Shed Assistant's work, upside only	7 am-3 pm	50	124	1,365

GREAT WESTERN RAILWAY

Divisional Superintendent's Office, Paddington Station, W2.

October 19th 1943

Regulation of Trains: Oxford area.

To commence 25 October 1943.

The regulation of ALL trains, passenger, parcels, freight, military, naval and R.A.F specials, empty stock, light engines in the area bounded by:

Sandford and Wolvercot Junction inclusive

will be vested in Traffic Regulators who will be employed continuously at Oxford Engine Shed box.

The closest co-operation must be maintained by these units with the Station Masters, Reading Control (Traffic and Relief), Signalmen, Yard Inspectors, Didcot Relief Supervisors and Traffic Regulator Didcot East Junction in order that the maximum beneficial effect in train working may be obtained.

The Regulator must confer with the Oxford Station Master and/or Platform and Yard Inspectors especially when there is congestion at the station which is likely to cause delay.

The employment of Traffic Regulators will not relieve signalmen and others of the duty of regulating trains normally associated with their grade but is designed to co-ordinate the efforts of all concerned to achieve the best results. In cases referred to the Traffic Regulators and also those instances where the men act on their own initiative, the ruling of the Regulator must be accepted and acted upon.

Investigation over a lengthy period has shown that the majority of delays in the Oxford area are due to freight trains stopping for relief of trainmen or because of inadequate road knowledge of the crews without the signalmen being aware of the circumstances. The Regulators must therefore specialise in this aspect of the operating requirement and keep themselves fully informed as to the way all freight trains are manned which pass through their area contacting Reading Traffic and Relief Controllers and the Didcot Relief Supervisor as may be necessary.

IT WILL BE THE DUTY OF ALL CONCERNED TO KEEP THE TRAFFIC REGULATORS FULLY INFORMED OF ALL PHASES OF THE WORKING WHICH WILL ASSIST THEM IN MAKING THEIR DECISIONS.

Source of advice

Sandford. Down.
Signalman to advise passing/departure times from Didcot North Jc., for all passenger and parcels trains. To advise passing times at Sandford for all freight trains and light engines and whether via Main or Loop.

Kennington Jc. Down.
Signalman to advise the time all trains pass Morris Cowley *en route* for Oxford.

Hinksey (South). Up.
Signalman to advise the passing/departure time all up freight and route via Main or Loop.

Hinksey (South). Down.
Must obtain Regulator's permission before allowing any freight train to proceed Down Main to Oxford South. [Re-named Hinksey North in 1944.]

Hinksey Yard. Inspector to advise:
Up freight. Identify time ready to leave and time of departure.

Hinksey Yard. Inspector to advise:
Down freight. Identity and time of arrival, time ready to leave and actual time of departure and to what point is the train manned.

If any Down freight train has to stop in the Oxford area for relief after it has left Hinksey Yard the Regulator MUST be advised beforehand.

Oxford North Jc. Up.
Passing, arrival, departure time of all trains and light engines from the LMS. Including trains arriving/leaving Port Meadow Loop.

Oxford North Jc. Down.
Passing, arrival and departure times of all trains and light engines to the LMS. Time all engines 'blow-up' to leave for Yarnton and whether they go by Main or Loop.

Wolvercot Sidings. Up.
Departure of all freight trains and light engines diverted Loop to Main. Time all freight trains enter Loop at Wolvercot Jc.

Wolvercot Sidings. Down.
Departure of all freight trains and light engines diverted Loop to Main. Time all freight trains leave the Loop at Wolvercot.

Wolvercot Jc. Up.
Identification and passing time of all trains and light engines at Fritwell & Somerton.

Yarnton Jc. Down.
Identification and departure times of all freight trains and light engines from the Fairford branch or Yarnton yard, also identification and passing times from Bruern Crossing of all trains and light engines.

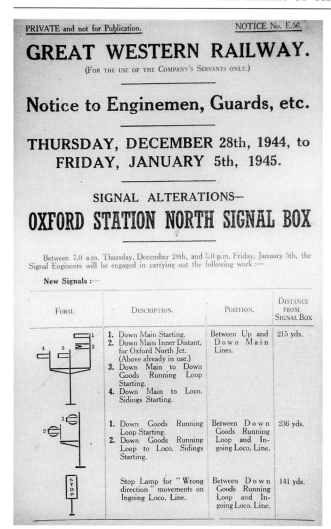

GREAT WESTERN RAILWAY.

(FOR THE USE OF THE COMPANY'S SERVANTS ONLY.)

Notice to Enginemen, Guards, etc.

THURSDAY, DECEMBER 28th, 1944, to FRIDAY, JANUARY 5th, 1945.

SIGNAL ALTERATIONS—

OXFORD STATION NORTH SIGNAL BOX

Between 7.0 a.m. Thursday, December 28th, and 5.0 p.m. Friday, January 5th, the Signal Engineers will be engaged in carrying out the following work :—

New Signals :—

FORM.	DESCRIPTION.	POSITION.	DISTANCE FROM SIGNAL BOX.
	1. Down Main Starting. 2. Down Main Inner Distant, for Oxford North Jct. (Above already in use.) 3. Down Main to Down Goods Running Loop Starting. 4. Down Main to Loco. Sidings Starting.	Between Up and Down Main Lines.	215 yds.
	1. Down Goods Running Loop Starting. 2. Down Goods Running Loop to Loco. Sidings Starting.	Between Down Goods Running Loop and In-going Loco. Line.	236 yds.
	Stop Lamp for " Wrong direction " movements on Ingoing Loco. Line.	Between Down Goods Running Loop and In-going Loco. Line.	141 yds.

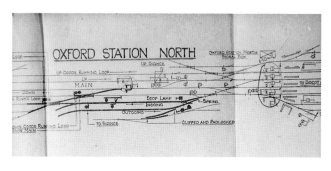

spaces assisted its operation by two men. Commencing on 25 October 1943, each shift was given a Traffic Regulator and also a Lad Telegraphist (booking boy) to keep the detailed 'train register book'.

The Regulators were appointed from the senior signalmen, Joe White, Alf Baston and Bill Perriman. Bill then became ill and was given a light job in Hinksey Yard ground frame, his place being taken by Edgar Smewin from Station South box. Edgar was also a 'Regulator of the King's Peace' as an Oxford magistrate. He became a City Councillor in 1934,

Sheriff of Oxford in 1943-44, and Lord Mayor from November 1946 until May 1948. Normally a Councillor was Mayor for one year, from November, but the month of appointment was altered to May during Edgar's term of office. A photograph was published in the *Daily Mirror* of him in full robes, hat and chain, pulling levers in Station South box.

After the promotion of White, Baston and Perriman, the signalmen were G. E. Mackenzie, F. R. Blackall (who later became a DI at Reading), Bert Hawtin (who became a Special Class Relief man and finished his time in the late 1960s helping in the Oxford DI's office and opening the, by then, boarded-up Yarnton Junction for the daily trip to Witney), Bert Allen and A. G. Tritton.

On 23 November 1944, these five wrote to DI Stacey at Didcot asking him for the night shift to be made 'double-handed'. The DSO deferred the application until it could be seen how much easier the new layout would be to work - perhaps the men would not mind being 'single-handed' on nights - but after the Night Regulator had been withdrawn on 4 March 1946 the men renewed their application.

The total number of trains handled in the course of seven days were:

Weekending	Trains
16.2.46	1,649
13.4.46	1,603
17.8.46	1,756
19.10.46	1,846

The detailed census of work carried out by the Station North signalmen took place over the 24 hours of Thursday 28 November 1946. In total there were 143 through trains and 148 starting/terminating trains, a total of 291. (And if that seems busy, it is worth recording that during the 24 hours 5/6 June 1923 the signalmen had dealt with 338 trains.)

There were now five 'triple-ended' points - levers 9, 30, 51, 65 and 81 - and these levers were operated 439 times. The total number of lever movements over the 24 hours was 6,078, and the marks earned per hour were 322.

On 29 January 1947 the DSO, C. T. Cox wrote to the Superintendent of the Line, Gilbert Matthews:

'The census confirms that the work is heavier - per man - between 11 pm-7 am - although not greatly exceeding that performed by the early turn assistant. On this basis it is doubtful whether a case could be established for the provision of an extra man on night shift but it is necessary to take into account that between 6 am and 10 pm the services of a Traffic Regulator are available to the signalmen which considerably eases the situation and leaves them free to concentrate on the work of signalling trains. There was a Night Regulator until 4 March but he is now withdrawn.

'I recommend that an additional signalman be provided on the night turn but that they do their own booking and dispense with the Lad Telegraphist. There is an increasing difficulty in obtaining suitable lads as Telegraphists and there is also the restriction imposed by the "Employment of Young Persons" Act to be considered. It would be to the Company's advantage to be released from the anxiety of finding lads for night work.'

Matthews was very slow to reply to this recommendation. Meanwhile the men's representatives asked the DSO what was happening and Cox wrote to ask Matthews for a decision. On 21 February 1947, Matthews replied:

'In the light of conditions obtaining at other boxes in the London Division, what special circumstances exist at Oxford Station North to justify the employment of an additional Special Class man? I appreciate that recruitment of Lad Telegraphists is becoming increasingly difficult and as an alternative perhaps the Telegraphist's post

could be filled by a disabled adult at Grade 2 Porter's wages instead of employing a second, Special Class signalman.'

Matthews finally agreed to the extra post being created on 24 February 1947. It was filled by Basil Marchant from North Junction, and Station North remained 'double-handed' until about 1966.

Three of the Lad Telegraphists or booking boys who worked in Engine Shed/Station North during and/or just after the war were John Hemmings, Keith Smith (always known as 'Felix') and a lad called Drewitt, whose first name has been forgotten. Keith became a porter on the station when he became 'adult' and is particularly remembered by the old hands for the day he was told to exercise a very valuable greyhound that was in transit. Somehow it slipped its lead and shot off northwards, off the platform and along the loop with Keith in hot pursuit. Surprised signalmen saw the dog and the young man passing, and disappearing down the line. Keith ran as far as Wolvercot Siding, by which time the dog had completely vanished, so he trudged dejectedly back to the station.

The signal box crew at 3.17 pm on 27 February 1949, looking south from levers 80 to 1. Basil Marchant, who had been a semi-professional boxer, is under the clock, Jerry Trevis is on the frame and Peter Hemmings is the booking lad, on the Dickensian stool in front of a miscellaneous row of vintage telephones. Note the tall Tyers/GWR 'Permissive Block' instruments on the shelf nearest the camera. Basil is standing by a standard issue GWR signal box stove; both stoves are polished with 'black lead', and both have an oven above the fire in which to heat or even cook food. This was especially important when signalmen worked 12-hour shifts. *R. H. G. Simpson*

Basil Marchant on the 'box to box' phone, Jo Jones, Traffic Regulator, answers a bell and Jerry Trevis moves a lever on 27 February 1949. The signal levers operating ground discs or semaphore arms on the platform lines or sidings are painted half and half red and black, or they carry a black patch at their centre. The 'Permissive Block' instruments working with North Junction for 'Jericho' and the Down Goods Loop are by Jo Jones's head. *R. H. G. Simpson*

Left The box interior seen from the same spot as the previous photograph, some six years later in 1955. All signal levers are now painted plain red. The 'Permissive Block' instruments working with North Junction have been removed from the North Junction end of the shelf and re-located, most illogically, at the Station South end. The group of Oxford University Railway Society members at the far end of the room are watching shunting movements. The levers reversed nearest the camera - points and bolts 25, 26, 30 and 31 - have 'set the road' for a movement from Down Main to engine shed; signal 24, controlling the movement, has been replaced and the signalman is hurrying to replace lever 72, the ground disc at the junction of the engine shed/carriage sidings. Also reversed, just beyond the central division in the frame, are levers 41 and 44, the bolts for the 'scissors' facing points. Besides these levers, 50, ground disc for points 58, 52, 53, 54, 55 and 58 are reversed; this route is Up Bay to Down Main, 58 being the Up Main to Down

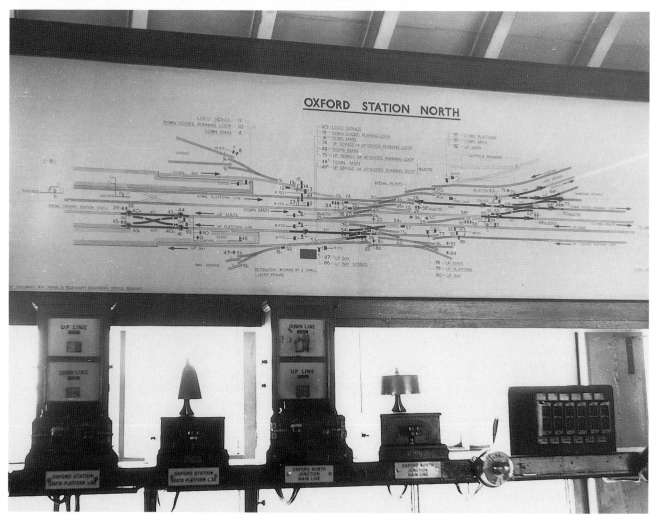

Main crossover. Signal 46, which started the movement from the Up Bay, has been replaced. *Peter Barlow/AVC*

Below left The 1945 layout represented in a diagram drawn at Reading under BR(WR) auspices. The style is very similar to that adopted in 1936, the greatest difference being that the ground disc symbol is simpler. Photographed in 1955. *Peter Barlow/AVC*

Right A GWR man in BR(WR) days: Special Class Relief Signalman Sid Mumford at the booking desk in Station North box in 1968. Sid was 100 per cent devoted to 'The Job' and, like many of us, resented intensely the completely unnecessary 'supervisions' of woefully inexperienced 'managers' who appeared on the scene in the later 1960s onwards. *AVC*

Drewitt was working in the box with Basil Marchant when a very strange and terrific noise outside brought them to the rear window. Down on the canal two swans were fighting to the death. One swan took a blow to its head and collapsed, apparently dead, whereupon the other swam away. Drewitt raced down the stairs to the track, down to the canal path, into the canal and out with the dead swan. It had been knocked unconscious. He took it back to the box and made a bed for it. It regained consciousness and for three days convalesced in the box until it was walking; he then replaced it in the canal.

Young Drewitt is also remembered as possessing a sort of double-jointed agility. The speed at which he went down the signal box steps to rescue the swan was unusual, not merely as a feat of acrobatics - his

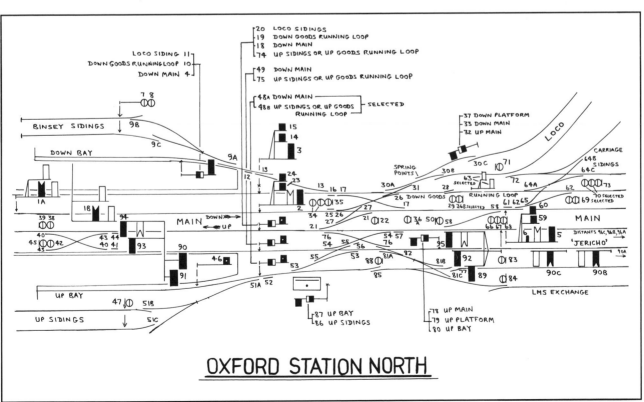

OXFORD STATION NORTH

normal exit from the box was to step out of the window and slide down the guy-wire supporting a telegraph pole very close by.

Where there were booking boys there was usually some horseplay between them and the signalmen. At Station North the toilet was outside, in a little cubbyhole of a place on the landing at the top of the stairs. One morning Drewitt went to use it, and while he was in there one of the signalmen tied the door. The only means of escape was a small window at the rear, and from this window to the ground was a drop of about 20 feet. It seemed as if Drewitt was imprisoned at the signalmen's pleasure - but no. He slipped through the ventilator-window, on to the roof of the loo and jumped down on to the stairs landing - free 'in a single bound' within moments of the signalman returning to the box!

As at Station South, the operation of Station North signal box was complicated by (a) lack of braking distance between the Down Distant and Down Home signals and (b) because the clearing point of the Up Home (440 yards ahead of it) landed 90 yards inside the Oxford Station South section on both the Up Platform and on Up Main lines.

As a result of condition (a) Regulation 4A was used, when required, for Down Through trains. As a result of condition (b) the Special Instruction for the signal box ordered that: 'Permission must not be given for Up trains to approach unwarned (from North Junction) until "Train out of Section" has been received from Station South box.' Given this proviso, Station North could give 'Line Clear' to North Junction on the Up line because Station North's Distant was far enough away to provide a proper braking distance.

To give 'Line Clear' on the Down Platform line to Station South for a down train, the road had to be clear for 440 yards ahead of the Down Home, No 3. This clear space of 440 yards could be through points 17 from Down Platform to Down Main, or, if this was not available, it could be directly along the Down Goods Loop. If neither was available the approaching train would be accepted under the 'Warning'.

The use of the 'Warning Arrangement' was liberally permitted - on the Up Main, Down Main and Down Platform lines - provided that there was no passenger train within the clearing point; however, a down train that was booked to stop at Oxford could be accepted under the 'Warning' when a passenger train was coming out of the Down Bay. If a down train not booked to stop at Oxford was 'asked' at the time that the road was set to bring a passenger train from Down Bay to Down Main, the 'Is Line Clear?' signal would be 'refused', or, in non-railway parlance, ignored.

The signalman at Station North did not 'ask the road' to North Junction for down trains at the Down Platform until the Platform Inspector 'rang them out' -

probably by means of a plunger on the wall of the station that rang a bell in the signal box. When North Junction 'gave the road' for the down train, he at once 'asked it on' to Wolvercot Siding, who 'gave the road' if conditions were right, but did not 'ask on' at that stage.

Down trains of any class booked to pass the station non-stop were 'asked on' as soon as the 'Is Line Clear?' bell was received from Station South. Any down train for the Banbury direction was signalled with the standard bell code for its class - 4, 3-1, 3-2, or whatever - but trains to and from the 'West Midland' (Worcester) and Fairford lines were signalled as a 1-2 (Branch Goods) or 1-3 (Branch Passenger). Trains for Bletchley were 3 beats.

There was as much or more shunting of passenger stock to do at Station North as at Station South. Trains of empty coaches could be propelled from North Junction to the station over the Up Main after the signalman at North Junction had 'asked the road' of Station North with the special 2-3-2 code, and engines with or without vehicles attached could run in the wrong direction between Station North and South, either under the bell code 1-6, 'May an engine or engine and vehicles run Down the Up Line?', or 4-2, 'Ditto Up the Down Line?'.

It was permissable for a shunting movement to occupy the section in advance after the bell code 3-3-2, 'May train shunt towards your home signal?', had been sent, the line up to the Home signal at the box in advance was clear, and the 3-3-2 acknowledged by the box in advance. (3-3-2 superseded 1-3-1 when the latter became the standard code for a parcels train in May 1950.) For example, there would be occasions when, in order to bring the rear of a long train clear of a set of points, prior to reversing over those points, the train would have to draw up to and beyond the Starting signal and into the section in advance.

Station North had the same instructions as Station South as regards the working of the 'scissors' crossings and the admitting of one train in behind another at a platform. It should be pointed out again that all these special dispensations from the standard rules at any signal box (in this book or not) were always modified or prohibited in fog or falling snow.

Station North had extra work because of the bays platforms, and also the engines on and off the shed. An engine requiring to come off the shed would stop at the shed exit signal and the fireman would phone in to say what or where he was for. The signal box booking lad would enter this in the train register, the time the message was received and the time the engine was let out. But there were also scheduled trains to run, and the Pilot to shunt vehicles to and from trains and sidings, and it was not always possible to let an engine out at once. The next engine would

Right Looking north from the signal box in 1949. The LNWR signals in the right foreground are Rewley Road's Up Starting with North Junction's Distant below. A very rusty connection from the LMS to the GWR passes behind the signal. Between the telegraph poles and GWR signals coaches are standing on 'Jericho Loop' and also on the LMS Exchange Siding. *R. H. G. Simpson*

Below right A rear view of the box from the ex-LMS line. The signal gantry was erected during an 'occupation' lasting from Sunday 1 November to Thursday 12 November 1959.

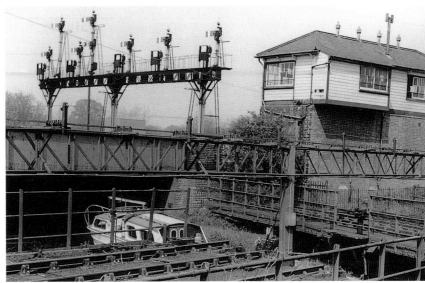

pull up behind the first and soon a queue of three or four had formed. A particularly busy time was around 11 am. My friend the late Sid Mumford reckoned that there had been occasions when he was working the box that he had turned 11 engines off the shed at 11 am.

The signalmen carried out their shunting to the instructions of the 'passenger shunters', or simply because the various trains had a set routine of attaching or detaching vehicles, the work going ahead without anyone having to say anything - signalmen, shunters, drivers and guards all knew what was expected of them. The signalmen watched from the lever frame as the vehicles cleared the various points, or they went to the window to watch or shout messages, or give or receive hand signals. The job worked because they knew what was required not only now but also in 10 or 20 minutes' time.

'Jericho Loop', the Up Goods Loop, was used exclusively for carriage stabling rather than as a Goods Loop, although there was a Grimsby-Swindon fish train that used it around 2.30 am. Coaches, horses boxes or other vehicles could be propelled - ie pushed with the engine at the rear - along this loop from North Junction after the 2-3-2 bell code had been used. From 'Jericho' they could be propelled directly on to the rear of an up train. If a movement had to come from the Up Platform or Up Bay into 'Jericho', the signalman first asked the man at North Junction, using 1-6 on the bell, and if North Junction replied by repetition the Station North man pegged his instrument to 'Train on Line' before setting the road for the movement to take place.

The tremendous amount of shunting that was done with light engines and engines with vehicles, and the hundreds of lever movements per hour that the signalmen were required to make, did sometimes lead to mistakes, and the derailment of an engine or coach. In order to work the station, everyone concerned - signalmen, drivers, shunters - was used to moving fast, slamming over the points smartly behind a shunt, moving away the instant the signal came off; sometimes the well-stressed 'jumped the gun'. There are no figures for the frequency of these incidents, but they were not rare. From GWR internal accident reports it is known that derailments of this kind occurred on 22 March and 21 August 1947.

On the former date, at 4.00 pm, the shunters were working with the Station Pilot engine, No 4973, and were taking two three-coach sets and two spare coaches from the Up Sidings to the Down Bay. The train was so long that, when the rear coach was against the Down Bay buffers the engine and two coaches were outside the Down Bay Starting signal. The signalman 'closed the road' into the bay at 4.5 pm and pulled off for the 3.30 pm Oxford-Birmingham to leave the Down Platform.

Meanwhile, the shunter had uncoupled the engine from the coaches and waved the driver forwards. The driver gave it not a thought but went ahead, and came off the road - all wheels, engine and tender - at the trap protecting the Platform line. The word went out to Oxford shed foreman, 'Trouble on the double - get an engine on the vans!', and 4973 was re-railed at 7.50 pm. As at Dunkirk, the British are at their best when getting out of cock-ups!

The derailment caused delays to four trains and caused seven more to be cancelled. The shunter and signalman were reprimanded for not working properly together, but the driver was held to be blameless.

On 21 August 1947 No 6868 was on the Back Road at 'Binsey' Sidings. It was the engine for the 10.25 pm passenger to Banbury and was waiting for the train engine of the 6.25 pm Paddington-Oxford to place its empty coaches on the Middle Road in 'Binsey'; these would then form the stock for the 10.25. When the coaches were stabled, No 7 ground

signal was lowered and the engine off the 6.25 pm Paddington went to shed at 10.5 pm.

No 6868 followed it out, but the driver was too quick off the mark in moving his engine forward, passed No 7 at 'Danger' and came off the road, one wheel, at No 9 points. Questioned later he said that he had expected the signalman to at once lower No 7 signal after the other engine had gone, as was the usual way. The vans were called at once and the engine's bogie wheel was re-railed at 10.27. The 10.25 Banbury left at 10.35.

The station was overloaded with work and the men worked under pressure. 'You didn't hang around,' the old hands told me. They tried - and managed most of the time - to fit a quart into a pint pot.

Oxford Station North box was closed by the Oxford MAS scheme on 7 October 1973.

Operating Oxford Station North

As we have already seen, train movements at Oxford were complicated. Station North had the greatest complications and I will attempt to give a flavour of the working there. I have drawn my information from the Train Register Book (TRB) written up, minute by minute, bell code by bell code, during 20 November 1946. This was given to me by the late Sid Mumford, Special Class Relief Signalman at Oxford, as a going away present when I escaped from the about-to-be-modernised Oxford for the mechanical signalling delights of deepest Somerset. I have also used the Oxford Station Shunting pamphlet for June 1947, the Special Instructions for working the signal box, dated 1953 but which had applied in 1946, and the memories of Stan Worsfold and Albert Walker who worked the box. Clearly, it would be better if all these documents were of the same date, but Stan and Albert are agreed that in 1946 or 1953 there was no difference in the way the box was operated, although, of course, a slightly different train service obtained year by year. I am going to use signal box vernacular to assist authenticity.

The TRB does not record all movements made at Station North; shunting moves that did not go into adjoining block sections are not recorded because they were not signalled on the bells and instruments. The fact that the signalmen did unrecorded shunting movements is shown in the register when 'Is Line Clear?' was asked by Station South or North Junction

and the Station North signalman 'refused the road' for a reason not at all apparent from reading the TRB; sometimes they refused the road for 11 minutes.

Engines from the shed were always recorded, even if they did not go beyond Station North's jurisdiction. The time that an engine's fireman called up from the shed signal to identify his engine, its duty and the fact that they were ready to leave, and the time it was 'let off' the shed, were all noted so as to provide a record in case the Traffic Department was blamed for an engine being late on to its train.

At 6 am on Wednesday 20 November 1946 the night shift of Signalman Horace Walton and his son Maurice, the Lad Telegraphist (booking boy), was relieved by Signalman Horace Gunningham and booking boy John Stone. The new shift was briefed on what was happening: there was a 3-3 'Block' on the Down Platform (3-3 was sent by Station North to Station South, and upon acknowledgment North pegged 'Train on Line', thus blocking the platform for shunting movements), and a 1-3-1, 'Shunt into forward section', on the Down Main to North Junction. This was because the Pilot engine was marshalling parcels vans and empty milk wagons for the 5.50 Worcester parcels (the empty milk tanks and churns were for the processing plant at Moreton-in-Marsh) and the Down Platform, Down Bay, 'Binsey' Sidings and the Down Main were being used for this.

The Morris Cowley Pilot was on the Up Main at

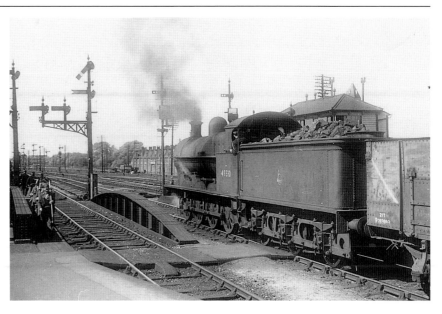

No 49330, an ex-LNWR 0-8-0, Mr Bowen-Cooke's 'G1' Class or 'Super D', heads for North Junction and the Bletchley line, passing pure GWR signalling at Oxford Station North on 20 June 1957. A post-Nationalisation view of a scene common enough at Oxford from 1940. *H. C. Casserley*

Station South, the Hinksey Pilot was on the Up Main at No 94, 'waiting the road', and the 3.10 Leamington goods had been accepted on the Up Main under the 'Warning' and was standing at the Up Home, No 95. Let's follow the sequence of events.

The Cowley Pilot clears Station South at 6 am; Horace immediately 'asks the road' for the Hinksey engine (2-3 on the bell), sends 'on line' (2 beats) at the same time, and pulls off 94. He puts back 94 and pulls 95 to start the Leamington. The Hinksey engine clears at 6.3 (2-1 on the bell), so Horace 'gets the road' for the Leamington (3-2) and pulls 94. The Leamington passes at 6.4. Horace sees something wrong with the train and sends 7 beats, 'Stop and Examine Train', to Station South.

At 6.5 the Abingdon engine is called up 'ready' at the shed signal and Horace sends 8 beats, 'Shunt Withdrawn', to North Junction as the shunting movement withdraws from North Junction's section - he at once 'asks the road' to North Junction for the 5.50 Oxford-Worcester parcels (5 beats) out of 'Binsey' Sidings, and sets the road - points 9, 13 and 17 reversed, and bolted with 12 and 16 reversed. The engine is probably outside the Sidings' Starting disc 7, but Horace will pull it to prove the detection, along with signal 5, Down Main Starting. The Parcels leaves at 6.8, 2 beats to North Junction, and Horace then restores to 'Normal' (replaces) in the frame 7, 12, 16, 13, 17 and 5.

He now gets the road from Station South on the Up Main for the Abingdon engine (2-3) and sets the road off the shed: pull points 21, 26, 27, 30 and 31, and signals 32 and 94. The Abingdon engine is 'on line' to Station South at 6.9, so the route is restored at 6.10.

While Horace is doing this the 10 pm York is 'asked' by North Junction, 4 beats. Horace refuses it, but does 'ask on' to Station South. An engine for the shed is accepted on the Down Main at 6.13, and the York is accepted at the same time.

The road on to the shed and into the Up Platform is now set. To go to shed from the Down Main requires bolt 25 pushed normal, points 26 reversed, 25 reversed, points 31 and 30 reversed, signal 24 lowered. To get into the Up Platform, bolt 57 is pushed normal, points 54 reversed, 57 reversed, signals 91 and 92 reversed. The engine goes on to shed at 6.17. Horace sends 2-1 to Station South at 6.17, and receives 2-1 from Station South for the Abingdon engine at the same time.

The York arrives at 6.21, 95 minutes late, nothing unusual in that for the York. The road is restored, 'Train out of Section' sent (2-1), and North Junction at once 'asks' the 4.45 am Banbury, 3-2. Horace gives the road 'full Line Clear', asks on to Station South and receives the reply 2-2-2, 'Line Clear to clearing point only'. When the Banbury is in sight Horace pulls his Home and Starting signal, 94 and 95, thus ensuring that the goods has had all Distant signals against him. The Banbury creeps past North Junction at 6.26 and takes a full 2 minutes to crawl past Station North.

A 50-wagon goods train composed only of four-wheel open and covered wagons will be 333 yards long - longer if all the couplings are drawn out tight. If such a train is stopped at Station South's Up Home signal its brake van will extend at least to the north end of the station platforms, seriously hampering the signal's operations at Station North. If it is a 70-wagon train stopped at Station South the brake van will be at least as far back as No 54 points and 'block up the shop'. This is a good example of the cramped, inadequate accommodation at Oxford.

At 6.29 the 6.52 Oxford-Risboro' passenger engine calls up 'ready' at the shed signal, and the Banbury goods clanks through on the Up Main between 6.28 and 6.30, just as the 7.10 Oxford-Paddington engine calls up 'ready'. The engine off the 6.52 is to take over the 6 am Banbury-Risboro', and the engine off the Banbury will go forward with the 7.23 workmen's to Didcot.

G.W.R. "Block Telegraph Train Register" Book, for Double & Single Lines.   UP TRAINS. (1043)

G.W.R. "Block Telegraph Train Register" Book, for Double & Single Lines.   DOWN TRAINS. (1043)

Pages from the Train Register Book for Oxford Station North in November 1946, showing the various movements described in the text.

As soon as the tail of the Banbury goods has cleared 94, that signal is restored and the road set from shed to Up Main for the Risboro' engine: pull points 21, 26, 27, 30 and 31, and signal 32. The engine goes up to stand at 94 while Horace restores No 32 signal and points 21, 25, 27, 31 before pulling points 13 and 30, disc 34 and signal 37. The 7.10 engine comes out and runs to the Down Bay, stopping just inside signal 10. Horace pushes back levers 32 and 34 and pulls points 72, disc 71 and Bay Starting signal 10; the engine is now cleared to go into the Carriage Sidings to collect its coaches.

Horace replaces 71 and 10, and as he is finishing this the 4.45 Banbury goods clears Station South at 6.32 and at once he 'asks the road' for the 6.52 Risboro' engine. He is given 'full Line Clear' (Station South knows that the engine is standing at Station North's Starting signal), and the engine is put 'on line' at the same time and clears Station South at 6.37.

At 6.38 Station South 'asks the road' for the 2 am Slough, 3-4-1, and Horace refuses it while 'asking on' for it to North Junction. North Junction refuses it until 6.41. Station South 'knocks out' (2-1) on the Up Platform for the 10 pm York at 6.41.

Horace is making some un-booked shunting movements across all roads because, at 6.43, when North Junction 'asks the road' for the 6 am Banbury passenger (3-1) he refuses that too, although he does 'ask on' for this to Station South and is given the road. He 'gives the road' to North Junction for the Banbury passenger and to Station South for the Slough goods at 6.44. For the latter he pulls signal levers 5, 2 and 1. For the up passenger he pushes over bolt 57, pulls points 54 and bolt 57, and signals 91 and 92.

As the Banbury passenger approaches, the 7 am diesel car for Kingham calls up 'ready'.

At 6.46 Horace puts a 3-3 'block' on the Down Platform and sets the road from the shed: points

30 reversed, disc 34, signal 37. The Banbury runs into the Up Platform at 6.47 as the streamlined railcar runs off shed into the Down Platform, to stop short of the discs at the down 'scissors', controlled from Station South.

At 6.47 Horace has replaced signals 92 and 91 behind the Banbury passenger and 'knocked out' (2-1) to North Junction. At once the latter 'asks' for the Kingham 'auto', 1-3. Horace accepts it 'full Line Clear'.

The Slough goods is put 'on line' from Station South at 6.48 and passes Station North between 6.49 (2 beats sent forward) and 6.50 (2-1 sent to Station South). Signal levers 1, 2 and 5 go back into the frame as the train clears them.

As soon as Station South receives the 2-1, he 'asks the road' for a light engine. A telephone message from Station South advises that this is the engine off the Banbury passenger, returning to the Carriage Sidings to collect the empty coaches for the 7.23 workmen's. Horace pushes bolt lever 61 into the frame, pulls points 62, 64 and 65, reverses 61 and pulls signals 60 and 2. Readers will have noted the constant walking along the frame, particularly for this latter move.

The road into the Up Platform remains set, ready for the Kingham 'auto', which is brought nearly to a stand at 92 before it is lowered, the platform ahead being occupied. It runs into the Up Platform at 6.52 as the engine on the Down Main runs into the Carriage Sidings. Horace replaces the signals behind both trains and sends 2-1 for both.

At once Station South asks the road for a 3-4-1, the 2.5 am Southall goods. Horace refuses this because he is preparing to bring the stock for the 7.10 Oxford-Paddington across from the Carriage Sidings,

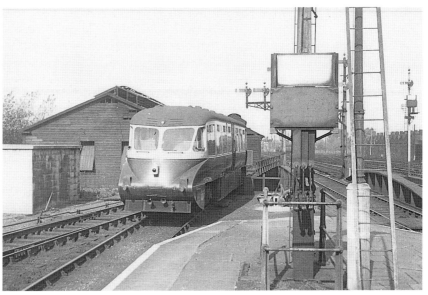

A Hereford diesel car leaves the Down Bay *circa* 1947. On the left is the GWR engine shed, and on the far right the LMS shed. In the foreground is the route indicator, working with the Down Bay Starting arm (out of shot). Note the three vertical 'blades' (driven by levers 4, 10 and 11 respectively), each attached to its own stencil. When the lever is pulled the blade is driven upwards and will display an abbreviated route indication against the translucent white background. At night an oil lamp shines through the white glass. *R. H. G. Simpson*

a movement that will block all roads. He has most of the route already set; he replaces levers 2 and 60 and then needs only to pull points 58.

By now the Kingham 'auto' has come to a stand in the Up Platform at 91 signal. When it is empty it will form the Woodstock branch train. Horace asks 'Is Line Clear?' for it (1-3) to Station South, and receives the 'Platform Line Occupied' acceptance, 2-4-2, at 6.53 - obviously the 6.52 to Risboro' is late leaving and still occupies the southern end of the Up Platform. 91 signal is then lowered, there being no special 'Calling-on' signal. Once the 'auto' has passed beyond 91 the signal is restored to 'Danger' and disc 70 is pulled at about 6.55 to start the 7.10 Oxford-Paddington empty stock from the Carriage Sidings.

Just at that moment North Junction asks the road for the 2 am Oxley, off the Worcester line and belled up as a Branch Goods, 1-2. Horace accepts this under the 'Warning', 3-5-5, as the 7.10 Oxford, perhaps 'Hall'-hauled, barks across the layout. When it has come to a stand at signal 91, Horace 'asks the road' to Station South, 2-2-1, and is accepted 2-4-2 at 6.56.

Immediately Station South completes that transaction, he asks for a 3-1-3 on the Down Platform. This is the ex-Kingham 'auto', coming into the Down Platform for Woodstock. Horace accepts it, 2-4-2, at 6.56; it will come to a stand behind the 7 am diesel car to Kingham.

The 2 am Oxley is put 'on line' from North Junction, after being all but stopped there and warned, at 7 am. At this Horace 'asks on' to Station South, and receives 3-5-5 in reply.

Although he does now have an acceptance, he does not pull off. He may have some shunts to make and certainly has to bring the 7.23 workmen's to the Up Platform from the Carriage Sidings. Having the job 'at his fingertips', and thinking ahead, he does not want the delay, just then, of having to give the 'Warning' to the Oxley, neither does he want the lengthy wait as it drags on to a stand at Station South with its tail coming back and blocking the crossings at his box; so he leaves it 'outside'.

At 7.0, just as the second signalman, Freddy Blackall, comes into the box to take up duty, the Kingham diesel railcar is 'rung out' by the Platform Inspector. Horace pushes over bolt 16, reverses points 17 and reverses 16, 'asks the road' to North Junction for a Branch Passenger, 1-3, gets 'full Line Clear', and pulls off signals 3 and 5.

From now on Horace will be in charge of the down side layout and Fred Blackall the up side. Each layout is separate and can be worked without interfering with the other side, until crossovers 21 or 58 have to be used.

The rail car down to Kingham leaves at 7.3. Levers 16, 17, 16, 3 and 5 are restored behind it, and at once the road is set from the Carriage Sidings to the Up Platform for the Pannier tank and four empty coaches of the 7.23 workmen's: bolts 56, 57 and 61 pushed into the frame, points 64, 65, 62, 58 and 54 and bolts 57 and 56 all reversed, followed by discs 70 and 66. The 7.10 is scheduled to have eight coaches; this means that the last two will be on the Station North side of No 91 signal. The 7.23 has four coaches, so will fit in behind it.

Once the coaches are into the Up Platform, at about 7.10, the two men restore the route from the Carriage Sidings, 12 lever movements, and Fred lowers 92 to start the 2 am Oxley. Horace sets the road from Down Platform to Down Main for the Woodstock 'auto'.

The 7.10 Oxford clears the Up Platform at 7.12 and at 7.13 Fred asks and receives 'Line Clear' from Station South for the empty workmen's coaches. Immediately Station South has given 'Line Clear', he 'asks' for a light engine, 2-3. The clearing point on the Down Main is fouled because the road is set to come out of the Down Platform, so Horace accepts the engine under the 'Warning', 3-5-5. Station South 'takes' this and puts the engine 'on line' at the same time.

A phone message from Station South to the booking boy advises that the engine is for the shed. Horace at that moment is getting the road from North Junction for the Woodstock 'auto'.

Fred lowers 91 signal for the 7.23 coaches to run into Station South's section; then he goes to the window, indicates the 'Warning Acceptance' to the driver of the Oxley goods with a green flag, gets an acknowledgement, and lowers 94.

'Train out of Section', 2-1, is sent to North Junction for the Oxley at 7.14 and at the same time 'on line' is sent by Station North to North Junction for the Woodstock 'auto'. Horace then restores the route from the Down Platform: signals 3 and 5, bolt lever 16 pushed into the frame, point 17 restored, and 16 reversed; then bolt 25 into the frame, points 26, 30, 31, bolt 25 reversed and signal 24 to get the engine, waiting at No 2, to the shed.

By now it is 7.15. North Junction asks the road for a Branch Passenger, 1-3, the Kingham railcar. This is not due in until 7.26, so Fred refuses it in order to keep himself free to carry out station shunting moves.

Horace puts a 3-3 'Block' on the Down Platform at 7.15; the reason is not apparent in the TRB, and what levers were required for this movement cannot be known. The engine on the Down Main clears on to the shed at 7.16 and the engine for the 7.45 Oxford-Worcester is reported 'ready' to come off shed at 7.16. Horace puts a 4-2 on the Down Middle at 7.17 to ask Station South if an engine can run to the South, up the Down Main. Station South acknowledges the 4-2 and thus gives permission for the 'wrong road' movement. The route is set - all that is required is to pull signal 32. The 7.42 engine leaves at 7.22 and clears Station South at 7.25.

Fred has finished his shunting at 7.22 and 'gives the road' to North Junction for the Kingham. The 4-2 up the Down Main clears Station South at 7.26, and Horace's shunt on the Down Platform, protected by the 3-3 'Block', is cleared at 7.26 with 2-1, 'Obstruction Removed'; at once Station South 'asks the road' for the 7.4 Didcot-Birmingham. It is accepted and arrives on time at 7.27.

In the 90 minutes since 6 am, 30 trains or engines passed the box and an unknown number of shunting movements were made. Thus the work went on, non-stop, minute by minute, hour after hour, as the signalmen, knowing what was required at that minute - and in the minutes ahead - tried to make hundreds of constantly correct decisions. If their concentration slipped, and a wrong decision was made over which shunt to allow or which train to bring on into their section, it would cause delays. They were mentally and physically very fit and felt very satisfied with the job they were doing.

Oxford North/North Junction

There was a signal box at 63 m 74 ch by 1884, and probably as early as 1874; it was known then as Oxford 'A'. A new box for this site was ordered from Reading Signal Works on 2 September 1894; this was built, but was sent to Llanganyd. On 28 November another box was ordered from the Works, and supposedly this came into use the following year. This was of timber construction with a floor 22 ft 5 in by 12 feet, raised 10 feet above rail level. The number of levers in the frame, as new, is given in GWR records as 25. The box controlled Up and Down Main lines, and those connections to and from the North End Yard and engine shed on the down side; on the up side it controlled the connections to a through siding leading to Engine Shed (later Station North) box, known as 'Jericho Siding', and a through 'Exchange Siding' connected to the LNWR.

In June 1900 an Up Goods Running Loop was brought into use between Wolvercot Junction, North box and Engine Shed box. Between North box and Engine Shed box this became known as 'Jericho Loop' and the original 'Jericho Siding' became 'Jericho Middle'.

North box was worked by one signalman per shift and full booking was done. Under the GWR the box was classed 'Special', earning 34 shillings a week for each signalman in 1914. Under the post-1919 national system it was placed in Class 3, earning 70 shillings. When the marks were taken in 1920, 1925 and 1929, the census form gave the number of levers in the frame as '34 including 2 detonator placers, no spares or spaces'.

Oxford North was, by all accounts, a pig of a place to work. The account of the box given by the Divisional Superintendent in May 1922 describes the hectic work of the signalman and the ridiculous situations that arose there as a result of the bad layout at Oxford.

'There is no doubt,' wrote Mr F. R. Potter, 'that the North box, 34 levers, at Oxford is a difficult one to work and there can be no doubt that the men feel the hardship of being placed in a lower class than Oxford Goods Shed box, 47 levers, which is easier to manage and in which the signalmen prefer to work.

'The North box man has to regulate all Down goods trains from Didcot* owing to the limited shunting room at Oxford and they have also to regulate all Up goods trains through Oxford to ensure they have a margin to reach either Oxford South End Yard or Didcot. Didcot North and Oxford North also telegraph train advices to each other and the other Oxford boxes make their inquiries from North box. Down goods trains with traffic for Oxford put off at the North End Yard. Most engines to and from Oxford shed go on and off at North box. The signalman has frequently to divide goods trains in the Down loop to clear the points leading to and from the engine shed and allow engines on or off shed [!].

'All empty coaches are put away at North box end. All transfers between the GWR and LNWR are made from North box. Lastly there is the fact that the North box signalman has to keep a train register and a separate book in which the train running advices are noted. Goods shed box, which is also Class 2, does not do booking. If it is possible to make any alteration in the classification of Oxford North box I recommend

* Apparently, therefore, Didcot North Junction signalman asked Oxford North man if it was all right to let a down goods 'run' and did not let it go without Oxford North releasing it.

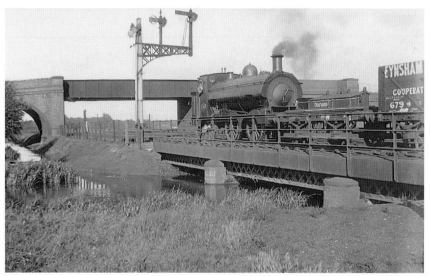

5¼-inch centres. In the course of 24 hours they handled 114 through trains and another 96 that started or terminated with them, giving a total of 2,211 lever movements. The men's difficulty in getting into the higher grade was that the box was relatively quiet on night shift. The early turn man had 77 trains/714 levers; late turn, 112/998 levers; night shift, 39/499. In the course of seven days a total of 1,315 trains were handled. On the day of the census the box was working on average at 209 marks per hour and did not qualify for re-grading.

In 1931 a 43-lever frame was installed - 41 working and two spares. These were interlocked with the standard pattern vertical tappet machine, with levers at 4-inch centres. The work became even busier. The men continued to ask for an increase, in 1929, 1936 and 1938. The latter census showed that in the 24 hours ended Wednesday 26 October, 181 through trains passed the box and 87 trains started or terminated there. There were seven Pilot 'trips' to the LMS, through the Exchange Sidings, and the total lever movements were 2,864. In 1937/8 the average number of trains per week - through and starting/terminating - handled by the signalmen was 1,597.

The marks were to have been re-taken in October 1939, but the war intervened. A letter from C. T. Cox's office on 5 December reads: 'The marks were not taken having regard to the emergency train service and the running of special trains through Oxford. I did not consider a record of work taken in October would represent normal conditions.'

The new box and double-track junction with the

that it be done.' (It is hard to imagine modern railway managers recommending pay rises for the men!)

The Divisional Superintendent forgot to mention that the 1922 Local Instructions for Oxford laid it down that 'Engines must be sent to the Locomotive Shed from the North End. They must not enter at the South End unless the entrance at the North End is blocked.' Traffic-jammed lines was a frequent occurrence at Oxford.

The man who made the work census on 7 June 1929, W. G. Taylor, wrote on the census form, 'This is a particularly aggravating one to work owing to the phone inquiries and crossing to and from sidings, shed, LNW loop, etc.'

The signalmen who had the working of this 'particularly aggravating' box were F. East, H. Woods and T. Maslin. In 1920 they had a frame of 34 levers, including two detonator-placer levers but no spares or spaces. This was a 'double twist' frame, with levers at

LMS were by then under construction and the signal-men deferred further attempts at a pay rise. The new box was begun around 14 June 1940 by contractors Brown & Son of Shepherd's Bush and opened as 'Oxford North' on 3 November 1940. It was a GWR 'ARP' design with a floor 45 by 13 feet, 11 feet above the rails, housing a frame of levers numbered to 88, of which, at opening, 68 were in use. It controlled, amongst other things, a dou-ble-line junction between the GWR and LMS; when the junction was required the signalman pulled lever 38 to switch into the LMS block telegraph circuit between Port Meadow and Oxford Station (Rewley Road) boxes. Civilian passenger trains were not permitted to use the junction until 1949.

The full layout was not complete until 18 October 1942, when the number of working levers was 71. 'Junction' was added to the name of the box on 22 May 1944, according to GWR papers. Again the sig-nalmen cannot agree with this, believing the name to have been changed in 1940.

There were three signalmen at the box,

not for Publication.   NOTICE No. E.89.

GREAT WESTERN and LONDON, MIDLAND & SCOTTISH RAILWAYS.

(FOR THE USE OF THE COMPANY'S SERVANTS ONLY.)

Notice to Enginemen, Guards, etc.

SUNDAY, NOVEMBER 3rd, to FRIDAY, NOVEMBER 8th, 1940.

BRINGING INTO USE NEW DIRECT DOUBLE JUNCTIONS BETWEEN G.W. AND L.M.S. LINES AT

OXFORD

Commencing at 12.5 a.m. on Sunday, November 3rd, until 5.0 p.m. on Friday, November 8th, the G.W.R. Signal Engineer will be engaged in carrying out the following work :

NEW DIRECT DOUBLE JUNCTIONS BETWEEN THE G.W. AND L.M.S. LINES WILL BE BROUGHT INTO USE.

SEE DIAGRAM APPENDED.

THE SPEED OF TRAINS RUNNING THROUGH THESE JUNCTIONS MUST NOT EXCEED 20 M.P.H.

AT THE SAME TIME A NEW G.W. SIGNAL BOX AT OXFORD NORTH WILL BE BROUGHT INTO USE.

The New Signal Box will be situated on the same side of the Line as the existing Signal Box, 16 yards nearer to Oxford Station.

The existing G.W. Oxford North Box will be removed.

New Signals :—

FORM.	DESCRIPTION.	POSITION.	YARDS FROM NEW BOX.
1 A	1. Down Main Inner Home. 2. Down Main to Up L.M.S. Home.	Down Side of Down Main.	17.

Membury, Pegg and Allen, and, from March 1941, three booking lads. F. Membury, aged 38, entered service on 26 January 1914; he became a signalman on 28 September 1922 and moved to Oxford North on 31 December 1936. S. W. Pegg, aged 46, entered service on 8 January 1912, becoming a signalman on 13 January 1913; he moved to Oxford North on 18 January 1937. E. A. Smewin, aged 44, joined the railway on 27 September 1909; a signalman since 14 October 1913, he worked in Oxford North from 27 October 1931. Smewin was promoted to Oxford Goods Shed, Class 1, on 7 February 1938, and his place was taken at Oxford North by A. T. (Bert) Allen from Wolvercot Junction.

The latter was born at Bedwyn and had come on to the GWR because of this fact, it being well known on the pre-war GWR that any young man born in Bedwyn - provided he was clean, upright and God-fearing - could apply to Sir Felix Pole, the General Manager of the Company from 1921 to 1929, for a job on the GWR. Sir Felix, the son of the village schoolmaster at Great Bedwyn, operated this system as a sort of private charity. The last Station Master of Wantage Road, Mr Harding, came from Bedwyn and told me, with pride, that he had come on to the GWR through the influence of Felix Pole.

The box had 88 levers including 17 spare and was still Class 2. The marks were taken in November 1940 and fell short of Class 1 by 9 marks. On 13 January 1941 the three signalmen applied to be re-graded 'Special' Class. As part of their case they pointed out that they would be in switch with the LMS and would be required to 'pass the LMS rules' with the LMS Inspector as well as knowing GWR rules.

Some of the 24-hour daily totals of trains handled by the signalmen in 1941 were as follows:

Feb 10	214	April 21	214
Feb 11	211	April 22	237
Feb 12	249	April 23	241
Feb 13	248	April 24	242
Feb 14	238	April 25	231
Feb 15	243	April 26	233
Total	1,403		1,398

During those two weeks in February and April 1941 the number of times the box was switched into the LMS to pass troop and other Government trains was as follows:

Feb 12	4	April 23	5
Feb 14	1	April 24	4
Feb 15	2	April 25	4
April 21	3	April 26	5
April 22	2		

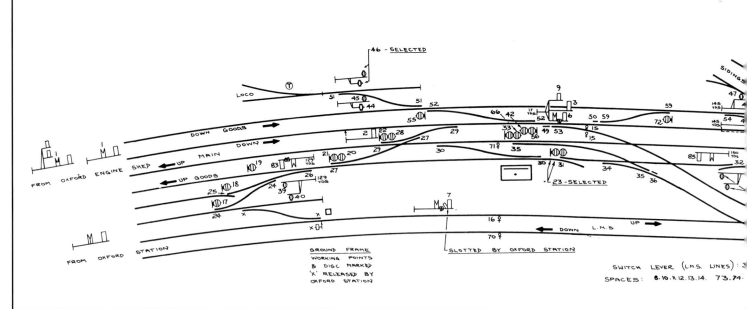

Some time in March 1941 the signalmen were relieved of the chore of keeping the train register by the appointment of a booking lad on each shift. One lad was Albert Walker.

The census was taken over the 24 hours of 4/5 June 1941. It showed, amongst other things, a total of 152 through trains, 68 trains starting or terminating at the box and a total of 3,264 lever movements. Nineteen 'wrong direction' movements were made over the Up or Down Main or Up or Down Goods Loops under the bell codes already described in the section on the Station boxes.

During this census 20 trains were signalled and then cancelled; amongst these were two occasions when an up (ie northbound) LMS light engine was 'asked' to Port Meadow by North Junction, then cancelled. This was because the engine, coming from Rewley Road, ran only as far as the trailing end of the junction points at North Junction (GWR), and there reversed to the GWR line.

North Junction's No 7 signal was his Up Home on the LMS, protecting the junction, and was also the Advanced Starting signal for Oxford Rewley Road - No 33 lever in that box. In the case of the light engine, the Rewley Road signalman asked 'Is Line Clear?', 'got the road' and pulled his signal levers, including 33. This action raised the counter-balance weight (the 'slot') holding the signal arm at 'Danger', but the signal did not move because North Junction's 'slot' - lever No 7 - was still down, holding the arm in position. This signal No 7 gave admission into Port Meadow's section; to be able to pull it and thus 'clear' the signal, North Junction had to get 'Line Clear' from Port Meadow. Having 'got the road', the North

Junction signalman pulled No 7 lever, the 'slot' was lifted and the arm fell to 'All Right'. The engine then ran forward clear of the LMS/GWR junction and reversed to the GWR, leaving the North Junction signalman to send 3-5, 'Cancel Train', to Port Meadow.

Below No 7 signal was Port Meadow's Up Distant signal, which was controlled by the upper arm; it would not be proper for the Distant signal to be lowered if the stop signal above it was still at 'Danger'. Thus the counter-balance weights, the 'slots', of Rewley Road and North Junction also controlled the counter-balance weight driving Port Meadow's Distant. There was therefore a great deal of ironmongery at the foot of the signal post.

The June 1941 census for North Junction showed a decrease in telephone work, and on 21 July Gilbert Matthews wrote to C. T. Cox, the Divisional Manager: 'The question arises as to the necessity for the employment of Telegraphists [booking boys]. Please let me have your comments.'

Cox replied to Matthews on 21 August: 'With the alterations proceeding at Oxford and the increase in traffic I am unable to agree that the Telegraphists should be dispensed with but I will look at this again should circumstances alter.'

Once again, it seems was if Cox was defending his signalmen. He had tried to get their wages increased against the findings of the traffic census before the war, and now he defended the need for the booking

A fine array of signalling instruments in Oxford North Junction box in 1955: Tyers/GWR 1947 block instrument, brass-cased track circuit repeaters and two LNWR-style block instruments for working to Port Meadow/Rewley Road. *Peter Barlow/AVC*

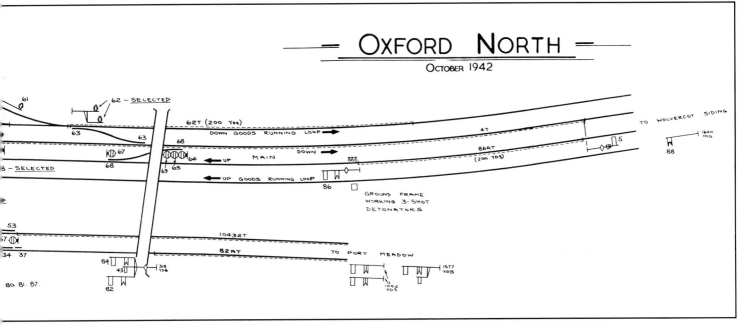

= OXFORD NORTH =
OCTOBER 1942

Preparing the foundations for the new coaling stage on the site of North End Yard on 11 August 1944. The work of the yard has been largely transferred to Hinksey, but there are still dozens of wagons of locomotive coal stored here. Oxford North Junction box is on the extreme right; the old North box has been cut down and turned into an enginemen's relief cabin, in which fresh crews waited to take over trains from tired men. *GWR*

boys. However, the effect of having the assistance of a booking boy was that the signalmen's wages remained in Class 2.

On 28 September 1942, upon the transfer of goods shunting work from the North End Yard to the new Hinksey Yard, the booking lads were transferred from North box to Engine Shed (Station North) box. The North box signalmen at once re-applied for an increase in wages; the extra work of keeping the Train Register, answering the telephone and making telephone inquiries, quite a chore in a busy box, would get them the extra marks they needed to rise into Class 1.

Now Mr Cox refused to allow a new census. Mr Matthews wrote to Cox on 11 December asking if the men were justified in their request, and on 28 December Cox replied 'No' in a rather roundabout way: 'When Hinksey Yard was brought in it was the intention for the whole of the working at North End to be transferred to the new yard, but owing to congestion of heavy traffic it has been necessary to take back some of the work to the North End temporarily. Certain Pilot trips are therefore running between Oxford North and South and two goods trains start from North End. It is anticipated that this will only be temporary and soon there will be no work in the yard. I am of the opinion that it would be reasonable to base the present classification on the June 1941 assessment, Class 2.'

The new works in the old North End Yard - to redevelop the site as an improved locomotive yard with proper coaling facilities and a better entrance/exit at the station end, and to provide carriage sidings at the north end, had not been autho-

rised by 14 April 1943 (letter from C. T. Cox to G. Matthews).

Four applications were made for upgrading from 23 November 1942 until 3 August 1943. On 16 August Mr Cox could still see no point in re-taking the marks because it seemed to him that the box now had less work to do; perhaps he thought that the assessment might be to the detriment of the men. He wrote, 'The North End Yard is used for loco coal wagon storage, cripples and traffic held back from Fairford line. There is no regular work done there and it is possible that the 24 hours chosen for the census could pass without a train going in.'

But the men continued to insist, and the assessment was made over the 24 hours ending 24 November 1943: 148 trains were signalled through, 101 trains started or terminated from the box, and 29 trains were signalled and cancelled; there were 3,827 lever movements. The box was working at 315 marks per hour and raised to Class 1 in January 1944, backdated to August 1943.

The junction to the LMR was inspected for use with civilian traffic on 7 July 1948. Lt-Col Wilson RE inspected on behalf of the Ministry of Transport - accompanied by 'a great crowd' of GWR and LMS officials*, to quote my friend, the late Sid Mumford, who was on duty in the box that day. Lt-Col Wilson told Sid that in his opinion the box ought to have had a booking boy because of the 88-lever frame and the constant work.

The signalman was authorised to use the 'Warning Acceptance (3-5-5 on the bell) against down trains provided that there was not a passenger train in the clearing point, and coaches could be propelled from North Junction to the station on the Up Main after the 2-3-2 code had been sent and acknowledged.

After 1 October 1951 all passenger services to and from the ex-LMS line were diverted to the ex-GWR

* Pictured in North Junction box in *Rail Centres: Oxford* by Laurence Waters, page 60.

station, increasing the work because now the box was permanently switched in to the LMR and the junction had to be reversed more often. At this juncture the signalman was permitted to use the ex-LMS line towards Rewley Road as his clearing point, if, at the time that 'Is Line Clear?' was asked from Port Meadow or Oxford Road Junction, he did not have a clearing point in the direction of the ex-GWR lines. In connection with this permission, if he had given 'Line Clear' with the junction set towards Rewley Road, he was permitted to re-set the facing points towards the ex-GWR line, provided that 'Train Entering Section' had not been received for the train and he had obtained permission from Station North for the train to proceed.

Right No 6949 *Haberfield Hall* coasts briskly southwards into Oxford past North Junction's Down Main Starting signal in 1955; Port Meadow's Up Home signal is on the right. *Peter Barlow/AVC*

Below An LMR 'Crab' coasts across the junction from the down Western to the up London Midland Region lines at Oxford North Junction in 1955. Note Port Meadow's fixed Distant below North Junction's Starting signal. The locomotive coaling stage, seen under construction in the previous photograph, is on the far right. *Peter Barlow/AVC*

Also, from 1 October 1951 the points previously operated by a ground frame released from Oxford Rewley Road box were put on the North Junction frame. Lever 13 worked the points with ground discs 11 and 14. Trap points were installed in the up and down LMR lines in advance of No 7 signal, but to the rear of the double junction. Crossover 68 was taken out of use about 1955; it was a long way from the box, heavy to pull and not used very much.

Oxford North Junction was taken out of use under the Oxford MAS scheme on 7 October 1973.

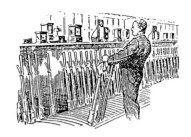

NORTH FROM OXFORD

Wolvercot Siding

The line ran northwards out of Oxford, skirting the eastern edge of the wide, grassy, acres of Port Meadow, with the Oxford Canal very close to the eastern side of the line. A rough track from a public road crossed the canal by a bridge and the railway on the level*, and a signal box existed here, on the down side, close to the 65¹/₂ milepost, by 1884 and probably since 1875. It controlled the crossing gates and also a short siding on the down side that was accessible from the Up Main through a reversing movement.

A new signal box, on the up side at 65 m 47 ch, 1 m 53 ch north of Oxford North, was opened in June 1900 with the introduction of the Up Goods Running

* OS reference: 495097, Sheet 158 of 1967.

Loop from Wolvercot Junction to Oxford North; a trailing crossover gave access from the Up Loop to the Down Siding. The new box was a brick 'Type 7' with a floor 29 by 12 feet, 11 ft 11 in above rail level, housing a frame of 29 levers, interlocked with the 'double twist' mechanism. There were several spaces or spares.

An ash path crossed the meadow, and the siding existed as a loading point for farm produce; hay and straw was for years sent away Mr H. O. King, a hay and straw wholesaler. It was also there for the Wolvercote papermill - coal and paper pulp came in by rail, and finished paper went out.

A porter from the Goods Agent's Department at Oxford came out for a couple of hours every weekday to manage the siding. He booked the wagons in and

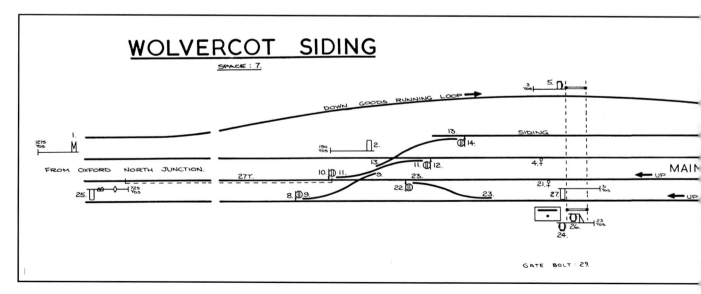

out so that demurrage could be charged if they occupied the siding for longer than three days; he also sheeted wagons, and made out the waybills.

In 1936 the 9.45 am Oxford-Aynho 'J' headcode goods was booked to call 'as required' daily at 9.52-10.2. It 'stopped main line', 'cut off behind' the siding

Wolvercot Siding signal box, looking north from the Up Main in 1955. No 6120 stands on the Up Goods Running Loop with an up 'H' headcode goods. *Peter Barlow/AVC*

traffic, went ahead and reversed into the siding. After berthing the traffic it came out again. The men had to look sharp and get on their way, for behind them was the 8.40 am Paddington-Birmingham 'A', off Oxford at 10.15. The goods was booked to refuge at Kidlington at 10.12.

The return trip, 1.25 pm Aynho, was not booked to call at the siding at all. Instead, in the up direction the siding was serviced by the 10.35 am Fairford-Oxford 'K' headcode, which came from Wolvercot Junction along the Up Goods Running Loop at about 4.40.

The Down Goods Running Loop was brought into use on 3 March 1942, but without any connection to the siding, together with a 'turn-out' from the Up Goods Loop to the Up Main. These additions left the frame with one space, No 7.

The box was Class 3 in 1923, working then at 120 marks per hour, and remained in that class until it was taken out of use on 7 November 1962.

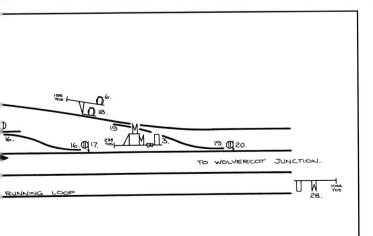

Left Looking south from the Down Siding as No 4903 *Astley Hall* approaches on the Down Main with an 'F' headcode train in 1955. Note the GWR wooden-post, ringed-arm signal - a March 1942 addition - on the Up Goods Loop. *Peter Barlow/AVC*

Below left Looking north from the Up Goods Loop before the war; these are the same signals as in the previous photograph, but before the connection between Loop and Main was added. This 15 August 1929 view is very little changed from 1900. Wagons for Wolvercote papermill stand on the left, and below the Siding box's Starting signal in the distance are Wolvercot Junction's 'splitting' or routing Distants. The Oxford Canal is on the extreme right.

In the far distance beyond the bridge a lineside house is just visible. This was occupied by a platelayer and his family who, in the days before the universal telephone, had the additional after-hours duty of acting as callman should the fogmen, snowmen or Signal & Telegraph Department linemen be required. All these men lived in Wolvercote village, and the platelayer earned a nice bit extra walking out to get them. There was a trembler bell in the house, operated from Wolvercot Junction, and each person was identified by a code of rings.

There were two linemen with Districts extending north and south of Wolvercot, covering many signal boxes. Once alerted the Lineman got on his bicycle and rode to the nearest signal box to use the phone and find out what was required. During the day the callman was working on the track and his wife had the job of listening for the bell. If she heard the appropriate code, she placed on the wall below an upstairs window one of the ancient GWR 'S' plates specially designed for the purpose of calling the Lineman. If he passed by on a train (railwaymen travelled about their business by train in those days - a novel idea!) he looked at the house to see if the plate was exhibited. Reg Gardener was the callman from 1945, and the system remained in force into the 1960s. *GWR*

Below Looking south from Wolvercote Lane bridge in May 1929, before the Down Goods Running Loop was added. A 'Star' Class express engine is on the lowliest duty, and the 5-foot-long arms of the signal indicate to the driver that he is 'right away' at Wolvercot Junction for Banbury. *Dr Jack Hollick/AVC*

Bottom Work in progress for the new Down Goods Loop on 24 February 1942. *GWR*

The finished job, and the 1942 replacement for the wooden signal, seen in 1955. No 6976 *Graythwaite Hall* heads a train bound, perhaps, for Sheffield - it has a Gresley Buffet Car. *Peter Barlow/AVC*

Wolvercot Junction

Wolvercot Junction came into being from June 1853 with the opening of the Oxford, Worcester & Wolverhampton Railway. The facing points in 1879 were at 66 m 21 ch; later they were moved 66 yards south to be directly outside the signal box. The Worcester and Birmingham lines split at the facers and ran parallel for about 220 (later 286) yards north of the facing points before commencing the divergence proper.

The junction was re-positioned at 66 m 32 ch early in 1900, when the new Up Goods Running Loop was added and a new signal box, a brick 'Type 7', was opened. This had a floor 29 by 12 feet, 11 ft 11 in above the rails, and housed a 35-lever frame (with some spaces), the levers interlocked by the GWR 'stud' locking, placing the levers at $5^{1}/_{4}$-inch centres. There were two detonator levers in the frame.

The 'stud' interlocking was replaced by a GWR standard vertical tappet machine on 29 August 1941 without alteration to the look of the frame in the operating room. The Down Goods Running Loop was added on 3 March 1942, the track running directly to the Down Worcester line with a crossover from the Loop to the Down Main for Banbury. These additions required seven more working levers, and thus more interlocking. This is one good reason why the old and rather restricted 'stud' system of interlocking was replaced.

The box was Class 3, working at 136 marks per hour in 1923 with one signalman on each shift, seven days a week, 24 hours a day. Trains in the following numbers passed the box during 1944/5:

Weekending	Trains
22 April 1944	1,118
19 August 1944	1,153
14 October 1944	1,261
17 February 1945	1,065

In the 24 hours ending 6 am on 12 April 1945 196 trains passed the box and eight started from or terminated there, making 204 in all; the signalmen made 1,858 lever movements. The eight trains were those either 'going dead' in the loop, or those being re-started with a fresh engine and men after going dead. The reason for this was probably that Banbury yard had 'blocked back' and could not accept any more trains, or that the men on the train had been on duty for very long hours and simply had to pack it in since there was no relief crew to take over.

The Instructions for Wolvercot Junction dated 1949 (which were printed with the GWR typeface) show that down trains bound for the Yarnton direction on the Worcester line were 'asked' to Wolvercot Junction as 1-3 or 1-2, 'Branch passenger' or 'Branch

Goods'. The Wolvercot signalman 'asked on' to Yarnton using 1-3 or 1-2 if the train was bound for the Fairford line, but if it was bound for what was always called 'the West Midland', ie the Worcester main line, a 1-3 became a normal 3-1 (Stopping passenger) or a 4 (Express passenger), and a 1-2 was changed to the appropriate freight bell code.

For trains *from* the Worcester or Fairford lines, the Wolvercot Junction signalman asked 'Is Line Clear?' to Wolvercot Sidings as soon as he had given 'Line Clear' to Yarnton Junction; Yarnton used normal 'Is Line Clear?' codes to Wolvercot and the latter signalman changed them. Any passenger trains from Yarnton were 'asked

on' as 1-3, and any goods as 1-2, this code being repeated up to Oxford Station North box.

The entrance to the Up Goods Loop from the Up Main Banbury line was laid north of the Worcester line junction, and the interlocking was so arranged that the facing points from Up Main to Up Goods

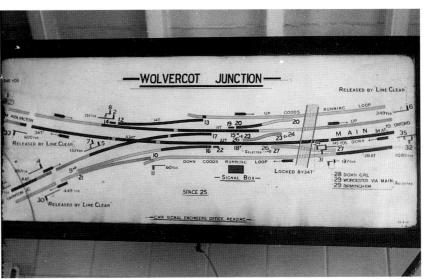

Right The 1942, GWR, diagram, photographed in 1965. *AVC*

Below Wolvercot Junction from the A40 overbridge in 1955, with the 8.55 Worcester coming over the junction. *Peter Barlow/AVC*

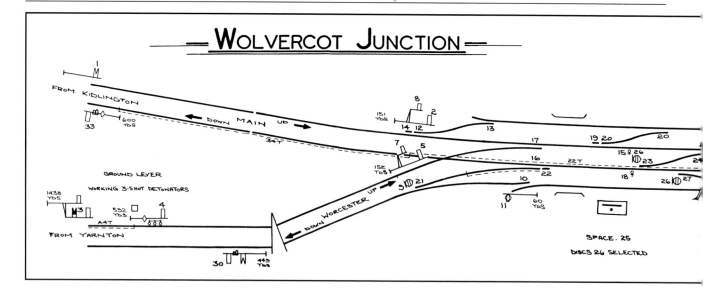

Loop had to be set for the loop before the route could be set from Up Worcester to Up Main. The signal box Instructions permitted the signalman to accept any train from Kidlington with the points set for the Up Goods Loop, provided that the loop was clear for 440 yards ahead of the Home signal.

However, this permission was more or less useless. If an Up Main Banbury line train had been accepted from Kidlington with the points set for the loop, the Wolvercot signalman would have been obliged by the rules to bring it to a stand at his Home signal before he could alter the points from Up Loop to Up Main. He might just as well 'refuse' the road to Kidlington until he had a proper clearing point up the Main. He had no authority to use the 'Warning Acceptance' to Kidlington. If an Outer Home had been sited on the Up Main 440 yards in rear of the Inner Home there would have been no problem.

On the Up Worcester line trains were running on a falling gradient for 30 miles from Moreton-in-Marsh. At Yarnton, just as the train crossed the junction to the LNW/LMS, the grade steepened from 1 in 240 to 1 in 127 as far as Wolvercot's Home signal protecting the main line.

GWR signalling regulations required a Distant signal to be 1,000 yards from its Home signal when on a falling gradient. In 1909 and until 1940 the distance from Wolvercot Junction's Up Distant to outermost Up Home was only 687 yards, and was a lower arm below Yarnton's Up Advanced Starting signal. To give

The signal box in 1965, with 1905-pattern GWR block instruments for the main lines to Banbury, Worcester and Oxford and 1947-pattern 'Permissive Block' instruments for the Goods Loops. All the track circuit repeaters are old GWR types. *AVC*

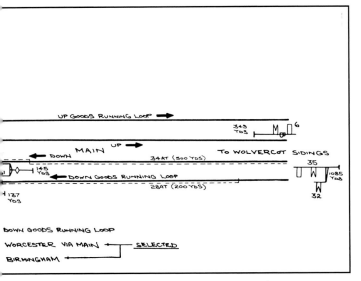

the regulation 1,000 yards braking distance, Distant arms would also have been necessary under Yarnton's Up Starting signal and Up Home, a relatively expensive proceeding.

However, to improve matters Yarnton's Up Advanced Starting signal was abolished during the later 1930s, well before the new yard began construction in 1940. This enabled an Outer Home for Wolvercot Junction to be raised, while Wolvercot Junction's Up Distant was put on Yarnton's Up Starting signal. This Outer Home signal was exactly 440 yards to the rear of Wolvercot's Home, so the main line was properly protected from trains approaching from Worcester and the Wolvercot Junction signalman could allow trains to approach him simultaneously from Worcester, Banbury and Oxford - provided that his clearing points were unoccupied and that he did not lower his Outer Home.

The braking distance on the Worcester line from the Up Distant to its Outer Home was still only 846 yards. Given this lack of braking distance, the GWR Signalling Regulations required the signalman to use the procedures of Regulation 4A (already described) to accept a train from the rear when he could not get the road from the box in advance. My friend Stan Worsfold worked Yarnton from 1939 to 1942 and later worked Yarnton and Wolvercot Junction as a relief man. Albert Walker also worked Wolvercot Junction and both men are quite sure that Regulation 4A was never used by Wolvercot Junction, neither before nor after 1940. Furthermore, the 1949 Instructions for Wolvercot make no mention of the need to use Regulation 4A.

The only answer to this curious inconsistency is that there was a 40 mph permanent speed restriction from Yarnton station to Wolvercot Junction, which reduced the danger of over-running signals at 'Danger', but Regulation 4A recog-

Wolvercot Junction's Worcester line Down Starting signal, with Yarnton Junction's Distant below it, in 1955; a classic GWR signal with 5-foot arms. *Peter Barlow/AVC*

nised no such condition. However, wise drivers, working loose-coupled freight trains, did not wait to pass Distant signals at 'Caution' before they started braking, and they treated the approach to Yarnton/Wolvercot with particular respect, knowing too well the lack of braking distance. Charlie Turner used the bridge carrying a farm track across the line* as the point at which he began to brake so as to be well under control should he find Wolvercot Junction's Up Distant at 'Caution'. This was 1¼ miles before Wolvercot Junction's Distant and about 350 yards before passing Yarnton's Up Distant.

There were occasions when drivers neglected to do this. One night a signalman at Wolvercot gave 'Line

* OS reference 460120, Sheet 145 of 1953.

Clear' to Yarnton for an up freight and later 'gave the road and pulled off' for a 'Down Birmingham fast'. Freight and 'Fast' were 'on line' together, the fast clattered past and the signalman had just re-set the road to bring the freight off the Worcester line when it went rumbling by. This caused considerable astonishment to the signalman since he had not yet lowered his Up Worcester line signals. Taking matters in his stride, he pulled off his Up Starting signal and sent 'Train out of Section' to Yarnton.

The Yarnton-Wolvercot 'box to box' phone rang.
'Did that up one stop at your signal?'
'No.'
'I didn't think he would,' came the laconic reply.
Wolvercot Junction box was taken out of use on 14 October 1973.

Kidlington

Between Wolvercot Junction and Kidlington there were three gated level crossings worked from ground frames, each with their own Distant signals: Yarnton Lane, 67 m 40 ch*; Sandy Lane, 67 m 78 ch; and Roundham, 68 m 41 ch (approx)**. Sandy Lane's Down Distant was a few yards north of Yarnton Lane Crossing and Roundham's Distant on the up line was below Kidlington's Up Starting signal. Each crossing's

* R. A. Cooke, *Track Plans: Oxford*, Vol 27.

** OS reference 484140, Sheet 145

ground frame hut contained the gate bolt levers, Distant signal levers and a repeater block instrument working in circuit with the Wolvercot Junction-Kidlington instruments, so that the crossing-keeper would know when a train was coming. The three huts were of standard design.

Kidlington station centred on 69 m 5 ch and the signal box was situated on the up side of the line at 69 m 17 ch*. There had been a signal box here since about 1882, but the box referred to here was the second and last at the station. This was a brick 'Type 5', brought into use when the single-track Woodstock branch was opened from here on 19 May 1890.

The box had a floor 31 ft 9 in by 11 ft 6 in, raised 8 feet above the rails, housing a 51-lever frame, of which 13 were spares. Branch trains were at first worked with the Train Staff & Ticket system with a block bell and instrument, but between July 1901 and July 1902 the Webb-Thompson Electric Train Staff was introduced. The box was Class 4 in 1923, at 102

Yarnton Lane, the first of the three level crossings between Wolvercot Junction and Kidlington, looking north in 1955; Sandy Lane's Down Distant signal is 'off'. *Peter Barlow/AVC*

Great Western men at Kidlington, 5 February 1921. Nearest the camera is 'Ol' Pom', Woodstock branch driver Bill Pomeroy. He worked the line for many years and became quite blasé about the job. On the engine is Fireman Ted Harmon, who moved to Slough and was a driver from London area sheds. The other man is the then Station Master, William Thomas Cook, who was nicknamed 'Traffic' Cook because of his general enthusiasm for business and also for the 'Traffic Department' against the 'Loco' in the event of disputes over delays. He was what Berkshire people used to call 'a good old boy', a devoted, hard-working, cheerful, rough 'n' ready, unpompous person without a Gestapo-like regard for the Rule Book - just my sort of person. While he undoubtedly took a relaxed view of the rules, he simply would not have understood a railway that has rules coming out of its ears - and turns away traffic.

Cook was born on 9 May 1862 and entered the GWR as a Lad Porter at Oxford station in June 1876. He portered at Radley and became Booking Porter at Burghclere in November 1883. Here he got into some difficulty over the Train Staff and was fined 10 shillings in May 1886. He was promoted to

Booking Porter at Aldermaston one year later, and was promoted to Station Inspector at Kidlington, a new post created because of the opening of the Woodstock branch. He remained here for the rest of his service, merely because he was happy where he was, getting into trouble very occasionally and retiring after 51 years' loyal service in 1927. *W. L. Kenning/AVC*

marks per hour, being upgraded to Class 3, 158 marks, in July 1924.

The branch line ran north alongside the Down Main for about a mile to cross the River Cherwell, before swinging due west and climbing over the Oxford Canal. From 1891 until 1906 there was a crossover from the Down Branch to the Down Main 166 yards north of the signal box, which enabled the branch to be used as a goods loop* - a rather curious and unusual feature for several reasons. There were eight trips in each direction over the branch, so the signalman would have to be sure, when he used the branch as a goods loop, that he could have it clear before the branch passenger train wanted the road.

Until 1906 there was no facing connection from the Down Main to the Down Branch/Loop, only a trailing connection from the Up Main, reversing into the loop - thus an up goods train would have to reverse across the Down Main into the loop. A down goods would have been obliged to make a double shunt - reverse from Down to Up Main, then forwards into the loop.

The pre-1906 method of protecting the branch line before it was occupied by a main-line goods trains is not known. Perhaps the Kidlington signalman merely 'refused the road' to Woodstock if the latter asked 'Is Line Clear?' for a branch train during the time the loop was occupied by a main-line train.

The Train Staff & Ticket system was superseded by the Electric Train Staff between July 1901 and July

1902, which system permitted greater control of movements on the branch, but a more certain method of protecting the single line was not adopted until 1906.

In that year facing points were installed from Down Main to Down Loop, and the points from Down Branch to Down Main at the northern end were repositioned 70 feet north of the farm track overbridge*, making the loop approximately 250 yards long. Before the Kidlington signalman could unbolt the facing points from Down Main to Down Loop, he sent the bell code 5-2 to Woodstock. Woodstock replied, holding down his morse key on the final stroke. This sent a current to lift the lock on an Annett's key in Kidlington box. The signalman turned the 6-inch brass key in its lock and removed it. The Electric Train Staff circuit was now broken, the staff instruments inoperable, and with the Annett's key the signalman unlocked the facing point bolt lever.

Early in 1928 the signal box at Woodstock was abolished along, therefore, with the Electric Train Staff. This was replaced by a wooden Train Staff and 'Only one engine in steam' working. In PRO Rail 250/454 (Record Office, Kew), the entry for 28 July 1927 shows that the GWR gave an undertaking to this effect with the Ministry of Transport. Passenger trains still ran on the line - no fewer than 18 a day in

* R. A. Cooke, op. cit.

Above On the Woodstock branch, about 700 yards north of Kidlington station, the signalling arrangements enabled the passenger branch to be used as a Down Goods Loop. The signal for Woodstock on the extreme left is lowered - just - and there is what appears to be a non-standard arm to route trains from Branch (or Loop) to Down Main. In the far distance on the branch can be seen the Up Branch Outer Home giving a clearing point to permit acceptance of a train from Woodstock when the loop was occupied. Photographed in 1952. *W. L. Kenning/AVC*

Top The Woodstock branch train, running 'mixed', leaves Kidlington for Woodstock in 1954. The view is looking north from the up side. The engine and its 'push-pull' coach are close-coupled and vacuum-braked, and the window of the driving-end of the coach is visible. Behind that come the unbraked, loose-coupled freight vehicles, with a manned brake van or 'Toad' on the rear. If the trucks should break away from the coach the guard will screw down his hand brake and prevent a runaway or a collision. The 'Toad' is branded 'RU' (Regular User); below this the wording appears to be 'Blenheim & Woodstock Oxford', and below that 'Not in common use'. *Peter Barlow/AVC*

Above left The view north off the road bridge in 1954. In the foreground is Kidlington's Up Starting signal, with Roundham Lane's electric-motor-worked Distant beneath it. No 2259 runs through on an up 'H' headcode freight. The signal on the left is the Up Branch to Up Main junction signal. *Peter Barlow/AVC*

1936 - so to protect a goods train in the Branch/Loop from the approach of an Up Branch train an extra stop signal was provided on the Up Branch 600 yards on the Woodstock side of the Branch to Main points.

In May 1942 the Goods Loop was extended by re-siting the Branch to Main points 679 yards further north; the Up Branch Outer Home would have been re-positioned accordingly. The points were then operated by an electric motor using hand-generated current from a Westinghouse 'Type C' ('hurdy-gurdy') machine in the signal box.

Extra traffic came to the station from November 1923* when Oxfordshire Farmers Ltd opened a rail-connected bacon processing factory behind the station.

Kidlington signal box was closed on 16 September 1968.

* R. A. Cooke, op. cit.

Yarnton Junction

Yarnton Junction - its layout, it history, its remoteness - had a wonderful 'atmosphere' and a curiosity that fascinated enthusiasts and even some of its signalmen. Much of its early history has been described in the history of Oxford and its railways (pages 16-17).

The first junction created on the Yarnton site came into use on 1 April 1854 at 67 m 12 ch from Paddington, when the LNWR opened the link from its 'Buckinghamshire Railway', giving Euston access to Worcester. Then on 1 August 1859 the Witney Railway (WR) was incorporated by Act of Parliament to build 8 miles of standard-gauge single track from Yarnton 'Witney Junction', 67 m 28 ch; this was opened on 14 November 1861 from a very simple station. Indeed, it seems that there was little more than bare platforms.

The independent East Gloucestershire Railway, incorporated on 7 August 1862, built a single-track extension from Witney to Fairford, 14 m 10 ch, opened on 15 January 1873. Both these little companies were purchased by the GWR on 1 July 1890. The full length of the line from Yarnton to Fairford is given in the GWR Working Time Table (WTT) as 22 m 57 ch, and in the GWR Company History (McDermott, Vols 1 and 2) as 22 m 23 ch. Until the demise of the GWR, the WTT for the branch was entitled 'Witney & East Gloucestershire Branch'.

By circa 1880 the two junctions at Yarnton were worked by separate signal boxes, rather than by policeman and ground levers. The erstwhile 'Buckingham Junction' was worked by 'Yarnton, Oxford Road Junction' (which worked with the LNWR box 'Oxford Road Junction'), situated in the 'V' of the junction; the other, 'Yarnton, Witney Junction', was sited by the main-line facing points.

On 13 June 1909 the GWR brought into use a central signal box. It was a wooden 'Type 7' with a floor 25 by 12 feet, raised 14 feet above rail level on a narrow, brick pedestal. At that stage it housed a McKenzie & Holland frame of 50 miniature levers set at $2^{1}/_{2}$-inch centres, in a raised console. Lever interlocking, as at Didcot North, was mechanical. All the point bolts, fouling bars and signals in the layout were operated by battery-driven electric motors, activated by the operation of the miniature levers, the battery house and generator room being situated on the up platform. This pioneering installation was replaced by a conventional GWR-design frame of 51 levers on 30 July 1929.

The single line to Fairford was controlled by Tyers No 7 Electric Tablet instruments from Yarnton to Eynsham, Witney and Bampton (re-named 'Brize Norton & Bampton' on 1 May 1940), and by the Webb-Thompson Electric Train Staff from Bampton to Lechlade and Fairford. This was still the case in the summer of 1953, but Yarnton (and perhaps the others also) lost its Tablet instrument by the end of that year. It was replaced by the 1914-designed GWR Key Token instrument.

The oldest Instructions I have for Yarnton Junction are from 1944. These permitted the signalman to use the 'Warning Acceptance' for Up Branch and Up Main line trains, provided that there was not a passenger train within the clearing point. However, it seems likely that the earlier Instructions superseded by the 1944 issue permitted the use of the 'Warning' without any restrictions. I think this because the 1936 WTT schedules three occasions when passenger trains' timings clashed at the junction, and the only way to keep the trains running at all would have been by the use of the 'Warning' - under circumstances that were forbidden by the 1944 Instructions. There was a noticeable trend in the latter days of the GWR, and by BR, to reduce the number of places were the 'Warning' could be used, and to restrict the circumstances in which it could be used.

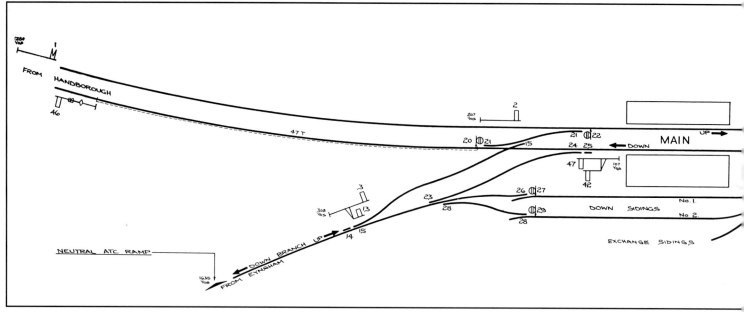

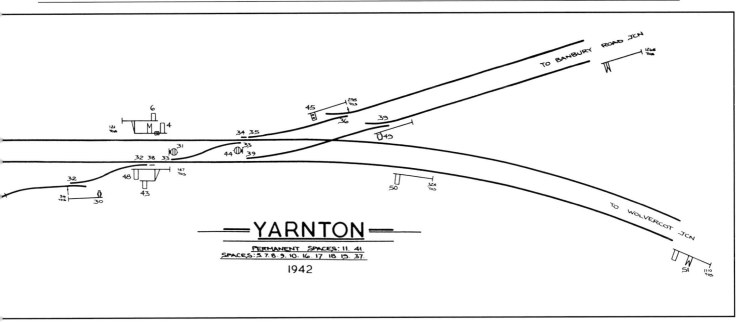

In the up direction Handborough 'asked the road' to Yarnton when he received 'Train Entering Section' ('TES') from Charlbury; Charlbury to Handborough was 6 m 16 ch, and from Handborough to Yarnton 3 m 16 ch. Yarnton 'gave the road' (if the line was clear) and at once 'asked on' to Wolvercot Junction. The latter could 'give the road' as already described; if the circumstance were favourable he could at once 'ask on' to Wolvercot Siding.

In 1936 a theoretically impossible sequence of events was timetabled for Yarnton between 7.21 and 7.41 pm. The 4.10 pm Wolverhampton (6.10 Worcester) express was 'asked' from Handborough, and simultaneously the 6.32 pm Fairford passenger was 'asked' from Eynsham. Yarnton would have 'given the road' to Handborough and 'refused' the road to

Left Signalman Eric Davies and Yarnton Junction signal box in 1955. *Peter Barlow/AVC*

Right The splendid interior of the box in January 1954. Nearest the camera there is an LNWR-style instrument on brass columns, its bell situated underneath the cabinet; the instrument is labelled 'Oxford Road Junct. LMS'. The central knob is turned to operate the lower needle of the pair, which also operates the needle at Oxford Road Junction. When the bottom of the needle is pointing to '5 o'clock' it indicates 'Line Clear'; '7 o'clock' indicates 'Train on Line'. This is a 'Permissive' line, allowing more than one train to occupy it, and a small window above the knob contains a counter; each time a train is sent 'Entering Section' from Oxford Road Junction, the Yarnton signalman turns the knob one notch.

Beyond the GWR Absolute Block instrument is the bell for the single-line tablet instrument - a Tyers No 7 - which stands at the far end of the frame. *Peter Barlow/AVC*

Eynsham, but the 6.32 Fairford was scheduled to leave Eynsham at 7.28½, 30 seconds after the up express was due to pass the box. If the express ran late, Yarnton would still have to refuse the road to Eynsham - unless he was allowed to give Fairford the 'Warning' - because his clearing point was going to be fouled by a passenger train.

After the up fast had passed Yarnton, the signalman gave 'Train out of Section' to Handborough and, according to the WTT, was immediately 'asked' for the 2.50 pm Moreton-Oxford 'pick-up' goods. The 6.32 pm Fairford-Oxford passenger had also to be 'given the road' as it would be standing at Eynsham - and again, unless the Yarnton signalman was permitted to use the 'Warning' for the goods, with a passenger train signalled to foul the clearing point, the goods would have to be 'refused' until the Fairford passenger had cleared towards Wolvercot, thus preventing the goods from keeping its schedule. Both trains were scheduled to arrive at Yarnton at 7.40. Clearly this was impossible, and unless the GWR made a mistake in its timetabling the Yarnton signalman must have been allowed to accept the goods under the 'Warning' in spite of the clearing point being fouled by a passenger train.

There were two other, similar, occasions: the 2.12 pm Fairford clashed with the very important 12.50 pm Hereford express, and the 4.38 pm Bampton clashed with the 'crack' 3.40 pm Malvern. Timetables after 1944 seem to include these clashes, which would be in keeping with the 1944 Instructions regarding the use of the 'Warning Acceptance'.

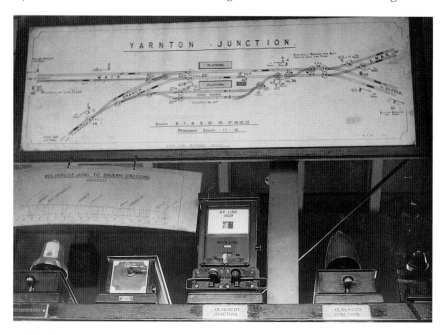

Above left The diagram is dated 24.7.28 and is in the 'AK' style, but no tracer's initials can be seen. The second instrument from the left is the switching-out device, the 'block switch', at the 'In' position. Photographed in January 1954. *Peter Barlow/AVC*

Left The single-line Tablet instrument, with its hooped carriers hanging below, has been, or is about to be, superseded by the Electric Key Token instrument alongside in this 1954 photograph. The 'new' instrument (it was invented in 1914) has a key token in the lock, displaying the legend 'YARNTON JCT - EYNSHAM'. *Peter Barlow/AVC*

'The LNW Loop'

Even after the Euston-Worcester passenger service was withdrawn from 31 September 1861, Yarnton Junction remained an interchange for freight and minerals between South Wales and the GWR Black Country, the southern part of the LNWR and East Anglia. What follows is a combination of information drawn from the GWR WTT and the working Instructions for Yarnton and the accounts given to me by Sid Mumford, who was a porter-shunter at Yarnton prior to 1939, and Stan Worsfold, who worked the box 1939-41.

The line to Oxford Road Junction was known as the 'LNW Loop', and even in BR days the men called it the 'LMS Loop'. 'Fixed' (ie permanently fixed at 'Caution') Distant signals were provided on the approaches to Yarnton and Oxford Road Junctions. Prior to 1940/1 there were three hand-worked crossovers along the loop; one was a long train's length from the GWR line, the second was situated a little to the west of the Woodstock Road level crossing and the third near Oxford Road Junction. When a train was going to occupy the loop, the LNW/LMS signalman and the GWR signalman conferred and agreed by telephone.

The usual traffic over the loop from the LNW/LMS was iron ore, bricks and coal empties for the GWR in South Wales or South Staffordshire, and from those districts came iron ore empties, brick empties and loaded coal. LMS freight traffic off the Bletchley line for Reading or Bristol did not go to Yarnton, but was taken to Oxford North and put on to the GWR there.

During the Depression of 1929-33 the coal and iron industry in South Wales declined severely and the train service suffered accordingly, but from 1935, when recession began to lift as Britain prepared for war, iron, coal and bricks and the trains to haul them were in demand again. During the week-ending 3 July 1938 300 wagons were sent from the GWR to the LMS, and 521 wagons came in the opposite direction*.

In 1936 the only GWR through freight *scheduled* to put off traffic on the loop was the 2.20 am (MO), 3 am (MX), Pontypool Road 'J' headcode, 4-1 on the bell, booked at Yarnton from 12.57 to 2 pm. A similarly timed train had called at Yarnton as far back as 1910. There were, of course, 'specials', so on some days the loop was busier than others.

Traffic for the LMS was marshalled next to the engine. Nothing was detached on the GWR Up Main

- the whole train ran on to the Up Loop until the brake van was 50 yards beyond the catch points protecting the Worcester line. The guard secured the rear section of the train, uncoupled behind the LMS section and waved the driver forward until the rear of the last wagon was clear of the first crossover. The wagon brakes were then pinned down, the engine cut off and run forward over the second crossover on the far (east) side of the Woodstock Road. The guard altered the points, the engine reversed to the down line and ran back to the first crossover, crossed again and went up behind the LMS wagons. Now these were propelled over the Woodstock Road crossing, beyond the second crossover, wagon brakes pinned down, and left for collection by the LMS.

In 1932 the Instructions did not allow the men to run their engine 'down' the 'up' line, even though this was occupied by the rear of their stationary train and, indeed, the whole loop was nothing more than a glorified exchange siding. Once it had been the Main Line to Euston, and the formalities had to be observed. The engine therefore re-crossed to the down road, to the first crossover, then re-crossed, backed on to its train and, when No 45 signal was lowered, pushed back out on to the Up Main. A similar procedure was carried out by the LMS to leave one of its trains on the Down Loop. LMS engines did not normally come on to GWR metals at Yarnton at this time.

There was one shunter on duty during the day at Yarnton. His duty was (as best old memory serves) 8 am-4 pm or 9 am-5 pm. He was relieved by a Porter-Shunter, such as young Sid Mumford, who worked from 5 pm to, say, 9 pm. The shunter's job was to assist the guard of a train shunting on the loop, organise the stabling of wagons on the RCH* sidings and to take the number of every wagon exchanged between the two companies.

The 3.15 pm Didcot-Yarnton 'J' called at Radley if required to pick up Abingdon empties for Oxford North End Yard. At North End it collected empty wagons belonging to the LMS or LNER companies or 'private owners' on those lines. It also brought down the 'iron ore brake van'. This was a 25-tonner, especially for use on these very heavy trains; the LMS brake van did not work through. The 3.15 terminated at Yarnton at 5 pm, and the wagons were stabled on the RCH sidings behind the box, or perhaps its engine and men transferred them to the LMS Loop. It was scheduled to return to Didcot at 5.50 pm, calling at Oxford North to collect LMS transfer traffic.

---

* RAIL 421/9 (Record Office, Kew), LMS Chief Operating Manager's Report. Quoted by M. Christensen in World War 2 Railway Study Group.

* So-named because the Railway Clearing House kept account of inter-company transactions such as wagon mileage over 'foreign' lines.

Whether any passenger train ever worked over the loop after October 1861 is not known*, but contingency plans were included in the Local Instructions of 1922 - and probably earlier. In the event of a complete blockage of the GWR route between Oxford North and Wolvercot Junction, Worcester line trains, including passenger trains, would have been worked to Yarnton Junction via the LNWR, going through the Exchange Siding at Engine Shed (Station North)

* A passenger train chartered by the LCGB passed over the line in 1965 (see the accompanying photograph).

box to Oxford Road Junction. The effect of this was to take the train around a triangle and reverse it. On arrival at Oxford Road Junction a waiting GWR engine would reverse on to what had been the rear of the train and draw it over the loop and to Worcester, while the engine that brought the train from Oxford waited to bring the next southbound GWR train into Oxford.

Before the loop could be used for passenger traffic it had to be walked by a competent person to make sure that both lines were unobstructed. He then issued a certificate to this effect to the signalmen at Yarnton and Oxford Road and only then could the trains pass over the line.

The curious thing was that the Instructions did not permit the line to be worked by the Absolute Block method, using telephones, to say when the line was clear; a telephone or single-needle telegraph circuit must have existed between the two boxes. Instead the time-wasting - and not entirely safe - 'Time Interval' method was used. One train could not follow another over the same line until an interval of 30 minutes had elapsed between them.

In September 1938*, contingency planning for the forthcoming war recognised the Cambridge-Bedford-Bletchley-Yarnton line as being of strategic importance, bypassing London, which would undoubtedly be bombed heavily, and cutting across all the major routes radiating northwards from London. Traffic from the LMS and

* M. Christensen, op. cit.

Above left The view south in January 1954, with the old Tablet instrument alone and in silhouette. The slide of the instrument is out, proving that a tablet has been withdrawn for a branch train to Eynsham. Just beyond the approaching train the 'LMS Loop' swings away to the left. *Peter Barlow/AVC*

Left A clearer view of the Loop junction, as a regular Fairford branch engine approaches with a down branch train. Note the 3-foot arm as the signal to the 'LMS Loop' - the loop was only a goods line and did not warrant a full-size arm. It's a very cold, murky morning in January 1954. *Peter Barlow/AVC*

Surely the last passenger train ever to run from Yarnton to Oxford Road Junction? The magnifying glass shows that the GWR's precision in placing a 3-foot arm on the junction signal has been abandoned by the WR - there is now a 4-foot arm to the loop. The date is 15 August 1965. *Hugh Ballantyne*

LNER for the Southern Railway, Central Section, was to come across to Yarnton, reverse and go south through Oxford and Reading West. In 1940 connecting curves between the north/south and east/west routes were laid at Sandy and Claydon/Calvert, and the 1854 South Curve at Bletchley was re-laid. Swanbourne marshalling yard opened 10 August 1942*.

Enlarged exchange facilities were built at Yarnton during 1940/1. They consisted of five exchange sidings, two reception sidings (connected at their buffer-stop ends with a crossover to allow the engine that had brought the train in on one line to escape through the crossover along the other line), a cripple wagon siding, a turntable road, and a locomotive water supply. An austerity brick building with an office, shunters' accommodation and a store was erected along with buildings for the Carriage & Wagon Department men. This was brought into use on 5 May 1941**.

The 'No Block' method of working the LMS Loop was replaced with LMS 'Permissive Block' regulations. An ex-LNWR 'Permissive Block' instrument was installed on the instrument shelves at Yarnton and Oxford Road Junctions, together with bell communication, and the three hand-worked crossovers were removed from the loop, made redundant by the facilities of the New Yard.

'Wrong direction' working was now permitted on the loop as follows: 'When the Down Loop is occupied, LMS engines for Yarnton GW yard may run over the Up Loop between Oxford Road Junction and Yarnton GW signal boxes in accordance with LMS Block Regulation 36. This working is not permitted during fog or falling snow.'***

Now there was a regular booked service of trains

across the loop, and 'specials' as well, of course. The wartime traffic was very heavy*, both in terms of numbers and sheer weight - iron ore, bricks, coal, steel, military stores, ammunition and vehicles. The loop was always fully occupied, as was a shunting engine at Yarnton yard. My friend Driver Don Kingdom recalls that this was usually a 2-6-0 tender engine, or 2-8-0/2-8-2 tank, because of the weight of the trains.

Don Kingdom and Stan Worsfold remember that the Fairford branch was used as a head-shunt. The line fell steeply from the sidings to the branch and heavy trains dropping down, engine leading, on to the branch often had great difficulty backing up. Some idea of what went over the line can be gathered from the 1953 WTT details shown in the accompanying table.

Traffic from Yarnton to South Wales consisted of heavy-weight trains, and the climb to the Cotswold ridge was over 30 miles long and almost continuous, followed by steep descents. Not only hauling power but braking power was required. Most trains off Yarnton Loop went to South Wales: via Kingham and Stow-on-the-Wold; via Honeybourne and Toddington; and even via the exchange siding at Evesham to the LMS via Ashchurch. All these routes brought the trains to Cheltenham to go on for Gloucester and Chepstow. Others went all the way to Worcester, then south-west through Hereford to Newport (Mon). These trains were often hauled by

* M. Christensen, op. cit.

** RAIL 421/9, LMS Chief Operating Manager's War Report regarding the yard, states: 'Date facilities became available: 19.5.41. Cost £18,852.' Quoted in M. Christensen, op. cit.

*** GWR 'Additional Instructions for Yarnton Junction'.

* Wagons exchanged at Yarnton, week-ended 28.6.41:
From LMS to GWR, 1,821; increase on 1938 507%
From GWR to LMS, 1,871, increase on 1938 259%
From RAIL 421/9, quoted by M. Christensen, op. cit.

Scheduled trains, Yarnton to LMR, 1953

Depart Yarnton	To	Days run	Load	WR feeder
1.15 am	Toton	SuO	Empties	11.45 pm Didcot
1.15 am	Desford	SuMX	Empties	11.45 pm Didcot
3.00 am	Irthlingborough	SuO	Empties	3.30 pm Rogerstone
3.10 am	Irthlingborough	SuMX	Empties	2.00 am MO, 12.30 am MX Rogerstone
7.55 am	Swanbourne	Mon-Fri	Goods	7.30 pm Pontypool Road
10.15 am	Swanbourne	Mon-Fri	Mineral	
11.00 am	Cambridge	SuO	Goods	2.25 pm Severn Tunnel Junction
7.45 pm	Swanbourne	SX, Mon-Fri	Empties	
	Toton	SO		
9.35 pm	Swanbourne	SO	Goods	4.35 am Pontypool Road
10.50 pm	Northampton	Mon-Fri	Goods	4.35 am Pontypool Road

LMR to Yarnton

Train	Depart Yarnton	Days run	WR connection
8.20 pm Irthlingborough	1 am	SuMX	4.55 am Yarnton-Rogerstone
12.35 am Bletchley (Light engine)	2 am	SuO	-
9.43 am Cambridge	2.55 pm	Mon-Fri	3.50 pm Yarnton-Severn Tunnel Junction
11.30 am Wellingborough	5.5 pm	Mon, Tues, Fri, Sat	8.40 pm Yarnton-Severn Tunnel Junction
12.45 am Wellingborough	5.55 pm	Wed, Thurs	8.40 pm Yarnton-Severn Tunnel Junction
2.00 pm Irthlingborough	7.35 pm	SuX	11.55 pm Yarnton-Rogerstone

SuO/SuX = Sundays Only/Excepted
SO = Saturdays Excepted

2-8-0 tender engines of GWR, GCR and WD origins - and even double-headed by 2-8-0s. Also used were GWR 2-8-0 and 2-8-2 tank engines. The LMS engines that brought the trains into Yarnton went up to Oxford (GW) shed for servicing before returning to Yarnton or to Port Meadow loop for their return working.

While the value of the Cambridge-Bletchley-Yarnton to South Wales route had been recognised as early as 1938, the traffic persisted long after the war was over. But after 1953 the road haulage industry was unleashed, while the heavy industries served by the railway changed or even declined. The great days were gone by 1960, and a twilight existence settled over the place.

The Fairford branch was closed to passenger traffic on 18 June 1962 and was cut short at Witney. A daily goods ran into Witney Goods station - the original terminus of the line before the East Gloucestershire extension was built. When the goods was steam-hauled the tank engine went to the passenger station to take water.

The 'LMS Loop' was closed on 8 November 1965, and the once busy four-way junction lay under a curiously melancholy air. The signal box was switched out except for the time it was required to allow the Witney goods access to and from the branch, the windows were then completely boarded up. I have a very clear memory of my trips with Don Kingdom down to Witney with a Pannier tank on the goods and seeing Bert Hawtin coming down the stairs with the wooden Train Staff as we approached. If it was a fine day he could sit out on the top landing and enjoy the view; on a cold or wet day he sat inside the boarded-up room with the light on and the door closed.

The Witney branch was closed completely on 2 November 1970, which for all practical purposes closed Yarnton Junction signal box. It was officially abolished on 28 March 1971. Today the site of the busy exchange yard is a water-filled hole in the ground.

Right Looking towards Worcester, with the Fairford line forking left, a profusion of flowers on the down side and topiary on the up. The ivy-covered house was erected by the OWWR to house the person in charge of the station, the booking office and waiting room(s). The house could not be closer to the lineside and passengers on trains approaching the junction from the branch felt that their train was going to run into it until the line began to curve round to join the main line.

In 1931 the resident porter/booking clerk/gardener was Ernie Carter. He had been wounded in the Great War and was the porter here until the place closed; he may have come here as early as 1920. The house was demolished about 1935 and the GWR moved Ernie and his family into a new house that it built especially for him in Yarnton. The magnifying glass reveals Ernie and the signalman standing in the 'gothic' arched doorway to the booking office. One man is bending to speak to a child standing by a light-weight gate that (hopefully) prevents precipitate access to the railway line. *L&GRP 13790*

Centre right Yarnton new yard and the Fairford line, seen across the Worcester line in 1955. The 'austerity' yard office is in deep shadow on the far right. The wagons seem to go to the horizon around the sharp curve - as a result the rostrum on the extreme left was provided so that a shunter's hand signals could be seen by the train crew. *Peter Barlow/AVC*

Left On the same day ex-LMS '4F' No 44540 turns on LMR metals at Yarnton Junction. The little 'backing' signal is operated by lever 45 in the signal box. *Peter Barlow/AVC*

Eynsham

The first signal box at Eynsham station, 70 m 52 ch, was closed in 1893 and a second was erected. This was situated on the platform, measured 18 ft 6 in by 9 ft 6 in, and contained a frame of levers numbered to 19. There were probably several spaces in the frame because its layout was very simple - a connection to a couple of sidings, and the level crossing.

The station was once robbed by a pair of desperados called Brown and Kennedy. It happened in the mid-1920s. After the last train had left Eynsham these two men attacked the signalman, tied him up and took the keys to the safe and the till before dumping him in the ground frame hut 220 yards along the line towards Witney. They stole all the money they could find and made their escape in a car they had parked along the railway line. They drove along the track with one pair of wheels in the '4-foot' until they came to a farmer's occupation crossing, where they turned on to the public road. The reason for this eccentric means of departure is obscure, but perhaps they thought that they would not be seen on the road near the site of the station.

At any rate, their subterfuge did them no good, and they were arrested and imprisoned. Stan Worsfold, who told me this story, was a schoolboy at Fairford when it happened, but it was still a popular topic of conversation several years later when he went to work at Bampton.

Sidings were laid on the down side of the line between the 69¾ milepost and 70 m 7 ch during the 1930s in connection with the sugar beet industry. Access was through a single connection worked from a ground frame at 70 m 7 ch, the levers being released from Eynsham box. In November 1940 this site was enlarged for the War Department with a second ground frame at the 69¾ milepost.

On 13 July 1944 a new 17-lever frame was installed for use with a new crossing loop, about 450 yards long, which was brought into use in August. The 1944 Instructions for the box show that the signalman was permitted to accept down trains from Yarnton under the 'Warning', 3-5-5 on the bell.

The branch was closed 18 June 1962 and the signal box, the crossing loop and sidings were taken out of use on 11 July.

Above left Eynsham station looking towards Yarnton on 1 May 1956. *H. C. Casserley*

Left Looking back at Eynsham station from an Oxford-bound train. *H. C. Casserley*

The rest of the Fairford branch

Witney was allowed to use the 'Warning' for up and down trains. When the signalman there wanted to work a train into the Goods station from the passenger station, this required the train or engine to occupy, briefly, the single line between him and Eynsham. Before this movement could take place it had to be protected by the Witney signalman removing a Witney-Eynsham Tablet from the instrument. The Tablet was handed to the driver and the train set off accompanied by a porter, riding on the engine. The train drew up clear of the points, the porter worked the point and bolt levers at the ground frame, and when the train was 'inside' the Goods station, clear of the 'main line', the porter 'shut him in' and walked the Tablet back to the signal box.

When the train wanted to come out of the Goods station, the porter walked the Tablet back along to the junction. If the train had come from Oxford the porter met it at the junction, operated the ground frame, took the Tablet and walked it back to the signal box.

The Fairford branch had known peak times before the war, when extra trains were run, but when the Second World War came it was often crammed to capacity - first with trains of materials to construct the vast aerodromes for bombers, particularly that at Brize Norton. The girder work for the hangars came in by rail from Oxford, while materials for the base at Fairford are thought to have come by road from the railheads at Cirencester.

Having built the bases they had to be supplied with troops and bombs. Traffic along the branch was considerable, the layouts at several of the stations along the line were enlarged.

The 1944 Instructions for **Brize Norton & Bampton** station, 79 m

11 ch, have one word printed on the paper, in a half-inch-tall, very heavy type-face: NONE. This must surely have been for security reasons, because there must have been a lot of extra Instructions for working the place. In my notebook I have the diagram, copied from the original, which shows two runways crossing the line, a stop signal on the western side worked by an electric motor, and a 'Gateman's hut'. When planes wanted to use the runways the gates across them had to be swung away. These gates were locked by Annett's key, and the gateman asked the signalman for a release. The signalman reversed his No 4 lever, which electrically released an Annett's key. The gateman took out this key and used it to unlock a second Annett's key, which was used to unlock the runway gates. There being a war on, the air base must have asked 'Is Line Clear?' for their planes many times a day, and the planes must surely have taken precedence over the trains - on this and other questions that spring to mind, the Instructions for Brize Norton & Bampton and Carterton signal boxes are silent.

The two runways crossed the railway at 79 m 69 ch, 58 chains to the west of Brize Norton station. Lechlade, the next block post, was 6 miles to the west of the runways, and after an up train had left that station there was plenty of time, in 6 miles of running, for some emergency to occur on the runways that would obstruct the line - and no way of stopping the train. Thus a completely new signal box and crossing loop was built at **Carterton**, 80 m 43 ch, 54 chains or 1,188 yards west of those runways. The effective length of the loop was 800 feet*, and flanking it were

* GWR 'Notice to engine drivers and others'.

Witney goods yard on 24 September 1925. Sixteen vans of Witney blankets are bound for the Oxford Street, London, store of Maples. The advertisements on the engine claim that 'Witney blankets cover the world'. The engine is No 1336, taken over from the Midland & South Western Junction Railway and re-boilered by the GWR, and will be changed for a larger one at Oxford. Advice of the loading, engine number, and time of departure of the train will be telegraphed to Oxford and from there relayed to Paddington. At Paddington Goods the blankets will be loaded on to the GWR's drays and hauled through the streets of London, covered in slogans for Marriot's blankets and the GWR, by the finest draught horses Paddington's 'Mint' stables can provide. *GWR*

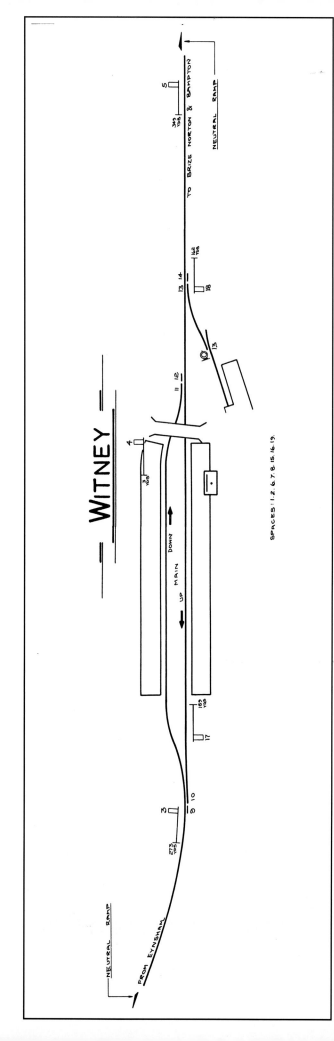

bare platforms. One of the original signalmen here was Ben Davies, who transferred to the job for health reasons after being an engine driver at Oxford.

Carterton's Up Starting signal was 410 yards in advance of the signal box and thus 778 yards from the runways. They were now closely protected on each side. The ATC ramp was 880 yards in rear of the Up Home signal, or 1,235 yards from the signal box. In the down direction the ramp was 880 yards from the Down Home, 958 yards from signal box, the line here rising towards Fairford at 1 in 230. The block sections east and west were worked with the Electric Train Staff. Carterton was permitted to accept up trains under the 'Warning'.

Lechlade was not a crossing place until 27 October 1944. After a week of work, from the 22nd to the 27th, the old Down Siding, with points to the single line at its western end, was converted to an 'each way' goods loop by installing facing points at the eastern end. A goods train could be placed in this to allow a passenger train to pass on the main line, but it was forbidden to cross two passenger trains.

It was the Lechlade signalman's responsibility to advise the Little Faringdon level crossing keeper when an up goods train left Lechlade. The signalman was permitted to use the 'Warning' for down trains, but this permission was withdrawn in 1957.

The 1944 Instructions for Fairford did not permit the use of the 'Warning'.

The Fairford branch ATC

The Fairford branch was equipped with the GWR's 'Audible Distant Signal' system in December 1906*, and on the Lambourn line in September 1909. This was an electro-mechanical system that blew a steam whistle in the engine's cab when the Distant signal the train was approaching was at 'Caution', or gave an 'All Right' bell if the signal was cleared. In 1913 the device was improved so as to apply the train's brakes if the driver did not acknowledge a warning siren - the steam whistle warning was abolished. Atmospheric pressure rushing into the vacuum brake system was used to work the siren. At this stage the system was re-named 'Automatic Train Control', or 'ATC'.

The system was very widely installed on double- and quadruple-track lines, but the only single-track lines to have it were the Fairford and Lambourn branches. The original intention was that the Audible Distant Signal/ATC would entirely replace semaphore Distant signals, but that happened only on these two branches. When the ATC was removed from the Lambourn line in March 1929, semaphore

* See my *Great Western at Work 1921-1939*, Appendix 2.

Witney, looking towards Fairford, on 1 May 1956. Porters wheel away the four-wheel barrows as the train leaves. *H. C. Casserley*

The 4.26 pm Oxford-Fairford stands at Witney on 11 June 1962; the view is towards Yarnton. There's a nice gas lamp on the signal box wall. *Hugh Ballantyne*

4.18 pm Oxford-Fairford arrives at Carterton on 2 June 1954; Signalman Ben Davies, the first man to work the box, walks to pick up the Staff. Ben began his railway career as a cleaner at Lydney in 1918 and transferred from footplate work to Carterton for health reasons. *Hugh Ballantyne*

'Fixed' Distant signals were re-erected. The Fairford branch lost its Distant signals in 1906 and never regained them when the ATC was removed after the closure of the line to passenger trains.

On double-track routes, where trains normally only ran in one direction along each track, each Distant signal was relevant to the progress of the train and the ATC device was relatively simple. On single lines, however, trains ran in both directions over one track and therefore not every Distant signal applied to the direction in which the train was running.

An up train leaving Fairford would first pass over the ramp for Fairford *Down* Distant signal, which was of course of no interest to the driver of an up train, and later would pass the Up Distant for Lechlade, which *was* of relevance. The driver required no signal at all from the first ramp, but required a siren from the second. This was achieved by making the Fairford down ramp 'live' with positive polarity current and leaving the Lechlade up ramp electrically 'dead'.

On the locomotive the solenoid (temporary magnet) holding shut the aperture into the train pipe was held closed by current from a battery. When the locomotive passed over the ramp, that current was interrupted, but the magnet remained energised with the positive current from the ramp - the bell worked off negative polarity and therefore made no sound. There was, therefore, no reaction, as far as the driver was concerned, from his ATC equipment when it passed over an irrelevant ramp.

Passing over the 'dead' ramp the battery current to

the magnet was interrupted and there was no current to replace it. The magnetism was destroyed, the air valve opened and atmospheric pressure entered the train's vacuum pipe, applying the brake and causing the warning siren to sound. The driver cancelled the brake application by acknowledging the siren; he lifted a latch, closing the air valve which was then held shut by the re-energised magnet, the engine by now having passed beyond the ramp.

Every train on the approach to any station equipped with stop signals met a 'dead' ramp, this being the equivalent of a semaphore 'Fixed' Distant. The level crossings at Little Faringdon and South Leigh had no semaphore stop signals, only the red target on the gate and the red lamp on the top bar. At these places the Distant ramp was the equivalent of a working Distant signal - it could give the driver an 'All Right' bell or 'Caution' siren.

The crossing-keeper had three levers: 1 and 3 polarised the down and up ramps respectively, and 2 locked the gates across the road. The gates had to be properly locked before either 1 or 3 could be reversed, and both levers had to be 'Normal' in the frame before 2 could be reversed to unlock the gates.

In the sections worked with the Electric Train Staff the electricity supply to the ramps was polarised by an interlocking lever, which was painted red on the top half and blue below. If the signalman at Fairford wanted to get a Staff out of the instrument, he asked 'Is Line Clear?' to Lechlade. Lechlade replied in the normal way, and held down his tapper on the last stroke of the code. This sent a current to release the interlocking lever - No 9 - at Fairford, and the signalman pulled it over. This action had three functions: it released the lock inside the Staff instrument to permit removal of a Staff; it polarised positive the down-direction ramp at Fairford; and disconnected the up ramp at Lechlade.

When the train arrived at Lechlade, the Staff was handed to the signalman who placed it into his instrument. He sent 2-1 on the bell, holding down on the last beat, enabling the Fairford man to restore the interlocking lever 'Normal' in the frame.

Those block sections worked by Tablet or, later, Token did not have an interlocking lever in living memory, the action of removing the Tablet or Token effecting the necessary switching of the ramps. However, in the original 1906 arrangement Yarnton had a Tablet instrument and an interlocking lever - No 41.

Above left Fairford station seen from the main road (numbered A417 from 1921) looking towards the end of the line *circa* 1890. Carts of milk churns, coal in sacks and merchandise are drawn up in the station yard, while lady passengers in ground-length skirts wait on the platform. The Home and Starting signals are lowered; below the latter there is a second 'Shunt Ahead' arm, distinguished by a large, white metal 'S' (from the rear this 'S' appears to be an ellipse). It is a matter of some curiosity as to what was happening when the picture was taken. The coaches in the distance are beside the 'run-round' loop by which the engine gets round them, then draws them into the platform, but the points are set and the signals are lowered for the coaches to be pushed into the platform - with the engine still at the wrong end. If a 'shunt' was required, the 'Shunt' signal should be lowered. I wonder if the 'main line' signals were lowered purely for the photographer's benefit? *GWR*

Left Fairford station in January 1932, precisely as Stan Worsfold saw it as a young GWR employee on his way to catch the train for Oxford. *GWR*

Handborough

There was a signal box at Handborough by 1883 and probably by 1874. The signal box pictured here dates from *circa* 1883 and is categorised as 'Type 4B' by the SRS. It has a steeply pitched roof and is a relatively rare style taking the GWR as a whole, the design being concentrated on the ex-OWWR line or in the West Midlands. Handborough signal box had a floor 20 ft 6 in by 10 ft 6 in and was 10 ft 4 in above rail level. It housed a 42-lever frame, with, I imagine, several spaces. The box was closed on 22 June 1966.

The signal box, 15 February 1964. *Roger Webster/AVC*

Handborough station looking towards Worcester, with an up 'H' headcode goods behind No 2899; 19 October 1957. *R. M. Casserley*

OXFORD LMS

Oxford Road Junction

The first 'Oxford Road Junction' signal box was introduced to work the junction at 27 m 69 ch from the Bletchley-Oxford line to the GWR at Yarnton Junction. Thirteen chains to the north was the level crossing of the Oxford-Banbury road, and the gates were operated by a crossing-keeper. In February 1876* the junction was moved 10 chains northwards and a new signal box brought into use to dispense with the crossing-keeper and give control of the gates to the signalman. The signal box was open continuously. In 1913 the box contained a frame of 16 working levers and five spares. It was a Class 5 - a grade from which the signalmen continuously tried to escape, but without success.

From 9 October 1906 until 25 October 1926** there had been a wooden halt installed in connection with the steam rail-motor running between Bletchley and Oxford; the down platform was located south of the

* R. A. Cooke, *Track Plans: Oxford*, Vol 27.

** Laurence Waters, *Rail Centres: Oxford*.

level crossing, the up platform to the north. In 1923 the signalmen were O. Justain, R. Lambourne and W. G. Starr. By June 1927 Lambourne had gone, to be replaced by A. D. Barden. Their Inspector was Mr H. Lambourne of Bletchley.

The line was not a busy one; the average number of trains dealt with during daily 24-hour periods during 1922/3 were:

Weekending	Trains
19.8.22	46
14.10.22	44
17.2.23	46
14.4.23	45

The old box at Oxford Road Junction in 1954, seen from the 1935 Banbury road bridge. A trace of the old level crossing can be seen on the left, and the markings for the foundations of the new 'Banbury Road Junction' signal box can be made out on the right beside the old box. The complete lack of ground discs might also be noted. The 'Yarnton Loop' diverges right, then runs parallel to the main line to Oxford. *Peter Barlow/AVC*

In June 1927 the noise of cars over the crossing was getting on the signalmen's nerves and in spite of the fact that they had lost the rail-motor traffic they wrote to Mr Smith, Station Master, Oxford (LMS): 'Our rate of pay is 50/- per week. We get thousands of motor cars over this crossing every day and it is very difficult to get the gates shut across the public highway at times. The shunting into the Down Siding has increased. If you could arrange for some one to watch the traffic over this crossing any day and see how the shunting is done we think you would see that we are really worth 55/- a week.

'Hoping that you will kindly put this application to Headquarters.'

The letter went to the Chief General Superintendent at Derby, who told the Bletchley Inspector (Wickes?) to investigate. His reply to Derby on 7 July is interesting and even (at this distance in time) slightly amusing.

'The traffic at Oxford Road Junction is about normal compared with 1923 except that owing to the rail-motor trips between Bicester and Oxford being discontinued the trains are fewer now than at that time. The men do not ask for the marks to be taken but they contend that road traffic has increased over the crossing - it is a fact that 3,000 vehicles a day pass over the line - and that they should be paid for the higher responsibility that rests upon them.

'It has been pointed out to them that it makes no difference to them how many motor-cars cross the railway until they have to reverse the gates.'

Mr Smith wrote to the signalmen to tell them they needed railway work to the extent of 75 marks per hour to get into Class 4. The racket of cars on the crossing remained with them in their otherwise peaceful little signal box until 1935, when a bridge was built to carry road traffic over the line.

Even when wartime traffic arrived, the box still could not get out of Class 5. In 1940 the signalmen were J. Aspinall, R. Martin and A. Barden. In 1940/41 they were dealing with these numbers of trains:

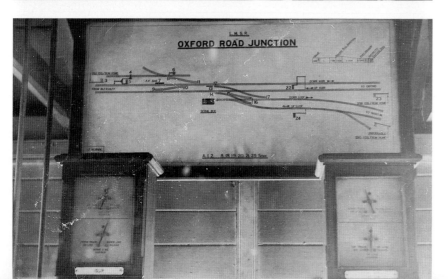

Above left The signal box interior in 1954. The floorboards are worn like water-washed sand from 80 years of footsteps. Note the LNWR 'stirrup' handles that the signalman pressed down to raise the lever latch - awkward things. The 'Permissive' instrument working to Yarnton is that nearest the camera. *Peter Barlow/AVC*

Left The diagram, up in the gloomy roof, did not photograph well in 1954. The block instruments beneath it show that a down train has left Islip and that Oxford Road Junction has got 'Line Clear' for it from Port Meadow; also that an up train is in the section between here and Islip. *Peter Barlow/AVC*

Weekending	Trains
13.4.1940	288
17.8.1940	290
19.10.1940	369
15.2.1941	248

On 29 May 1941 the signalmen applied for upgrading to Class 4 because of the additional wartime traffic, the installation of the 'Permissive Block' instrument to Yarnton Junction and the addition to the Working Time Table of nine regular freight trains in each direction over the 'Yarnton Loop'. The men also asserted that the Yarnton signalmen had already been given a pay rise due to the extra work, but this was not true.

A census of trains dealt with was taken for every day during the week-ended 14 February 1942. At the end of the week the box had dealt with 410 trains. Between midnight on Sunday 8 February and 6 am on the Monday five trains had been signalled; on the early turns that week they had handled between 25 and 32, while the late turns handled 18 to 26 and the night turn 16 to 28 trains. The great fluctuation must be due to freight trains for Yarnton. In the 24 hours 11/12 March 1942 the total of trains going up or down the Yarnton Loop was 26, with 48 through trains to and from Oxford. In spite of the extra work the marks were not sufficient and they remained a Class 5 box.

A brand new 'modernistic' signal box was opened here in November 1956 and was renamed 'Banbury Road Junction' on 15 September 1958*, rather belatedly, to avoid confusion with the Oxford Road Junction on the 'Berks & Hants' line at Reading. The layout was typically under-signalled by the LNW/LMS, in spite of its role as a shunting place.

There were no starting signals and only one ground signal where there was a need for about six.

The signal box was abolished under the Oxford MAS scheme during October 1973.

Woodstock Road Crossing

Nearly three-quarters of a mile west of Oxford Road Junction, along the 'Loop' to Yarnton, the Woodstock Road (A34) crossed the railway on the level. There were gates here and a crossing-keeper's cottage, the latter situated on the south or down side of the line, touching the western side of the road. On the eastern side of the road stood the ancient LNWR signal box shown in the photograph. Note that a few yards to the east of the ground frame the trackbed of the OWWR 'Woodstock Curve' turned east to south towards Oxford LNW station. Obviously it was from this site that the facing points to the curve were once operated.

The level crossing gates were protected in each direction by a 'Fixed' Distant signal and a working stop signal. This is typical LNWR signalling practice for the 1850-60s - the electrical instruments were housed in the hut and the levers, with their interlocking, were deliberately placed out in the weather. It was the Oxford Road Junction signalman's responsibility to advise the crossing-keeper of the approach of up and down trains. Perhaps it was cheaper to install the telephone in the crossing-keeper's house and abandon the old signal box, saving its maintenance. The last train ran over the 'Loop' on 27 October 1965*, the line was closed on 8 November* and taken up on 26 October 1966*.

* R. A, Cooke, op. cit.

Woodstock Road Crossing, looking east towards Oxford Road Junction, in 1930. The ancient LNWR junction signal box (now the level crossing ground frame) is on the right, and just beyond it can be seen the trackbed of the OWWR curve to join the 'Buckinghamshire Railway' north of Wolvercot Tunnel and permit OWWR trains to work between Worcester and Oxford, independent of the GWR. In true 19th-century LNWR style, the levers are outside the signal box. A train of coal is on the up road, awaiting collection by the LMS - who will also have to provide a brake van. The post of the down road stop signal protecting the level crossing can be seen.
Dr Jack Hollick/AVC

Port Meadow

This signal box stood about 100 yards on the Oxford station side of the 30 milepost and came into use on Sunday 29 March 1942*; it was Class 5, and was intended to be opened continuously. On the same day the existing Up and Down Sidings were

* LMS Chief Operating Manager's Report, RAIL 421/9 (Record Office, Kew): 'date facilities became available'.

converted to Goods Loops. The signal box then had all its 30 levers in use and was scheduled to be open from 6 am Monday until 6 am the following Sunday (LMS Signalling Notice). The original signalmen were F. Stone, S. G. Sellers and D. Goudinson, and their District Inspector was M. A. Cassels.

A traffic census was taken over the week from 6 am Monday 13 April until 10 pm the following Saturday, and this showed a very fluctuating train service. The early turn signalman dealt with between 14 and 17 trains per shift, 15 to 18 trains per late turn and between 7 and 13 trains per night shift.

The loops were often used to stable trains while awaiting fresh engines, fresh crews or a 'margin' through Oxford GWR. The chief memory seems to be of long trains of tanks (armoured fighting vehicles) standing there. The layout was comprehensively signalled with plenty of ground signals to 'detect' the points - for safer shunting!

The signal box was taken out of use 28 August 1960*.

* R. A. Cooke, op. cit.

Above left Port Meadow signal box in 1955. *Peter Barlow/AVC*

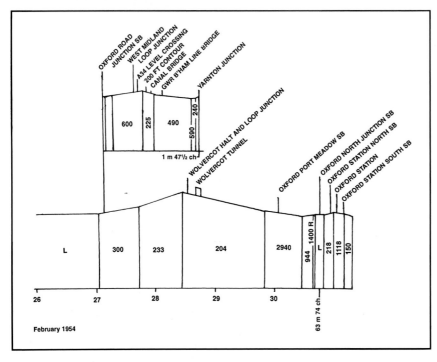

February 1954

Left The gradient profile of the 'Yarnton Loop' and the LMS line from Oxford Road Junction into Oxford Rewley Road.

Rewley Road

There had been a signal box here since January 1853 - when the GWR were still working trains with top hat and truncheon. There was a frame of levers numbered to 36, with one spare and a gong lever to alert the station staff to the approach of a train.

The line came into the station over the 'Cut' between the Oxford Canal and the Thames, necessitating a swing bridge. Four point rods and five signal wires crossed the water by a gantry fixed above boat roof level The swing bridge was bolted in position by Lever 16.

There was opposite the box a stone-cutting plant where Cotswold limestone boulders were cut into regular planks and slabs. A crane was used to swing the stone on to the sawing bench, and in so doing its jib fouled the Down Main line. To pro-

tect the trains and the crane, the latter was locked out of harm's way and could only be swung when unlocked by a key held in the signal box. When the key was taken out of its lock in the box the signalman could not lower his signals for a down train.

The ex-LMS station ceased to handle passenger traffic after 1 October 1951, the service then running to and from the ex-GWR station. Freight still worked in, and the signal box remained a block post until 31 July 1959, when it was reduced to ground frame status - that is, it was retained to operate points and ground signals.

It was finally taken out of use on 2 May 1978.

Right The interior of Rewley Road station on 1 May 1940. *LMS*

Below Rewley Road goods station and the GWR passenger station up the approach road on the left, photographed on 6 December 1935. Two cars are whizzing past a GWR hoarding announcing Mr Buckingham's special offer: 'Exceptionally cheap evening tickets from Oxford station to London each weekday by any train from 4.30 pm. 7/6 and 5/-.' This allowed theatre-goers, for instance, to catch the 4.30 pm express to Paddington, calling only at Reading (for 6 minutes) and arriving at Paddington at 5.50 pm. *GWR*

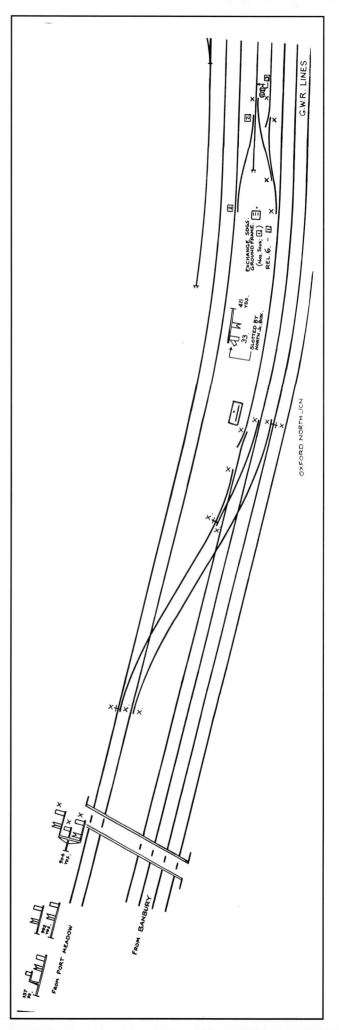

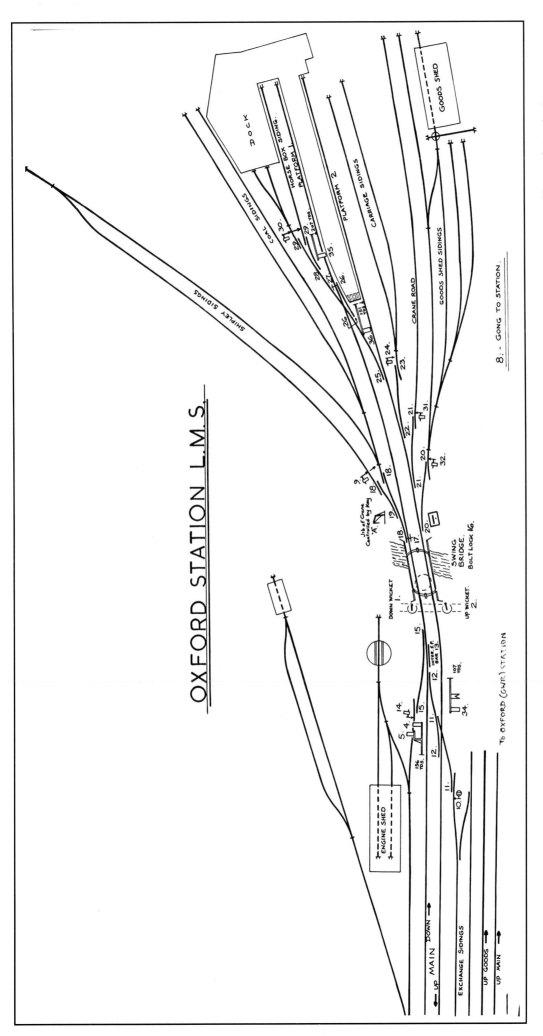

OXFORD STATION L.M.S.

Top left Rewley Road passenger station from the main road on 6 December 1935. *Top right* The swing bridge and the gantry to carry point rodding and signal wires The GWR station is up the approach road on the extreme left. *GWR* across the canal, *circa* 1900. The back of Rewley Road signal box can be seen behind the trees. *GWR*

Top The swing bridge open to allow passage of a boat in 1954. *Peter Barlow/AVC*

Above left A close-up of the hand-cranked gearing for the bridge in 1968. *AVC*

Above Lurking at the back of the LNWR shed, seen from across the Oxford Canal on 24 April 1930, is 'Experiment' Class 4-6-0 No 5464 *City of Glasgow*, once the pride of the LNWR but now relegated to secondary duties. *Dr Jack Hollick/AVC*

INDEX